LAITY:
BEAUTIFUL,
GOOD AND TRUE

Laity: Beautiful, Good and True

Hans Urs von Balthasar's theology of the Laity

Bevil Bramwell OMI

Contents

Introduction 1

1. The Church is not a Refuge from the World 25
2. The Scriptural Archetypes and the Laity 67
3. The Church living out the Archetypal Life 109
4. Laity: Fruitful in the World 145
5. The Drama: Laity on Fire 185
6. The Word is the Goad 231
7. The Drama of Life: Finitude, Suffering and Death 265
8. Brought Home to the Mansions of the Father 299

Selected Bibliography 337

Acknowledgements

So many people have generously given me their time to make this text come together. So I would like to thank my original Thesis Board at Boston College where the whole project started and then those who subsequently have so kindly read the manuscript in its various incarnations and passed along their comments.

Libraries have been so helpful here too, particularly the Boston College Library and the Oblate School of Theology Library in San Antonio TX and the Library of the Catholic University of America.

Thank you to the various communities of the Missionary Oblates of Mary Immaculate who have hosted me during the long writing process.

And last but not least I want to thank the people with whom I work at the Catholic Distance University for providing the intellectual environment in which this kind of research can be done.

The ideas are those of Hans Urs von Balthasar but the presentation and its errors are mine. He has been an inspiration.

The Feast of the Holy Family, December 30, 2012

TO MY MOTHER AND FATHER

Introduction: The Theology of the Laity: A Spiritual Crisis

In 2005, Joseph Ratzinger (now Pope Benedict XVI) spoke at Subiaco, Italy. He described the spiritual crisis of modern man. He said that "the splendor of being an image of God no longer shines over man which is what confers on him his dignity and inviolability, and he is left only to the power of his own human capacities. He is no more than the image of man—of what man?"[1] The implication is that western man particularly no longer understands his own situation. This was not Ratzinger's insight alone.

In the 1960's the Second Vatican Council itself felt obliged to present a detailed theological anthropology as an initial step in aiding the understanding of man. (GS 4-45). The Council sometimes did not offer a deeper theoretical framework but it did occasionally refer to historical experience.

In a similar vein, the Swiss theologian Hans Urs von Balthasar (1905-1988) described the state of modern man as "*anima technica vacua*" (empty technocratic spirit).[2] By this short phrase he—and the pope—were proposing that modern man has emptied his soul (*anima vacua*) and so lacks the real sensibility about who man is. This hollowed-out form manifests itself as harshness to all that is outside of the individual because everything 'outside' of the individual is viewed from a technical manipulative point of view (*technica*).[3]

Responding to this situation, von Balthasar proposes a radical vision of the Christian layman (who then speaks to all men) that is an intellectual response to this crisis.

The radicality of Hans Urs von Balthasar's approach can best be summed up in the fact that he works ontologically, that is he uses the reflection on

---

[1] See Joseph Ratzinger, Speech at Subiaco, April 1 2005 at http://www.zenit.org/article-13675?l=english. The same conclusion appears in *Spe salvi*, 16ff. as well as in his *Meeting with the Representatives of Science*, University of Regensburg, September 12, 2006.

[2] Hans Urs von Balthasar, *Epilog*, (Einsiedeln: Johannesverlag, 1987.)

[3] Cf. David L. Schindler, "Christological Aesthetics and *Evangelium Vitae*: Towards a definition of liberalism", *Communio* 22 (Summer, 1995), 193-273.

the *being* of man. He goes back to the metaphysical relationships between truth, goodness, and beauty to reach the proper description of the lay man. Note, for example, how he speaks of the being of the lay person:

> The Christian layman bears witness to Christ in the place in which he is rooted, not through the proclamation of doctrine, not through direct publicity, propaganda, addresses and conversions, but primarily through the example of his life, the silent and consistent total Christianization of his secular task entrusted to him as father and mother of a family, citizen, scientist, artist, and so on.[4]

Now strictly speaking, von Balthasar's approach is not a novel one. For example, the Second Vatican Council used ontology in the answers to the questions that they considered. As Joseph Ratzinger explained in his commentary on the *Constitution on the Church in the Modern World*: "the tradition of Christian metaphysics forms the real intellectual background to the text" of this particular document.[5] Consider some words from the *Constitution* itself: the council lamented that: "Often refusing to acknowledge God as his beginning, man has disrupted also his proper relationship to his own ultimate goal as well as his whole relationship toward himself and others and all created things." (GS 13) The council has given us an ontological description, that is, one that relates to *being* itself. In this case to *human* being, and its ultimate theological meaning.

Van Balthasar's approach can be best appreciated, first of all, by situating it within the landscape of other efforts in the second half of the twentieth century. Then as a second step, I want to indicate the different dimensions of the ontological approach. The critical exposition will form the rest of the book.

---

[4] Hans Urs von Balthasar, *The Laity and the Life of the Counsels: The Church's Mission in the World*, trans. Brian McNeil C.R.V. with D.C. Schindler, (San Francisco: Communio Book with Ignatius Press, 2003), 149.
[5] Joseph Ratzinger, *Commentary on the Documents of Vatican II*, vol. V, Herbert Vorgrimler gen. ed., W.J. O'Hara trans., (London: Burns and Oates, 1969), 132.

A Brief Historical Sketch

The Church's tradition contains numerous efforts to explain aspects of a lay person's life from the *First Letter of Clement to the Corinthians* (First century A.D.), to the extensive writings of Saint Ambrose and Augustine (Fourth and Fifth centuries), to Saint Thomas Aquinas (Twelfth century), to Saint Francis de Sales (Seventeenth century), and the Curé of Ars (Nineteenth century), and so many others. This is not to mention the thousands of teachings from the official Church, specifically from popes, bishops, and councils! In these teachings, the specific references to lay life always form part of a larger whole, because within the Church, the lay person has always been envisaged as being part of the larger whole of the Church and the *humanum* itself. It was only as the secular nation states developed that the theology of the lay person as a separate treatise came to the fore. This process appears to have been concurrent with the increased need for treatises on the nature of the Church itself. These arose as the Church became obliged to explain its fundamental differences from other institutions in society.[6]

From the Enlightenment to our own time, one finds that as the separation between the Church and the state became more pronounced, the explanation of the nature of the Church and, of course, the explanation of the nature of the lay person in the Church became more urgent and more difficult.

Many current theologies of the laity start from very limited starting points driven, I suspect, by the fractured nature of the modern view of the world. This view expects that reality itself is fragmentary and indeed that its meaning is subjective. Consequently the meaning of reality can be assembled according to the personal preferences of a particular author.[7]

The modern view of the world is the result of a trend that started at the end of the Middle Ages with

---

[6] Henri de Lubac S.J. explains the development of the custom of writing treatises on the Church as being driven by society's loss of appreciation for the Church. See Henri de Lubac S.J., *Splendor of the Church*, (San Francisco: Ignatius Press, 1999), chapter one.

[7] For a history of the development of the isolated individual or as Charles Taylor terms him "the buffered individual," see Charles Taylor, *A Secular Age*, (Cambridge Massachusetts: Belknap Press of Harvard University Press, 2007)

atheist writers such as Benedict (Baruch) Spinoza[8], who began to assemble the available elements of naturalist and mechanistic thought (that can even be found scattered in the writings of ancient Greece and Rome) and arrange them into systematic denials of the integral structure of reality (of Being) to the degree that David Hume (Eighteenth century) criticized these denials as "eliminating Divine Providence and governance of the world".[9] The materialism of Spinoza led him to the theory of a purely material world.

The purely naturalist and materialist view of the world spurred the ever larger distance between the Church and the life of the state. It left the lay Catholic having to scramble to learn how to function as a citizen within a secular and agnostic state, while being a member of the Church at the same time, remaining always obedient to revelation and its interpretation by the Church. The naturalist and materialist view, coupled with the rising importance of historicism as the discipline of history came to dominate the academy, led in turn to an analysis of the Scriptures that imagined them to be merely freestanding secular texts and not sacred texts written within the Spirit-filled ecclesial community, in order to be read there. The theologian Henri de Lubac S.J. called these limited approaches "confusions of mode."[10]

Consequently, many works in modern theology isolate the 'Jesus of History' and the 'Christ of Faith', leaving the former to historicist writers like Albert Nolan O.P. and Edward Schillebeeckx O.P, for example, while the writers on the 'Christ of Faith' were left with a purely subjective devotional image of Christ.[11]

---

[8] See for example, Jonathan I. Israel, *Radical Enlightenment: Philosophy and the Making of Modernity 1650-1750*, (Oxford: Oxford University Press, 2002).
[9] This is the paraphrase of Hume's views by Jonathan I. Israel, 159.
[10] Henri de Lubac S.J., *The Splendor of the Church*, Michael Mason trans., (San Francisco: Ignatius Press, 1999), 26.
[11] See for example Albert Nolan O.P., *Jesus before Christianity*, (Maryknoll NY: Orbis Books, 2001) and Edward Schillebeeckx O.P., *Jesus: An Experiment in Christology*, (New York NY: Crossroads, 1981), for example. On the 'spiritual' side see Friedrich Schleiermacher, *The Christian Faith*, (Edinburgh: T&T Clark, 1999) for example. For a critique of the trend of separating the Jesus of history from the Christ

However Christology is the fundamental issue for a theology of the laity. In Paul's words: "And he put all things beneath his feet and gave him as head over all things to the Church, which is his body, the fullness of the one who fills all things in every way." (Ephesians 1:22, 23)[12] The Church and all that is in it is eminently Christological. Even Christian views of the world are ultimately Christological!

If we follow up on the line of thought that separates the Jesus of history and the Christ of faith, we can, for example, study Kenan Osborne OFM and his *Ministry: Lay Ministry in the Roman Catholic Church*.[13] As we will see, the derived theology then depends on the historical-critical method itself. To take one 'pure' historical-critical point: he claims that: in early Christianity, "some new criterion has had to be *introduced* in order to determine which of the above [people featuring in the Scriptures] should be considered 'cleric' and which should be considered 'lay'."(Emphasis added.)[14] His hypothesis is that this criterion did not exist in the time of Jesus.

Without giving all of the contrary argument, because we will see it later, for von Balthasar and the Magisterium of the Church, Jesus' simple act of calling the twelve (eg Matthew 4:19), *already* indicates a criterion that arises out of the historical event itself— that is within the actual historical *being* of the disciples in their lives with Jesus Christ. Furthermore Jesus did not make the same appeal to everyone he met. This is an argument from within the living relationship of Jesus to his followers as witnessed by the Scriptures. Even in such a simple illustration, it is apparent that something about the actions of Jesus is not the same as the actions of other human beings. By contrast the commonly used historical-critical-method of reading the Scriptures starts out with a particular philosophy of history and then imposes this on sacred history. In support of this conclusion, Hans Urs von

---

of faith, see Martin Kähler, *The So-Called Historical Jesus and the Historical Biblical Christ*, (Minneapolis MN: Fortress Press, 1964).

[12] Hans Urs von Balthasar, "The Layman and the Church," in *Explorations in Theology II: Spouse of the Word*, (San Francisco: Ignatius Press, 1991), 315.

[13] Kenan Osborne OFM, *Ministry: Lay Ministry in the Roman Catholic Church*, (New York: Paulist Press, 1993).

[14] *Ministry*, 18.

Balthasar argues that "secular history . . . cannot, in its secular meaning, be indifferent as regards sacred history, for it has in its totality been impregnated through and through by the Word."[15] We will return to the historical-critical-method and the way that metaphysics throws the flaws of this method into high relief. (Chapter One)

On the positive side, the twentieth century saw many efforts to explain aspects of the theology of the laity. So for example the official Church has published extensive teaching on such subjects as labor unions (e.g. Pius X, *Singulari quadam*, 1912), on marriage (e.g. Pius XII, *Casti conubii*, 1930), on Catholic education (e.g. Pius XI, *Divini illius magistri*, 1929), on Catholic action (e.g. Pius XI, *Non abbiamo bisogno*, 1930), the social order (e.g. Pius XI, *Quadragesimo anno*, 1931; John XXIII, *Mater et magistra*, 1961; Paul VI, *Populorum progressio*, 1967; John Paul II, *Solicitudo rei socialis*, 1987), combating atheism (e.g. Pius XI, *Divini redemptoris*, 1937; Pius XII, *Anni sacri*, 1950), regulating birth (e.g. Paul VI *Humanae vitae*, 1968; John Paul II, *Evangelium vitae*, 1995) to name just a few of the vital issues affecting the laity. These are just a few titles taken from a long list of encyclicals that could be named! Of course, there have been many other levels of ecclesial documents on the laity, but a survey of their contents would be far too long. Nevertheless, the point can be made that the complex nature of lay life has been addressed, in great detail, by the Magisterium.

However the number of documents specifically on the global concept (already I am pointing to the need for a specifically ontological approach—with its constant reference to the whole of Being.) of "laity" *per se* is much smaller, not because of any lack of interest on the part of the Magisterium, but rather because the Magisterium has always viewed the laity as a vital part of the Church. So the laity have been viewed as recipients of the thought of the teaching Church *alongside* the other members of the Church. (Even a document to bishops has all kinds of implications for the laity.)There was also the expectation that the laity

---

[15] Hans Urs von Balthasar, "The Implications of the Word," A. V. Littledale with Alexander Dru trans., *Explorations in Theology I: The Word made Flesh*, (San Francisco: Ignatius Press, 1989), 67.

would be taught about the meaning of their lives, as members of the baptized community, by the religious and the clergy to whom many of the documents were addressed. So throughout the two millennia of teaching, there has always been an *assumed* theology of the laity, but rarely were there specific documents that dealt with the underlying principles of the explicit general theology of the lay person, other than the fact that they were baptized and had shouldered the often very difficult task of being holy in the world.

The first time that the principles of the theology of the laity *qua* laity were considered on a conciliar basis was at the Second Vatican Council (1963-1965). The council issued substantial teachings on the theology of the laity. Strictly speaking there was a chapter in the *Constitution on the Church* (*Lumen gentium*) and then the whole of the *Constitution on the Church in the Modern World* (*Gaudium et spes*). The latter was devoted to the laity and issues that involve the laity directly, such as marriage, family, politics etc. Finally, the council issued the *Decree on the Apostolate of the Laity* (*Apostolican actuositatem*). Subsequent to the council, there is the great apostolic exhortation on the laity *Christifideles laici* (1988), from the hand of John Paul II and issued after the Synod on the Laity (1987).

As we have said the Second Vatican Council worked ontologically and understood the being of the lay person as involving the individual, as well as the network of relationships to his or her spouse, to the children of the family, to one's neighbors and friends, at work, to a whole spectrum of organizations within society, most notably within the Church that grounds and nourishes the rest. We saw this broad spectrum of relationships illustrated in the titles of the documents listed above.

Now a Catholic theology of the laity has to help a layperson appreciate the way in which his/her own existence, and the living out of these relationships as an authentic Christian, is the way to become holy. So for example, Vatican II taught that "all the faithful of Christ of whatever rank or status, are called to the fullness of the Christian life and to the perfection of charity; by this holiness as such a more human manner of living is promoted in this earthly society."(LG 40) When holiness is conceived in this way then it is not simply a 'compartment' in a person's life. Instead, it is a concept of the holiness of a *whole* life before God. In Christianity, a person's life comes to fullness and wholeness as it draws on the integrity granted it as part of the life of Jesus Christ and his Church. Integrity is a quality of being itself and the concept of the integrity of a life with the relationship between all of its parts will be presented in Chapter Two. Emphasis on the insight about the integrity of life is particularly urgent in the twenty-first century, when eclecticism dominates most views of the world in our time.[16]

As the last part of our quick overview of the field of the theology of lay life, there are some other Catholic theologians who need to be singled out for special note as we proceed.

Yves Congar O.P.

In addition to the work of the official Church, during the twentieth century, some noted theological writers have tried their hand at formulating a theology of the laity. The most significant of these efforts were by Hans Urs von Balthasar, who is our interest here, and by Yves Congar O.P. and Karl Rahner S.J., who were *periti* at the Second Vatican Council.

Yves Congar worked largely with what he had learned from Saint Thomas (1225-1274), and consequently he structured his thought around lay participation in the Offices of Christ who is Priest, Prophet and King. This is the theological 'design' that was followed by Vatican II's *Lumen gentium*. Not surprisingly, this is also the approach of cert-ain parts of the Scriptures. Congar's thought appeared in his *Laypeople in the Church*, as well as elsewhere.[20]

Nevertheless, von Balthasar criticized Congar for his apparent reduction of the ontological tension between the cleric and the layperson by transposing it onto the tension between the ecclesiastical elements

---

[16] See for example Hilton Kramer's judgment of the modern period in *The Triumph of Modernism: The Art World 1985-2005*, (New York: Ivan R. Dee, 2006). However he does not go far enough, for example in his critique of Robert Maplethorpe, where the flawed principle driving the eclecticism manifests something derogatory and corrupt.

[20] Yves Congar O.P., *Laypeople in the Church*, (Westminster MD: Newman Press, 1963).

belonging to 'structure' and to 'life' respectively.[21] As we will see, von Balthasar argued that the structure of the lay person's ecclesiastical being is not as easily isolated as this. Just to highlight one dimension that he brings in—in the words of Jacques Servais: "[von Balthasar's] main objection to Congar's ecclesiology is that the 'supersacramental' reality of the Church as Eucharistic and Mystical Body is neglected."[22] The communion which is the communion in Christ and consequently with the Divine Trinity—the suprasacramental—is underplayed. To make the counter-proposal all too briefly here: the grounding of the theology of the laity in the analogy between created being and uncreated Being, overcomes this perceived flaw of 'ignoring' the suprasacramental level of the Church because of the nature of comm.-union that is intrinsic to the Divine substance.[23] This point will resurface again later.

Instead of starting with participation in the Offices of Christ as Congar had done, von Balthasar rooted his theology in the theology of the Divine Trinity and the corresponding *analogia entis* with created being that is concretized in human history in the Incarnation itself. For von Balthasar, the eternal relations between the Divine Persons are imaged in some lesser, finite way, in the intersubjective relationships between finite human beings. This leads ultimately to a vision of the lay person as finding his being in a network of ontological relationships within the union of Christ and his Church, to bear fruit for Christ in the world. So for instance, just as the divine Persons in the Trinity are not interchangeable, neither are the clergy and the laity in the work of von Balthasar. And so I would argue that von Balthasar's theology preserves the distinctive character of both the clergy and the laity. At the same time, his work follows the ontology of the Second Vatican Council with great respect for its nuance.

---

[21] Hans Urs von Balthasar, *Laity and the Life of the Counsels*, 146.
[22] Jacques Servais, "The lay vocation in the world according to H.U. von Balthasar," *Communio* 23 (Winter 1996), 671.
[23] Hans Urs von Balthasar, "The Layman and the Church," 315.

Karl Rahner S.J.

Another influential theologian, from the second half of the twentieth century, was Karl Rahner S.J., another of the *periti* at the Second Vatican Council. One example of Rahner's thought can be found in a 1963 article: "Notes on the Lay Apostolate".[24] The article has many helpful points including details of the notion of 'layman' in the Church. For example, Rahner's approach sounds very similar to von Balthasar's ontological approach when he says: "[the lay man's] being-in-the-world . . . is now both the material for his very being as a Christian and the limit of this being, as far as his exterior life and the structure of his state are concerned."[25] However, von Balthasar did have a bone to pick with Rahner and that was that he offered a theology of the layman that was entirely eschatological.[26] Certainly eschatology is *one* of the dimensions of theological ontology, but it is not the only one. What this means, in von Balthasar's eyes, is that there was no room in Rahner's view for laity who live the life of the counsels in secular institutes, something that was a significant interest of von Balthasar. Even the above quotation indicates the limits that Rahner would impose on the lay man.

In contrast, I would classify von Balthasar's approach as a subtle interrelation of the essentialist and the existentialist approaches, where essence unfolds in existence and this means the lay man's existence even and most especially *before* the eschaton.

Other Approaches to the Theology of the Laity

Rahner's work illustrates a way of thinking that is based on a single dimension of the life of the baptized. Some authors have focused on discipleship, for example.[29] Now, 'discipleship' as it is usually understood, is not a free-standing absolute all-embracing concept, the philosopher's stone for every issue related to the theology of the laity. As important as it is, it does not immediately establish the grounds

---

[24] Karl Rahner S.J., *Theological Investigations II: Man in the Church*, Karl-Heinz Kruger trans., (New York NY: Crossroads, 1963).
[25] Karl Rahner, "Notes on the Lay Apostolate," 324.
[26] *The Laity and the Life of the Counsels*, 148.
[29] Cf. Kenan B. Osborne, *Ministry – Lay Ministry in the Catholic Church*, (New York: Paulist Press, 1993).

for each of the relationships that exist in the life of the lay man.

One problematic area in considering the discipleship of the baptized: how does this concept indicate the mode of participation in the Sacraments? Once again, the participation in the sacramental *communion* comes to the fore and communion (communio) is a complex phenomenon in itself as we shall see.

Then there are some attempts that start from the canonical status of the lay person within the Church[30], or from the gifts of the Spirit[31], or from the increased liturgical activity of laity.[32] These elements are all relevant elements of the life of the laity, but they are distinctly limited as the foundations of theories of the theology of the laity taken as a whole. These defects will become more apparent as we proceed.

Von Balthasar himself

Finally, let us turn to the theologian who is to be the focus in this work.

I propose that the elements of an extensive and detailed theology of the laity can be found in von Balthasar's work. The reason why he did not simply write one text on the laity seems to be both due to the fact that laity live in an exceedingly complex world, and perhaps more significantly, because his attention was taken up in pursuing so many theological

---

[30] This is a flawed approach noted by Karl Rahner in his introduction to his far more substantial—and indisputable—proposal that in fact a theology of the Laity has to be grounded in Jesus Christ. That he does not get to the deep meaning of the actual relationships between the members of the Church is a critique of his work, and also a reminder of the impetus that von Balthasar received from his interest in phenomenology, that acts as a corrective to what I would classify as the more essentialist approach of Rahner. (See Karl Rahner, "Notes on the Lay Apostolate,") For von Balthasar's phenomenology, see Hans Urs von Balthasar, *Theologic I: The Truth of the World*, trans. Adrian Walker, (San Francisco: Ignatius Press, 2000).

[31] William J. Rademacher, *Lay Ministry – A Theological and Spiritual Handbook*, (New York: Crossroad, 1963), chapter nine.

[32] This is the thrust of Osborne's arguments in his *Ministry*. Cf. Section C: "The Tria Munera," 540ff.

issues.³³ One central question concerning the laity for von Balthasar was the establishment of secular institutes in which lay people committed themselves to the evangelical counsels. (See Chapters Three and Eight)

In fact it is the relationship between lay life and the life of the counsels, in a secular institute, that illuminates the peculiar situation of all laity who are 'in the world' and so is worth mentioning here. In von Balthasar's view, the situation of laypeople, at the present time, involves "the coming of age of a competent laity and their acceptance of the full spirit of the Church."³⁴ The lay person has to face the characteristic nature of the world as secular, in the negative sense of being divided up into at the very least agnostic political and economic systems. However this is a very reduced view of the secular as we shall see.³⁵ As von Balthasar noted: "the material of the secular society is not merely secular but also Christian (and thereby ecclesial)."³⁶ However the *saeculum* is also the world that Christ died for. This is where the lay man or woman comes in.

Going back to the quotation in the previous paragraph: the two key terms are 'competent'—which has to do with the lay person's functioning in the world—and 'the full spirit of the Church'—which relates to the fully functioning lay person in the Church. Then the fully functioning lay person is, in some sense, living the life of the counsels, even if his embrace of the counsels is only in the analogous sense of showing the proper relation to the goods of the world (poverty), the proper use of sexuality (chastity),

---

[33] The closest to a single volume presentation of the theology of the laity in his work is his *The Christian State of Life*, trans. Sister Mary Frances McCarthy, (San Francisco: Ignatius Press, 1983). Future references to this text will use the abbreviation *CSOL* followed by the page number.

[34] *CSOL*, 358.

[35] Benedict XVI offered a more positive sense of the secular that fits with what von Balthasar has said. Benedict said: "one risks viewing secularity solely in the sense of excluding or, more precisely, denying the social importance of religion. . . . There is thus an urgent need to delineate a positive and open secularity which, grounded in the just autonomy of the temporal order and the spiritual order, can foster healthy cooperation and a spirit of shared responsibility." (*Speech to the Members of the Diplomatic Corps*, 11 January 2010)

[36] "The Layman and the Church," 316.

and proper response to God's will (obedience). The Evangelical Counsels show the meaning of a life in the full spirit of the Church as the Spouse of Christ.[37]

To start with the subject of competency in the world: qualified and experienced laity know important things about the world. Historically, the dilettantism of clergy and religious with regard to worldly matters, in von Balthasar's opinion, led for example "to those medieval fiascoes" such as the Crusades. So in his view the laity should not look to the Church "for ready-made solutions" to problems in the world for which *they* themselves are responsible.[38] However, there is probably also some anachronistic thinking here on von Balthasar's part regarding the Crusades![39] Now the laity *are* indeed to be helped by religious and clergy to form their consciences, but it is the laity who are to *work* for a Christian world order, something that the clergy and religious can only do indirectly. This formation of the conscience and cooperation with grace happens within the Church through its teaching and the sacraments. Here clergy and religious are most helpful and indeed essential!

Note here the upholding of the *communion* of grace and truth. Taking this point a little further, the document *Gaudium et spes* from the Second Vatican Council follows this bipartite structure of the formation of the lay conscience within the Church, followed by the working out of the lay individual's life in the sphere of the world. So in Part One of the document, the Fathers of the Council presented 'The Church and Man's Vocation', so that Christians could understand who they are as persons and what it means to have a conscience, to sin, or to live morally. Then in Part Two, the document goes on to some urgent issues facing lay Christians, namely marriage, culture, economic, and social life, the political community, contributing to peace among nations. Both parts of the document return to Jesus Christ and

---

[37] *The Laity and the Life of the Counsels*, 162.
[38] Ibidem
[39] See Jonathan Riley-Smith, *The Crusades, Christianity and Islam*, (New York: Columbia University Press, 2008). Witness for example Riley-Smith's judgment that "Western Christendom shares responsibility for a movement that was dependent for its very existence on the cooperation of men and women from all sections of society." (5) That is, the crusades were not merely at the urging of clergy!

his teachings as the foundation and source of the thinking in each different area of life. The document both outlines the foundations of the thinking as well as giving some of the consequences of the thought for the individual Catholic layperson. Von Balthasar works in a similar way, but spends considerably more time on the foundations than he does on all of the details of what follows from the fundamental theology. Since von Balthasar is so in harmony with the tradition of the Church, I would direct the reader to the Church documents for many of the consequences as they have been expressed in Church thought.

Backtracking a little, we are now in a position to appreciate the unique contribution of the consideration of the theology of the secular institute—something that von Balthasar was singularly situated to appreciate both historically and personally. (See Chapter Eight) Members of a secular institute unite both the contemplative Christian impulse to reflect on Christ (who is poor, chaste and obedient) within the communion of the Church, and the active human impulse to cultivate the world, and to do it, in this case, in the Spirit of Christ. So the mention of secular institutes and the theology behind them places the focus on the special character—the secularity—of the laity and the way that they are to be formed in Christ, through his Church, and they then contribute to transforming the world in their unique way.

+++

The Design of the Book

Von Balthasar's reflections are widely spread throughout his work so they did need to be gathered together in an organized way. This book is a humble initial attempt at this task.

To establish a context complete enough to describe the rich and profound role of the laity in the Church and the world, one needs a method equal to the object being reflected upon. This leads to von Balthasar's recovery of metaphysics and its application to divine revelation in history. [40] As Peter Henrici S.J. so cogently summed the approach: "According to the mutual indwelling of the transcendentals, the nature of truth is seen in the encounter between the lover and the beloved, truth manifests itself thus as revelation,

---

[40] Cf. Cornelia Capol, *Hans Urs von Balthasar: Bibliography*, (Einsiedeln: Johannes Verlag, 1990).

as unveiling, but also as sheltering participation."[42] So at the foundation of all the abstract statements that will have to be made to explain the complexity of lay life, lies the loving relationship of God to his people whom he has created out of love and accompanied in their history in love. God's revelation of himself takes place out of love and leads to man's loving participation in God.

The details of this application of metaphysics starts out in a practical vein as viewed through the life of a notable French lay man Georges Bernanos in Chapter One. There we will also see some of von Balthasar's theory of the Church and the world, that makes his theology of the laity intelligible. The chapter also introduces the transcendentals of Beauty, the Good and the True. They establish the three main themes of the book and indicate the three sections into which I have divided von Balthasar's theology. This approach is suggested by the great man himself in the structure of his last work, the so-called 'trilogy,' about which more later.

At this point, it must be noted that we will describe his theology and also move beyond a simple exposition into a critique of the assembled theology. This critique will work, both from the relations between the elements themselves, as well as through relating von Balthasar's propositions to the Catholic tradition. Often the critique is in the endnotes so as not to disturb the 'flow' of the presentation of what is a detailed and intricately thought out theology.

Another comment on the writing: this work began as an attempt to render my doctoral thesis into a form that could be published, but in fact there are so many themes in von Balthasar's theology of the laity that it has meant selecting only some of them and rewriting each chapter that was finally used. Some were written specifically for this work. The presentation starts with a detailed reflection on the philosophical and theological anthropology and then shows some of the consequences of these thoughts.

Obviously the consequences of each theme are far more extensive than can be presented here, but the

---

[42] Peter Henrici, S.J., "The Philosophy of Hans Urs von Balthasar," *Von Balthasar: His Life and Work*, David L. Schindler ed., (San Francisco: Communio Books, Ignatius Press, 1991), 151.

basic premise is that the lay people should reach a deeper understanding of their state in life, and then through their creative application of their conception of their state of life, they can participate as free and responsible laity in the Church and in the world.

There are some additional points about the theology of the transcendentals that are needed by way of introduction.

The Transcendentals themselves

The four transcendentals that qualify Being are the One, Beauty, the Good and the True. Von Balthasar handles them not simply as interrelated qualifications of created being but as grounded in the uncreated being of God himself. Created being can then be discussed by analogy with the fullness of Being which is God, most especially, since God has shared his life with us in Christ: "Of his fullness we have all received, grace upon grace." (John 1:16) God had filled his people in Christ and given them form (beauty) in self and in life. This results in the first great theological reflection, the reflection on God's glory manifested in the world in Christ and his brothers and sisters. (See Chapters One through Four)

Returning to the absolute centrality of God's relationship to man, the second great theme appears and this is God's action in terms of manifesting the good. Corresponding to God's actions is the human response. The fundamental category for von Balthasar is *drama* and more precisely *theo-drama*. Within the category of theo-drama there is an absolutely fundamental ontological dimension and that is intersubjectivity. Our study of theo-drama forms the basis of the second major part of this book, the drama of lay existence in the world. (See Chapters Five, Six and Seven) Here in my view lies the main reason for paying attention to von Balthasar's theology. The time-bound intersubjective character of human existence, imaging as it does in some sense the eternal divine interpersonal relations, is the foundation of a theological recovery that responds to the problems of three somewhat flawed theological enterprises namely neo-thomism, process theology, and historical theology.

Furthermore the very turning to drama is a practical application of von Balthasar's fundamental intuition that "theology should take seriously and . . .

it should cherish the explicit or implicit philosophy man employs when thinking about the meaning of the world and of existence and it should pursue its own reflection upon the biblical revelation in association with this mediating philosophical reflection."[43] The drama of salvation, as it unfolds in Scripture and the tradition of the Church needs to inform philosophy and at the same time be regulated by the rigor of philosophy. Von Balthasar has situated the role of philosophy as an essential mediator of the meaning of the world and of human existence itself. One immediately has to qualify this statement: philosophy is to mediate the reflection on God's revelation but only in correlation with and guided by revelation itself.

There is a way in which the reflection on revelation uses the assistance of the reflection on existence, but which at the same time the reflection on existence is elevated and corrected by the reflection on revelation. This brings philosophy to its true flowering as the love of wisdom, where as the *Book of Wisdom* tells us, "those who gain this treasure [wisdom] win the friendship of God." (Wisdom 7:14) Then too, as a corollary, with wisdom—as Joseph Ratzinger noted: "what is involved is man's very humanity."[44] The core principle of this work is that it is through metaphysics illuminated and corrected by Scripture that one approaches the meaning of humanity itself.

Thus the reflection on human existence can show us that our existence finds its ultimate meaning (truth) in Christ's work of salvation of all of created being, and that is to bring man to God.

In this way, we come finally to the third great theme in von Balthasar's work and that is truth, and that Henrici prepared us for above! Von Balthasar trusted that Being already speaks, because in some way it already manifests the creator God who speaks his Word and in whose image it was made. Hence the philosophical experience participates in the unveiling of truth that is completed in God's revelation.

---

[43] Hans Urs von Balthasar, *Theodrama II: Dramatis Personae: Man in God*, (San Francisco: Ignatius Press, 1990), 193. Please note that once a volume in the *Theodrama* has been referenced, subsequent references will simply use the abbreviation *TD* followed by the volume number.

[44] See Joseph Ratzinger, *Commentary on the Documents of Vatican II, vol. V*, Herbert Vorgrimler gen. ed., (London: Burns and Oates, 1969), 133.

By working in this way, von Balthasar has returned to a philosophical and theological method that has had its vicissitudes in the modern period. He goes back to an understanding of being that he finds, for example, in Saint Thomas Aquinas' writings. In his summing up of Aquinas's work, he understands Aquinas to have come to the following concept of Being: "Being (*esse*), with which he is concerned and to which he attributes the modalities of the One, the True, the Good and the Beautiful, is the unlimited abundance of reality which is beyond all comprehension, as it, in its emergence from God, attains subsistence and self-possession within the finite entities."[45] This is also the best formulation of the theory of being that von Balthasar uses and it provides the metaphysical grounding for the theology of the laity. But the method goes back further than that, it is ultimately Patristic—without being merely a slavish return to that period— and much, much more is it scriptural, but more about that too later.

So then for von Balthasar, lay persons are baptized Christians whose being in the world manifests the goodness, beauty and truth of Christ in his Church for the world. But what of the One? Von Balthasar says that "all the transcendentals equally determine the whole of being—not only to underscore their inseparability (cf. Plato, *Philebus* 64e), reciprocal interpenetration, and mutual implication, but also, and for the same reason, to highlight the fundamental transcendental quality of unity."[46] In other words the meaning of the being of the individual is only found by reference to the whole unity of being itself. We can see why the theologies of the laity based on single aspects of lay life already compromise the source of the meaning itself.

Now von Balthasar's analysis of the manifestation of beauty, the good, and the true, comprise the series of the works known collectively as

---

[45] Hans Urs von Balthasar, Oliver Davies, Andrew Louth, John Sayward and Martin Simon trans., *The Glory of the Lord - A Theological Aesthetics V: The Realm of Metaphysics in the Modern Age*, (San Francisco: Ignatius Press, 1991), 12. Please note that once a volume in the *Glory of the Lord* has been referenced, subsequent references will simply use the abbreviation *GL* followed by the volume number.
[46] *TL I*, 7.

The *Glory of the Lord*, the *Theodrama* and the *Theologic* respectively. Given the primary nature of comments on ontology, the transcendentals can be the organizing principle for all of the comments on the laity in von Balthasar's other writings.

The organizing principle offered by ontology—and this is an ontology rooted in the Scriptures—also does justice to the different literary genres that von Balthasar has drawn into his theology of the laity. His first resources are, of course, the Scriptures and the Tradition of the Church, but then he has also studiously examined a vast array of texts from the worlds of philosophy and literature. We do keep in mind that von Balthasar's approach to the laity is not *primarily* ontological—as if the meaning of lay life is a merely philosophical project! Instead it comes from a serious meditation on revelation in Christ, and then ontology is the tool for maintaining rigorous thought about the data of revelation.

There is another reason why the preoccupation with Being is significant. Lay people live out their roles and discover their salvation in the world, where they have their homes, and their businesses, and where they play baseball, and where they take walks. Consequently the focus on the whole, on Being itself, keeps the theology of the laity centered on its true locus, in the world, although the world itself is only finally understood in the light of God's revelation of himself in Christ.[47] After all, Jesus Christ died for the world, so the world is not neutral in these considerations. For this reason von Balthasar argued that lay theologians are going to be the most successful theologians in the modern period, simply because they are dealing with the situation in the world in which they are immersed rather than with more narrowly academic or clerical questions.[48] Thus

---

[47] The metaphysics of light in use here parallels the thinking of *Gaudium et Spes* (eg. GS 15). Joseph Ratzinger argued that the Augustinian intellectual tradition in evidence here is also the background to the whole of the constitution. See Joseph Ratzinger, *Commentary on the Documents of Vatican II, vol. V*, Herbert Vorgrimler gen. ed., (London: Burns and Oates, 1969), 132.

[48] Hans Urs von Balthasar, Andrew Louth, Francis McDonagh and Brian McNeil C.R.V. trans., *The Glory of the Lord – A Theological Aesthetics II: Studies in Theological Style: Clerical Styles*, (San Francisco: Ignatius Press, 1984), 15.

lay theology and by implication the theology of the laity itself, offers "an understanding of revelation in the context of the history of the world and the actual present."[49]

Lastly, Hans Urs von Balthasar offers a theology of the laity that argues for laity's integral *manifestation* of the transcendental qualifications of being. Examining the form of one's life (beauty) always reverts to the good (action) that one does to bring the form about and the truth of existence that is manifested through one's form of life. For heuristic purposes, in this text, the transcendental qualifications of lay life will be dealt with as separately as possible, so this work will examine the life of the baptized Christian sequentially from the perspective of the good, beauty and the true.

With these preliminary comments, we can summarize the life of a Christian as follows: the life of a Christian lay person is a life of doing the good *in the power of Christ* that gives rise to a beautiful form of life in the world. This form of life speaks of an inner truth which is the truth of God's revelation in Christ to the world. The lay person is simply defined as someone who belongs to the general state of the baptized in the Catholic Church, but does not belong to the State of Election (religious or cleric).[50]

The notion of 'state' in itself is itself complicated. In von Balthasar's work, the word 'state' refers to where one takes a *stand* within the Church, "where there is room for all to stand, [in] many contrasting and mutually supplementary states of life."[51] As the Latin *status*, it appears in the work of Thomas Aquinas. In the very early years of the Church, she adopted terms from civil society with its pagan terminology. However, that did not mean that the terms could not be absorbed and adapted to identify Christian realities, once they had been purified of their pagan associations. In Roman society, citizens belonged to the *status*, while officials belonged to the *ordo*.[52] So priests and religious in the early Church were held to belong to various *ordines* or orders. However, von Balthasar expanded the meaning of

---

[49] Ibidem.
[50] Cf. John Paul II *CL*, 9. Cf. Second Vatican Council, *LG*, 31.
[51] *CSOL*, 11.
[52] *CSOL*, 11, Footnote 6.

status by using an insight that is found in both Aquinas and Suarez, namely that of *status* as 'state of life'. Specifically, the layperson lives in the "general Christian state'.[53] From the most ancient tradition, this meant living the life of the commandments. There is much that can be learned from this distinction, but it will be left to Chapter Three.

These are just a few preliminary comments about some concepts that appear in the work.

+++

A brief Overview of the Chapters

The complex situation of the lay person in the Church and in the world, involves searching for a method that will do justice to describing such a reality. Thus *Chapter One: The Church is not a Refuge from the World* starts out by putting a face on the thinking about being a lay person, entering into the subject through the life of Georges Bernanos. Then we explain the interplay of God's revelation in history, and the analysis of the contemplation of this history in terms of metaphysics. This methodology opens the way for some fundamental comments on the nature of the Church, and world, and of the notion of laity itself.

Starting with the form of lay life we have: *Chapter Two: The Scriptural Archetypes and the Laity*. We focus on the heart of the form of Christian life namely its ecclesial aspect. Christian life is rooted in the foundational community formed by Jesus Christ around himself. Von Balthasar's use of metaphysics uncovers descriptions of Jesus Christ's being in the world as expressed in the network of Jesus' Christ's personal relationships.

These relationships constitute the Church and form the basis of the chapters that follow. So Christ's relation-ships with Mary, Peter, and the others, are examined to give us the basic relations that constitute the Church for all time. (The relationship between Jesus and John as fundamental for the existence of religious life is the only dimension of this analysis that cannot immediately be found in the teachings of Vatican II.)

Specifically, it is Jesus' relation to 'the Multitude' that founds Christ's relationship to the lay members of his Spouse the Church for all time, always with the proviso that Christ (and Mary who lives in his

---

[53] *CSOL*, 239.

grace) founded lay life by living it, before he entered the State of Election to found it in turn.

Moving on: Chapter Three *The Church living out the Archetypal Life* examines how the relationships within the scriptural community of the Church continue into subsequent epochs. So the chapter describes the relationships of the states of life in the Church. These states rest upon the relationships in the community of Jesus himself. The notion of *relationship* (founded on intersubjectivity in the created order) is important because it is the eternal foundation of the Trinity and is reflected in the communion of the Church in the relations between the different states of life in the Church.

The preceding chapters sketch out the formal ecclesial aspects established by the network of relationships around Jesus. Next we consider the mission of the Church to the world. The two aspects are simply different dimensions of the one lay person's life (and indeed of the one Church's life!), but they are separated for heuristic purposes. Thus *Chapter Four: The Fruitfulness of Lay Life* covers some of the features of lay life in the world under the scriptural rubric of fruitfulness. The issue of sin is an important one as it fundamentally contradicts fruitfulness. The formal aspect of lay life as radiant with the glory of God, and the proportion between all of the elements of lay life contribute to its fruitfulness. The final part of this consideration examines the 'hour of the laity' in more detail, and concludes the aesthetic reflection on lay life.

The theo-dramatic reflection starts by analyzing the scriptural theme of fire in *Chapter Five: Laity on Fire*. This consideration establishes the meaning of the theo-dramatic approach. Then follow the formal elements of the 'location' of the drama in the heavens and on the earth, and the formal elements of the lay person's experience as elect, called, and sent in Christ. The conclusion of the chapter draws out some of the implications of this understanding for being a Christian.

It is in the actual day-to-day life of the lay person that *"the Word is the Goad,"* which is the title of Chapter Six. The chapter analyzes the different ontological dimensions of lay life as rooted in the cosmos, as spirit, and body, as man and woman, and as member within as community. It is the Christological transformation of each of these natural dimensions that concerns us here. Von Balthasar's treatment of the question of gender not only has existential implications but also substantial theological implications for the understanding of God's relationship to the world, the individual and to his Church.

The everyday life of the lay person also has eschatological implications. Three of the most important are considered in Chapter Seven: *The Drama of Life: Finitude, Suffering and Death*. Repeatedly in studying these major elements of human experience we find that the Cross of Christ ultimately offers the only hermeneutic capable of grasping the meaning of finitude, suffering, and death. This chapter also concludes the theo-dramatic section of the book.

The final chapter considers three possible life options for a lay person, the married life, the virginal life, and membership of a secular institute. These are treated from the theological perspective, to illustrate what it means to say that lay life manifests the truth of God in Christ. This chapter is entitled *Being Brought Home to the Mansions of the Father*. This theo-logical consideration presents the truth of lay life and most importantly it presents the circumincession of the transcendentals.

This is where the conclusion of all of our study lies as it must. As God eternally manifests an internal Word (truth), he has expressed his Word within created history. The whole of creation that came to be through the Word has to come to express the truth of God. So theologically this is the most accurate and noble way to pay homage to the circumincession of the transcendentals.

So then for the laity, each person is called to a life of reaching for a beautiful form of life offered by Christ to his followers. Such a life is achieved by dramatic action, in the proper sense of fulfilling the drama of life through making choices, so as to embrace the supreme good both for oneself and for others. This dramatic exercise of life manifests the truth of God that he has spoken to the world in Christ.

+++

Christ said: "These things I speak in the world so that they may have my joy made full in themselves." (John 17:13)

Chapter One: The Church is not a Refuge from the World

1. Georges Bernanos: Layman
2. Jesus Christ: in History and in the Church
3. Metaphysics: The philosophy that purifies thinking
4. History: Human being in Time
5. Scripture and Tradition
6. The Layperson with Georges Bernanos: In a movement in history

1. Georges Bernanos: Layman

The French Catholic layman Georges Bernanos (1888-1948) was one of Hans Urs von Balthasar's favorite lay figures because he was passionately Catholic and deeply involved in his vocation as an author with many notable works including *The Diary of a Country Priest* and *Dialogues of the Carmelites*, as well as a vocal analyst of the cultural and political scene of his time.

Von Balthasar said of him:

> Like few Christians, perhaps even (when you consider the enormous effect of writers) like few priests in our time, the Christian creative writer Georges Bernanos became a minstrel, an interpreter, and a mediator of divine grace. Already in the trenches of the First World War we see him acting as an apostle, and through his assiduous correspondence, we see him increasingly become a kind of lay father confessor to countless seekers. The letter of August 1947 shows how intelligently and frankly he could even help priests. . . . The grace of God shines forth from this life, a life that great and merciless trials "drove home to the foot of the Cross" but that in the process lost none of its fullness of freedom and grandeur.[1]

So he is a worthy reference point when considering what it means to be a functioning Catholic layperson

---

[1] Hans Urs von Balthasar, *Bernanos: An Ecclesial Existence*, (San Francisco: Ignatius Press, 1996), 55.

as we work with von Balthasar to understand it in all of its complexity.

Some words of the chapter title come from Bernanos' essay *Freedom, for what?* One of his concerns—contained in the notion of 'freedom *for*'—was that we might reduce the Church to a haven from which "through her windowpanes one may take pleasure in watching the passers-by—the people who belong outside, those who aren't paying boarders of the house."[2] The vision of the Church that he is advocating—and one that fits the tradition of the Church—moves irrepressibly outward to take on the world, to challenge it to meet Jesus Christ. Hence the Church must not be perceived as a refuge!

One can see this rich evangelizing dynamism of the Church in Bernanos' frank references to the saints. For example:

> What matters most is to know what exactly a Christian person is. For there does exist a 'type,' or model, of the Christian person and this type is determined by the Church herself: it is the saint. The saints are the army of the Church. The Church in arms is the Church in deployment, with the saints in the first line of battle.[3]

For Bernanos (and von Balthasar) the saints are not removed from the world. They are not delicate plaster figures but rather real people who cooperate with the grace of the Church more than we do and so are worthy and challenging models of Catholic life in this world of ours. This was the vibrant and forceful community in which Bernanos understood himself to be.

In von Balthasar's words:

> no one can keep him from being a thinking Christian—a courageously thinking Christian—of our time. No one can keep him from having derived his faith, not from textbooks, but from the catechism and a stormy prayer life, from the reception of the sacraments and the daily wounds inflicted by the sin and blindness of the world: his faith was to him the living truth,

---

[2] Georges Bernanos, *La Liberté, pourquoi faire?* 267-269 B 252.
[3] Georges Bernanos, *Lettre aux Anglais*, 245 B 265.

which must suffice in mastering the most terrible questions of existence.⁴

This is an inventory of the signs of the ecclesial existence of Georges Bernanos, and fortuitously, they give us the key insights in the theology of the laity in the work of Hans Urs von Balthasar himself. Technically then we can say that they refer to a concrete historical figure (Georges Bernanos) within whose life there is an identifiable historical form (great author and social observer in early twentieth century France) with a dramatic character that radiates Christian truth. This form, this drama, and this truth come from the fact that the lay person is being constituted more deeply as a person in the history of salvation because he is a member of the Body of Jesus Christ (the Church), the Savior and Redeemer of the world.

2. Jesus Christ and the Church in History

There is a very close union between Jesus Christ and the Church. As the Second Vatican Council expressed it: "Christ, the one Mediator, established and continually sustains here on earth His holy Church, the community of faith, hope and charity, as an entity with visible delineation through which He communicated truth and grace to all." (LG, 8) This community came forth from the Old Testament People of God and was informed by Jesus Christ right here in human history as a visible community.

The Church then *mediates* the extension of the Christ-event (with all of its implications) through history in the power of the Holy Spirit. When speaking of the mediation of the Church, von Balthasar says that "it is . . . the expression, itself the vesture and message of the power of the incarnate God [Jesus Christ] speaking to and governing the course of world history."⁵ Here, on the one hand, von Balthasar illustrates the close link between being and history, where the events of salvation history have universal significance, because they are real (historical) and they transform the being of the world (metaphysical). This

---

⁴ Hans Urs von Balthasar, *Bernanos: An Ecclesial Existence*, trans. Erasmo Leiva-Merikakis, (San Francisco: Communio Books – Ignatius Press, 1996), 17. (Henceforth referred by the abbreviation B)

⁵ Hans Urs von Balthasar, "The Word and History," *ET I*, 33.

will be our constant framework of this reflection on the meaning of the life of a Catholic lay person.

On the other hand, we are hearing something important about the Church as well. We could find the meaning of what von Balthasar is saying about the meaning of the concrete presence of the Church, just as well, in a quotation from the First Vatican Council (1870). In the document entitled *Dei filius* (Son of God), the council says:

> To the sole Catholic Church belong all of the manifold and wonderful endowments which by divine disposition are meant to put into light the credibility of the Christian faith. Nay more, the Church by herself, with her marvelous propagation, eminent holiness and inexhaustible fruitfulness in everything, that is good, with her Catholic unity and invincible stability, is a great and perpetual motive of credibility and an irrefutable testimony of her divine mission. (*Dei Filius*)[6]

This is the Church, present and convincing in the unfolding history of the world, as the Body of Jesus Christ. Paul wrote to the Romans: "so we, though many, are one body in Christ and individually parts of one another." (Romans 12:5) Here we are as a community of meaning generated by Jesus Christ!

The continued grounding of the life of the community and the individual Catholic in the presence of Christ is important for what follows so that the reality of the Church does not get separated, in our minds, from the ever-present Jesus Christ. So, for example, when von Balthasar speaks about Jesus Christ he can say: "The potentiality that he realized in the incarnation even to the total renunciation of obedience unto death on the cross had its foundation in the pure actuality of the eternal life of the Blessed Trinity."[7] It is this potentiality that he has unleashed in the world. This is a massive achievement with many, many consequences but we are going to follow just one, and we will do that by answering the question: what does this amazing thing that Jesus is accomplishing in his person in the world mean for the life of the Catholic lay person?

---

[6] J. Neuner S.J., J. Dupuis S.J., eds., *The Christian Faith*, (Dublin: The Mercier Press, 1976), 46.
[7] *CSOL*, 189.

To answer the question: first of all: "in the first thirty years of his journey through the world, the Lord exemplified the secular state" of life, which is the life of the lay person.[8] What does this mean? It means that Jesus Christ is "the genuine . . . model of the worldly state because within a genuine human framework and in genuine obedience to the laws of natural family and society, the Son exemplified the possibility of taking one's stand as child, youth and adult in the Father and his will and mission."[9] This genuineness resides in the fact that everything, the world, the laws of nature, and so on, is all created through the Divine Son at the will of the Divine Father. (cf. John 1:3) We are always obedient to something even if it is only our own appetites as destructive as that might be. What von Balthasar is pointing us towards, is what the Church leads us to and that is becoming obedient to higher and higher principles until finally we are obedient to selfless love.

Hence importantly for us, the meaning of Jesus' historical life rests in the fact that it is the expression in time of his eternal existence as the one begotten by the Father and then "conformed to this world".[10] The existence of the Divine Son is eternally generated by the Father and eternally returning all that he is to the Father, in the eternal relations of Paternity and Filiation respectively.[11] So then these two eternal divine relations form the "basis of time and temporality as these apply to the Son in his creaturely form of existence."[12] Among the many clues to the nature of Jesus' existence, as it is described in the Scriptures, is his refusal to anticipate the will of the Father, for example. (Cf. Mark 13:32) He receives his earthly life from the Father in due time. He does not rush ahead of the Father's will for him. Or one might point to Jesus' allocution to his disciples before the Passion. Speaking to the Father, he said: "Now they know that everything you gave me is from you, because the words you gave to me I have given to them, and they accepted them and truly understood

---

[8] *CSOL*, 194.
[9] *CSOL*, 195.
[10] *Theology of History*, 31.
[11] See Thomas Aquinas' treatment of the eternal existence of the divine Son in *ST I* and the existence of the Son in the Incarnation in *ST III*.
[12] *Theology of History*, 33.

that I came from you, and they have believed that you sent me." (John 17:7, 8) One can see the strong indications of God's paternity in these words.

Perhaps this sounds very theoretical so let us turn to one practical result of this line of thinking, Jesus' perspective on time, just to show how this wonderful life of the divinity unfolds right here in our world. In the life of Jesus Christ—von Balthasar again!—, "there is no such thing as empty time, available for filling with some indifferent content or other. To have time means, for him, to have time for God, and is identical to receiving time from God."[13] The Incarnate Son's life on earth is the expression of his existence as Incarnate Son and so every element, every relationship, is significant because it has been drawn into the revelation of the inner life of the divine Trinity to the world in history.

For the lay person, who is living in the Spirit of Christ, time then has the same meaning. There is no 'compartment', so to speak, of 'neutral' time that has no meaning, and hence there is no lay activity that is just empty. Interestingly, when the philosopher Joseph Pieper speaks of leisure, the opposite of *acedia* (listlessness or torpor), he speaks of it as being "the cheerful affirmation by man of his own existence, of the world as a whole, and of God—of Love, that is from which arises that special freshness of action, which would never be confused by anyone with any experience with the narrow activity of the 'workaholic'." This is the meaning of a genuine human life.[14] Then too Christ's life on earth—now enveloping all of creation and time—was the completely authentic lay person's life.

Returning to the Church itself: the Church is the custodian of God's revelation to mankind. This custodian-ship is naturally articulated in the study of theology and especially in the theology of the laity. In fact, according to the Second Vatican Council: "She has always maintained, and continues to do so, [that the Scriptures] together with sacred tradition, as the supreme rule of faith, since, as inspired by God and committed once and for all to writing, they impart the

---

[13] *Theology of History*, 40.
[14] Joseph Pieper, *Leisure: The Basis of Culture*, Gerald Malsbary trans., (South Bend IN: Saint Augustine's Press, 1998), 29.

word of God Himself without change, and make the voice of the Holy Spirit resound in the words of the prophets and Apostles."(*Dei verbum*, 21) God speaks to the world through his Church—another theme of the theology of the lay person that we will return to again and again. Here too, for the first time, we see the close interaction between Scripture and Tradition. This interact-ion will be seen to regulate our study of the laity.

If we were to ask the council what tradition is, we would find the following: "what was handed on by the Apostles includes everything which contributes toward the holiness of life and increase in faith of the peoples of God; and so the Church, in her teaching, life and worship, perpetuates and hands on to all generations all that she herself is, all that she believes." (DV, 8) These elements are elements of life in the church community.

So at this point if I were to sum up the theology of the lay person as we have developed it thus far, I would say that it is a theology that is done *within* the Scriptures and the Tradition of the Church. We do this to uncover the meaning of the life of Christ, who is, after all, the perfect example of lay life! So, as we move forward, let us look both for the meaning of the Scriptures and the tradition of the community that enfolds the Scriptures.

Now, when we go to the Scriptures, we are not just hearing stories. There has to be a rigorous way to 'unpack' their meaning in a way that respects the deeper meaning that can be found there. In this regard, John Paul II explains something that will be very useful for us. He says that: "The Acts of the Apostles provides evidence that Christian proclamation was engaged from the very first with the philosophical currents of the time." (*Fides et Ratio*, 36) Then, reading on,—and this is where we discover the next step to take after looking at the narratives of the life of Jesus—at its best "one of the major concerns of classical philosophy was to purify human notions of God. . . . Superstitions were recognized for what they were and religion was, at least in part, purified by rational analysis. It was on this basis that the Fathers of the Church entered into fruitful dialogue with ancient philosophy, which offered new ways of proclaiming and understanding the God of Jesus Christ." (*Fides et Ratio*, 36) The ancient philosophy is what Aristotle called 'first philosophy' and what we have introduced as metaphysics (*Introduction*). This book is going to apply metaphysics to what we know about Jesus Christ. Von Balthasar gives us three principles that specifically set Scripture within a dynamic symbiosis with metaphysics in the tradition of the Church where the metaphysics keeps our thinking accurate and rigorous. Let us start with what metaphysics is.

3. Metaphysics: The Philosophy that purifies thinking

How does von Balthasar understand metaphysics, the description of the nature of created being? His answer actually sets up the structure of this book so we will spend some time on his response to this question. He says: "Metaphysics must be taken here in its most original and broadest range . . . [as] not separated from the 'holy knowledge about the origins of the world' . . . and in the breadth of the aspects of what is ἀληθές ('clear, true'), ἀγαθόν ('good') and καλόν ('sound, healthy, beautiful')."[15] Now, first, the quotation speaks of the 'holy knowledge,' this is the knowledge that all ultimately owes its existence to the divine, to revelation. Then too, being is seen to be beautiful, good and true. Von Balthasar is calling for a recovery of this ancient understanding of metaphysics, because it is only such a metaphysics in its Christian variant, that can show the true meaning of being (of what is), and when this happens then that which was "once thought lost again [is] drawn forth anew from the scriptural revelation," which is where the historical dimension of existence comes in.[16] Not surprisingly, this will then involve the Scriptures because of their witness to the history of salvation which is a genuine history and not simply a collection of stories.

The quotation from von Balthasar on metaphysics, for the first time, shows the full breadth of the proper metaphysical description of Christian existence that he seeks. This book will examine the ontological nature of the lay state from the perspectives of the beautiful, the good and the true.

Delving more deeply into thought in metaphysical terms itself, the quotation above said that

---

[15] Ibidem.
[16] Ibidem.

metaphysics unites the 'holy knowledge' and what is beautiful, good and true of all that is. But *why* are we interested in this? Von Balthasar answers quite simply that "the path to being is the path to God."[17] In terms of the initial argument in this chapter such an approach is the faithful response to revelation. So the metaphysics is not a 'foreign' philosophical intrusion in the human project of finding meaning. Acknowledging being is acknowledging reality, *as it is*, while at the same time not turning to a post-modern *construction* of what 'is'. The establishment of this point early on, not only recognizes von Balthasar's commitment to being as it is, but it is also his reaction to a long lasting academic 'blind alley' in the work of understanding of the Scriptures, and that is the accusation that the Church 'hellenizes' the reading of the Scriptures by 'introducing' philosophy into the process.[18] Moreover, at this level, being is both that which is and that which is experienced. It is the understanding of the *experience*—in our case the experience of being a lay person— that involves philosophy.

Now being is characterized by the circum-incession of beauty, the good and the true. But through grace all created being has been redeemed in Christ. An apt quote from von Balthasar says it all: "that which is beautiful and whole never lacks that which is morally sound or the radiance of truth in its

---

[17] Hans Urs von Balthasar, "Philosophy, Christianity and Monasticism," *ET II*, 352.

[18] The claim is false for a number of reasons, but chiefly that the makers of such claims miss the "truly thought out universality" of metaphysics in that it can aid us in appreciating the whole which is not the same as manipulating it! See *GL IV*, 16, 17. Joseph Ratzinger (Benedict XVI) also reacted to the same claims by saying that historically the Church had to say 'which God it had in mind'. And that the Church chose 'the God of the philosophers' and not 'the gods of myth'. By this he means that the Church did not follow the religious trend of a withdrawal from reason into religious myth. He cites Tertullian: "Christ called himself truth not custom." (97) Real religion is connected with the truth! There is a felicitous congruence between those philosophers who sought the meaning of being and the thinking about Christ who is the logos of the world. See the *Gospel of John*. For more see Joseph Ratzinger, *Introduction to Christianity*, (San Francisco: Ignatius Press, 1990).

work of reconciliation and healing by grace."[19] Hence, this book will explore the beauty, goodness and truth of the layperson in the Church, and in the world, and the way in which lay life (from the perspectives of beauty, the good and the true) has been redeemed and sanctified in Jesus Christ. It is precisely a reflection on created and redeemed being—which can only result from the meta-physical reflection nourished and regulated by the data of revelation—that will take us into the deepest possible reflection on the grace-filled possibilities of the lay state of life.

At the same time this approach is the only possible authentic approach to understanding lay life. To at least demonstrate this point in a brief way: the theologian David Schindler judges von Balthasar's contribution concerning the present spiritual crisis that has distorted theology itself. He says: "Through the union of truth and goodness termed beauty, Balthasar answers at a fundamental level the split between arbitrary subjects (will) and mechanized objects (intelligence) which 'structures' the sin of the 'culture of death'."[20] Evidently by returning to metaphysics, von Balthasar resolved the intellectual split between subjects and objects that, if they are separated arbitrarily, loses the way in which subjects and objects are related to each other in their existence and meanings. The split became a common piece of intellectual furniture after the Enlightenment. Now by separating subjects and objects so that the operation of the subject is not regulated by the meaning of the object, we unleash subjects who are not working in terms of the truth of the objects around them.

Going to our author and specifically to his book on phenomenology, we find that:

> only a man who has learned to renounce his own self-concocted judgments and norms and, in the most intimate association with God, to look at the world, as it were through God's eyes (assuming God commissions and empowers him for the task) grant objects their truth and

---

[19] *GL IV*, 21.
[20] David Schindler, "Christological Aesthetics and *Evangelium Vitae*: Toward a definition of liberalism," *Communio* 22 (Summer, 1995), 205.

tell them what they both are and should be in the sight of the Absolute.[21]

All of this thinking of course is very abstract because it has to apply to all kinds of situations—how else do we view all of the other parts of God's creation? However just to illustrate von Balthasar's point with a very disturbing concrete example: the people who ran the Nazi concentration camps in Europe in the thirties and forties had separated subject from object. They had isolated themselves as subjects who could then assign meaning to the objects, to the prisoners whom they saw in front of them. They could first classify those who were in fact fellow human beings as subhuman and then they were free to torment and kill them without too much remorse.

Technically speaking, the Nazi way of thinking uses an ontology of the will. People who operate in this way choose to break the bonds between subject and object where the meaning of the object cannot be imposed by an act of will ('these people are subhuman'). They are deciding (will) the way being is by imposing a meaning on it eg. Jews are bad; people with mental problems are bad and so on. They are not letting being teach them what it (being Jewish) means. In our distressing example, they should have operated from the fact that they were dealing with precious irreplaceable human beings. When being is allowed to assert its own meaning, for example, that this prisoner is a human being just like me, or that pregnancy involves a new and genuine human life with all of the rights that that entails—then the human relation between subject and object is allowed to manifest meaning the way that it was created to do. As a consequence being is protected: these human beings, no matter what their state in life are worthy of my best care and attention regardless of what some demagogue says.

So von Balthasar is first of all advocating returning to the metaphysics of being and secondly, he is posing a serious critique of the ontology of the will! We are going to learn a theology of the layperson that comes out of the ontology of being. We may have taken a long journey to get to this conclusion but in fact,

---

[21] Han Urs von Balthasar, *Theologic: I: The Truth of the World*, Adrian Walker, trans., (San Francisco: Ignatius Press, 2000), 61.

even through this very abstract analysis, von Balthasar has ended up at what he was saying about Georges Bernanos. Von Balthasar places Bernanos in a unique category among authors: "Bernanos is the only one [author] . . . who has in full earnest seen the real fusion and indeed, the *ultimate identity that exists between the truth of literary creation and the truth of salvation*. And not only did Bernanos see this identity; it was on the basis of it that he both wrote his works and lived his life."[22] (Author's emphasis.) When von Balthasar considers Bernanos' works and life, he highlights two dimensions of Bernanos' being in the world. The emphasis on an ontology of being obviously is pointing us in the right direction.

Beauty, goodness and truth are called the 'transcendental' qualifications of being because they are 'transcendental', that is "each of them holds sway over the totality of being."[23] This perspective was commonplace in the period prior to the Enlightenment. (von Balthasar devoted two entire volumes to a study of the history of thought on the transcendental, most particularly that of beauty.)[24] Consequently the transcendentals provide the organizing principle for the major monument in von Balthasar's life's work. This is the so-called 'trilogy' of the *Glory of the Lord*, the *Theodrama* and the *Theologic* and, of course, we must include his *Epilog*.

The categories of beauty, the good and the true offer perspectives from which to examine being—remembering that being a layperson is a state of being in the world. Being a lay person is a global quality that informs every moment of lay life and consequently von

---

[22] B, 169.
[23] Ibidem. For more details on this complex issue, see D. C. Schindler, *Hans Urs von Balthasar and the Dramatic Structure of Truth: A Philosophical Investigation*, in the Perspectives in Continental Philosophy Series, (New York: Fordham University Press, 2004), 350 – 421.
[24] See Hans Urs von Balthasar, *The Glory of the Lord – A Theological Aesthetics IV: The Realm of Metaphysics in Antiquity*, trans. Brian Mc Neil C. R. V., Andrew Louth, John Saward, Rowan Williams and Oliver Davies, (San Francisco: Ignatius Press, 1989) and Hans Urs von Balthasar, *The Glory of the Lord – A Theological Aesthetics V: The Realm of Metaphysics in the Modern Age*, trans. Oliver Davies, Andrew Louth, Brian McNeil C. R. V., John Saward and Rowan Williams, (San Francisco: Ignatius Press, 1991).

Balthasar's vast output of theological work on the laity can be fruitfully organized in terms of beauty, the good and the true.

Very briefly then, von Balthasar's theology of the laity can be expressed as follows: the life (the being) of a Christian lay person is a life of doing the good as part of the mission of Christ. Such activity generates a beautiful form of life in the world that expresses the truth of God's revelation in Christ to the world.

So then von Balthasar's theology of the laity becomes an adaptation of his basic proposal at the beginning of the *trilogy*, where he says that "in order to maintain the right balance, a 'theological aesthetics' should be followed by a 'theological dramatics' and a 'theological logic'."[25] These several studies do, in some sense, separate into studies in terms of the individual transcendental, but in fact, "they cannot, therefore, be marked off from one another but indwell each other and make their voices heard in each other."[26] This indwelling will be evident in the frequent references to the other perspectives throughout this study. The three perspectives give this book its logical structure. The studies of lay life under the rubrics of aesthetics, dramatics and logic comprise the chapters Two, Five and Eight respectively, with more specialized reflections forming the intervening chapters.

However there is one earlier point that we have not explored. We advocated the recovery of the metaphysical approach to finding meaning.[27] By why did von Balthasar choose this approach to finding the meaning of a lay person's life? Von Balthasar made this choice because it was the best response to some of the major flaws that developed in later understandings of how history works.[28]

---

[25] *GL I*, Foreward.
[26] *GL IV*, 21.
[27] *GL IV*, 14.
[28] There is another issue here that I do not want to get into because it would fill another book, and that is Kevin Mongrain's proposal that von Balthasar's work is a 'retrieval' of the principles developed by Irenaeus. See Kevin Mongrain, *The Systematic Thought of Hans Urs von Balthasar – An Irenaen Retrieval*, (New York: Crossroad Publishing, 2002). I would propose that one could develop a response to Mongrain along the following lines: both von Balthasar and Joseph Ratzinger (now Benedict XVI) understand the

Very briefly, there were those who overemphasized the metaphysical side of the enterprise of finding meaning. Such an approach exaggerates the power of reason in 'penetrating' the meaning of God's plan. The work of George Friedrich Hegel is a prime example.[29] Then there were those who overemphasized the role of history (more specifically scripture) in the understanding God's plan. In von Balthasar's estimation, one influential example would be the work of Martin Luther (1483-1546).

Out of curiosity, how do these two mistaken ways influence thinking about the laity? Briefly, almost in the form of a caricature: the overemphasis on philosophy would have people thinking that they could simply reason to what they are going to do, and then simply 'dip into' the scriptures once they had decided what they were going to do. Hegel did that in his *Phenomenology of History*. Marxist thinkers did the same in their theology of liberation. The Vatican's *Instruction on Certain Aspects of 'Liberation Theology'* offers the following criticism of liberation theology:

> The 'theologies of liberation' make wide use of readings from the book of Exodus. The exodus, in fact, is the fundamental event in the formation of the chosen people. It represents freedom from foreign domination and from slavery. One will note that the specific significance of the event comes from its purpose, for this liberation is ordered to the foundation of the people of God and the Covenant cult celebrated on Mt. Sinai. That is

---

Patristic period as a whole *and* as a response to the Scriptures. (See for example, Joseph Ratzinger, *Principles of Catholic Theology*, 147.) These concepts, while not diminishing Irenaeus' influence on von Balthasar, do recognize his grasp of patristic theology as a whole. The notion of the patristic teaching *as a whole* is crucial to the priority that Ratzinger attributes to the Patristic period and to its theoretical description of its connection to the Scriptural period, as a response to Scripture. It is worth noting that Jacques Servais specifically lists the *Epistle to Diognetus*, Origen, and Basil the Great as influences on von Balthasar's theology of the Lay vocation in the world. See Jacques Servais, "The Lay vocation in the world according to H.U. von Balthasar," *Communio* 23 (Winter 1996), 656ff.

[29] Cf. Roch A. Kereszty O. Cist., *Jesus Christ: Fundamentals of Christology*, J Stephen Maddux ed., (New York: Alba House, Communio Book, 1991), 243-249.

why the liberation of the Exodus cannot be reduced to a liberation which is principally or exclusively political in nature. (*Instruction*, August 6, 1984)

So evidently, the overly philosophical approach strips away the more important aspects of the events in salvation history and simply reduces the meaning of events to politics.

Alternatively, an overemphasis on the Scriptures, without the benefit of rigorous thinking about their content, can lead to biblical fundamentalism where lines out of the bible are taken out of context to 'tell me' what to do. The problem with Luther's theology, as far as one can identify a systematic line of thought, is that his focus is so exclusively on Sacred Scripture that the intellectual reflection (in von Balthasar's terms the 'metaphysical reflection') is critically unaware. Informed as it must be, and guided as it must be by the scriptural reality, the metaphysical reflection is regulated by the philosophy of being. When both elements are active, then and only then can the reflection be aware of itself and its strengths and limitations. It is noteworthy that Luther also rejected the contribution of the Fathers and gave the priority in his thought to the Scriptures alone.

In contrast to these two extreme ways of doing things, Christian metaphysics—as von Balthasar understands it—consists in an ongoing metaphysical reflection on the history of God's work (scripture and tradition), and as such is the one that can best be a response to the awesome fact that it is *God* who is acting in the world, and also telling us the meaning of his actions.[30]

---

[30] The conception of history that is being used here is also skillfully described in the chapter on "The Method of Biblical Christology," in Roch Kereszty O.Cist, *Jesus Christ: Fundamentals of Christology*, (New York: Alba House, 1991), 3-20. The same 'marriage' of the contemplation of Scripture and the metaphysical reflection on the results of this contemplation can be identified in the work of Thomas Aquinas. For example, Giles Hibbert says: "the words with which the revelation of God is handed on are human and have a potential metaphysical content, what is handed on by way of them has a direct personal relevance—'encounter content' it could be called—in making God known to man. But of course it is necessary that this content be actualized

So we have made an argument as to why metaphysical thinking about lay life is important. Now we have to look at von Balthasar's understanding of history. This will also help us flesh out his ontology because human beings are inevitably historical beings—beings whose lives unfold in history.

4. History: Human Being in time

We have to appreciate that history is a unique characteristic of human being so when we study being a lay person we need to grasp what history is so that we can speak about the laity correctly.

The theologians Adolf Darlap and Jörg Splett explain that history is

> the peculiar nature of human existence (gathering up world and time into one) by which man stands between a past which is imposed on him, with enduring effects and yet beyond his reach, and an outstanding future on its way to him which he must try to procure.[31]

So history is a defining characteristic of human existence. This is important for us because the lives of laypeople unfold in history. The past has happened and yet has lasting effects. This of course applies in a special way to the death of Christ and the existence of the Church. Then too there is a future that will be with Christ.

In von Balthasar's terms: "Whatever the content of historical time in the past or the future might be, this content, seen from the point of view of creation, will always be embraced and measured by the form of the salvation time of Christ and, thus, by the form of his substantial, human-divine, dying and resurrected word."[32] In other words, the heart of *all*

---

and brought to life . . . A genuinely metaphysical theology will make it live." (Giles Hibbert O.P. "Mystery and Metaphysics in the Trinitarian Theology of Saint Thomas," *Irish Theological Quarterly* 31 (1964) 189.)

[31] Adolf Darlap and Jörg Splett, "History," *Encyclopedia of Theology*, ed., Karl Rahner, (New York: Seabury Press, 1975).

[32] Hans Urs von Balthasar, *A Theological Anthropology*, (New York: Sheed and Ward, 1967), 242. By conceiving of history in this way, von Balthasar is correcting more than two centuries of historicism in the academy. In an extended treatment of the method of biblical Christology, another author Roch Kereszty O. Cist. explains that the theologian's work seeks "a meaning which transcends the historian's field

history and its meaning is the Incarnation, Life, Death and Resurrection of the divine Son of God. There are not two separable histories, a secular history and a separate history of salvation that only applies to our group but to no one else.

Thomas Aquinas had a very similar vision of history. He recognized the structure of history in terms of the stages of salvation that he listed as "the state of nature, the state of grace and the state of glory."[33] These stages can be described as the unfolding of the event of salvation, starting with the creation of the world and ending with its return to God. This applied to the whole world. This is also the structure of the *Summa Theologica* (a survey of theology) itself.

Expanding on this concept, according to M. Seckler, the history of salvation "itself carries within it the fundamental theological design."[34] In other words, "it is the order of salvation that structures theology" and so for our purposes, very specifically, the theology of the laity.[35] In support of this point, it is useful to recall that Thomas Aquinas frequently cited the text from Saint Augustine's *City of God*:

---

of competence". (12) So much so that one has to turn to a new field so that "our main source and model for this enterprise is the New Testament itself." (12) Then comes the central insight that is so congruent with what von Balthasar proposed, namely: "the writers of those documents [the texts of the New Testament] were inspired by the Holy Spirit, who made them 'congenial' to the Christ event, that is capable of understanding its meaning for God's plan of salvation." (12) See Roch Kereszty, *Jesus Christ: Fundamentals of Christology*, (New York: Communio Book – Alba House, 1991).

[33] M. Seckler cited by Fr. Jean-Pierre Torrell, O.P., "Saint Thomas et l'histoire: État de la question et pistes de recherches," *Revue Thomiste*, 105 (2005), 363. (My translation.)

[34] Ibidem. Seckler, Thomas Aquinas and von Balthasar hold the same basic viewpoint, namely that ecclesial relationships are *essentially* structured by the actions of Christ. On the other hand, for Thomas O'Meara, O.P., for example, the perspective from which to examine ecclesial relationships, and hence the understanding of ministry is largely "human and historical". See Thomas O'Meara, O.P., "Theology of Ministry," (New York: Paulist Press, 1983), 98. This is based on his claim that "ultimately the Church is not a belief or a law but a social reality." (11)

[35] Ibidem.

> We see then that the two cities were created by two kinds of love: the earthly city was created by self-love reaching the point of contempt for God, the Heavenly City by the love of God carried as far as contempt of self. In fact, the earthly city glories in itself, the Heavenly City glories in the Lord. The former looks for glory from men, the latter finds its highest glory in God, the witness of a good conscience." (*City of God*, XIV, 28)[36]

Augustine was referring to the two dynamics in the history of salvation that of the human heart left to its own devices (the City of Man) or that of the heart that seeks the grace and light of God (the City of God). The echoes of these themes in the writing of von Balthasar himself on the laity will become apparent in what follows.

Now because salvation history is primary in revealing the meaning of history, the history of the archetype of all that it means to be a human being before God, namely Jesus Christ in his Life, Death and Resurrect-ion, grounds the ultimate meaning of every single event, most especially every single event of the history of the lay person in the Church.[37] So then, the historical life of Christ (as it is known from the Scriptures and the Tradition of the Church) is the foundation of the theological understanding of the Church and of the life of the lay person.

Now for von Balthasar (and the Church) Jesus Christ, not surprisingly, is the center of the Scriptures and of course here he means the way in which the Old Testament converges on Jesus Christ. That is to say that Jesus'

> life is a fulfilling of Scripture. . . . As his life proceeds two things stand out: the Word becomes more and more flesh, inasmuch as he imparts to the abstract nature of the law and the expectancy of prophecy the character of a divine, factual presence, and the flesh becomes more and more Word, inasmuch as he increasingly unifies the scriptural words in himself, making his earthly life the perfect expression of all the earlier revelations of God.

---

[36] Saint Augustine, *Concerning the City of God against the Pagans*, Henry Bettenson trans., (London: England, 1984)
[37] See Hans Urs von Balthasar, *Theology of History*, (San Francisco: Ignatius Press, 1991), 42ff.

He is their living commentary, their authentic exposition, intended as such from the beginning.³⁸

In short then, we are learning that Jesus lived 'inside' Scripture as it were. What I mean to say is that the teachings of the Old Testament formed a kind of framework for all that he said and did. This is not wishful thinking. Jesus even understood his life this way himself. So he, the Word, 'unifies the scriptural words in himself.' In the *Gospel of Luke*, for example, it says: Jesus "said to [the disciples on the way to Emmaus], 'Oh, how foolish you are! How slow of heart to believe all that the prophets spoke! Was it not necessary that the Messiah should suffer these things and enter into his glory?' Then beginning with Moses and all the prophets, he interpreted to them what referred to him in all the scriptures." (Luke 24:25- 27)

Now look at the phrases: 'he is their living comment-ary," "their authentic exposition'. Here is the core of the understanding of lay life. The life of a layperson is a commentary on Scripture as Jesus did. He or she expounds the Scriptures in life just as Jesus did. We started by generally looking at what history is and now we find that Jesus' history was a living commentary on the truth of Scripture. His life authentically expounded the truth of the Scriptures. Then, for one thing, we can appreciate that if this applies to Jesus then *lay life* in Christ too should be a commentary on the Scriptures. Catholic Lay life should be an exposition of the Scriptures.

But to do that we have to appreciate how we study the Scriptures—and I don't mean to get a doctorate but simply to appreciate what they mean. This is where things get complicated very quickly because we also have to make a good case that our thinking is valid.

First of all, according to von Balthasar, when we do theology of the laity then the metaphysical understanding of human being (as good, true and beautiful) depends on its constant reference to the whole, the totality of revelation, for its accuracy. In other words, "the proportions of the structure of theology must be governed by those of revelation, that

---

38 Hans Urs von Balthasar, "The Word, Scripture and Tradition," *Explorations in Theology I: The Word made Flesh*, (San Francisco: Ignatius Press, 1989), 13.

is to say, not of Scripture as a book, but of the event described in Scripture."[39] Because we are focusing on *events*, we can bring the events of Jesus' life up against the events of an individual layperson in the Church to understand their meaning and to act as a benchmark for the value of the lay person is doing. [40] We do this because Jesus is the fullness of the meaning and the value of human life. The reasoning is this: as Paul wrote to the Colossian church community in the first century: "See to it that no one captivate you with an empty, seductive philosophy according to human tradition, according to the elemental powers of the world and not according to Christ. For in him dwells the whole fullness of the deity bodily, and you share in this fullness in him, who is the head of every principality and power." (Colossians 2:8-10) So we are constantly to refer ourselves to the fullness of human life because we have been gifted with a share in this fullness! It is by comparing the events in lay life with *the* fullness of meaning that we find in the events of Jesus' life that we will see what the events in the life of a layperson mean and how to judge their enduring value.

Then as a second principle for reading Scripture: we discover that the Church is the inescapable part of this searching for meaning. Following our author, the divine Being of the Spirit of God is "the Spirit of missions and special functions within the mystical body, [the Church,] the Spirit who in fulfilling the Old Testament, continues its historical course, in which ever new unforeseeable tasks sent by God erupt."[41] The mystical body is, of course, the Church

---

[39] Hans Urs von Balthasar, *Explorations in Theology I: The Word made Flesh*, (San Francisco: Ignatius Press, 1989), "The Place of Theology," 156.

[40] There is interesting support from Henri de Lubac for the recognition of this consciousness. For example: when speaking about the Church in the early period, he says: "From the very start you feel that she has an extraordinarily deep awareness of her own being." *The Splendor of the Church*, Michael Mason trans., (San Francisco: Ignatius Press, 1999), 17. The Church had a consciousness that fulfilled the requirements of a reflection on being. On the same page he speaks of attempting "to grasp the mystery in its totality."

[41] "The Place of Theology," 158.

and the Spirit of God pours out of her in missions to the world.

Look at the meaning of mission: Georges Bernanos has one of the characters in his *Dialogues of the Carmelites* (1949) say in a homily: "The Lord always did live and still continues to live among us like a poor man, and the moment always arrives when he decides to make us poor like himself."[42] We will later see how this is poverty in a particular sense involves the recognition of being in the Church and of being obedient to the Church as our mission from Christ discovers us.

Just to whet your appetite concerning mission: our author says the following: "Bernanos always portrayed the Christian person in the act of commitment and in the vulnerability endemic to Christian judgment and action—something that often enough takes the form of suffering what is inflicted."[43] Here is one dimension of taking on the mission. There will be some suffering involved! Now we still have to identify the third principle . . .

The two principles that we have seen so far keep us facing God's revelation, complete as it is, in ever new situations as it meets us today. However, thirdly, there is also the *tradition* of the Church who has faced revelation (in scripture and tradition) for over two thousand years. The Church has a great storehouse of reflections done at various times in the Spirit of Christ through the ages. Thus "the theology of today must have such certainty and fullness—derived from the eternal fullness of revelation, of the Spirit given at this time, and of the fullness of the tradition received—as to embrace the riches of past theology as a living thing."[44] In other words, these three principles honor the sheer scale of God's revelation to us where the contemplation of the Scriptures respects the Scriptures (the divinely inspired witness to salvation history) and the tradition of the Church respects the life lived in the Church! Both are lights for our path.

This approach to meaning might be called an 'oscillation' between historical being (Jesus /the layperson) and the meaning of existence (the thought-out reflection on life) and it echoes through the

---

[42] Bernanos, Dialogues des Carmelites, 145-146, B 262.
[43] B, 115.
[44] "The Place of Theology," 159.

Scriptures themselves and in the works of the Church Fathers and the teaching of the Church.[45] So there is something very fundamental about his approach.

Von Balthasar explained that this approach is valid because if an event has a universal claim then it must have "its roots both in the historical sphere (only things that exist are real) and also in the metaphysical sphere (only as being is that which exists universal)."[46] In short, the meaning of the event unfolds in a metaphysical reflection. Now the truth of this approach will become more evident as we proceed but even at this stage one can make an initial point about lay life, and that is that, from the existential perspective, lay life is in its most basic sense an 'oscillation' between being and meaning and it happens in private prayer, in the celebration of the sacraments (if we are looking for it!) and in day-to-day events.[47]

---

[45] This insight is not reserved to von Balthasar. See for example, Joseph Ratzinger's (now Benedict XVI) comment that "the beginning and end of this new history is the Person of Jesus of Nazareth, who is recognized as the last man (the second Adam), that is, as the long awaited manifestation of what is truly human and the definitive revelation to man of his hidden nature; for this very reason it is oriented toward the whole human race and presumes the abrogation of all partial histories." This is from Joseph Cardinal Ratzinger, *Principles of Catholic Theology: Building Stones for a Fundamental Theology*, trans. Sister Mary Frances McCarthy S. N. D., (San Francisco: Ignatius Press, 1987), 156. Here Ratzinger, now Pope Benedict XVI, is indicating the way in which metaphysics of being and history are closely interrelated in the understanding Jesus Christ's action in the world.

[46] Hans Urs von Balthasar, *The Glory of the Lord – A Theological Aesthetics IV: The Realm of Metaphysics in Antiquity*, trans.,Brian Mc Neil C. R. V., Andrew Louth, John Saward, Rowan Williams and Oliver Davies, (San Francisco: Ignatius Press, 1989), 12. Please note that von Balthasar is showing the very close connection between theology and philosophy. This view is again a recovery of a method that has been falling into disuse in the modern period. See Martin Bieler, "Meta-Anthropology and Christology: On the Philosophy of Hans Urs von Balthasar," *Communio* 20 (Spring, 1993), 129 - 146.

[47] As Joseph Ratzinger explains: "the problem of God is not a supplementary question of metaphysics, but is posited with the question of being itself." *Commentary on the Documents of Vatican II vol. V*, 132.

This 'oscillation' is the search for meaning in historical being. This is a milestone in our search to understand a lay person's life. At its heart it is the "foundational spiritual act of the creature . . . one of pure receptivity, astonished at its depths that it is: for some unfathomable reason, it has been thought by God to be worthy of being allowed to exist."[48] Being allowed to exist is wondrous. To find the meaning of this being in Christ is more wondrous still.

Acknowledging this manner of uncovering meaning means respecting being (events in history) in a way has massive repercussions. Consider, just to take one example, the German author Reinhold Schneider's (1903-1958) statement on the presence and impact of Saint Boniface (died 755) in Germany. He said that from the years that Boniface spent in what is now Germany: "the existence of the Germans had an inseparable relationship to the work of redemption, which had been inserted into history."[49] There is a particular Judeo-Christian understanding of history here where nothing is lost due to the ontological unity of salvation history. The actions of Boniface (and in our example it could have been anyone else) radically change history. Germany would never be the same again. In a strange way then Jesus' words come back to us: "Are not two sparrows sold for a small coin? Yet not one of them falls to the ground without your Father's knowledge." (Matthew 10:29) This is the perilous nature of human action in history. Both for good or ill our actions have consequences that we cannot imagine.

The experiences of people in history have light to shed on us even a thousand years later! Schneider's simple comment finds companions in the statements of Joseph Ratzinger (now Benedict XVI) on the cultural crisis in Europe, for example, where Europe "excludes God from the public conscience" by not repeatedly making the connection between the Europe of today and its Christian past.[50] Specifically, because of the

---

[48] Hans Urs von Balthasar, "Beyond Contemplation and Action?" *Explorations in Theology IV: Spirit and Institution*, (San Francisco: Ignatius Press, 1995), 300.

[49] Hans Urs von Balthasar, *Tragedy under Grace: Reinhold Schneider on the Experience of the West*, trans. Brian McNeil C.R.V., (San Francisco: Ignatius Press, 1997), 198.

[50] Joseph Ratzinger, (Benedict XVI) *Speech at Subiaco*, April 1st 2005. Text from Zenit 26th July 2005.

loss of the contact with the Christian past, Ratzinger noted that "the splendor of being an image of God no longer shines over man . . . [and] confers on him his dignity and inviolability, and he is left only to the power of his own human capacities."[51] It is this splendor to which von Balthasar calls the laity—as witnessed by choosing Georges Bernanos as a fitting example—while he develops his theology of the layperson in the life of the Church. But how do we get a perspective on this life?

5. Scripture and Tradition

To start with Bernanos our model layman: "For me the Catholic faith is an element out of which I could not live any more than a fish out of water."[52] Bernanos had a dynamic experience of Catholicism and it is the dynamic Catholic experience that we are seeking to describe in this section. Now when von Balthasar is explaining this project, he says: "if we don't want to misunderstand Bernanos at a fundamental level, we will have to grasp that everything depends on this: God's revelation in Christ, in his Church and in his saints—in the whole of Christian life—*cannot and will not provide readymade recipes* for overcoming the problems of the world, of history, of the development of culture, the State, technology and so on."[53] (Author's emphasis.) Here is the subtle dynamic that we are exploring: it is the lived experience of the lay person in both the Church and the world.

There is no simple blueprint for what we are studying. Rather we are pointing to the experience and reflecting on the experience of *this* individual Catholic in the 'water' in which he now swims. Nevertheless there are some constant elements to Catholic experience.

The first constant is Catholic history. Each Catholic joins the history of Catholicism. Just look at Boniface! At the heart of this history lies God's revelation and von Balthasar explains:

> the one and only thing God's revelation does provide us with are archetypes or models that necessarily and in keeping with their very

---
[51] Ibidem.
[52] Freedom, B 36.
[53] B 33.

essence stand above the level of worldly questions and' like stars, shed their light down upon them. If Christ himself wasted hardly a word concerning the State or culture, and no word at all concerning art or science, it was so as not to commit the blunder of meddling in the Father's work of creation, and also in order not to rob man, the laboring king of creation, of the earnestness of his accomplishments by applying some magical formula.[54]

Here is the role of the human being in God's world. He or she is not passive in all of this. So how do we bring the rich scriptural and traditional (historical) content of the concept of the laity to living expression in a formal theology of the laity aided by metaphysics?

Well, let us see how he does it: for him there are two stages in the metaphysical method that make it valid. The validity arises because these moments demonstrate that reflecting philosophically on the results of the contemplation of the Scriptures is a proper response to the reality being presented. Interestingly, these two moments also turn out to be the constitutive moments in how the Church understands things as well, and this is the direction in which this presentation has been moving. But first, let us flesh out the two moments themselves.

The first moment in our relationship with God is that "the living God [is] the only subject of the act of revealing, law-giving and the bestowal of grace."[55] This is letting God be God! Then, continuing this point, access to this revealing subject is through the Scripture and the Tradition[56] of the Church. The

---

[54] B, 33.

[55] *GL IV*, 24.

[56] The term 'Tradition' here alone refers both to the Tradition as commentary on Scriptures (the sense of Tradition in DV) as well as what the documents of the Second Vatican Council referred to with the lower case 'tradition' namely, ministries (LG, 20), the apostolic tradition (LG, 20), liturgical rites (LG, 21) and so on. In the Constitution on Divine Revelation, the list is more substantial: "Now what was handed on by the Apostles includes everything which contributes toward the holiness of life and increase in faith of the peoples of God; and so the Church, in her teaching, life and worship, perpetuates and hands on to all generations all that she herself is, all that she believes." (DV 8)

dynamic relationship between Scripture and Tradition shows the essential role of the Church with its Magisterium so that "the inspiration of the Scripture necessarily passes through, while never being reducible to, the participation of the Church . . . in Jesus Christ's original act of traditioning."[57] In these words lies the answer to the two more extreme methods of finding meaning that were mentioned above. We have transposed our approach to events (and laity are always trying to make sense of events in their lives!) by avoiding the extremes of an overly philosophical or an overly scriptural way of seeing things and instead by placing the lay person in an ongoing symbiosis between Scripture and the Tradition of the Church where *both* Scripture and Tradition have a part to play in helping the lay person to see the deeper meaning of events.[58] The lay person is consciously located 'within' this symbiosis at many levels. As Benedict XVI describes it: "Their insertion into this context also involved a sharing in both the liturgical and external life of the communities, in their intellectual world, in their culture and in the ups and downs of their shared history." (*Verbum Domini*, 29) He is referring specifically to exegetes but the dynamic is the same for the layperson looking for meaning and lay people cannot avoid this search. The fact is that every lay person "needs to develop through an ever more conscious Christian way of life capable of "accounting for the hope" within us (cf. *1 Pet* 3:15)." (*Verbum Domini*, 84)

Now on to the second moment in our relationship with God! When God has been acknowledged to have the necessary and continuing

---

[57] Adrian Walker, "Fundamentalism and the Catholicity of Truth," *Communio* 29 (2002), 5 - 27

[58] Benedict XVI explains this symbiosis this way: "*the primary setting for scriptural interpretation is the life of the Church*. This is not to uphold the ecclesial context as an extrinsic rule to which exegetes must submit, but rather is something demanded by the very nature of the Scriptures and the way they gradually came into being. "Faith traditions formed the living context for the literary activity of the authors of sacred Scripture. Their insertion into this context also involved a sharing in both the liturgical and external life of the communities, in their intellectual world, in their culture and in the ups and downs of their shared history." (Verbum Domini 29)

priority then there is the second moment to the relationship: "only then can man who is the object of God's action become a subject whose action is a reply to God."[59] Here is the recognition of the role of the human person. After acknowledging the primacy of God, we can acknowledge the existence and responsibility of the human person. He or she is not a passive bystander. The subject reflecting (metaphysics) on the fruits of the contemplation of Scripture (and the history that it embraces)[60], acknowledges that man's response is most definitely subsequent to God's actions. Incidentally the sequence indicates the flaw in the rationalism and the relativism of the historical-critical approach to the Scriptures when it is not applied correctly.[61]

(Looking ahead: This line of thought also suggests a further concept that will be developed in the theodramatic study, and that is how man becomes a real subject in the divine-human drama, precisely because God has taken the initiative and addressed him. Only thus does man become a participant in salvation history. This involves intersubjectivity, a

---

[59] Ibidem.
[60] See Hans Urs von Balthasar, "The Word and History," *Explorations in Theology I: The Word made Flesh*, trans. A. V. Littledale with Alexander Dru, (San Francisco: Ignatius Press, 1989), 27 ff., and Bevil Bramwell, "Hans Urs von Balthasar's Theology of Scripture, *New Blackfriars*, vol. 86 no. 1003 May 2003.
[61] See too David Schindler's conclusion that there is a "need for an appeal to some principle other than history as a necessary condition for the possibility of advancing normative interpretations." This comes from his reading of Van Harvey and David Tracy that need not concern us here, except to say, that there are internal flaws in the historical critical-method of Harvey that leave him open to the serious accusation that his work is either a relativist or a dogmatic use of history. Cf. David l. Schindler, "The historical-critical claims of modernity: on the need for metaphysics," *Communio* XXX (Spring 1979), 85. This conclusion also echoes the thought of Maurice Blondel: "Since philosophy cannot claim to substitute itself for the real even in its own domain, the field lies open for a dogma which governs life and thought in virtue of a quite different title, and speaks the language of the absolute," in *The Letter on Apologetics and History and Dogma*, trans. Alexander Dru and Illtyd Trethowan, (Grand Rapids MI: William B. Eerdmans, 1994), 185.

concept that has such an important part to play in von Balthasar's *Theodrama*.)

6 The Lay Person: In a Movement in History

Since Georges Bernanos has been our model for the layperson, let me now use his life to draw together what we have seen so far. First some quotations from Bernanos' own words: "My books and I are one."[62] Then in a different place: "It seems to me I've respected my vocation. . . . We must both be saved together . . . by fulfilling each other to the end."[63]

Our study of metaphysics finds its concrete exemplar in the life of Bernanos. He lived his vocation as a writer. He knew the struggle to put bread on the table: "The trials that poverty has imposed on me have been fewer than the follies she has spared me."[64] He experienced the First World War as a volunteer and came out as a brigadier. He moved his whole family to South America once the fascists began to rise in Spain, offended as he was by the excesses of Catholic Fascism there. The financial struggles continued and many friends came to his aid. He supported the French resistance through radio broadcasts. Finally he returned with the family to France in 1945 to take up the cudgels again on behalf of finding spiritual values in the post-war world. He died in 1948. His last work was a film script for *Song at the Scaffold*, the story of the Carmelite martyrs during the war.

We have studied history from a technical point of view and in Bernanos' life we see the man responding to historical events. His insights are manifold but for example: "only Christianity can raise nature to the full measure of man and of man's dream."[65] Here is Salvation History in practical terms, the lived version. Accompanying this understanding there is also the recognition that:

> There is in man a secret, incomprehensible hatred, not only of his fellowmen, but of himself. We can give this mysterious feeling whatever origin or explanation we want, but we must give it one. As far as we Christians are

---

[62] From a Letter to Amoroso Lima, March 5, 1939. Cited in B 211.
[63] Letter to Amoroso Lima, March 13, 1940. Cited in B 211.
[64] *Les Enfants Humiliés*, cited in B 609.
[65] *Journal d'un cure de campagne*" cited in B 220.

concerned, we believe that this hatred reflects another hatred, a thousand times more profound and lucid: the hatred of the ineffable spirit who was the most resplendent of all the luminaries of the abyss and who will never forgive us his cataclysmic fall.[66]

As neat a summary of the theology of Satan as I have ever seen! It is gleaned from his own going to Mass and his own reflections. This text is found in his book *Freedom: To do what?* It is his reflection on the nature of human freedom and includes, of course, a reflection on original sin and its origins.

This is all to do with human life as it is spoken of in the Scriptures as they are understood in the Tradition of the Church. Now let me try to list some of the implications of what we have seen so far:

First of all, apparently being a lay person is not a concept that is simply 'added on', so to speak, to some other conception of man, whether it is my own private idea of who I am, or whether it comes from my social class or from the political situation in my country. So a Catholic does not start by considering himself or herself as a business man, or a lawyer, or a wealthy citizen who then also in addition belongs to the Church.

The ontological understanding of being Catholic means that we start with the lay person as redeemed and sanctified by God. This is the first qualification of the baptized person. Then these other things (occupation, politics, class concerns) come 'later' and are critiqued and amplified by the Catholic meaning of lay life. The lay person's grasp of the meaning of his/her life develops in the Church from the metaphysical reflection on Scripture within the Tradition that is constantly being done by the Church in liturgy, in councils and by the Pope.[67]

Secondly: the Scripture and the Tradition of the Church come from the all-powerful God acting and revealing himself in the world and causing salvation history to unfold. So in the Old Testament and then in its fulfillment in the New Testament, God has begun to

---

[66] *La Liberté, pour quoi faire?* Cited in B 220.
[67] See Thomas O'Meara O.P., *Theology of Ministry*, (New York: Paulist Press, 1983). O'Meara O.P., does not see the scriptures as showing the principles for the later history of relationships in the Church. For him "theology is grounded in history". (17)

weave a new reality, the New Creation, in this world. Lay people are part of that and can choose to immerse themselves in the New Creation. All else, the lay person's way of thinking, the choices he/she makes, follow from and are ordered by, this most basic truth: the infinite, incomprehensible all-loving God acting in his creation to redeem and sanctify it, because "he destined us for adoption to himself through Jesus Christ, in accord with the favor of his will, for the praise of the glory of his grace that he granted us in the beloved." (Ephesians 1:6)

Third: This concerns man's reply to God. We learned from the second stage of using metaphysics that man's (woman's) reply is not solely a faith-filled *intellectual* response to the True. There is an accompanying *moral* component as well. (The Good) The will is organized by the intellect's knowing, where the person knows that he/she is to live a life of charity, precisely because he/she knows that God loves him/her in Christ and that love is the proper response. The tropological sense of the Scriptures comes into play here. There is a definite moral sense to Scripture. In his work on the medieval understanding of the senses of Scripture, Henri de Lubac S.J. mentions Elmer of Canterbury's words: "that which Scripture commemorates historically about the earth seems to belong morally to hearts."[68] Knowing Christ through the Scriptures and the Tradition of the Church should lead, by its own inner necessity, to laity leading a more moral life and giving themselves more and more fully to Christ's mission. Such a life involves an ongoing discovery of God's intimacy with the individual lay person, in and through his Son, in his Body the Church. The Good which is God himself thus informs the good of the hearts and minds of lay people through their participation in the Church of Jesus Christ.

Fourthly, although it would take too long to detail here, the Second Vatican Council actually used the method of theological ontology that is being put forward in these pages so von Balthasar is not just making things 'more academic,' as it were. If I may just

---

[68] Henri de Lubac S. J., "Quotidie ["Daily"] in *Medieval Exegesis 2: The Four Senses of Scripture*, (Grand Rapids MI: William B. Eerdmans, 2000), trans. E. M. Macierowski, 134.

illustrate what I mean: in the *Constitution on the Church*, to take one example, the council said:

> All the members [of the Church] ought to be molded in the likeness of [Christ], until Christ be formed in them. For this reason we, who have been made to conform with Him, who have died with Him and risen with Him, are taken up into the mysteries of His life, until we will reign together with Him. On earth, still as pilgrims in a strange land, tracing in trial and in oppression the paths He trod, we are made one with His sufferings like the body is one with the Head, suffering with Him, that with Him we may be glorified. (LG 7)

The council was describing the being of the members of the Church united with the being of Christ. Then too, the members of his Body are 'taken up into the mysteries of his life'. The being of the individual members of the Church is accurately described as 'pilgrims', 'in trial and oppression'. Notice that the Church does not appear as a refuge from the world! This is the ontological approach in action, recognizing the individual's development in goodness, beauty and truth as he or she participates in the history of Christ *in the world*.

On a practical note, the endnotes will point to the parallels between von Balthasar's thought and the formulations of the council. What he has done is to provide a plausible theological argument to substantiate the theological statements of the council. The council fathers did not go into the underlying theology that grounded their statements. That is not customary in conciliar statements!

Point number five: the lay person is a member of the Body of Christ and the Bride of Christ. He or she is constituted as a Catholic lay person by the Sacrament of Baptism and so the lay person is a member of the Body of Christ. As such the lay person lives within the life of Christ and has Christ as the Head of his life. In Paul's words: "in him you have been made complete, and he is the head over all rule and authority." (Colossians 2:10)

The lay person is who he/she is as part of the Church. His way of life is not a private one. It is shared and it is public. The corporate dimension of being Christian involves everything from genuinely worshipping, as part of the Body of Christ, to being part of the community, to continuing to extend this recovery of corporate human life in Christ into one's family, the community and into one's business, social and political life. The spiritually corporate way of being in the world, as Church, means being one's brother's keeper (Genesis 4:9), loving one's neighbor (Luke 10:27 ff.), and knowing how to truly love everyone: "Love is patient, love is kind. It is not jealous, [love] is not pompous, it is not inflated, it is not rude . . . it bears all things, believes all things, hopes all things, endures all things." (1 Corinthians 13:4-7)

Sixthly—and we are going to have to spend some time on this— lay people are in the world. This is where they will build their sainthood. The Church is in the world, it "does not exist for itself alone, but for the ultimate redemption of the world."[69] However one must ask about the nature of the world. How do we describe it? Chapter Four will have more to say, but significantly all theologies of the laity refer to the specifically *secular* nature of lay life. It is fundamental to John Paul II's *Christifideles laici* for example. So what is meant by terms like 'secular' and 'world'? Von Balthasar's answer is theological and it is complex.

Distinguishing between the Church and the world is difficult because "the Church is only Church in the world," and the world is only "created through [Christ] and for [Christ] (Colossians 1:16)."[70] So there is no *a priori* concept available to help us distinguish between them. Von Balthasar noted Paul's words to the crowd at the Areopagus: "[God] made from one man every nation of mankind to live on all the face of the earth, having determined their appointed times and the boundaries of their habitation, that they would seek God, if perhaps they might grope for him and find him, though he is not far from each one of us."(Acts 17:26, 27) Von Balthasar concluded that God is immanent in his creation "which is the basis of our immanence in him."[71] Here is the true situation of the world—something that we can only know from Revelation— and it does not change. So the believer,

---

[69] *CSOL*, 345.
[70] Hans Urs von Balthasar, "Encountering God in the World," *Explorations in Theology III: Creator Spirit*, trans. Brian McNeil C. R. V., (San Francisco: Ignatius Press, 1993), 299.
[71] "Encountering God in the World," 300.

living in the world, is placed under somewhat of a burden, because modern society leads man to view the world as separate and isolated from God.

The modern technological mindset means that man no longer rises in contemplation to God by wondering at the Creator from the evidence of his creation, but instead, looks down on a world that is given meaning only when man assigns it.[72] Looking back, the contemplation of being that is part of metaphysics, returns man to the first way of relating to the world, as manifesting the beauty of the creator.[73] Restating another point: the reflection on the being of the world is not isolated at any point from the evidence of historical being and the revelation about historical being found in the Scriptures.[74] The Scriptures are a complex expression of being. The meaning of being uncovered by contemplating the Scriptures both regulates the metaphysical approach to this meaning and provides much of its content as well. It does this because the Scriptures (history of salvation) contain things that can never be deduced by philosophical means. They testify to a personal God who has chosen to relate personally to his creation and they give evidence of the radical new meaning of the world because of the Incarnation.

In his theology of the laity, von Balthasar recovers the ancient and indeed scriptural attitude, towards the world at large of looking "through things upward."[75] These 'things' are people and relationships as well as material things. Consequently, the world with its 'natural' elements and structures is not rejected. Instead God can be 'seen' through the 'ordinary', 'everyday' fabric of life. Then since God took flesh in *this* world, through the Incarnation as Jesus Christ, the relationship between the Church and the

---

[72] "Encountering God in the World," 302. See also Saint Bonaventure's *Itinerarium Mentis in Deum*.

[73] Hence the importance of the notion of the world as gift. See Nicholas J. Healy III, "The World as Gift," *Communio* 32 (Fall 2005).

[74] This is an important point because of what Joseph Ratzinger (Pope Benedict XVI) has called a step in the 'stock idea' of Jesus Christ, namely the claim that Hellenisation has contributed to the content of Catholic thought. See Joseph Ratzinger, *Introduction to Christianity*, trans. J. R. Foster, (San Francisco: Ignatius Press, 1990), 158-159.

[75] "Encountering God in the World," 302.

world is not merely dialectical. Instead, because of God's action, the Catholic understanding of the world is founded on the principle that unfolds in revelation and that is *gratia supponit naturam*.[76] God has done so much more than to simply providentially place human beings in the world, "in a marriage, a profession, as a member of a people, a state, a native land, humanity."[77] The Incarnation has changed everything so that God has "establish[ed man] in a quite different relation to himself, that of personal love, which demands not merely [his] action but [his] heart, not merely [his] 'works' but [his] 'faith' (i.e. the gift of [his] heart)."[78] Von Balthasar's theology of the laity describes "the working of God the creator [as] . . . not contradicted by the working of God the redeemer but rather perfected therein."[79] Thus the world is not neutral. Instead, it is intimately taken up in the working out of the history of salvation, through the Church, as well as the working of the Spirit beyond the visible confines of the Church. More formally, the world has been brought under the sway of the order of grace.

So the revelation of God's love in Christ does not trivialize the world or its relationships. On the contrary "they remain what they are, viz., essentially demands made by the order of creation, and for this reason they may not simply be equated through a logical short-circuit with the demands of the order of

---

[76] Hans Urs von Balthasar, "Forgetfulness of God and Christians," *Explorations in Theology III: Creator Spirit*, trans. Brian McNeil C. R. V., (San Francisco: Ignatius Press, 1993), 322.

[77] Hans Urs von Balthasar, "Secular Piety," *Explorations in Theology III: Creator Spirit*, trans. Brian McNeil C. R. V., (San Fran-cisco: Ignatius Press, 1993), *Explorations in Theology III: Creator Spirit*, trans. Brian McNeil C. R. V., (San Francisco: Ignatius Press, 1993), 357.

[78] Ibidem.

[79] Hans Urs von Balthasar, *The Glory of the Lord: A Theological Aesthetics IV: The Realm of Metaphysics in Antiquity*, trans. Brian Mc Neil C.R.V., Andrew Louth, John Saward, Rowan William and Oliver Davies, (San Francisco: Ignatius Press, 1989), 24. This and the other books of von Balthasar's great trilogy, *The Glory of the Lord*, the *Theodrama* and the *Theologic* will be referred to by the abbreviations GL, TD and TL respectively each time after the first full reference to a particular work has been made.

grace or of revelation."[80] Instead, the secular situation of the baptized person in the world does not mean that one 'realm' answers (or substitutes) for the other, so to speak, but in fact, as Jesus taught, it is the duty of man to "render to Caesar the things that are Caesar's; and to God the things that are God's." (Matthew 22: 21) The two realms are so intertwined that the lay person has to attend to them in an ordered way, with the order of grace being recognized as the inner principle of the order of nature through Christ. In the background is always the fundamental principle that God has "order[ed] man to himself [that is God's self] and creat[ed] nature for the sake of grace."[81] Essentially then in a concept that was summed by Thomas Aquinas and cited by von Balthasar: "A being is all the more noble the higher its end be toward which it strives by the definition of its essence, even if it can no longer reach this goal by its own power."(*ST Ia IIae*, q. 5, a. 5)[82] The true nobility of the lay person comes to be realized through the cooperation with the grace of Christ, who includes the lay person in the work of his Church through the Holy Spirit.

Seventh: we have to now describe the activity of a lay person. When he describes the *relation* between the Church and the world more formally, von Balthasar speaks of a process of "osmosis" between them.[83] As in biology, he sees that the single process, of the relation between the Church and the world, has both a systolic and a diastolic mode. The former assimilates the world as it is brought under grace. The latter involves the Church transcending itself and reaching out still further into the world—"go[ing] to meet the world outside it"—as von Balthasar expresses it.[84] The lay person participates in both of the modes of the 'osmosis', so that he/she has to cooperate with the grace and truth of the Church in the first mode, and then secondly, see his/her mission to reach still further into the world through Christian action. (The Church is not a refuge . . .) The lay person cooperates in the Church's radical Christian transformation of the

---

[80] "Secular Piety," 358.
[81] Hans Urs von Balthasar, "Who is man?" *Explorations in Theology IV: Spirit and Institution*, trans. Edward T. Oakes, (San Francisco: Ignatius Press, 1995), 26.
[82] Hans Urs von Balthasar, "Who is man?" 25.
[83] *CSOL*, 347.
[84] Ibidem.

world (systolic mode), as well as in the diastolic missionary approach to the world that is still 'other' in relation to the Church.

Eighth: so that we do not see lay activity as mere activism, von Balthasar notes that these two are fundamentally immeasurable, relying as they do on the 'yes' of Mary (systolic mode) and the "Passion [of the Word] by which he destroyed the world's dominion." (dyastolic mode.)[85] These modes lie deep within the grace of God. Lastly, on this question, the systolic mode relates to von Balthasar's understanding of the traditional term 'contemplation', while the diastolic mode refers to the 'active' mode of life. Both modes will be shown to be integral to lay life! The lay person lives out the receptivity of Mary within the Church, while at the same time suffering in the world because of a genuine love for the beings of the world in Christ.

An important note: what we have been doing here is a reflection on nature and grace. A significant principle for doing this reflection properly is the Analogy of Being. As Thomas Aquinas explained: "Although it may be admitted that creatures are in some sort like God, it must nowise be admitted that God is like creatures." (*ST I* q.5 a.3) The understanding of the relationship between uncreated and created Being is actually the foundation of the theological method being described here. In other words, recognizing the analogy between created and uncreated Being safeguards the continual respect for the priority of God's action in the world and of the openness of created being to its perfection in grace. But there is more: the notion of 'similarity' in the analogy "makes the finite the shadow, trace, likeness and image of the Infinite."[86]

The Analogy of Being tells us something crucial about finite being: finite being does not first of all constitute itself as an acting subject by making its choices, and then subsequently choose to pass on some good. Instead the finite being of the person is constituted as a subject precisely through respecting

---

[85] CSOL, 351.
[86] Hans Urs von Balthasar, *The Glory of the Lord V: The Realm of Metaphysics in the Modern Age*, trans. Oliver Davies, Andrew Louth, John Sayward and Martin Simon, (San Francisco: Ignatius Press, 1991), 627.

being, that is, having the right metaphysical relationship to all being, whether it is in the family or in society or in the natural world. This right relationship, according to von Balthasar, involves man in an "*ekstasis* out of [his] own closed self."[87] He is to relate to the God who loves him. This *ekstasis* is borne by the unmerited love of God. Divine being redeems and elevates created being and allows it to reach its true goal, union with God. This is the encounter between the lover and the beloved that Peter Henrici S.J. mentioned in the *Introduction*.

The encounter is grounded in the fact that Uncreated Being takes the initiative and freely gives existence to created being, so that there is then a "correspondence between worldly 'beauty' and divine 'glory' . . . between worldly, finite freedom and divine infinite freedom . . ., between the structure of creaturely truth and the structure of divine truth."[88] Expanding on the manifestation of truth in being, Peter Henrici S. J. explained that "according to the mutual indwelling of the transcendentals, the nature of truth is seen in the encounter between the lover and the beloved; truth manifests itself thus as revelation, as unveiling, but also as sheltering participation."[89] The encounter in love grounds the whole theology of the laity that we will uncover in the work of von Balthasar. *That* is where the refuge is—in the truth, in revelation.

Less abstractly, consider that von Balthasar often speaks of the nature of the world, because it is in the world that the laity find their place, and work out their salvation within the relationships of the world. The lay person does this in the systolic and the diastolic movement of the Church.

Nineth: to illustrate this point, take the example of time. We are interested in the notion of the quality of lay time (and not just place). The lay person takes time for God and for prayer (systolic) as well as time for secular occupations (diastolic). The mature

---

[87] Ibidem.
[88] Hans Urs von Balthasar, *Theologic I: Truth of the World*, trans Adrian J. Walker, (San Francisco: Ignatius Press, 2000), 7.
[89] Peter Henrici S. J., "The Philosophy of Hans Urs von Balthasar," *Von Balthasar: His Life and Work*, ed. David L. Schindler, (San Francisco: Communio Books – Ignatius Press, 1991), 151.

Christian lay person spends time properly. Lay people who do their work competently, for example, demonstrate that competence and they show how to use time well. Both competences owe a lot to love. They do what they do with love. The 'natural' requirements of being in the world find their supernatural fulfillment when they are done lovingly.

Tenth: Laity in the World (place). Someone who reflected on this attitude to how we live in the world was Saint Ignatius of Loyola (1491-1556). He influenced von Bathasar (a former Jesuit!) regarding the meaning of some dimensions of the receptive stance of the lay person vis-à-vis the being of the world. Von Balthasar owes a debt to Saint Ignatius of Loyola of whom he was—in Henri de Lubac's words—a "fervent disciple."[90]

Learning how to stand in the world and getting better at doing it is called conversion. Conversion is at the heart of Ignatius' *Spiritual Exercises* and it is a conversion with respect to God that then has implications for the individual's relationship to the world! The depth of the individual's conversion rests on Ignatius reminder about the disponibility of the baptized to grace. Ignatius only serves as a *reminder* on how to work with grace because the characteristic disponibility had already been clearly expressed in the Old Testament, ("But now, O Lord, you are our Father, we are the clay, and you our potter; And all of us are the work of your hand." (Isaiah 64:8)) and the same structure of the faith of Abraham continued to be realized in the New Testament ("By faith Abraham, when he was called, obeyed by going out to a place which he was to receive for an inheritance; and he went out, not knowing where he was going." (Hebrews 11:8)).

As a faithful mirror of the Tradition of the Church, Ignatius wrote in his *Spiritual Exercises*: "Man is created to praise, reverence, and serve God our Lord, and by this means to save his soul. All other things on the face of the earth are created for man to help him fulfill the end for which he is created. From this it follows that man is to use these things to the extent that they will help him to attain his end.

---

[90] Cited by Werner Löser in his "The Ignatian Exercises in the Work of Hans Urs von Balthasar," *Hans Urs von Balthasar: His life and Work*, 103.

Likewise, he must rid himself of them in so far as they prevent him from attaining it."[91] Ignatius has described the posture of the Christian in relation to the gifts that God has given. The Ignatian concept of disponibility sums up the posture of every Christian before God who is the real value and the real satisfaction for the creature.

Disponibility has a specific influence on the choices that Christians have to make. Drawing again on the *Spiritual Exercises*: "I ought to choose whatever I do, that it may help me for the end for which I am created, not ordering or bringing the end to the means, but the means to the end: as it happens that many choose first to marry—which is a means—and secondarily to serve God our Lord in the married life— which service of God is the end."[92] Hence, Christians must choose the means that will help them reach their end. They cannot choose the means first, simply because that is what they would like to do, and then try to turn it into a means of their salvation.

Ignatius was laying out the level of choice, of indifference, and of obedience that is involved in the operation of a baptized person. These two attitudes comprise the fundamental openness that lies at the heart of being a lay person in the Catholic Church. It is both biblical ("Take my yoke upon you and learn from me . . ." (Matthew 11:29)) and one of the "Catholic objectivities" down through the ages.[93] But as Ignatius and his disciple, von Balthasar knew, the choices are not blind.

Indifference is not with respect to nothing. The obedience is not blind. The lay person is—in von Balthasar's words—"one who has been struck by the splendor of Christ—and, in him, of the triune God— [and then] is next introduced into the lived answer that this experience requires."[94] The choice, the

---

[91] Saint Ignatius, *The Spiritual Exercises of St. Ignatius*, trans. Anthony Mottola, (New York: Doubleday, 1964), 47.
[92] *The Spiritual Exercises of St. Ignatius*, 83.
[93] Hans Urs von Balthasar, "Die Kirche lieben?" cited in Werner Löser's "The Ignatian Exercises," *in Hans Urs von Balthasar: His Life and His Work*, ed. David L. Schindler, (San Francisco: Communio Books Ignatius Press, 1991), 110.
[94] Hans Urs von Balthasar, *Theologic: I: Truth of the World*, trans. Adrian J. Walker, (San Francisco: Ignatius Press, 2000), 20.

indifference, and the obedience of the lay person, are all parts of the lived answer to the mission of the Incarnate Son of God. Salvation history is initiated by God prior to the life of a particular individual. A lay person lives a life of particular response in his situation and time. So according to von Balthasar, the response of the Christian requires an 'attunement' in grace to "the mysteries of salvation."[95] This attunement must both be "prayed for" and "created and acquired by man himself."[96] Importantly, Ignatius' reflection on the Scriptures uncovers a religion that is neither based on feelings nor is it rationalistic.[97] Instead, Christianity is a way that is the "higher middle way which we can call 'existential Christianity'."[98] Von Balthasar's theology of the laity is a theology of an existence transformed in Christ through his Church.

Furthermore the life of Christian response takes place within salvation history. Note that Ignatius structured the meditations of the *Spiritual Exercises* following the narrative of the Scriptures. By doing this, he showed the importance of encountering in meditation the aesthetic dimension of the Scriptures, and this takes place by being faithful to their very structure. Aesthetics is part of ontology! Similarly Thomas Aquinas takes the student of theology through the sequence of the events of the life of Christ *in the world* and draws out their meaning.

The meditations in the *Spiritual Exercises* help the Christian develop his attunement to God in Christ in the Church. However, the Christian continues to grow in attunement *in the world* rather than in the cloister. Ignatius was not training people for the cloister. He also gave the *Exercises* to a number of lay people.[99] He was helping them precisely to be Christ-like in the world.

Now Henrici's words (above) lead us to the final point in this chapter. He said that the beauty, goodness and truth of the lay person are transformed through the inner principle of participation in the

---

[95] *GL I*, 298.
[96] Ibidem.
[97] See his theology of the place of feelings, *GL I*, 241-244.
[98] *GL I*, 298.
[99] See the comments of the historian John W. O'Malley, *The First Jesuits*, (Cambridge: Harvard University Press, 1993), 37ff.

beauty, goodness and truth of God who is transforming his beloved in a boundless outpouring of grace. This wondrous process is taking place within the "Christological and Trinitarian disclosure of absolute being".[100] But the world is blind to this 'wondrous process'. Such blindness places the Christian in a very special and unique position.

For von Balthasar, there are two consequences to this general blindness: first on the metaphysical level, "the Christian even today must accomplish and exemplify in his life the inalienable experience of being."[101] This actually means attending to being, to the structures of being that are revealed in the daily experiences of contingent being. At the risk of using yet another quotation, von Balthasar says that "finite being [has] the consistency, vitality, and dignity that elevate it beyond mere facticity and make it the object of unquenchable interest, indeed, of a reverent, astonished wonderment."[102] This wonder at being is elevated through the Life, Death and Resurrection of Christ, so that secondly, "the Christian will be the responsible guardian of glory as a whole, just as once the Jew was, as he sang the psalms . . . and so was the responsible guardian of the glory of covenant *and* of creation."[103] The Christian mission is to show that the glory of God does shine through the redeemed world.

The principles so briefly sketched out here introduce the first of the studies proposed by von Balthasar, namely a 'theological aesthetics', which is to examine the theology of the laity from the perspective of Beauty.

---

[100] *GL VII*, 432.
[101] *GL IV*, 17.
[102] *TL I*, 9.
[103] *GL IV*, 17.

Chapter Two: The Scriptural Archetypes and the Laity

Introduction
What is a Form?
God works through Archetypes
The Relationships in the Christ-Form
    (1) Mary
    (2) The Office of Peter
    (3) John
    (4) Paul
    (5) The Multitude
The Time of Jesus and the Time of the Church
Conclusion: Laity and the Archetypes

Introduction

    We began our journey to discover what it means to be a lay person in Chapter One. We learned to value metaphysics when reflecting on the Scriptures in a rigorous way. This will help us in this chapter so that we can appreciate Jesus as *the* lay person, the archetype of the lay person. In addition we learned about the Church as the Body of Christ and the 'place' where we meet Jesus Christ.

    So where do we go from here? The *Introduction* pro-posed that a lay person's life has a beautiful form, generated by doing the good, through participating in the mission of Christ, and this form expresses the truth of existence. In this chapter we will examine just the first part, the beautiful form of life and the reason for it. However, once again, Christian being is described by all three transcendentals at the same time, and they can only be separated for the purposes of presentation. The aspect of form (beauty) appears somewhat static until it develops into a vital structure in the theo-dramatic study (Chapter Five).

    When von Balthasar says that "to be a Christian is precisely a form," he means that being a Christian is a total reality, an indissoluble whole.[1] All

---

[1] *GL I*, 28. Here is the foundation of the theology of the distinction between the Church of Jesus Christ and Christian ecclesial communities. (Note *Dominus Iesus*, 17, for example.) The Catholic Church contains all of the relationships and elements that constitute the mystery of the presence of Jesus Christ. Those properly called 'particular

of its relationships and principles are defined with respect to Christ and his Church rather than being made up of a personal and arbitrary selection of principles, charitable acts and devotions—which describes a life that is only partially *form*-ed in Christ. But where does the notion of form come from and what does it mean for the study of the laity?

What is a Form?

At the philosophical level, von Balthasar defined giving form to one's life as "the self-relativisation of the intraworldly and mortal existence at the service of an idea."[2] So the historical form of a person's life grows through words and deeds, the relationships and objects, according to the idea that gives them their integrity as a form. However, this is still only a philosophical formulation.

The next step involves theology and more specifically biblical theology and Saint Thomas Aquinas. Von Balthasar's summation of Aquinas' thought is as follows: "The metaphysics of Thomas [with regard to beauty] is . . . the philosophical reflection of the free glory of the living God of the Bible and in this way the interior completion of ancient (and thus human) philosophy."[3] Thomas' achievement (that von Balthasar follows up on) was to bring together the philosophical reflections up to his time, and to show how when suitably developed so as to recognize the divine subject, they can be applied to the manifestations of God in the Old and the New Testaments. Moreover in the philosophical tradition in general, any form has integrity, (wholeness) proportion, (relation between the parts) and radiance, (the light of its own essence radiating from it) and this is so even though it is not possible to 'define' the transcendentals as such![4]

However, Thomas did not see a thing having a form just of itself. Instead in von Balthasar's estimation: "God, [Thomas] says, is the ultimate principle of all beauty in so far as he causes

---

Churches' have all of these elements except the recognition of the Petrine Office. Then 'ecclesial communities' are those who do not have the valid episcopate or the true understanding of the Eucharist.
[2] Hans Urs von Balthasar, "The Christian Form," *ET IV*, 44.
[3] *GL IV*, 406.
[4] See *GL IV*, 411.

consonantia [proportion] and *claritas* [light of being]. He is the cause of *claritas* in that he lets things participate in his own primal light; the cause of *consonantia* in two senses, first of all because God orders and turns all things to himself and calls them home . . . and secondly because he orders and assembles things in relation to one another."[5] This means that created things—like the lay person's life—imitate the characteristics of divine beauty to some degree.

Theologically then, if the 'idea' that lies at the heart of a form of life is considered as the divine idea, the divine Word, then as the Divine Word draws the elements of the world into a new form and makes the meaning of worldly things relative because he transcends the world and is God's self-expression in the world.[6] Or, recasting this thought in terms of the glory of God, the "glory [of God] is the intruding lordliness of him to come to confront the world, both judging it and gracing it."[7] (One must hasten to add that in the case of God's self-expression, von Balthasar identifies 'glory', 'beauty' and 'form'.) Such intrusion happens, for example, in the celebration of the Sacraments, or in the lives of the saints, or when the pope issues an encyclical. God intrudes in the world a mediated way and confronts it.

Just one illustration to make the point clearer: Saint Bonaventure (1221-1274) wrote a biography of Saint Francis of Assisi (1181-1226). In Francis' experience of the stigmata, Bonaventure explains that the wounds were "*vere divinitus expressa*"—truly divinely expressed—and then "*in corpore ipsius (Francisci) impressum*"—impressed in his (Francis') body.[8] The wounds of the Passion of Christ were present for the world to see in Francis' day. They have also marked history itself ever since, not least because of the effects of the presence of the Franciscans in our history. The Spirit of God transformed the body of

---

[5] *GL IV*, 410.

[6] De Lubac explains that we can only 'believe in' a divine person strictly speaking according to the meaning of the phrase 'credo in' as it originated in the *Gospel of John. Splendor of the Church*, 33.

[7] Hans Urs von Balthasar, *The Glory of the Lord VI: The Old Covenant*, Brian McNeil C. R. V. and Erasmo Leiva-Merikakis trans., (San Francisco: Ignatius Press, 1991), 14.

[8] *Legenda S. Franc.* 13. 10, cited in *GL II*, 271.

Francis so as to manifest the goodness of God (who died for us in the Passion) to the world.

Now back to God's intrusion in the world: perhaps surprisingly, when he is reflecting on the scriptural theology of form (glory), von Balthasar uses the words of Karl Barth (the most noted of the twentieth century Evangelical Protestant Church theologians) to explain what the glory of God means. In fact, his points fit well with Thomas' insight precisely because of both of them are faithful to the scriptural record.

Following Barth and his drawing on the data from the Scriptures, von Balthasar proposes that God's manifestation of his glory can be described in three steps. They deepen the way we understand the indwelling of the divine in the created earthly forms like lay life manifest the divine glory.

First, the glory of God (whence the title of von Balthasar's work on theological aesthetics!) manifested in the world is the key to understanding God's revelation.[9] It also aids us in understanding why lay life is expressive, that is as bearing the glory of Christ and giving glory to God! Like Karl Barth before him, he drew this conclusion on biblical grounds. In fact, von Balthasar simply cited Barth:

> God's glory is, first, 'the dignity and justification proper to God, not only to assert that he is who he is, but to demonstrate this and make it known . . . in a certain measure to make it obvious and not to be overlooked; second to 'obtain acknowledgement for himself'; and this, . . . with divine power.[10]

The fact that God's revelation into human history expresses God's own self means that it too has form. God is after all Beauty and the expression of his glory in the world takes on the '*materia*' of the world, whether it is smoke and fire, (Exodus 19:18) or the life of a prophet, (Isaiah 42:1ff.) or when he becomes a human being (John 1:14).[11] God's absolute self-revelation in Jesus Christ is described as having a

---

[9] According to Oëtinger, "God's glory constitutes not only the chief concern, but also the formal foundational character of Scripture. *Theosophie*, C. A. Auberlin ed., 1847, 33 cited in *GL VI*, 10.

[10] *GL VII*, 21. Von Balthasar has summarized Karl Barth's *Kirchliche Dogmatic II/1* (1940), 722 – 762.

[11] See *GL VI* and *VII*.

concrete form so, for example, the Word of God "pitched his tent among us." (John 1:14) Even God's manifestation within the soul takes on the form of feelings or experiences.[12]

Second, considering the believer who experiences God's revelation, the Bible texts describe the life of the believer as a *response* to the manifestation of the glory of God. For example, Paul wrote to the Corinthian community: "It is the same God that said, 'Let there be light shining out of darkness,' who has shone in our minds to radiate the light of the knowledge of God's glory, the glory on the face of Christ." (2 Corinthians 4:7) The experience of the believer is to be caught up in the ongoing manifestation of the glory of God, to join the form of this manifestation, and to become part of it in the world and so give glory to God.

Third and last, the Bible is clear about the source of the form of a believer's life. For example, Paul says that "we with our unveiled faces reflecting like mirrors the brightness of the Lord, all grow brighter and brighter as we are turned into the image that we reflect; this is the work of the Lord who is Spirit." (2 Corinthians 3:18)[13] Now for von Balthasar (and the Church), even as a sinner man retains his nature as the *image* of God even though he loses the radiance of the glory of God because of his sin. Again this is a scriptural lesson from Paul who wrote: "all have sinned and are deprived of the glory of God." (Romans 3:23) Now these Pauline insights illustrate that the origin of the glorious form of a believer's life is God working in the person participating in Christ in the Holy Spirit.[14] However the intra-worldly form alluded to here is not the final glorious form of the resurrected person in the end time.

Note that these three steps do not ignore the individual's personal decision and action. Von

---

[12] See, for example, Jordan Aumman's *Christian Spirituality in the Catholic Tradition*, (San Francisco: Ignatius Press, 2001).

[13] Cited twenty-one times in *GL VII*. For example, on pages 24, 241 and 264 among others.

[14] "The divine revelation of grace perfects created natures – both conferring on the complementary disclosures of beings their final meaning, and also revealing the transparency of all being in the world to the absolute ground of being." *GL II*, 12.

Balthasar followed Thomas Aquinas in his understanding of the relation between First and second causes through his use of the concept of co-creation to explain the individual's person's cooperation with grace.[15] So von Balthasar speaks neither of a person 'dissolving' into the One (e.g. Buddhism) nor of the 'indifference' of God to man's actions (Deism). In Christianity, the Spirit of God works through Christ in the heart of the one who is faithful. Jesus said: "A pupil is not above his teacher; but everyone, after he has been fully trained, will be like his teacher" who in this case is Christ himself. (Luke 6:40)

So then von Balthasar describes participation in Christ's mission as participation in the 'Christ-form'[16] or in the 'christological-form'.[17] Rooting the participation in Christ himself safeguards the important consequence that for all that we have said so far, "an overall view of the relationship between Christ and his disciples, Christ and the Church . . . Christ and the Old Testament, is not possible."[18] The measure of this participation and hence the 'overall view' of what is going on ultimately remains *with* God. However he does argue that working from the perspective of the Christ-form offers a better christology than one that isolates Christ and treats the other figures in his life in separate treatises.[19] He calls the theory of the Christ-form a "symbolic doctrine of the Church."[20] It is this approach that illustrates the defects in Osborne's conclusions such as his claim that: "The New Testament could be described in contemporary language as the 'people's book,' not the 'hierarchy's book'."[21] He has missed the interplay of relationships and the meaning that the New Testament attributes to them. This interplay is safeguarded only

---

[15] Thomas Aquinas: "It does not belong to forms to be made or created, but to be co-created. What indeed is made by the natural agent is the composite." *ST Ia* 45 a. 8 *Respondeo* . . .. Yves Congar O.P. restates this principle in his work on the Laity. See Yves Congar O.P., *Lay People in the Church*, 60.
[16] *GL I*, 459.
[17] *GL I*, 303.
[18] *GL I*, 304.
[19] *The Office of Peter and the Structure of the Church*, 136-137.
[20] *Office of Peter*, 132.
[21] *Ministry*, 110.

by an ontological reflection. This is *theological ontology*.²² It is also a recognition of the category of experience, which is where the phenomenological reflections will play their part!

Going back to the theology of form and the Church: the category of 'form' indicates two elements needed for an understanding of the theology of the laity. One is the nature of the Christ-form itself which adds the essential dimension of form to the ecclesiology that was developed in Chapter One. As we will see it establishes the relationships in the Church that are archetypal for the Church through the ages. This helps the lay person to situate himself within the actual structure of the Church. The other element to be considered is the human *participation* in this form. These points will be dealt with in succession.

To appreciate the nature of the Christ-form, an explanation of archetype is needed.

God works through Archetypes

The concept of an archetype is ancient. The word refers to the originating type ($αρχη$-origin) that gives order to the subsequent realities that spring from it. Here we are back at metaphysics once again but the concept of the archetype also points to something that is crucial for understanding salvation history and that is first of all, that God's revelation uses historical contingencies such as certain individuals and certain historical situations because it is intrinsic to historical contingencies that they are by their very nature open to "the transcendence towards the Absolute and Unconditional."²³ Furthermore the historical nature of man himself means that "man cannot simply be thought of as self-sufficient and autonomous," since he lives both a life that is assigned to him and has a life to be assumed and these 'assignments' never do cancel each other out in practice.²⁴ These two features of history and historicity mean that even prior to God's revelation generating his own archetypes, it can be said that archetypal structures of people and

---

22 Cf. Hans Urs von Balthasar, Andrée Emery trans., *Office of Peter and the Structure of the Church*, (San Francisco: Ignatius Press, 1986), 136.
23 Adolf Darlap and Jörg Splett, "History," *Encyclopedia of Theology: A Concise Sacramentum Mundi*, ed. Karl Rahner S.J., (London: Burns and Oates, 1975), 624.
24 Adolf Darlap and Jörg Splett, "History," 622.

relationships in history do unavoidably intrude into the life of man and cannot be discarded. So, for example, if the Constitution of the United States is considered archetypal for life in the United States— and to some extent it is— then people living in the United States come under the sway of the Constitution whether they like it or not. However the Constitution is a pale shadow of the archetypal community that God has generated in our history.

In the Scriptures God himself works through archetypal structures of people and relationships and so, following from this insight, von Balthasar proposes that the circle of people around Christ represented in his time and represents today a particular kind of archetypal totality (called the Church united in Christ) that manifests the glory of the God-made-man and his mission to the world.

The archetypal existence of Jesus Christ and his community does not recede into the past. Let me quote our author again: "we must agree with Thüsing when he stresses that the 'future' element does not exclude the present, realized element . . . in fact in the community's awareness of time, the two necessarily belong together."[25] The archetype of the presence of Christ makes the present moment a realization of the archetypal presence of Christ until the *eschaton.*

To understand the role of the original circle around Jesus is to attend to the development of this circle and not go ahead of it in anticipation that something else of a different form will come along. This approach allows history to unfold as *God* wills it. It also allows that the Old Testament is 'propaedeutic' for the New.[26] The preliminary nature of the Old Testament also illustrates the sheer fact of the *datum* of the Old Testament that the New Testament contends with, as well as the salvific mandate that it contains.[27]

In the Old Testament, the chosen people experienced God in their history. There were "revelations to the whole people, even if these are apportioned to smaller groups of witnesses".[28] Their

---

[25] *TD III,* 131.
[26] *GL I,* 332. See too de Lubac's description of the continuity and fulfillment in *Splendor of the Church,* 58-65.
[27] E. Schillebeeckx O.P. uses the concept of a sacrament instead of archetype. See his *Christ the Sacrament of the encounter with God,* (New York: Sheed and Ward, 1963).
[28] *GL I,* 333.

cultic celebrations continued the contact with God 'made visible' in the sense that the Old Testament sensory experiences of God continue in some form through the cult. In the Old Testament the separation of the world into sacred and profane spheres passes away because "everything—even the sphere of sexuality, of the family, of sickness and death, and of the relationship with the members of one's tribe and with outsiders—appears as affected and regulated by the holiness of the present God of the covenant."[29] The list of experiences 'under God' can be extended by considering the mediators of the Old Testament, because "the place where the [Old Testament] mediator and intercessor stands is always the same; it is the heart and point of intersection of the covenant" and so on.[30] The Old Testament was the time of promise in the form of very specific historical events. So it was not some vague generic promise rather it constitutes a definite covenant with a specific people towards a specific end.

Von Balthasar contends that the Old Testament teaches us that "it is only history, which convicts man as a sinner and confronts God with the fact of the broken covenant that permits us to see the concrete reality of God's glory."[31] The theology of historical archetypes truly appreciates the meaning of this history, both sacred and profane, if the distinction can even be considered in the light of the Old Testament. The preceding theology says that it was in the history of the old People of God that God became visible, and so the archetypal sensory experience that must be seen as the character of the Old Testament manifestations of God will then continue in the New Testament.

So then Paul could write to Timothy speaking of the Incarnation: "Undeniably great is the mystery of devotion, who was manifested in the flesh [and] vindicated in the spirit." (I Timothy 3:16)[32] The earlier list of experiences led to the experience of the Old Testament mediators now the cultic experience of the New Testament continues the experience of the one manifested 'in the flesh', Jesus himself. As Paul asked

---

[29] *GL I*, 334.
[30] *GL VI*, 190.
[31] *GL VI*, 215.
[32] *GL VII*, 159, 261, 279, 355, 403.

of the Corinthians: "The cup of blessing that we bless, is it not a participation in the blood of Christ? The bread that we break is it not a participation in the body of Christ?" (1 Corinthians 10:16)[33] Then too the use of mediators and intercessors in the Old Testament continues in the New Testament. Witness the choice of the Apostles including Saint Paul but now they mediate the presence of Christ.

The heart of von Balthasar's (and the tradition's) theology of the archetypal nature of Old Testament events and hence of God's *modus operandi* comes down to one sentence: "these great archetypal experiences of God, which in their structure are an anticipated Christology, are not, for all their proleptic character, to be classified as merely a lower stage which leads up to Christian experience."[34] God's chosen way of being with his people namely that of *a sensory and concrete presence in history* continues even as it comes to a whole new superlative quality with God's taking-on of human nature but the archetypal character of this taking-on already has the lines of its trajectory beginning in the Old Testament.[35]

Let us now detail the archetypal presence of God in the New Testament, after all these archetypes shape us today!

In the New Testament the circle of people around Christ is firstly *around* Christ himself. To explain something of what this means Irenaeus of Lyons said the following: "the perfect intelligence, the Word of God, begotten before the light: he was the founder of the universe (with the light) and the maker of man: he is all in all, patriarch among patriarchs, law in the laws, chief priest among priests, ruler among kings, the prophet among prophets, the angel among angels, the man among men, Son in the Father, God in God, king to all eternity."[36] In this 'pocket Christology,' so to speak, Irenaeus believes that the Old Testament types of the prophet, the priest and the king, find their fulfillment in Christ the archetype of

---

[33] *GL VII*, 182, 418, 460, 461.
[34] *GL I*, 336.
[35] Note his lengthy analysis of the lives of the Old Testament figures to show the things that they contain as they appear in the light of the Incarnation. See *GL VI*.
[36] Cited in H.A. Blair, "Allegory, Typology and Archetypes," *Studia Patristica XVII*, part one, ed. Elizabeth A Livingstone, (Oxford: Pergamon Press, 1992), 265.

prophecy, priesthood and kingship and thus these qualities continue to be present in a superabundant way. The Fathers of the Church explained the coherence of the Old Testament in terms of the economy (οικονμια) of salvation so that the types of the Old Testament show "the beauty of salvation-history radiating objectively through the veiled form" of the Old Testament.[37] In other words the types lead forward to the fulfillment of the type in Christ. He has the Offices of Prophet, Priest and King.

But there is a problem if the previous instances of a particular type are merely seen in terms of what is generally understood as continuity or discontinuity. Continuity could be construed simply in terms of a series of transitions that continue to occur. Thus one would expect yet another messiah, yet another gospel or yet another prophet, (Islam for example) because Christ is not the ultimate covenant between God and man. The other misunderstanding that can arise is when these transitions in continuity, from one instance of the type to another, are viewed simply as superficial changes.[38] Here one might see the line of prophets as basically the same and so the same reality just reappears in a new form. It is the theology of form, as recovered by von Balthasar, that alone avoids these two misconceptions and gives a method that respects the meaning of the history shown to us by the Scriptures.

Jesus Christ is the truly unique fulfillment of salvation history and so he is the archetypal form of the new form of salvation history, where the Lord of History is now present. Quoting Peter in the *Acts of the Apostles*: "let the whole house of Israel know for certain that God has made him [Jesus] both Lord and Messiah." (Acts 2:36)[39]

So what is the 'situation' of the Church? Here is "the decisive question" for ecclesiology.[40] How does the Church come about so as not to be understood as an intervening (interfering) third term between Christ and man? In line with what was said above, the

---

[37] *GL I*, 39.
[38] *GL I*, 641.
[39] See Vatican II: "It was in Him, before the foundation of the world, that the Father chose us and predestined us to become adopted sons, for in Him it pleased the Father to re-establish all things." (LG 3)
[40] *GL I*, 557.

Church is not just another institution in a succession of institutions ranging through history, (the first possible misconception above) nor is it simply a religious group that has had many different appearances throughout its history and will have more in the future (the second misconception). What makes the Church a unique institution—as far as it remains faithful to its originating principle—is that it is the extended presence through space and time of the glorified Christ whose life is the archetype of the Church.

Now let us turn to the foundational group itself. How was the archetypal circle of people around Jesus Christ formed? At minimum, one could imagine for example, that Jesus only left his followers with some "testamentary words", but how long would the group have remained faithful with just words to hold on to?[41] Or he might have gone further and poured out his own Spirit upon them when he died, so that he could share his very own understanding with the faithful. However would this not simply be a totally spiritual experience of a kind of infused knowledge? Should he not also be present in some tangible way? In his answer von Balthasar is already building on the suggestive structure of the Old Testament that had a concrete and sensory dimension to its experience of God. So he can say: the Church "would have to be something permanent and perennially timely, so constituted that, as a whole, it would point to [Jesus Christ's] own perennial timely existence, his loving self-giving to each man, his personal summons to each man, his availability to each man."[42] This is von Balthasar's understanding of Jesus' words "I am with you always, until the end of the age." (Matthew 28:20)

Put in other terms, this presence of Jesus Christ, as the ever-present archetype at the heart of the circle means that the Church continues "to manifest this presence and at the same time protect it from man's clutches and from any distortion."[43] The dimensions of his presence have at their heart the Sacrament of the Eucharist and other elements such

---

[41] Hans Urs von Balthasar, "The Church as the Presence of Christ," *New Elucidations*, trans., Sister Theresilde Skerry, (San Francisco: Ignatius Press, 1986), 88.
[42] "The Church as the Presence of Christ," 89.
[43] Ibidem.

as the Scriptures, the Tradition, the authority in the Church and so on that "render possible and transmit his immediate presence."[44] These dimensions are all conferred on the circle around Jesus himself in the time of his Life, Death and Resurrection.

Thomas Aquinas' thinking followed along these lines too. In the question about the visibility of the work of the Holy Spirit he noted that it "is said (1 Corinthians 12:7)—the manifestation of the Spirit is given to every man [for] profit—that is, of the Church. This utility consists in the confirmation and propagation of the faith by such visible signs." (ST I, q.43 a.7) Then Thomas explained further that "a mission of the Holy [Spirit] was directed to Christ, to the Apostles, and to some of the early saints on whom the Church was in a way founded." (ST I, q.43 a.7) Here is the extension of the archetypal existence of Christ to his "friends". Jesus said: "I no longer call you slaves, because a slave does not know what his master is doing. I have called you friends because I have told you everything I have heard from my Father." (John 15:15)[45]

This is where history and the Gospel give different answers to the question: what is the Church? Historical studies, with their usually somewhat arbitrary criteria uninformed by the theological issues, have led to very strange perspectives on the Church where, for example, Christ was simply a preacher who left us with important teachings that we have to follow as best we can. (Thomas Jefferson) Then the miracles of Jesus might simply become scriptural allegories to encourage us.[46] By contrast the New Testament

---

[44] "The Church as the Presence of Christ," 90.
[45] De Lubac reminds us of Paul's admonition: "Jesus Christ, yesterday and today, the same forever." *Splendor of the Church*, 89.
[46] See, for example, Rudolf Bultmann, *Jesus Christ and Mythology*, (New York: Prentice-Hall, 1997). See James Kay's comment that Bultmann's "continuing influence does not stem from a surviving school bearing his name, since the synthesis he achieved has unraveled. Rather his continuing influence is seen (1) wherever the NT is approached through historical and comparative methods involving other ancient texts and parallels known to the history of religions; (2) wherever the saving significance of Jesus Christ is identified not with historical reconstructions but with the preaching of the Christian gospel." Comment in James E. Kay, "Rudolf

routinely points to the continuing relative nature of the Church as the Body of Christ that has Christ as its Head. (eg. Romans 12:5)

These conclusions on the nature of the archetypal form that Christ creates around himself in this world are a triumph of the method that was proposed in the first chapter. They start with a reflection on the Scriptures but the reflection is kept authentic by the metaphysical demand for the integrity and proportion of what is being contemplated in history to be recognized and articulated.

Now the circle of people around Jesus is given a participation in the form of the Church by the words and deeds of Jesus. They will be our next focus of interest.

The Relationships in the Christ-Form

The group of disciples around Jesus became part of the appearance of God in the world through the words and deeds of Jesus, and so belong to the form of Christ and the Church.[47] Von Balthasar and the Fathers that he drew upon subsequently identified these parts of the form of the Church. For example in his very early work *Augustinus: Das Antlitz der Kirche in Menschen der Kirche: In Zeugnis und Urkunde*, von Balthasar organized extracts from the writings of Saint Augustine according to what they said about the Church.[48] Augustine too had identified the relationships that comprise the Christ-form. Von Balthasar grouped Augustine's texts under the heads of 'Christ and the Church,' and then 'Members and Functions.' He has sections on 'Mary and the Church,' 'Peter,' 'John,' 'Paul' and so on. He found that Augustine had considered these interrelationships as both real and continuing.[49]

Bultmann," *The Oxford Companion to Christian Thought*, ed. Adrian Hastings, (Oxford; Oxford University Press, 2000),84.

[47] Note de Lubac's admonition: "If the Church today is not the apostolic Church, she is not really carrying on Christ's mission and is not his Church." *Splendor of the Church*, 87.

[48] Hans Urs von Balthasar, *Augustinus: Das Antlitz der Kirche in Menschen der Kirche: In Zeugnis und Urkunde*, (Einsiedeln: Benziger Verlag, 1955).

[49] He also indicates two other sources who have come to the same conclusion and they are Francisco Suarez in his *De Statu Perfectionis* and Heinz Shürmann's *Der Jungerkreis*

For von Balthasar and his patristic sources, the individuals around Jesus are "not so much moral 'examples' (how could Peter's denial be that!) as prototypes (τυπος Philippians 3:17); only thus are they *synmetai*, fellow imitators (cf. 1 Corinthians 11:1) forming the Church thro-ugh history."[50] Hence, the theologian's recovery of the elements of the Christ-form involves identifying the relationships between the persons there at the foundation. Incidentally, this example will also serve to illustrate the more abstract general principle that the nature of a particular form depends on the relationships between its elements!

Von Balthasar's definition of the relation between the parts of a form is that a "form consists only of parts or aspects that are distributed and adapted (*pro-portio*) to one another, but in such a way that the parts do not have their ultimate measure from themselves but from the whole that is, at the same time, both the distributer and ultimate consumer of its own measuring."[51] Thus the Christ-event is the 'whole' for the Church and yields the theological validation of this philosophical formulation, even though the 'whole' consists of people, relationships, and events. It is a form where the people, events, and relationships only find their ultimate meaning in terms of the whole that is in terms of what Christ is doing at the behest of the Father, in the Holy Spirit.[52]

Highlighting the concept of form points to the distinctive ecclesiological tradition that von Balthasar is joining. This form effectively disposes of the idea

---

Jesu als Zeichen für Israel und als Urbild der kirchlichen Rätestandes. CSOL, 290-292.
[50] Hans Urs von Balthasar, *The Office of Peter*, trans. Andrée Emery, (San Francisco: Ignatius Press, 1986),148.
[51] *GL I*, 468.
[52] In developing his theology of Scripture, von Balthasar has united two understandings of Scripture. The older view was one that viewed Scripture as God's word to the Church and the more recent one is one that holds Scripture to be the reflection on revelation in faith. The unity of these two views is not a forced construction but it is actually required by the nature of form itself. Fundamentally, God's revelation is received "in the womb of human faith." (*GL I*, 56) And the unity of the objectivity of God's revelation and the believing subject that conforms to that revelation in the act of faith indicates that both views of Scripture have their role in aiding the understanding of the process of the believer's encounter with Scripture.

that the relationship between the master and his disciples can be understood in purely human categories (historical, socio-logical or moral), and definitively points us to the sense of the Church being receiving its form through the form of the Incarnation.⁵³ Von Balthasar called the Incarnation a 'law'. Christ taught his followers but in his case his teaching was himself: "since he is what he does, his disciples must also do what he does and is and, in so doing they actuate not themselves but Christ in them."⁵⁴ So the life of Christ gives the Christ-form its inner principle. It springs from this principle.

Now the meaning of the whole is fundamental if we are to understand the form that we are dealing with—the Christ-form/the Church. Working with the form of the Church means that one cannot 'slice up' the circle of disciples to isolate one or other element in the hope of a 'deeper' understanding of the Christ-event (and the Church born from it.). This is the problem with trying to base an entire ecclesiology on 'discipleship' or Canon Law, for example.

Von Balthasar's argument for the Christ-form and its five elements is the most fundamental difference between his ecclesiology and that of Yves Congar O.P.. Congar developed his theology of the laity in terms of the Offices of Christ as Prophet, Priest and King and the lay participation in these roles.

This is a rich and valid approach that is found throughout the tradition and in the teaching of the Second Vatican Council.⁵⁶ The principles underlying the theory of the participation in the offices of Christ

---

⁵³ Here, von Balthasar criticizes Yves Congar O.P.'s distinction between the infallible element and the existential element in the Church "which although it is lives within this [existential] structure, is at best an approximation of" the infallible element. This distinction is based on a modern conception of institution and is foreign to the ancient thought on the Church. See *Office of Peter*, 194.

⁵⁴ "Office in the Church," *Explorations in Theology II*, 93.

⁵⁶ See *Lumen gentium* for example. This approach is better for some aspects and not so good for others. One can understand the clergy as participating in ministerial priesthood through participation in the Offices of Priest, Prophet and King. One can get some dimensions of the life of the laity through their mode of participation. However the Marian dimension of the Church is not clear and neither is the role of religious. One also cannot directly make an argument for the male clergy.

unfold in two steps. First of all Christ is the fulfillment of the Old Testament mediations of God to his people through the prophets, priests and kings. So he fulfills all three offices superlatively: he is the Prophet, the Priest and the King.

Then secondly, in several places, von Balthasar lays out the theology of two modes of participation—the ordained and the lay—in the Offices and how they relate in a complementary way.[57] This ordered complementarity means two things, as the *Constitution on the Church* stated so succinctly: first there is the fact that the two modes of participation "differ from one another in essence and not only in degree" and secondly, the two modes are "nonetheless interrelated". (LG, 10) Von Balthasar grounds *his* argument for the presence of these two modes in the very eternal complementarity between the divine Father and the divine Son within the Godhead. This then leads directly to his argument for the 'masculine' male office and the complementary 'feminine' lay response to that office within the created realm as it images the Divine.

He is arguing that created masculine and feminine participations have ontological meanings because Fatherhood and Sonship do within the Godhead. (See Chapter Six.) 'Masculine' and 'Feminine' are his terms—and they have a good ontological basis—for the two modes of being. This derivation will be treated exhaustively in Chapter Six. Nevertheless at this point for the sake of completeness, it can be said that the participation in the Offices of Priest, Prophet and King forms the subtext of von Balthasar's theory of how the people in the circle around Christ become part of the Christ-form.

So while not ignoring the Offices of Christ, von Balthasar instead developed his theory of the laity in terms of the archetypal relationships in the New

---

[57] See his articles "The Church as the Presence of Christ," and "Women Priests?" in *New Elucidations*, trans. Sister Mary Teresilde Skerry, (San Francisco: Ignatius Press, 1986). Then there are his articles "Office in the Church," "The Layman and the Church," and "Priestly Existence" in his *Explorations in Theology II: Spouse of the Word*. And the articles, "The Priest of the New Covenant," and "Spirit and Institution" in his *Explorations in Theology IV: Spirit and Institution*. This is just a few of the many instances where he deals with the issue.

Testament community.[58] As we have seen this theory in turn is based on the relations of the perfect persons

---

[58] For example, the reflection on Peter and John, who are New Testament figures, reveals the objective priesthood and the subjective interior priesthood respectively. (See *Christian State of Life*, 280) John is both an archetype of the objective and the subjective priesthood at the same time! So our author discovers the two modes of participation in the Priesthood of Christ directly from the text of the New Testament. At the same time, he has identified what *Lumen gentium* insists upon namely that the two modes "differ essentially and not only in degree". (LG, 10). The hermeneutic key to the analysis of the states of life in the Church is relationship because von Balthasar traces all of theology back to the inner life (relationship) in the Trinity.

The reflection on the prophetic office arises through the reflection on obedience to the priestly office that has just been considered. Out of obedience, the Church is a listening Church. The Apostles speak 'for' Christ and von Balthasar cites Jesus' words: "He who hears you hears me." (Luke 10:16) (*Christian State of Life*, 157) The theology of the hearing Church starts with Christ living on the hearing of the will of his Father. Once again, we have the two complementary modes of participation in the Prophetic Office that are noted by *Lumen gentium*. (LG, 12)

Von Balthasar's thinking on the participation in the Kingly Office of Christ in the Church starts from the relation of Christ to his Father "which he demonstrates in his own person and brings once more to the consciousness of the world." (*Christian State of Life*, 258) Those who participate in the authority that he confers operate on the principle that "he who hears you hears me." (Luke 10:16) (*Christian State of Life*, 259) Then those who are obedient to this authority are obedient because the bearer of this authority "can make unconditional demands on the company of believers." (*Christian State of Life*, 259) This structure of obedience rooted as it is in the obedience of Christ to the Father is essential for the unfolding of salvation history. Compare this thinking with the teaching on the Kingship of Christ in *Lumen gentium*, 26.

Also note that Raymond Brown S. S. also distinguishes roles in the New Testament record, but in an historical-critical way. There he finds the disciple, the Apostle, the presbyter-bishop, and the celebrant of the Eucharist as antecedents to the priesthood. Raymond Brown, *Priest and Bishop – Biblical Reflections*, (New York: Paulist Press, 1970), 21. He has a far narrower objective than the work of von Balthasar, namely to find the foundations of the priesthood by historical-critical means. Von Balthasar's theory of form would suggest that trying to isolate one aspect of the Church—in this case the within the Godhead. The contemplation of Scripture led him to a different set of types from those used by Congar. They differ because they are the *New Testament* archetypes (the people around Christ) and are both intersubjective and open to phenomenological analysis, two characteristics that are important when understanding New Testament laity.[59] Both Congar and von Balthasar work with the principle of subsidiarity where the higher principle of Christ and the relationships that he establishes constitute the forms of life in the Church.

Once again, due to the very nature of a form, examination of lay participation in the Christ-form means dealing with the relationships between *all* of the elements of the Christ-form. (This is the degree of detail that he did not find in Congar's work.) In the Christ-event, *all* of the people around Jesus and their relationships are significant. It was on this basis that von Balthasar criticized Schelling, for example, who "does not even see the indissoluble relation between Peter and John, implied in the final chapter of John's Gospel."[60] Similarly, von Balthasar had problems with the ecclesiology of the medieval theologian Joachim of Fiore.[61]

For von Balthasar, the network of relationships indicated in the New Testament are the blueprint for the Church for all time. They stand at the center of ecclesiology and cannot be bracketed out in the Husserlian sense.[62] There is no way to consider any single element of the Church in isolation. If you want to consider the laity then you need to consider the clergy and the Scriptures and the Sacraments so on.

---

historical—is a method that yields very limited results! See also Chapter Four.

[59] The same recognition of the social dimension of salvation is clear in the documents of the Second Vatican Council: "God, however, does not make men holy and save them merely as individuals, without bond or link between one another. Rather has it pleased Him to bring men together as one people, a people which acknowledges Him in truth and serves Him in holiness." (LG, 9).

[60] *Office of Peter*, 148.

[61] Ibidem.

[62] See Brandan Leahy, "Theological Aesthetics," 31, in *The Beauty of Christ: An Introduction to the Theology of Hans Urs von Balthasar*, eds., Bede McGregor O. P., and Thomas Norris.

To prepare for the discussion of the Good that will be found in Chapter Four, we can point out that the network of relationships can best be understood as the participation in a drama. So then the category of intersubjectivity unfolds as fundamental for the whole divine-human drama of salvation history. But it also means that there is no neutral point on which to stand and observe the action. (These will be dealt with in more detail in the chapter on human action and the good. Chapter Five) Evidently examining all of the relations within the primitive Church is essential to actually situating the laity in the Church and the world. And so our interest is more than "antiquarian."[63] The identifiable 'constellation' or complex of relationships in the New Testament are the foundation of the Church for all time.

Moreover the constellation is not incidental to Christ. Given that the Divine Word took human nature upon himself, he does not take to himself a mere biological form but actual humanity and certainly "to be human means to *be with* others."[64] (Emphasis added.) This philosophical insight helps us to understand the scriptural data. The community around Christ is crucial to his exercising his being who he is even as he remains the sole mediator between God and man.

Then too, when the Church is conceived as an archetypal community then it is a *communio*, a Latin term with a complex meaning ranging from communion, to community and communication. We introduce the term here because it is at the heart of von Balthasar's notion of Church as well as that of the Second Vatican Council. Working from its ancient Latin roots: "'communio' means community in the concrete expressive sense of being brought together into a common fortification . . . but also into a common achievement . . . which at the same time can mean mutual satisfaction, gift, [and] grace."[65] Then von Balthasar explains that: "Those who are in 'communio,' therefore, do not enter into such a social relationship solely on their own initiative, each of his own private accord, determining its scope by the

---

[63] *Office of Peter*, 144.
[64] *Office of Peter*, 136.
[65] Hans Urs von Balthasar, "Communio," *Communio* 1981 XXX, 198.

stipulations that they make when they establish it."⁶⁶ The presence of Christ acts as the higher principle of the new *communio* to which the members are obedient. The members of a communion, even on the natural level, are 'mutually dependent' in order to achieve a 'common activity'.⁶⁷ How much more so are the members of the Body of Christ! They are only who they are in salvation history in relation to him and then to one other.⁶⁸ In fact, the different appellations, 'the communion of the Church,' 'the Christ-form,' and the 'constellation around Christ,' are all synonyms, and theological explications of the scriptural term 'the Body of Christ'.(1 Corinthians 12:27)

Now von Balthasar identified five notable relation-ships in the life of Christ: the experience of Mary; the experience of Peter; the experience of the Beloved Disciple; the experience of Paul, and lastly the experience of the multitude.⁶⁹ When we consider these, then "we [will] have spoken of the theologically relevant human "constellation" of persons around Jesus Christ . . .. In him they meet and take their places relative to each other."⁷⁰ The five aspects represent the five key relationships in the ecclesial *communio* to which the Scriptures testify.⁷¹ They are 'theologically relevant'

---

[66] Ibidem.
[67] Ibidem.
[68] See Vatican II: "By communicating His Spirit, Christ made His brothers, called together from all nations, mystically the components of His own Body." (LG 7)
[69] Note that John Paul II refers to the multitude in the most generic sense of the word in *Christifideles laici*, 1. In his case, he develops the image around the *Parable of the Vineyard*. The fundamental idea that he is proposing is the mission of the individual in the 'vineyard'. The notion of Christian mission will be introduced in the theodramatic section of the book.
[70] *Office of Peter*, 308. The 'experience of the multitude' is mentioned in the *Christian State of Life* but not in the *Office of Peter*, and this is probably for methodological reasons. He does not need a consideration of the 'multitude' to formulate the responses to the various objections to the Petrine Office that are the reason for the book.
[71] The metaphysical reading of the Scriptures that is evidenced here contrasts sharply with the historical-critical read offered by Edward Schillebeeckx O.P. who proffers a *sociological* explanation: "At a time when the local leaders had lost the great bearers of their traditions . . . they could best 'legitimate' their own leadership . . . by stressing that

because together they manifest the continuing concrete presence of the Risen Lord.⁷²

To keep it short we will only sketch the characteristics of these modes of participation in the Christ-form because they reappear in subsequent chapters. The list of relationships that we will study demonstrate the proportion of the relations between the different people and their ordering by the higher principle of the presence of Christ. As always the fundamental truth that is revealed in the Christ-form is Christ himself, the Incarnate Word.

Incidentally the theology of the Christ-form disposes of at least one false way of thinking and that is the minimalist view of the Passion and Resurrection as "nothing more than a symbolic visual aid in the instruction that God imparts to mankind."⁷³ Such a view ignores mankind's incorporation into Christ.⁷⁴ In the notion of the Christ-form, men are incorporated into the form and given a new possibility of life which

---

they were simply carrying on the work . . . [of] those who founded the community and gave it life." See his *Ministry: Leadership in the Community of Jesus Christ*, trans., John Bowden, (New York: Crossroad, 1981), 12. This reduces Jesus's actions so as to make them "pale and unreal and not credible form" to borrow some words from von Balthasar. (*GL I*, 534). The historical actions and relationships "denote . . . that aspect of an event that possesses authentic and permanent meaning for faith, that aspect which, in addition, 'evokes the irrefutable impression of fullness of reality'". (*GL I*, 534) (He is citing Martin Kähler.) These comments are specifically to summarize Kähler's position but do in fact touch the heart of the response to the flaws in the historical-critical approach as it is applied by Schillebeeckx. The fullness of meaning requires both the data of history and the perception of that history in faith. Something that Kähler was well aware of but which is missing in Schillebeeckx' historicist approach.

⁷² See Vatican II: "each individual part contributes through its special gifts to the good of the other parts and of the whole Church." (LG, 13) This 'good' is the presence of Christ himself for the world.

⁷³ *TD III*, 117.

⁷⁴ See elements of the aesthetic description of the Church in the teaching of the Second Vatican Council, for example, in the Constitution on the Church: "'For from Him the whole body, being closely joined and knit together through every joint of the system, according to the functioning in due measure of each single part, derives its increase to the building up of itself in love'. (Ephesians 4:15-16)." (LG, 30).

is already realized in Christ.[75] What is clear in the Scriptures is that the "inner effect" of Christ's Life, Death and Resurrection within the individual believer differentiates the community around Jesus and permanently constitutes the community as well.[76]

Before considering the constellation of people around Jesus, it is worth mentioning the difference between this approach to Scripture and the more historical-critical approach of someone like Kenan Osborne O.F.M., for example.[77] He claims for example

---

[75] *TD III*, 121.

[76] Ibidem. This research of the scriptural record contradicts the assertion of A. Faivre that "the Christian literature of the two first centuries does not know the opposition cleric/lay." *Revue des Sciences Religieuses* 57 Juilliet 1983, 195. (My translation.) He claims that it is only in the third century that "the texts begin to present two groups in the Christian church." (195) The analysis that is found in the work of von Balthasar recognizes that the New Testament texts have more substance than Faivre gives them credit for, and that the lack of the terms 'clergy' and 'Laity' does not mean that the realities that the words represent were not present at the times described by the narratives. The scripture texts show relationships that are determinative of the Church for all time and the reason that the relationships are determinative is because God does not act accidentally or arbitrarily. To attribute such actions to Christ would be to diminish the nature of the being of the Incarnate Son who follows the will of the Father at every moment.

It is also worth noting that Vatican II also saw the life of Jesus on earth as constitutive. For example, the council said that: "The mystery of the holy Church is manifest in its very foundation. The Lord Jesus set it on its course by preaching the Good News, that is, the coming of the Kingdom of God, which, for centuries, had been promised in the Scriptures: "The time is fulfilled, and the kingdom of God is at hand". In the word, in the works, and in the presence of Christ, this kingdom was clearly open to the view of men." (LG 7)

[77] Kenan Osborne, *Ministry*, 48ff. This is to put aside the erroneous statements such as his claim that: "Contemporary Roman Catholic theology deliberately tends to be far more scripturally based than its predecessor: the Tridentine and counter-reformation theology." 48. There are at least two reasons why this statement is erroneous: There is, first of all, the statement of the Council of Trent itself, from the fourth session, where the council said that it kept "always in view, that, errors being removed, the purity itself of the Gospel be preserved in the Church; which (Gospel), before promised through the prophets in the holy Scriptures, our Lord Jesus

that: "Neither the cleric/lay pattern nor the ordained non-ordained pattern is discernible in the New Testament."[78] This conclusion is based more on philology than on the interrelationships described by the texts. But just because a later term is not in the New Testament, this does not mean that the reality is not there. The philological approach only works with words and not with ontological relationships! The clear relationship between Scripture and the tradition of the Church brings out this ontology. The Scriptures and the tradition of the Church are interrelated as witness to the presence of the divine Word (Scripture) and the sheer overabundance of the presence of the Divine Word "available to the Church in the living Eucharistic presence of Christ; the necessary reflection of this vitality in verbal form is the principle of tradition" in the words of our author.[79] This is the theology of the close interrelationship of Scripture and tradition. The tradition has been reflecting on Scripture since the beginning of the People of God. As the Second Vatican Council explained:

> The words of the holy fathers witness to the presence of this living tradition, whose wealth

---

Christ, the Son of God, first promulgated with His own mouth, and then commanded to be preached by His Apostles to every creature, as the fountain of all, both saving truth, and moral discipline; and seeing clearly that this truth and discipline are contained in the written books, and the unwritten traditions." (Decree on the Sacred Scriptures. *The Council of Trent*, Ed. and trans. J. Waterworth (London: Dolman, 1848)) The fact that this was their view means that the council fathers *did* indeed have a grasp of the meaning of the Scriptures.

And secondly, it is well worth considering that while he does not advocate a return to medieval methods of exegesis, Henri de Lubac does devote three volumes to the intricacies of medieval exegesis and further he says: "I have always been of the naïve belief that—although it must be said that all of the teachings of the Church confirm me in this notion—that in the witness [different historical periods] give to their faith, no less than the witness they expect from us in return, all the Christian generations enjoy a oneness and solidarity." Mark Sebanc trans, *Medieval Exegesis Vol: 1 The Four Senses of Scripture*, (Michigan: Eerdmans, 1998) xxi. This oneness too suggests a flaw in Osborne's analysis!
[78] *Ministry*, 49.
[79] "The Word, Scripture and Tradition," *Explorations in Theology I: The Word made Flesh*, 19.

is poured into the practice and life of the believing and praying Church. Through the same tradition the Church's full canon of the sacred books is known, and the sacred writings themselves are more profoundly understood and unceasingly made active in her; and thus God, who spoke of old, uninterruptedly converses with the bride of His beloved Son; and the Holy Spirit, through whom the living voice of the Gospel resounds in the Church, and through her, in the world, leads unto all truth those who believe and makes the word of Christ dwell abundantly in them (see Col. 3:16). (DV, 8)

The Council gives an ontological understanding of Scripture and tradition. It is the Church's way of reading the Scriptures *within the presence of Christ as Church* that is missing in Osborne's analysis.

Now turning specifically to the presence of Christ, the five modes of participation are as follows. The analysis of Mary's participation will serve as a first presentation of von Balthasar's way of thinking:

1. Mary[80]

Mary's experience of Christ far surpasses that of all the others. In a sense her experience is archetypal for them all.[81] Consider that, for von Balthasar, the most fundamental image of the Church is the Church as Bride. Then the theologically 'nuptial' relationship between Christ and his Church is first realized in the relationship between Christ and Mary.[82] Her feminine person relates to the masculine person of Christ, and this is the fundamental internal relationship in the Church (a *proportio*) together with

---

[80] See also Brendan Leahy, *The Marian Profile: In the Ecclesiology of Hans Urs von Balthasar*, (New York: New City Press, 2000).

[81] Here is the source of the historical significance of von Balthasar's Marian ecclesiology. His work signifies the reconnection of two dogmatic treatises that had become separated after the Reformation, namely Mariology and Ecclesiology. See his comment in *TD III*, 300. The same restoration is evident in the *Dogmatic Constitution on the Church*, chapter viii. See also Thomas Aquinas' *Commentary on Psalm 23*: "*ecclesia fundata est super maria*". *Super Psalmo 23* n.1.

[82] Note the treatment of the links between Zion, Mary and the Church. *GL VII*, 60 – 66.

its organizing principle in Christ himself. This relationship is fundamental because "the Church flowing forth from Christ finds her personal center in Mary as well as the full realization of her idea as Church."[83] What von Balthasar means here is that the Church starting with Mary is a virginal subject, faithful and responsive, and answers God's initiative through the Holy Spirit both bodily and spiritually.[84] The Holy Spirit is the source of Mary's fruitfulness and so it is the source of the fruitfulness of the Church as well.[85]

The experience of Mary grounds the proper understanding of the relationship between the Church and the world.[86] So, for example, the Immaculate Conception of Mary demonstrates that the Church at her core is always pure and holy.[87] Even if some members of the Church are sinners, they remain Church "since the sinner has some velleity and is being borne by the suffering members of the Church."[88] The integrity of both Mary and the Church

---

[83] Hans Urs von Balthasar, "Who is the Church?" *Explorations in the Church II: Spouse of the Word*, 161.

[84] Compare with John Paul II's phrase: "the special presence of the Mother of God in the mystery of the Church". (*Mulieris dignitatem*, 2) Being more specific, *Lumen gentium*, explains, citing Irenaeus directly: "the mother of the members of Christ . . . having cooperated by charity that faithful might be born in the Church, who are members of that Head." (LG, 53) Here the council is quoting Irenaeus' *Adversus Haereses* (Adv. Haer, 111 24, 1) The archetypal role of Mary is not discussed by Mongrain in his *The Systematic Thought of Hans Urs von Balthasar: An Irenaean Retrieval*. Note Thomas' reflection on Psalm 23, where he sees a marian side to the psalm and says: "*Ecclesia, fundata est super Maria, idest super tribulationis.*" *Super Psalmo 23 n.1.*

[85] He cites without giving a complete reference Methodius' description of the Church as a womb giving birth to Christians and bringing them up. "Who is the Church?" 159.

[86] Vatican II said: "At the same time, however, because she belongs to the offspring of Adam she is one with all those who are to be saved. She is 'the mother of the members of Christ . . . having cooperated by charity that faithful might be born in the Church, who are members of that Head.'" (LG 53)

[87] Vatican II: "Wherefore she is hailed as a pre-eminent and singular member of the Church, and as its type and excellent exemplar in faith and charity." (LG 53)

[88] See Hans Urs von Balthasar, "Casta Meretrix," *Theological Explorations II: Spouse of the Word,*

is preserved by the grace of Christ. In addition, the devotion to the motherhood of Mary protects the understanding of the motherhood of the Church as the Mother of the Faithful.[89] Through a balanced Mariology, in which all of the mysteries of her life are included, the nature of the Church is understood in terms of its purity and it does not deteriorate into a mere sociological entity.[90]

Von Balthasar regarded the Mariology of the Second Vatican Council as being extremely positive, among other things, for its understanding of the motherhood of Mary and the Church.[91] The council returned to the notion of Mary as type of the Church after a long historical period in which the idea of Church had been held to be another-worldly "pseudo-gnostic hypostasis".[92] This conception could easily reduce the this-worldly entity to just another 'institution'.

Lastly, von Balthasar expected to find the Marian experience continuing in the Church for the reasons laid out above.[93] Take note that the category of experience is constitutive of the Church as a believing Church because here 'experience' means the encounter with Christ in faith. Then the Marian principle in the Church grounds the experience of everyone in the Church.[94] So it must be clearly said that the spiritual attitude of the laity is Marian. The laity can say the *Magnificat* (Luke 1:46-55) with her.[95]

---

[89] See his summary of the maternal imagery in the Scriptures, culminating in the vision of the woman in childbirth in *The Book of Revelations*, (*Revelation* 21:1-3). See *Office of Peter*, 188.

[90] The reference to a balanced Mariology is a reminder of the traditional approach to Mariology where the thinking "shows [the] power" of the consideration paid to Mary while not obscuring or diminishing the role of "the one mediator" Jesus Christ. (See LG, 60) See also von Balthasar's extensive analysis of the history of Mariology. (*TD III*, 292 – 360)

[91] See *Office of Peter*, 203ff.

[92] See *Office of Peter*, 203.

[93] Vatican II: "As St. Ambrose taught, the Mother of God is a type of the Church in the order of faith, charity and perfect union with Christ." (LG 63)

[94] Vatican II: "they turn their eyes to Mary who shines forth to the whole community of the elect as the model of virtues." (LG 65)

[95] See *GL VII*, 61. Quoting von Balthasar: "Her Magnificat show how much she stands as the embodiment of the entire

They receive the indwelling of the divine Trinity in faith just as Mary received the Holy Spirit in faith: "Whoever loves me will keep my word, and my Father will love him, and we will come to him and make our dwelling with him." (John 14:21)

Moving on: one member of this group with its Marian principle has an additional function and that is Peter.

2. The Office of Peter[96]

Theologically the Marian Church shows the Church as the 'receptive subject' and the individuals constituting the Church are individually participative receptive subjects in faith.[97] The receptive subject, the Church as Bride is open to, and 'contains,' and receives the Divine-human Bridegroom. Here too there is both the proportion of the 'masculine' and 'feminine' as well as the relationship to the whole that constitutes the form of the Church. At this point, von Balthasar makes the next step in his argument: the 'masculine' principle is the principle of sacrament and office.[98] When he says this, he is remaining consistent with the notion of the 'masculine' principle being 'masculine' simply because it gives. (See Chapter Six) The 'masculine' principle completes the nuptial union of the Bride and the Bridegroom in the marital image

---

people . . . it lets the voice of the personified Israel be heard . . . Finally, the Magnificat gathers all together into the original prophecy to Abraham, in whose person the whole of society was gathered in the beginning, as in the end times it is united once again in Mary."

[96] Note that von Balthasar has himself critiqued three flawed positions on the meaning of the Petrine office. He has titled them 'A Pope, But not this one,' 'A Papacy as it was before,' and 'Peter, but No Pope'. These are found in *The Office of Peter*, at pages 65ff., 70ff., and 75ff., respectively.

[97] Vatican II: "Piously meditating on her and contemplating her in the light of the Word made man, the Church with reverence enters more intimately into the great mystery of the Incarnation and becomes more and more like her Spouse." (LG 65)

[98] Vatican II: "He placed Blessed Peter over the other apostles, and instituted in him a permanent and visible source and foundation of unity of faith and communion." (LG 18)

of the Church.[99] Christ is the Bridegroom who is present to his Bride in his priestly ministers.[100]

Now one such 'receptive subject'—in the Marian sense—is Peter himself. The relationship between Christ and Peter became the second fundamental relationship for the ongoing form of the Church through Jesus' initiatives in his relationship with Peter.[101] Peter especially stands out because he loves Christ more than the rest. (John 21:15)[102] Therefore the narrative goes on to describe that Peter embodies the principle of masculine office ("Tend my sheep." John 21:16))[103] and Sacrament ("Feed my sheep." (John 21:17)) for the Church. In the scriptures, Peter and the twelve were singled out from the crowd by Christ.[104] They accompanied him and so formed a community with him and with each other. This community of the twelve was distinctive because it involved the renunciation of other possible lifestyles and it had a clear form.[105] (The configuration as

---

[99] See the—to date—only complete text on the male priesthood in the Catholic Church: Manfred Hauke's *Women in the Priesthood: A Systematic Analysis in the Light of Creation and Redemption*, (San Francisco: Ignatius Press, 1988). Hauke arrives at the same conclusions as von Balthasar.

[100] See the texts: Matthew 25:1; Luke 5:34; John 3:29 etc.

[101] The Second Vatican Council specifically referred to the moment when Jesus "commissioned Peter to shepherd" the Church. (LG, 8) And the council used the image of "the Chair of Peter" as the symbol of the continuing office. (LG, 13) Note also that Thomas Aquinas explained that "*Petrus post acceptum spiritum sanctum in statu perfectorum erat.*" *ST* II q.43 a.6. It is the role of those in the state of perfection to teach.

[102] Noted by Aquinas in *ST* I q.20 a.4.

[103] See Augustine's words explaining the meaning of Jesus' words 'Tend my sheep': "Let then carefulness be our [ministers] portion, obedience yours [Laity]; pastoral watchfulness our portion, the humility of the flock yours." *Sermon 96* on John 21:16.

[104] Note Augustine's explanation of Jesus words: "I am the Good Shepherd," (John 10:14). Augustine wrote: "What was Peter? Was he not a good shepherd? Did not he too lay down his life for the sheep? What was Paul? What the rest of the Apostles? What the blessed Bishops, Martyrs, who followed close upon their times? What again our holy Cyprian? Were they not all good shepherds." *Sermon 88*. They are all shepherding in the light of the Good Shepherd.

[105] *CSOL*, 148.

community and the renunciations involved will be shown to be the foundation of the understanding of religious life presented in Chapter Three.) Both Peter and the twelve were accorded a certain delegated authority. The scriptural record shows that they "were gifted with power" (Mark 3:15) and were "appointed" to a definite authority. (Luke 10:1)[106] But Peter loved "more than these". (John 21:15) Hence he was told by Jesus: "Tend my sheep." (John 21:17)[107] Peter's relationship to Christ differs markedly from that of John, for example, in that John is also an Apostle but has a completely different role in the historical narrative.[108]

To understand the case of Peter and his situation in the flock, von Balthasar appealed to a "Catholic tact" to understand the nuances of Peter's position as situated between the guarantee that "nothing will prevail" against the Church and the real temptations to power.[109] Three things characterize Peter's situation: (i) He was chosen by Christ for a specific position even prior to being gifted by the Spirit.[110] (ii) The demand placed on Peter was entirely excessive and dependent on grace.[111] (iii) And lastly, Peter took his position "matter of factly."[112] It is *this* Peter who had the position of authority.

It is in the loving response to this authority that the operation of the laity begins to manifest itself. The corollary to the office of Peter in the flock is Marian obedience ("I am the handmaid of the Lord." Luke 1:38) which is a core element in the Church when faced with the Petrine office. Judging from the tradition as it is expressed in I and II Peter, von Balthasar concluded that "through obedience the community, and hence the laity as well, becomes a 'flock' (I Peter 5:3)—first a flock of the 'elders' and through them the flock of the 'supreme Shepherd'

---

[106] *CSOL*, 147.
[107] See Thomas Aquinas, regarding Peter, "*sicut ei tota Ecclesia confitetur.*" *Catena in Mt.*, cap. 16 l. 3.
[108] See Aquinas treatment of the difference between the relation-ships of Christ and John and Christ and Peter. (ST I, q.20 a.4) Von Balthasar follows this treatment in his own thought.
[109] *CSOL*, 149.
[110] *CSOL*, 152.
[111] *CSOL*, 153.
[112] *CSOL*, 154.

himself. (I Peter 5:4)[113] As an obedient flock, the entire Church hears the kerygma in the community and is brought in turn into a 'priestly ministry' (I Peter 2:4, 9) in the lay mode in which they offer spiritual sacrifices to God and make Christ visible in the world. (I Peter 2:12)[114] (In Chapter Three this relation of authority and obedience is dealt with more fully in diagram three.) The next member of the Christ-form is Saint John.

3. John

The scriptural data indicates that John is closely connected with Peter because he was one of the twelve. But he is the 'other face' of the twelve with respect to Peter because if Peter is authority then John is love.[115] In fact, von Balthasar's exegesis of the *Gospel of John* uncovers a Johannine "coexistence of 'love' and 'office'."[116] John has the power of office because he is one of the Twelve. At the same time he is the "beloved" one. (John 13:24)

Von Balthasar also cites Augustine of Hippo's explanation of John's role in the *Tractates on the Gospel of John* where he says: "There are some who have entertained the idea— and those, too, who are no contemptible handlers of sacred eloquence— that the Apostle John was more loved by Christ on the ground that he never married a wife, and lived in perfect chastity from early boyhood. There is, indeed, no distinct evidence of this in the canonical Scriptures: nevertheless it is an idea that contributes not a little to the suitableness of the opinion expressed above, namely, that that life was signified by him, where there will be no marriage."[117]

---

[113] *CSOL*, 352.
[114] *CSOL*, 353.
[115] *Office of Peter*, 137 and 142. See also Aquinas' *ST I* q.20 a.4 "*Ioannem vero plus, quantum ad donum intellectus.*" Von Balthasar also noted that for Aquinas "the monk is not simply a passive recipient of the enlightening and perfecting action of the hierarch, he also turns to action." *CSOL*, 304. This can be found in his detailed historical study of the relationship between the Priestly state and the Religious state in the same volume, pages 292 – 329.
[116] *Office of Peter*, 159 – 161.
[117] Hans Urs von Balthasar, *Augustinus: Das Antlitz der Kirche: Menschen der Kirche*, (Einsiedeln: Benziger, 1955), 214-215. The translation is taken from *Nicene and Post-*

By examining the different parts of the Johannine corpus, von Balthasar concluded that John's experience was a synthesis of the earthly (Petrine), the heavenly-prophetic (Pauline) and the contemplative aspect of faith.[118] To appreciate this, it must be remembered that John encountered Jesus historically. This is the Petrine strand of his existence. Christ would then appoint Peter as his Vicar! Then there is the vertical visionary strand exemplified by Paul's life as a Christian. (See below.) This strand appears in John's experience is his visions of 'what will soon come to pass.' (Revelation 1:2) Lastly, the contemplative aspect of John's experience is shown by his experience of the Triune God in the *First Letter*. "We are in union with the Father and with his Son Jesus Christ." (I John 1:3) Here is the final goal of Christian experience, the union with the Triune God. This is also the goal of reflecting on the Scriptures using metaphysics, the method spoken of in the first chapter. This was a common experience for the Christian community that gathered around John as is indicated by his use of the plural pronoun 'we' in the *Letters*.

John also was a virgin. So von Balthasar reasoned: "If Peter, who was married, appears as the representative of the official priesthood, [then] the virgin Apostles John and Paul are the designated representatives of that personal and interior priesthood that is the explicit following of the High Priest 'who offered himself unblemished to God.'(Hebrews 9:14)"[119]

The nature of John's relationships became the foundation of the state of the evangelical counsels in the Church. So for example von Balthasar says: "It is of the utmost significance that John met the Lord's mother at the foot of the Cross and nowhere else; that he and no one else received her from the Son as his own; that this supernatural community, the original unit of all forms of religious life, was formed in the instant of love's ultimate sacrifice." The community he is referring to is the one in which he takes care of

---

Nicene Fathers, First Series, Vol. 7. Edited by Philip Schaff. (Buffalo, NY: Christian Literature Publishing Co., 1888.) Revised and Edited by Kevin Knight.
[118] *GL I*, 357.
[119] *CSOL*, 281.

Jesus' mother. But she lived the life of the counsels and so did John, hence the special character of the community in von Balthasar's eyes.[120] They will reappear in more detail in the next chapter.

4. Paul

The Pauline tradition offered the most comprehensive account of Christian experience available in the New Testament, and the heart of this tradition is the passing on of Paul's own experience.

Following the *Letters* and *Acts*, it is apparent that the Pauline mode of experience is 'vertical' in von Balthasar's parlance, which is to say that it comes from above. (Cf. Galatians 1:11ff.) As the *Book of Acts* narrates, "a light from the sky suddenly flashed around him." (Acts 9:3) So Paul's experience was a particular kind of eyewitness experience. He saw the risen and glorified Lord. This experience was direct and unmediated. It was 'not from any man' (See Galatians 1:12).

Pauline tradition also identifies the possibility of new charisms in the Church. It describes events such as conversions, new missions and 'great visions'. Von Balthasar even described these charisms as 'discontinuous' but with qualifications, since he was adamantly against Schelling's view that Paul was operating independently of Peter.[121] Von Balthasar argues that Paul constantly referred his experience to Peter because otherwise "it trivializes the 'right hand of fellowship' given in Jerusalem." (Galatians 2:9). Schelling "plays the two 'authorities' against each other and passes over Paul's real authority over the communities so as to make him an abstract principle of the (reformed) 'freedom from' the 'strict legalism' that Peter embodies and with which 'everything has to start'."[122] Apparently Schelling had even misunderstood the notion of law in the Petrine principle. The 'legal' position of Peter exists only within the entire Christian form—that is the entire Church. In

---

[120] *CSOL* 287.
[121] This is Friedrich Wilhelm Joseph von Schelling (19th century) who proposed that Peter, Paul and John were simply "abstract principles supposedly tending in opposite directions." *Office of Peter*, 146. Von Balthasar instead, as did his predecessors in the tradition, saw them as real symbols in the Church.
[122] *Office of Peter*, 147.

the scriptures the integrity of the Christian form is demonstrated because all charisms are referred in some way to the Petrine office.

Then Paul's experience of Christ as Head of the Church is always from above. (Cf. Ephesians 4:13; Colossians 3:1) Von Balthasar saw these texts as summed up in the knowledge that "Jerusalem above is free and she is our mother." (Galatians 4:26)

The significant Pauline contribution to the Christ-form lies in the fact that Paul was able to articulate a deep sense of the drama of his existence in Christ: "I fail to carry out the things I want to do." (Romans 6:15) Then too Paul is "in the eyes of all a living anticipation of the eschatological promise."[123] So he drew the whole community into his prayer, his experience of joy and his *parrhesia* (openness to God and to men, candor). This term describes the behavior of a Christian. As Paul explained to the community at Ephesus: "This was in accordance with the eternal purpose which he carried out in Christ Jesus our Lord, in whom we have boldness and confident access through faith in him." (Ephesians 3:11-12) Lastly Paul worked through personal contact and he demonstrated the unity between being an Apostle and being personally holy.

We now come to the collective figure of the multitude. The multitude is the type of the laity. This can be said without ignoring the fact that the laity *qua* laity are only fully and finally constituted by the Marian principle of their existence and by their relationship to Peter, John and Paul. It is this complete constellation of relationships that can most appropriately be called the archetype of the laity.

5. The Multitude

The 'multitude' or the 'crowd' or similar words refer to groups with some kind of common intentionality and are frequently gathered around Christ in the New Testament.[124] Two kinds of groups gathered around Jesus, those who are positively disposed towards Jesus (eg. Matthew 7:28; Mark 2:4) and those who are negatively disposed (eg. Mark 14:43).

---

[123] *GL I*, 355.

[124] Eg. Luke 6: 17 – 19; Mark 6: 13; Mark 5: 31; Mark 3: 9; Matt-hew 9: 36.

The scriptural texts show that the groups are actually differentiated by their encounter with Jesus. The fundamental text on the differentiation of the group around Jesus can be found in Luke's narration of the choosing of the Twelve namely: "He then came down with them and stopped at a piece of level ground where there was a large gathering of his disciples with a great crowd of people from all parts of Judea . . . who had come to hear him and be cured of their diseases . . . and everyone in the crowd was trying to touch him because power came out of him that cured them all." (Luke 6:17ff.) Consistent with his analysis of other parts of the scriptural narrative, von Balthasar treats each relationship in the scene as archetypal for the Church for all time.[125] The clue for him lies in the different directions of movement with respect to Jesus. There is both the movement of the Twelve—who are called to the Lord (the State of Election in Chapter Three)—and the pressing in of the people.[126] These are fundamentally different dynamics. But it is more complex still.

The additional element is the fact that the people are also sent away once they have received his grace.[127] Often the instruction to depart is qualified by an injunction to return "explicitly to [their] usual milieu."[128] So, for example, the instruction to the paralytic was to "get up, pick up your bed and go home." (Matthew 9:6)

Von Balthasar has identified two diametrically opposed movements among Jesus' followers.[129] The crowd in the Lukan scene—the type of the laity in the Church—move differently with respect to Jesus than those in the State of Election. (See Chapter Three.) The crowds 'dwelling place' is in the world. The dwelling place of those who stay with Jesus, namely the Twelve, is wherever Jesus is. So after the crowd has encountered Jesus Christ in the flesh, they return to

---

[125] *CSOL*, 143. Here 'symbolic' is being used in the sense of the reality, the Church of Jesus Christ, manifesting itself. Symbol is not being used to refer to an arbitrary connection to a reality that is absent.
[126] See texts mentioned in Footnote 102.
[127] Cf. Mark 2: 11; Mark 5: 34; Mark 7: 29; Luke 7: 50; John 8: 11; Mark 8: 13 etc.
[128] *CSOL*, 145. He cites Mark 5: 43; Luke 7: 15; Mark 5: 18 – 19.
[129] *CSOL*, 146.

their homes and their places of work. To sum up the uniquene situation of the multitude, von Balthasar wrote: "the people's way to the Lord is to search for him in their necessity; their dismissal is attended with healing and grace for their subsequent existence in the world."[130] He is emphatic that the difference between the two movements around Jesus does not indicate that one group loves Christ more than the other.

Now that we have seen the relationships that are part of the scriptural archetype of the laity in the Church, there is still one more scriptural source to be tapped if we are to flesh out our understanding of the laity. We now turn to the lives of Jesus and Mary themselves as the archetypes for the response in faith to the life situations of all Christians.

The state of the laity in Christ can be called the 'General State of life' without further qualification for the moment. (Cf. Chapter Three) Everyone initially shares this state in the Church. Christ and Mary both lived in this state at the beginning of their lives. Primarily, Christ exemplified the state of life as life before God 'in the world' during the first thirty years of his life. So everyone in the General State of life finds the meaning of being a child, a young person and an adult before God in the details of the early life of Jesus.[131] In each instance Christ lived according to the will of his Father. He fulfilled the commandments. Once he began his mission then he entered the State of Election that is only indirectly of concern to us here.

Turning next to Mary: the nature of the secular state is further clarified by the way that Mary lived it out during the first phase of her life. As with her son—and she is living always by his grace—she lived in obedience to God. She followed the law of the Old Testament and so was married to Joseph, indicating her following the natural laws of life. To quote von Balthasar: "It was a life bound by the prescriptions and rules of family, household, education and children and the thousand other anxieties of life in a poor family."[132]

---

[130] *CSOL*, 146.
[131] *CSOL*, 195.
[132] *CSOL*, 207. This taxonomy of the works of the Lay State fits well with the official conciliar teaching of the Second Vatican Council who stated that: "the Laity, by their very vocation, seek the kingdom of God by engaging in temporal affairs and by ordering them according to the plan of God.

With these archetypal parameters of the General State in mind, it is easy to identify what our author finds in his reflections on the multitude but there is a complication. Von Balthasar recognized that the words in the scriptures that indicate groups even when they refer to those who are positively disposed are used in a number of different senses. For instance, one group was known as the "seventy-two". (NAB Luke 10:1) Then there were the groups of women who followed Jesus. (See Mark 15:41, for example.) There were those who were simply positively disposed towards Jesus perhaps out of curiosity. (See Luke 6:17, for example.) All of these were distinct from the Twelve and could be grouped into the archetype of the multitude.

However the important point is that "no exact lines of division can be drawn between the understanding of the Apostles and that of the multitude" in terms *of their own* understanding in their "concrete situations".[133] The distinct-ions that were caused by Jesus among the people don't necessarily depend on their understanding of what was going on. The distinction is ontological and was caused by the actions of Jesus himself. He introduced a polarity between the two groups, those in the General State and those in the State of Election and this polarity stands. The hermeneutic here is aesthetic in the sense that it starts with the perspective of the form of the multitude around Jesus and it is also theodramatic in the sense that it depends on the actions of Jesus. We will study this second aspect in Chapter Six.

How did Jesus treat the multitude? He sought them out by traveling from place to place. (Matthew 4:25) He welcomed them. (Luke 9:11) Most significantly he recognized their condition: "Seeing the

---

They live in the world, that is, in each and in all of the secular professions and occupations. They live in the ordinary circumstances of family and social life, from which the very web of their existence is woven. They are called there by God, that by exercising their proper function, and led by the spirit of the Gospel, they may work for the sanctification of the world from within as a leaven. In this way they may make Christ known to others, especially by the testimony of a life resplendent in faith, hope and charity." (LG, 31)

[133] *CSOL*, 178.

people, he felt compassion for them, because they were distressed and dispirited like sheep without a shepherd." (Matthew 9:36) They pressed in to hear him and so he taught them. He fed them beyond their needs. (Matthew 8:19) Then they returned home. How did the crowd respond? They followed Jesus and gathered wherever he was. (e.g. Matthew 4:25; 8:1) They "were awestruck, and glorified God, who had given such authority to men." (Matthew 9:8)

Jesus made an interesting distinction in his teaching. The crowd was taught in parables (stories) while Jesus spoke plainly to his disciples. (See Matthew 13) However Jesus was not being obtuse when he acted in this way. According to the *New Bible Dictionary*: "the word 'parable' (Gk. *Parabolē*) by derivation means 'putting things side by side', and is similar to the word 'allegory', which by derivation means 'saying things in a different way'. The object of teaching by parables and allegories is the same. It is to enlighten the listener by presenting him with interesting illustrations from which he can draw out for himself moral and religious truth."[134] Just a quick point here—the lay person has to be very active in his reflection to draw out the moral and religious truth from the teaching he receives.

In Jesus' use of parables there is yet another difference between the General State and the State of the Elect. Von Balthasar noted that the "Apostles who know the meaning of the word in all of its divine clarity, have a greater responsibility for acting according to it than does the multitude."[135] The deeper instruction to the Apostles was given because they were to be "pattern[s]" for the people of God. (Philippians 3:17) However as our author hastens to add the difference between the two states is not merely one of laity copying a pattern laid out by the Apostles and their successors because above this relationship between the General State and the State of the Elect there is the "common calling to perfect love".[136] Once again the distinction and similarities between the states are apparent in the very structure of the scriptural narrative. (See Chapter Three)

---

[134] "Parable," *The New Bible Dictionary*, org. ed. J. D. Douglas, (London: Inter-Varsity Press, 1962), 932.
[135] *CSOL*, 176.
[136] *CSOL*, 178.

Returning to our consideration of the multitude: their behavior indicated both a proportion (or relation) with respect to each other in the sense that they encounter each other *in coming to Christ* and a proportion or relation *to the world* to which they return. Both relationships formed because Christ was concretely present to them. He changed the crowd by modifying their relationship to each other and to the world by his words and deeds. Their return to the world is a graced return since the members of the crowd are returning healed, forgiven or encouraged by the presence of the divine grace and truth and this puts them in a different relationship to the world from that they had before.

The Christian in the secular state lives in a state with two foci where he responds to the parameters of creation in the Natural Law as well as to the Christian command to love. The seventh chapter of the *First Letter to the Corinthians* recognizes that believers live in the world but not simply as directed by the rules of the society around them which is usually not the same thing as following the Natural Law. Human societies create their own structures of meaning and so Saint Paul had to explain that Christian were to act as follows: "those who buy, [are to act] as though they did not possess; and those who use the world, as though they did not make full use of it; for the form of this world is passing away." (I Corinthians 7:30-31)[137]

Von Balthasar's treatment of the different types in the primitive community around Jesus shows the rich tapestry of relationships of grace and truth that abound within the Church community. However is the Church of today simply *that* primitive community? Von Balthasar answered this question under the rubric of time.

The Time of Jesus and the Time of the Church

The difference between the time of Jesus and the time of the Church has confused people like John Calvin (one of the two founding figures of the sixteenth century Protestant Reform) who held that there was little from that primitive community that continued

---

[137] *CSOL*, 173.

from the time of Jesus.[138] But in fact Jesus' time embraced the whole of history or as von Balthasar put it so poetically, "he reaches out in the Cross and Resurrection over all chronologically future time and of the world."[139] The end of creation has already been fully achieved in Christ. The time of the Church is now in "the power of this gift of the Father and the Son. He, the Spirit, is the indubitable present tense."[140] The time of the Church is the time of living in this Spirit that brings the 'past' of Jesus into the present. The central line in the Eucharistic prayer at each Mass is: "Let your Spirit come upon these gifts and make them the Body and Blood of Jesus Christ". The Church lives in this 'past made present' and in the hope of the future coming of Christ. This synthesis of being and time is achieved by the Spirit of God himself.

The previous paragraph means the archetypal community around Jesus is present to us and includes us through the power of the Holy Spirit. A further point that will only be mentioned here: Jesus achieved this universality through his poverty and self-abandonment and so "the imprint of the time of Jesus implies therefore an objective dispossession of one's own life, eliminating in advance very act of the will or resistance: it implies a being taken into the end of time accomplished by Jesus" as participants in the archetypal community around him which is the Church.[141] These issues will be treated in the next chapter!

Conclusion

The scriptural picture of the multitude lays out the vast range of their experience of Jesus. They were nourished by his teaching and filled with his grace and then they returned home to continue their life as followers of Christ. Through this whole cycle of life they still participate in the Christ-form.

---

[138] See his treatment of the Sacraments in John Calvin, *Institutes of the Christian Religion 1 & 2*, ed. John T. McNeill in the *Library of Christian Classics XX & XXI*, gen.eds. John Baillie, John T. McNeill, Henry P. van Dusen, (Philadelphia: Westminster Press, 1960).
[139] *GL VII*, 177.
[140] *GL VII*, 177.
[141] *GL VII*, 181.

The differentiated archetypal community around Jesus shows the face of authentic Christian community centered on Christ and expressing his presence. The community is differentiated so every feature of Christ's presence is concretely manifested and impresses itself upon the world. There are numerous implications for laypeople's understanding of their role and will unfold as we proceed. The dominant notion is that the lay person understands his life of following Christ in relation to the Pope (Peter), to the bishops (Apostles) and clergy, to religious (John) and to other lay folk (Mary). Within this complete network of relationships the lay person meets Christ in concrete and personal terms and not in some idealistic and abstracted way. Holding to this concrete manifestation means that it is not at the level of an idea and cannot be bent into whatever shape is agreeable and easy to do. The abstraction that we find in the work of the historical-critical method illustrates the flaw that arises. It is primarily a method developed for texts other than the Scriptures. It allows the notion of discipleship to be separated out without regard for the other relationships that together make the Church. By contrast, the ontological perspective is respectful of the whole. The reality of these personal relationships is that they shape us into members of the Christ-form in ways that follow the mind of the Church and are beyond our imagining.

The meaning of the totality of these relationships will be brought out more fully in the next chapter.

Chapter Three: The Church: Living out the Archetypal Life

Introduction
The Foundation of the States of Life
    The Lay State
    The State of Election
The Relations between the States of Life
The Position of Secular Institutes
Christian Experience
The Christ-Form and the Church
Conclusion

Introduction

So far, in surveying von Balthasar's ecclesiology, the Body of Christ is understood as a community in Christ in which every lay person participates in the Marian principle of the community, under the authority of Peter and his successors, as well as the bishops who succeeded the Apostles, alongside the religious communities. Participating in the form of the Body of Christ gives form to the individual Christian's existence by enabling him or her to participate in the relationships that constitute the Body of Christ.

Put differently: the lay person is called to live according to the archetypal Christian life. This is fundamental to the Christian understanding of the *form* of lay life because the lay person no longer lives a separate, self-established private kind of life. He or she rather lives a form of life that only exists as a form *because* the lay person participates in the form of the Church. (However keep in mind that the lay state is a *general* state of life in the Church. It is based on the Sacrament of Baptism and exists in relation to Religious Life and the Priesthood.)

Two rather unique aspects of von Balthasar's theology of the laity flow from the previous paragraph. The first is that he has actually detailed the complex network of relationships that comprise the form of the Church. He does this from the personalist perspective but in fact each relationship can be found in *Lumen gentium,* for example. The Church consists of Christ's loving relationships in grace with Mary, Peter, John, and the Multitude that continue in the life of faith

(Marian faith), under the authority of the Pope (Peter) and so on. These are our concern in this chapter.

The second feature of von Balthasar's work is that he has analyzed the two dimensions of the lay experience of this form. (Cf. Chapter Four)

But before we proceed further, there is a warning in von Balthasar's writing that serves as the rationale for this chapter:

> today seems to be the time of the laity, which . . . needs an appropriate spirituality . . . But much of what has been done in this line is quite superficial and trite, since the ecclesiastical states are treated as though they were separate departments of a secular association, without due attention to the profound mysteries of the ontology of the Church, and the resulting circumincession of the various states."[1]

His examination of the ontology of the Church involving the interrelationships between the states of life in the Church appeared in the *Christian State of Life*, and resulted in the six different interrelationships between the groups. Studying them will form the body of this chapter.

These interrelationships are the *form*-al side of two concepts that will be developed in more detail later namely (i) the dramatic notion of the intersubjective relations in the group around Christ which will be seen to be the foundation of the relations between the three states of life in the Church—Lay, Religious and Clerical—in the Church now. Also, indirectly, (ii) the diagrams illustrate some features of the radiance, proportion and integrity (the characteristics of a form that were presented in the previous chapter) of the Church. Of course the formal character of the Church is that which manifests its beauty, and so we are doing an aesthetic study!

Furthermore, von Balthasar wanted to emphasize this integrity. He proposed to focus on the real subjects participating in the beginning of the Church precisely to correct

> the view prevailing in the late Middle Ages and the Counter Reformation . . . that hierarchical and sacramental structure of the Church is the

---

[1] Hans Urs von Balthasar, "Spirituality," *Explorations in Theology I*, (San Francisco: Ignatius Press, 1989), 222.

Church in the strict or formal sense . . . while the 'sheep' ruled by the hierarchy and merely receptive of the Sacraments belong only to the 'material' element of the Church.[2]

Here von Balthasar is highlighting a common flaw in modern ecclesiology. The flawed thinking attempted to distinguish between the formal and the material elements in the Church, whereas in his thought the formal exists *for* the 'material' dimension of the Church. This historical misconception apparently developed because some aspects of the concept of the Church as the Bride of Christ got lost during the Reformation and Post-Reformation period. They were also a reaction to the rise of the congregationalist view of the Church, where according to Yves Congar O.P., who treated the history of the concept extensively: "For Luther, for Zwingli particularly, or for Cranmer the Church was hardly more than civil society gone over to the Gospel and acknowledging the rule of Christ: a people, not an institution."[3] Congregationalism is the prevailing concept in the modern west and so we do need to appreciate the difference between it and the Catholic notion of Church.

Turning to the long sweep of European history, we might say that this approach contributed to somewhat of a "withering away of the master narratives of European history," if one may borrow a phrase from the historian Tony Judt.[4] One of the 'master narratives' of Europe is the continuing existence of the Christ-form. In contrast, the congregationalist model persists in popping-up, again and again, in the history of ecclesiological thought from the Reformation to the present day. Clearly, von Balthasar and the Tradition of the Church understand the Church as the Spirit-driven unity of Christ and his Church present in history. The idea of a narrative is

---

[2] Hans Urs von Balthasar, "Who is the Church?" *Explorations in Theology II*, (San Francisco: Ignatius Press, 1991), 157.

[3] Yves Congar O.P., *Lay People in the Church*, 36. This concept is treated in more detail in a chapter by Emile G. Léonard entitled "Le Protestantisme, religion laïque," in Bibliothèque des Centres d'Études supérieures spécialisés VI. *La Laïcité*, (Paris: Presses Universitaires de France, 1960), 99-114.

[4] Tony Judt, *Postwar: A History of Europe Since 1945*, (New York: Penguin Press, 2005), 7.

congenial to the theodramatic study that follows in Chapter Five.

Now another concept must be introduced: the word 'state' has appeared often in this chapter, and was first used in the *Introduction*. It is time to examine the term more deeply.

Generally the word 'state' refers to what follows from the Christian's election and vocation (more about this below) by God. It is significant for von Balthasar because it translates the German *stand* which is 'where one stands'. The word is also found in the lexicon of the *Spiritual Exercises*.[5] So Christians are 'enstated' by their inclusion in the unfolding of God's plan of redemption.[6] Their existence is very different from what it was before they joined the Church. Now it will be clear in Chapter Five that the Christian stands within the will of the Father, due to his election in Christ. However, particularly for the laity, it is a dramatic struggle for the Christian to find what this will is. Von Balthasar noted that, for example, the famed French Catholic writer, Georges Bernanos: "wrestled with God for the meaning of his life, but also for the spiritual meaning of the age and of the war" and, in this case, that meant the First World War.[7]

We have discussed the general state of the baptized and we can say that, in von Balthasar's work, the State of Election means being chosen for the life of the evangelical counsels or the priesthood. So people in Church are found in one of three related states of life, the lay (general) state, the clerical state, or the state of religious life, and the information on these states is to be found in the Scriptures and the tradition of the Church.[8]

The scriptural sources for this tradition are widespread. Briefly, in the *Book of Genesis*, human beings were made in the image and likeness of God (Genesis 1:27) and are like their archetype through grace. The Fall changed man's situation in relation to

---

[5] Saint Ignatius of Loyola, *The Spiritual Exercises of Saint Ignatius*, trans., Anthony Mottola, (New York: Doubleday, 1989), 15.
[6] His term is *in-Stand-gesetz*. *CSOL*, 133.
[7] Hans Urs von Balthasar, *Bernanos: An Ecclesial Existence*, trans. Erasmo Leiva-Merikakis, (San Francisco: Communio Book – Ignatius Press, 1996), 63.
[8] See von Balthasar's detailed summary of the history the Clerical and the Religious States in *CSOL*, 292-329.

God, the world and to themselves. (Genesis 3) This changed circumstance led to the need for the Church, starting with the Old Testament People of God (Exodus 19, 20) and coming to fulfillment in the New Testament People of God (e.g. 1 Peter).

As the result of Adam's sin the primordial state of subjective and objective (defined in the previous chapter) conformity to the will of God was split up into two states in the Church, the Religious and the Clerical states respectively. These formed the state of election which is biblically and patristically a "unity," in the sense that together they combine the internal spiritual dimensions of Christianity with its external expressions.[9] These terms will need further definition but the point here is that the differentiation of the states of life in the Church is God's answer to the Fall. They form the subjective (Religious State) and objective (Clerical State) components of God's response to the spiritual and bodily disorder resulting in man by the Fall.

This theology comes from "the meditations on the life of Jesus . . . based on a naïve confidence in the Gospel text that permits us to have immediate access to the person of Jesus in his intellectual and bodily existence, his feeling and his conduct."[10] What von Balthasar is referring to is the now familiar whole of the Christ-form made up of all the intersubjective relations in which Jesus was involved. These ground the archetypal experiences laid out in the previous chapter and are the source of the theodramatic dimension that we will study in Chapter Five.

When von Balthasar's describes the archetypal origins of the Church, he completely contradicts the historicist view found in the work of Edward Schillebeeckx (previous chapter). The essential structure of the Church *is* present at the time of Jesus, and so, everything that we know today is "implicitly present from the beginning". In this, he follows both Vincent of Lerins and John Henry

---

[9] *CSOL*, 303. Von Balthasar attributes this united view of the State of Election to its roots in the *Gospel of John* and then it reappears both in the work of Ignatius of Antioch and Dionysius the Pseudo-Areopagite.

[10] Hans Urs von Balthasar, "Two Modes of Faith," *Explorations in Theology III: Creator Spirit*, trans. Brian McNeil, C. R. V., (San Francisco: Ignatius Press, 1993), 92.

Newman.[11] In his work on the development of dogma, Karl Rahner S.J. did agree with von Balthasar on this point. He noted that at the time of the New Testament, "all was known, because men had laid living hold upon the total reality of God's saving act and now lived it spiritually."[12] So then theologically von Balthasar was able to make the proposal expressed in the first paragraph.

The Foundation of the States of Life[13]

The three states of life, the general state and the two parts of the State of Election, namely the Clerical and the Religious States, can be traced to theological structures generated by Jesus' Life, Death and Resurrection. Von Balthasar chose this theological base for his ecclesiology after examining two flawed approaches namely; (i) what he called the 'universal church' theory, which was his term for the reduction of the structure of the Church to what is agreed by the

---

[11] CSOL, 292. Note John Henry Newman's comment in his introduction to his *Essay on the Development of Christian Doctrine*, (Notre Dame IN: University of Notre Dame Press, 1989) where he says: "to be deep in history is to cease to be Protestant." (8) And to be more explicitly, "modern Catholicism is nothing else but simply the legitimate growth and complement, that is, the natural and necessary development, of the doctrine of the early Church and that its divine authority is included in the divinity of Christianity." (169)

[12] Karl Rahner, "The Development of Dogma," *Theological Invest-igations I*, (New York: Crossroad, 1982), 67.

[13] Thomas Aquinas' *Summa Theologica* has a section on the States of Life, (ST II II q. 184 – 189.) The two sections after the State of Perfection in General are on the Episcopal State and the Religious State. There is no incongruity here since the State of Perfection is primarily the perfection in love and "secondarily and instrumentally . . . perfection consists in observation of the counsels." (ST II II a.3.) As regards prelates, they "bind themselves to things pertaining to perfection when they take up the pastoral duty." (ST II II q.184 a.5) So the State of Perfection seems to be equivalent to von Balthasar's State of Election. Prelates and Religious belong to the State of Election. Is there a section on the General State? Yes. ST II II, q. 179, argues that life can be adequately divided into the active and the contemplative life. So then "all the occupations of human actions, if directed to the requirements of the present life in accord with right reason, belong to the active life." (ST II II q. 179 a.2.) This is the lay life.

majority and (ii) the theory that the 'Church as simply a contingent part of salvation history'.[14]

The latter is particularly pernicious because it makes the Church only accidental in the unfolding of salvation, instead of being *the* sign of the presence of Christ in the world. Obviously, neither view respects the origin of the Church in Christ and the community that he gathered to himself, or the role that the Church plays in the operation of his mission in the world. But returning to the Life of Christ . . .

For von Balthasar, Christ's life has two aspects. It is both the foundational state of the New Creation and Christ meant others to be included in that state.[15]

Let us now consider the three states of life in the Church that make these two aspects present in concrete history:

The Lay State[16]

To start with, we said that both Jesus and Mary lived in the general state of the faithful. The word 'general' means "related as a general state to particular states having their own distinguishing characteristics."[17] In the case of Jesus and Mary, and in the

---

[14] Hans Urs von Balthasar, *Office of Peter and the Structure of the Church*, trans. Adrée Emery, (San Francisco: Ignatius Press, 1986), 131. Yves Congar took the classical approach to this question. For him, the institution of the Church is the result of Christ's action (*sacramentum*) and the fellowship community of the Church is the making visible of Christ's life (*res*). These are two interrelated aspects. *Lay People in the Church*, 104.

[15] In Kenan Osborne's view, "if Jesus is the source, origin, model and measure of all Christian leadership, then Jesus himself cannot be seen as either Lay or cleric." Kenan Osborne, O.F.M., *Ministry: Lay Ministry in the Roman Catholic Church: Its History and Theology*, (New York: Paulist Press, 1993), 39. Von Balthasar has two ways to answer this view (i) through the archetypal nature of Christ's life: "People who have mastered the art of living manage to some extent to integrate the seasons of life . . . It is different when the Word of God becomes man. Then every period of his life acquires, even within its continuing unfolding, the character of a revelation of eternity." Hans Urs von Balthasar, *A Theological Anthropology*, 244. And (ii) through the 'masculine' (clerical) and 'feminine' (Lay) components present within the Christ-form. Cf. Chapter Six.

[16] Also see Footnote 13.

[17] *CSOL*, 329.

lives of those who were to follow, the general state was a life of observing the eternal law of God. Even prior to Jesus, this state had already been founded on the general election and vocation of the People of God. The people who would become the Jews of the Old Testament were chosen and called from among the non-believers to be God's people. Abraham was told: "I will maintain my covenant with you and your descendents after you throughout the ages as an everlasting pact, to be your God and the God of your descendents after you." (Genesis 16:7)

The Old Testament general state of life involved a double precept, namely the command in the order of nature to subdue the earth (Genesis 1:1-2:4), and the participation in the universal call to love in the order of grace (Deuteronomy 6:5). In the order of redemption, both of these commands are only fulfilled through Jesus Christ who shows the true relationship to creation and the natural order, as well as the real meaning of love. Jesus and Mary lived this initial state to perfection as examples that continue to instruct today. The Scriptures tell us that Jesus was "busy with [his] Father's business" (Luke 2:50), and Mary was "the handmaid of the Lord," (Luke 1:38) It was thus that they both waited on the will of the Father.

After the Life, Death, and Resurrection of Christ, the 'generality' of the state of the laity is primarily based on the general availability of Baptism as the requirement for participation in this state.[18] Everyone starts their life in the Church by being baptized. The Sacrament of Baptism has an in-*forming* effect and von Balthasar explains it using the Pauline text that describes Baptism as joining Christ in his death: "for if we have grown into the likeness of his Death, that we may also grow into the likeness of his Resurrection." (Romans 6:5)[19] Here is the form of Christian life. Then too, Paul draws on Greek Platonism to show that likeness does not indicate simple similarity, because even for the pagan Greeks, it indicated "the relationship of earthly imitative things to their heavenly archetypes."[20] In the New Testament, the sense of the term is stronger still as Christ 'impresses his form of life' on believers.

---

[18] *CSOL*, 329.
[19] His translation from the Greek. *GL I*, 577.
[20] *GL I*, 577.

A further feature of the general state is added by the Spirit sent by Christ, so the general state is not some kind of amorphous existence, but is animated by the Spirit who "distributes different gifts to different people just as he chooses." (I Corinthians 12:11) It is assumed that this text applies to all of the members of the community. Paul is also implicitly describing a "torrent of grace" falling upon members of the community.[21] To properly understand what this means one must realize that, "just as grace knows no upper limit, so its challenge knows no upper limit."[22] There is no passivity or dreary narrowness in von Balthasar's (and the Church's) vision of lay life. A lay person is filled with the grace of God and all of the infinite possibilities that that offers. In the words of his mentor Henri de Lubac S.J., the Church "will always reflect [Christ's] glory through the best of her children."[23]

Connected to this point, we have von Balthasar's concern that, on the one hand, this aspect of lay life has not been sufficiently emphasized, and on the other hand, this fact has not been grasped sufficiently by lay people, who in the "long-standing experience of the Church . . . often do not want to become mature in the Christian sense because Christian maturity does not mean just a serious obligation towards all of the ministries inspired by the Holy Spirit and also conferred as tasks: it also presumes a supernatural maturity that can be achieved only through much prayer and sacrifice."[24] This maturity is aided by the Sacrament of Confirmation, and in fact the wording of the Homily in the *Rite of Confirmation* does say the following: "Be active members of the Church, alive in Jesus Christ. Under the guidance of the Holy Spirit give your lives completely in the service of all, as did Christ who came not to be served but to serve."[25] This thought points to the examination of the lay life from the perspective of the Good, and that will be found in Chapter Five.

Returning now to the gifts of the Spirit: they are given for the growth of the Body of Christ, as it

---

[21] *CSOL*, 336.
[22] *CSOL*, 338.
[23] *Splendor of the Church*, 235.
[24] *CSOL*, 333.
[25] ICEL, *The Rites of the Catholic Church as revised by the Second Vatican Council, IA – Initiation*, (New York: Pueblo Publishing, 1976), 488.

expands in the world. Nevertheless, the nature of the teaching in this chapter of the *Letter to the Corinthians* indicates that the gifts are "for the most part transitory [and] cannot be the foundation of a state of life."[26] The life-form of the General State is distinguished from life outside of the Church by its participation in the Spirit of Christ and the concrete relationships of his life to Mary, Peter, John, and the Multitude respectively.

Finally, it must be said that in lay life in general, given the coherence of the work of the Spirit, the gifts that are offered by the Spirit of God never ever claim to compete with the objective ministries of those in the State of Election as ordained ministers.[27]

The State of Election

After their archetypal lay life, Jesus and Mary then lived in a different state, which von Balthasar, following the tradition, described as the 'State of Election'. Both Jesus and Mary were called successively from the lay state into a life that becomes the archetype for the State of Election. A specific election by God is the basis of this state.

Following the narrative of the life of Jesus—which means that his life is being taken as archetypal for life in the Church[28]—there are the following clues to what the State of Election looks like. To begin with, Christ left the general state to start his public ministry. He started a community of disciples. His new state was so distinctive that Jesus went to the extent of denying his earthly relationship to his mother and family in favor of his new family, about which he says: "Here are my mother and my brothers. For whoever does the will of God is my brother and sister

---

[26] *CSOL*, 330.

[27] See Vatican II: "The Church, which the Spirit guides in way of all truth and which He unified in communion and in works of ministry, He both equips and directs with hierarchical and charismatic gifts and adorns with His fruits." (LG 4) There is an implied concord of purpose in these words.

[28] In proceeding in this way and holding that Christ founds the states of life, von Balthasar is following both Aquinas and Franceso Suarez S.J. a great theologian in the sixteenth century. Of relevance here is Suarez' *De Statu Perfectionis*. For his general theory of the states of life von Balthasar also refers the reader to the works of Augustine, Chrysostom, William of St. Thierry amongst others.

and mother." (Mark 3:31)[29] The events at the wedding feast at Cana demonstrated the same distance between the state of his mother and himself, where Jesus says: "Woman, how does your concern affect me?" (John 2:4)[30] These clues indicate the difference between the general state and the State of the Elect.

At this point, the State of Election is the state of living *with Christ where he is*. The narrative tells us about the group (called disciples in many of the texts) who were always with him. In the *Gospel of Matthew*, for example: "He got into a boat and his disciples followed him." (Matthew 8:23) This is the central characteristic of the State of Election. Those in this state are *with* him all of the time.[31] This state means living poor, chaste, and obedient lives as Jesus did.[32] Poverty, chastity, and obedience came to be called the Evangelical Counsels because they summed up the life of Jesus in the world so perfectly.[33]

Now from the life of Mary we learn that the State of Election is a life of poverty, chastity, and obedience, so that the meaning of poverty, chastity, and obedience can be learned from her as well.

However the narrative does not stop there. Still to happen, we have the central events of Jesus' life, namely his Death, and Resurrection. The sacrifice of Jesus that is represented in the Last Supper, and takes place on the Cross the following day, ushers in the sacrifice at the heart of Christianity. Jesus offers himself for us, and he confers the ability to preside at the sacrifice on his disciples. Jesus' actions differentiate the State of Election into the Life of the

---

[29] See Thomas' note in his *Catena in Marcum, 31.6*, that this actions of Jesus is not rejecting his mother "*sed ostendens quod super omnem cognationem temporalem oportet propriam animam praehonorare.*"

[30] *CSOL*, 196.

[31] Note Thomas' conclusion: "The Apostles are understood to have vowed things pertaining to the State of Perfection when *they left all things and followed* Christ." (ST II II q. 88 a. 5.)

[32] Similarly Thomas says: "our Lord, in proposing the counsels, . . ." (ST I II q. 108 a. 4.) They are originating with Christ himself.

[33] Cf. "The evangelical counsels of chastity dedicated to God, poverty and obedience are based upon the words and examples of the Lord. They were further commanded by the apostles and Fathers of the Church, as well as by the doctors and pastors of souls." (LG 43)

Evangelical Counsels and the Priesthood.³⁴ In other words, Christ generates the basis of Catholic Priesthood through his own priestly state, as the one who offers sacrifice.³⁵ In fact, the *Letter to the Hebrews* describes Christ's role entirely in priestly terms: "Therefore holy "brothers" sharing in a heavenly calling, reflect on Jesus, the Apostle and High Priest of our confession, who was faithful to the one who appointed him." (Hebrews 3:1)

What is relevant here is that Christ's priesthood has the character of an office (from the Latin *officium* meaning duty or ceremony) in that it is concretely objective in its offering. Now it is possible to participate in the office of Priest in two ways. The foundations of both ways were laid in the life of Christ, and consequently in the lives of the Apostles John and Peter who, for von Balthasar, respectively characterize the religious priest and the secular priest.³⁶ This is to say that these two mens' experience of Christ in the

---

[34] Kenan Osborne says that the lay, cleric distinction occurred later than the New Testament period. *Ministry*, 21. More specifically, he claims that the distinction arose from the development of nomenclature. Von Balthasar does note that historically, the "first eleven centuries of the Church were basically acquainted with one single 'state of perfection,' which as a whole was the complement of the state of Lay persons in the world." *CSOL*, 296ff. He is referring here to religious priesthood. There were no secular clergy in the modern sense. Von Balthasar is basing his statements on the work of Ludwig von Hertling. However those in the state of perfection were clerics. The differentiation of those in the state of perfection into religious and clerics occurred in the "complete reorganization of the ecclesial states" in the aftermath of the Gregorian Reform. Ludwig von Hertling cited by von Balthasar, *Christian State of Life*, 298. The work of Kenan Osborne is simplifying a complex historical picture that does in fact consistently show elements of the three states.

[35] Raymond Brown reduces the phrase 'priesthood of Jesus' to the Christological statements in the *Letter to the Hebrews* instead of acknowledging the sacrificial character of every moment of the life of Jesus. Then he notes the paucity of such statements in the early New Testament. Raymond Brown S.S., *Priest and Bishop*, (New York: Paulist Press, 1970), 14. In contrast Thomas Aquinas demonstrated that it is fitting that Christ is a priest because "the office proper to a priest is to be a mediator between God and the people." ST III q. 22 a. 1. Here Christ *is* the priest by his nature.

[36] *CSOL*, 287.

New Testament offers significant clues to the meaning of religious and secular priesthood. Now von Balthasar is not saying that religious and secular priesthood existed *in their present form* in the early Church. In fact he does refer specifically to the "evolution of the two states of Election."[37] His position is nuanced because it takes into account the historical development of dogma and of life in the Church. What we are referring to are the *essentials* and these are traceable to the primitive community!

So he is saying that the *realities* that the states represent were present from the beginning, "even if only implicitly" and were "more 'lived' than reflected upon."[38] The underlying unity of the subjective and objective elements in the lives of those who followed Jesus meant that it took time for the differentiation of the two states in the State of Election. What they shared in common was the decision to follow Christ absolutely, which forms the basis of the state in terms of its stability.

The stability of a state had been argued for by Thomas Aquinas by reference to the man who "is said to have stability (*statum*) in reference to [his] own disposition in the point of a certain immobility or restfulness." (ST II II q.183 a.1) So the condition of the person in spiritual matters regards something that is established where a man finds that he is in a state of "freedom or servitude". (ST II II q. 183 a.1) Here Thomas means 'freedom' and 'servitude' in relation to sin and justice.

What is also helpful for the theology of the states within the Church is Thomas' careful presentation of the relationship between the states of life, in terms of the nature of the whole Church. The fact that there are different states of life, first of all, shows the Church in all of its fullness. This is because "perfection, which in God is simple and uniform, is not to be found in the created world except in a multiform and manifold manner" (a.2). True to his method, Thomas learned this from the Scriptures that say for example: "It was he who gave some to be Apostles, some to be prophets, some to be evangelists, and some

---

[37] *CSOL*, 292.
[38] Ibidem.

to be pastors and teachers." (Ephesians 4:11)[39] Thomas cited this text in his explanation of the diversity of the states of life in the Church.

Then further, the diversity of ecclesial states permits the diversity of actions that correspond to them. The diversity of actions is essential to the full expression of the existence of the Church. This is again a Pauline insight: "each of us has one body with many members, and these members do not all have the same function." (Romans 12:4, 5) (cited ST II II q. 183 a.2) Finally, this organic diversity "belongs to the dignity and beauty of the Church." (a. 2) As Paul wrote to Timothy: "in a large house there are not only gold and silver vessels, but also vessels of wood and of earthenware, and some to honor and some to dishonor." (II Timothy 2:20).

Summing up: When von Balthasar moves from explaining the organic unity of the states in the Church to showing the distinctions between them, he keeps returning to the fact that there is only ultimately one State of Election in the Church namely that of Christ himself. So then those who participate in the State of Election are taking part in *his* state of existence by his grace. The inclusion of others in the State of Election took place through the activities of Jesus himself. He called the Apostles, taught them the evangelical counsels, and led them as a group that lived these counsels.[40] The sheer fact of the calling of the Apostles differentiated them from the larger group of people who were following Jesus in other ways.

The Relations between the States of Life

The continuing of the Christ-form in the world requires all three states of life.[41] In a virtuoso piece of

---

[39] With regard to a related question, Kenan Osborne O.F.M. works hard to try to demonstrate that the Second Vatican Council "relativised the hierarchy." *Ministry*, 518ff. I am not sure that this extreme reading of the council's position fits the structure of *Lumen gentium*. In the sense of being related to the other states in the Church, the hierarchy has always been in the position being argued in this work.

[40] Von Balthasar cites Aquinas: "The Apostles are believed to have vowed what pertained to the state of perfection, when, having left all things, they followed Christ." (*ST II II* q.88 q.4 a.3)

[41] As the Second Vatican Council explained: "In virtue of this catholicity each individual part contributes through its

analysis, von Balthasar set out six interrelationships between the states of life. Since the Church is a theological mystery, there is of course no one single conceptual principle that will completely describe the relationships in the Church.[42] If one might use a physical analogy—weak as it is—then much as with the other forms that have already been discussed, one has to 'walk around' the Church and 'see' the relationships from other 'angles' to try and grasp what the Church is.[43] Each perspective that von Balthasar takes produces one relationship between the three states of life in the Church. To reiterate a point: what is being called the lay state in this chapter is the general state of the life of the command-ments, together with the "special gifts of grace, special inst-ructions and special demands of the Spirit".[44] It is 'general' in the sense that all who are called to the State of Election, as well as those who remain in the lay state, start their lives in the Church by living this form of life.

Now we are in a position to examine von Balthasar's conclusions about the relationships between the states of life. The first perspective views the relations between the states of life from the point of view of love.

---

special gifts to the good of the other parts and of the whole Church. Through the common sharing of gifts and through the common effort to attain fullness in unity, the whole and each of the parts receive increase. Not only, then, is the people of God made up of different peoples but in its inner structure also it is composed of various ranks." (LG, 13)

[42] Similarly John Paul II stated that "The Church . . . is mystery because the very life and love of the Father, Son and Holy Spirit are the gift gratuitously offered to all those who are born of water and the Holy Spirit (Cf. John 3:5) and called to relive the very communion of God and to manifest it and communicate it in history (mission)." (CL, 8)

[43] Once again, John Paul II concurs: "only from inside the Church's mystery of communion is the 'identity' of the Lay faithful made known and their fundamental dignity revealed." (CL, 8) Von Balthasar explains this point further in his *Theologic: I: The Truth of the World*, Adrian J. Walker trans., (San francisco: Ignatius Press, 2000), 8

[44] CSOL, 333.

(i) The mutual indwelling of the states with love as its ultimate form[45]

The first interrelationship shows that all of the states of life in the Church only exist for the fundamental service of love.[46] Jesus came to show God's love to the world. So this becomes the purpose of the existence of the Church.[47] As de Lubac would have it: "Christ . . . loves us in his Church."[48] This interrelationship points out the theological core of human life and its main purpose namely loving service of God and neighbor in Christ. Von Balthasar placed this particular relation between the states in the Church at the end of his presentation as a kind of culmination of all that he was saying. Here I have mentioned it at the beginning as a response to the

---

[45] The Second Vatican Council emphasized the love at the heart of the Church as follows: "The Church, further, 'that Jerusalem which is above' is also called 'our mother'. (Galatians 4:26; cf. Revelation 12:17) It is described as the spotless spouse of the spotless Lamb,(Revelation 19:7; 21: 2 and 9; 22:17) whom Christ 'loved and for whom He delivered Himself up that He might sanctify her',(Ephesians 5:26.) whom He unites to Himself by an unbreakable covenant, and whom He unceasingly 'nourishes and cherishes',(Ephesians 5:29.) and whom, once purified, He willed to be cleansed and joined to Himself, subject to Him in love and fidelity,(Cf. Ephesians 5:24) and whom, finally, He filled with heavenly gifts for all eternity, in order that we may know the love of God and of Christ for us, a love which surpasses all knowledge.(Cf. Ephesians 3:19)" (LG, 6) Note also the specific mention of Religious where: "The evangelical counsels which lead to charity join their followers to the Church and its mystery in a special way." (LG, 44)

[46] Note as well Congar's statement that "it is love that is its own reason and its origin, this is the love of the Father." (My translation.) *Sacerdoce et Laïcat*, (Paris: Les Éditions du Cerf: 1962), 13. The *Constitution on the Church* notes that love is at the heart of the Church: "He filled [the Church] with heavenly gifts for all eternity, in order that we may know the love of God and of Christ for us, a love which surpasses all knowledge. The Church, while on earth it journeys in a foreign land away from the Lord, is life an exile." (LG, 6) And then when discussing the different gifts and ministries the *Constitution* says: "Giving the body unity through Himself and through His power and inner joining of the members, this same Spirit produces and urges love among the believers." (LG, 7)

[47] Cf. "The Calling to Love," CSOL, 25ff.

[48] *Splendor of the Church*, 45.

constant suggestion from modern western culture that *power* is what is really important in institutions. Let us take an extreme example of power becoming the foundation of a culture: As Benedict XVI said so poignantly at the Auschwitz death camp (a peculiarly twentieth century phenomenon!): "By destroying Israel, by the *Shoah*, they ultimately wanted to tear up the taproot of the Christian faith and to replace it with a faith of their own invention: faith in the rule of man, the rule of the powerful."[49] More currently, for example, people in businesses can become obsessed with the bottom-line this in itself is an obsession with power as money supersedes other responsibilities that a business has.

But in fact, instead of seeking power, human beings were created to "love the Lord your God with all your heart, with all your soul, and with all your strength." (Deuteronomy 6:5) And further: "you must love your neighbor as yourself." (Leviticus 19:18) These commandments were given a new base in the New Testament: "I give you a new commandment, love one another . . . By this love you have for one another, everyone will know that you are my disciples." (John 13:34) But the initial demands of the Old Law were not changed by this new commandment. These two points are the reason for emphasizing the actual *relativity* of the states of life.

Von Balthasar also speaks of the 'dialectical' relationship between the states.[50] The service of love makes the different states found in the Church *relative* to each other, and at the *service* of each other, so that in Christ men and women are reconciling the world to God through the love of Christ. As von Balthasar reminds us, "Christ's primary intention was . . . to win men to that personal following of himself that leads to the reconciliation of the world with God by a renunciatory, even a crucified, love."[51]

That being said, the characteristics of the Christian form of being help us identify more of the meaning of Diagram One. A form radiates the depths that are the source of the form. Members of each state

---

[49] Benedict XVI, *Address by the Holy Father*, Auschwitz-Birkenau, 28th May 2006.
[50] Hans Urs von Balthasar, "A Theology of the Secular Institute," *ET II*, 431.
[51] *CSOL*, 12.

are members of the Church of Jesus Christ which represents on earth the love of the Divine Trinity made present in Christ.[52] Each state manifests an aspect shared by the other states in representing this personal love. For example, the state of the cleric makes concrete the redemption of Christ as concrete presence and sacrament in such a way that it is absolute. Christ as Priest, Teacher, and Shepherd is concretely present in the experience of those who encounter the priest.[53] The state of the evangelical counsels represents the possibilities of personal commitment in Christ as the poor, chaste, and obedient one in the Holy Spirit.[54] The members of the lay state practice love of God and neighbor in the world. All these are the actions of a person who has joined Christ's mission of demonstrating God's love to the world.

The five relationships that follow can only be understood together and in the light of Christ's love for us. Von Balthasar cites Paul's teaching: "There is a variety of gifts but always the same Spirit, there are all sorts of service to be done, but always to the same Lord; working in all sorts of different ways in different people, it is the same God who is working in all of them." (I Corinthians 12:22-27) Paul was telling each member of the Body of Christ that their place is related to everyone in the rest of the community, and is for the good of the rest of the community before God. Given that all three states interrelate in a service of love, each state contributes to the form of the Church and how it manifests the presence of Christ, can now be examined in turn.

(ii) The Intensity of Participation in Christ's Mission[55]

---

[52] See Benedict XVI's words: "In the account of Jacob's ladder, the Fathers of the Church saw this inseparable connection between ascending and descending love, between *eros* which seeks God and *agape* which passes on the gift received, symbolized in various ways." (*Deus caritas est*, 7)
[53] Cf. LG 20.
[54] Note also John Paul II: "Christ invites some people to share his experience as the chaste, poor and obedient one." (*Vita consecrata*, 18.) (VC) The character of Christ's life is described by the evangelical counsels.
[55] *CSOL*, 365.

The different states show increasing degrees of 'intensity' in following Christ. In von Balthasar's lexicon, 'intensity' means 'degree of analogy'.

The Religious State potentially has the fullest analogy to the life of Christ, the Clerical State the next fullest and the next is the Lay State. So we distinguish the states by their degree of analogy in the following of Christ.[56]

Now, in O'Donnell's view, expressing the distinction this way indicates that "it is clear that what stands closest to von Balthasar's heart is the elected state."[57] But this diagram is not a projection of von Balthasar's desires! O'Donnell does not recognize the sources of von Balthasar's theology. Every person in the Church has a vocation and a mission that will be realized, at the behest of the Father, in Christ through the Holy Spirit, but—and this is crucial—there is one mission from God to the world, and that is the mission of Christ himself.[58] This is the higher reality that regulates how people participate in it. There is no neutral position between God and human beings that can escape being defined in some way by the counsels that sum up so completely this concrete analogy of being. As was stated earlier: Christ is the "model for the analogy of being; he becomes the *concrete* analogy of being." (Original Emphasis.)[59] This is a rephrasing of the description of the hypostatic union that constitutes Jesus Christ. In other words each

---

[56] Vatican II spoke in terms of the totality of the call to the live the life of the counsels: "The faithful of Christ bind themselves to the three aforesaid counsels either by vows, or by other sacred bonds, which are like vows in their purpose. By such a bond, a person is totally dedicated to God, loved beyond all things." (LG 44)

[57] John O'Donnell, Hans Urs von Balthasar, (England: Geoffrey Chapman, 1992), 137.

[58] It is the nature of this mission as a mission to the world that challenges Osborne's ecclesiology. For him, "the sacrament of initiation . . . is an initiation primarily into the Church . . . not into the secular world." Kenan Osborne O.F.M., *Ministry*, 539. The problem is that the Church is for the world and the mission of a confirmed individual is to bring the world into the Church. The suggested words of the celebrant at the Rite of Confirmation are "The promised strength of the Holy Spirit . . . will make you more like Christ and help you to be witnesses to his suffering, death and resurrection." *The Rites: Initiation*, 162.

[59] *CSOL*, 192.

Christian life state is some approximation to the most complete possible state of human life before God namely that of Christ himself.

The gradation in the degree of analogy to Christ comes about as follows: the first division of the states of life was brought about when Christ called the Apostles from the commitment of their earthly ties in the general state of life. The Apostles then belonged to the State of Election. Those who participate in the State of Election are with Jesus where he is.[60] However, they can be with him both subjectively (in terms of conformity of spirit) and objectively (in terms of the external expression of conformity to Christ). Historically, these participations can occur in the same persons as in the case of the Apostles themselves. However, the subjective state is the qualitatively higher state namely the State of the Counsels because of its *interior* conformity of spirit to Christ. Here love as a life of poverty, chastity, and obedience indicates the character of the *complete* self-surrender of the Christian in Christ.[61] This form of existence reaches the highest level of analogy between Christ's self-surrender and the self-surrender that is possible for some of his followers.

Differentiating between the State of the Counsels and the Clerical State lies in the fact that the life of the counsels is the most direct following of the way of Christ.[62] By contrast, the Priesthood only

---

[60] The Second Vatican Council taught that: "The evangelical counsels of chastity dedicated to God, poverty and obedience are based upon the words and examples of the Lord." (LG, 43)

[61] Congar calls this line of argument the "Monastic notion" which views the states of life in terms of their moral demands. *Lay People in the Church*, 8. Cf. also John Paul II: "The identity of the consecrated person, beginning with his or her complete self-offering, [is] comparable to a genuine holocaust." (VC, 17)

[62] Thomas Aquinas would not agree with this ordering of the states: "the state of perfection is more perfect in bishops than in religious." (ST II II q. 184 a. 7.) However, this judgment is due to his understanding of the episcopate which is that "the priest or archdeacon does not pledge his whole life to the cure of souls, as a bishop does." (ST II II q. 184 a. 8.) So he would see as regards the good, the priest and archdeacon would be below the religious in the diagram. Von Balthasar by contrast does not consider the orders of participation in the priesthood in his scheme of things.

requires an indirect subjective following, although it does still require it. Hopefully a priest is good! Additionally, the priesthood on this scale lies between the general state and the Religious State because it participates in both in some sense.[63] Priesthood objectively mediates the following of Christ through an objective life of celibacy and obedience to the bishop. Priesthood also participates in the lay state in the sense that the diocesan priest does not take a vow of poverty and has the autonomy over his affairs that is necessary for his pastoral ministry.

The distinction between those in the general state and those in the State of Election is the distinction between those who do not receive a specific call and those who do. The lay state has its place in the scale of following Christ because it embodies the lowest degree of renunciation as expressed in the vows. Members of the general lay state cannot renounce the goods of this world and by definition are not called to do so. This is an instance of what Yves Congar called "laicality"[64] and what John Paul II called the "secular character" of lay life (CL, 15).

Lastly, this scale of analogical following of Christ summarizes the characteristics of the form of the Church. It is founded on the loving relation between the Incarnate Son, and the Father, through the Spirit. This is radiated in the Church through the State of the Evangelical Counsels. But the other states do manifest aspects of this subjective self-surrender, so that priests grow in holiness and laity can demonstrate a 'poverty', 'chastity' and 'obedience' through their ordered use of the goods of creation.

(iii) Obedience to the Priestly State.

Von Balthasar's third interrelationship describes the hierarchical dimension of the Church.[65]

---

[63] The judgment on the distinction between the Lay State and the Contemplative State is that "it is more meritorious to offer to God one's own soul . . . than any other external gifts" and this appears in Thomas' section on the Active and the Contemplative Life. (ST II II q. 182 a. 2.)

[64] *Lay People in the Church*, 20.

[65] With regard to the whole Church, the Second Vatican Council said: "Bishops, as vicars and ambassadors of Christ, govern the particular churches entrusted to them by their counsel, exhortations, example, and even by their authority and sacred power, which indeed they use only for the

Fundamentally in the logic of love, those "called to perfect love, are equally admonished to perfect obedience."[66] So obedience lies at the heart of the Church.[67] Christ called a specific group of followers, "the Twelve," who were to lead the rest of the followers to unity in Christ. The expectation is that the rest of the Church be docile to their leadership, but only through the "incurable humility" of the leaders, as illustrated by the continuous humbling of Peter. So while the State of the Counsels and the lay state only comprise part of the Church, the hierarchy is for the whole Church and hence its position must be considered.[68]

This reflection helps us illustrate the cleric-lay distinction in the Church. (Many religious are laity too!) The clergy embody the Offices of Christ as Shepherd, Leader, and Teacher for the whole Church and so they are shepherds, leaders, and teachers for those in the State of the Counsels and for those in the lay state. The continuing of the presence of Christ as Shepherd, Leader, and Teacher is the radiance to be identified here. This argument also indicates the importance of understanding roles in the Church in terms of the Offices of Christ, a question that has arisen already.

Lastly, the relationship of the rest of the Church with the clergy can be considered from the perspective of form. The presence of Christ gives the Church its proportion and integrity as a form. Given

---

edification of their flock in truth and holiness." (LG, 27) Specifically with regard to religious, the council said that: "It is the duty of the ecclesiastical hierarchy to regulate the practice of the evangelical counsels by law." (LG, 45)

[66] *Office of Peter*, 76.

[67] With regard to the Laity specifically, the Second Vatican Council said: "Let them follow the example of Christ, who by His obedience even unto death, opened to all men the blessed way of the liberty of the children of God. Nor should they omit to pray for those placed over them, for they keep watch as having to render an account of their souls, so that they may do this with joy and not with grief." (LG 37)

[68] Note the comment in the *Supplement* to the *Summa Theologica*, which was not written by Aquinas himself, but follows his thought: "a priest has two acts; one is the principal, namely to consecrate the Body of Christ; the other is secondary, namely to prepare God's people for the reception of this sacrament." ST Suppl. Q. 40 a. 5. Here is the priest serving the whole Church.

the 'masculine' and 'feminine' complementarity that comes about within the Church, between the two ways of participating in Christ's offices, there is a proportion between these two ways of participating in the Church. The laity exercise the 'feminine' side of this proportion and the hierarchy exercises the 'masculine' side. At the same time, the presence of Christ is the higher principle that makes this relation possible.

(iv) The interrelationship between the Clerical and the Religious States as the Model for the Lay State

The fact that two states—the Clerical State and the Religious State—exist within the State of Election means that their interrelation has a definite meaning for the lay state.

In a key sentence, von Balthasar wrote that "the secular state receives its ultimate substance and form from the State of Election."[69] This sentence sums up the meaning of the relationship with the clergy and religious and is a substantial claim to make. Clearly the relation between the general state and the State of Election is not simply one of example. There has to be more. The relationship is based on theological personhood which is a rich concept that will be explored more fully in the theodramatic study to follow.[70]

Theological personhood involves complimentary subjective (interior, spiritual) and objective (concrete) elements where the individual becomes fully a person within the history of salvation due to the grace of Christ. The Religious State demonstrates the subjective 'conforming' to Christ.[71] But at the same

---

[69] *CSOL*, 197.

[70] Vatican II expresses a similar thought. For example regarding the priesthood: "They likewise exercise that priesthood in receiving the sacraments, in prayer and thanksgiving, in the witness of a holy life, and by self-denial and active charity." (LG 10) Here you have the various objective elements in von Balthasar's sense. Then regarding religious, the council said that those in the "religious state and, tending toward holiness by a narrower path, stimulate their brethren by their example." (LG 13) This is the 'subjective' dimension in von Balthasar's sense.

[71] In just one example of many quotations from the Second Vatican Council we see the inward conformity that can be achieved through the life of the vows: "By his profession of the evangelical counsels, then, he is more intimately consecrated to divine service." (LG, 44)

time, the objective nature of the actions and presence of the priesthood manifest the concrete historical elements of the presence of Christ.[72] Hence these two states together show the lay state both the interior conformity to Christ and the need for concrete external actions showing participation in the work of Christ. Marriage, for example, involves both subjective and objective elements. It is a personal interior commitment that is expressed and completed in the external actions of the ex-changing of vows and consummation of the Marriage in sexual union.

The States of Election also present the tension between form and person for the laity. The members of the Religious State cannot ever totally appropriate their religious rule. It is a goal that always requires more to be fulfilled. Neither can priests fully achieve the objective ministry to which they are called. Both states can always learn to live more fully for God than themselves and more *from* God as well. Similarly the laity experience the tension between their faith and their prayer, in their trying to do their work ethically, and trying to fully develop their Marriage as a sign of the union between Christ and his Church.

Moreover, Christ is the foundation of all of the states, and the hiddenness of his early life models the dimension of hiddenness of the lay state. The people asked about him: "Is this the carpenter?" (Mark 6:3) Then Saint Paul, referring to the believers of the Church of Colossae, wrote: "You have died and your life is hidden in God." (Colossians 3:3) Laity live in the midst of the world, and the heroic dimensions of their lives are usually unrecognized in this world.

Lastly, the relation between the State of the Counsels and the priesthood is a source of *proportion* for the form of lay life. Christ's total self-surrender is subjectively and objectively to his mission for the Father is 'modeled' by the State of Election, and it is the higher organizing principle for the lay state. Lay people can learn how to live as Christians from the Priests and Religious that they encounter. When the full meaning of the State of Election is lived within the

---

[72] See the *Dogmatic Constitution on the Church*'s teaching: "Bishops thus, by praying and laboring for the people, make outpourings in many ways and in great abundance from the fullness of Christ's holiness." (LG, 26) The constitution then goes on to list the objective actions of the bishop.

community, then it radiates this total 'giving over' of the community to the mission of Christ with all that means in terms of being a holy people.[73]

(v) The Evangelical State as the Norm for the Lay State[74]

Now just as the Clerical State has a primacy in the Church due to its authority over the whole Church, the Religious State has a kind of primacy that must be noted.[75] This is not a primacy of authority but a normative one.[76]

Because of the total commitment of the person in the Religious State to the state of Christ, "[the Religious State] acquires thereby a normative function" with respect to the other two states.[77] Besides the perhaps unexpected general proposal that the lay person is in a direct relationship with the members of the other two states, the claim of the normative presence of Religious in the Church community is perhaps the most surprising. Religious are called to offer themselves as personal subjects who come to theological personhood by representing the poverty, chastity, and obedience of Christ to the world. It is their making present of the sheer possibilities of poverty, chastity, and obedience that is the issue in

---

[73] Cf. The Second Vatican Council: "Thus, as those everywhere who adore in holy activity, the laity consecrate the world itself to God." (LG 34)

[74] Note that the diagram shows that Religious stand with Christ. The Second Vatican Council explained: "The evangelical counsels of chastity dedicated to God, poverty and obedience are based upon the words and examples of the Lord. They were further commanded by the Apostles and Fathers of the Church, as well as by the doctors and pastors of souls. The counsels are a divine gift, which the Church received from its Lord and which it always safeguards with the help of His grace." (LG, 43)

[75] Note the Second Vatican Council's teaching that: "by their state in life, Religious give splendid and striking testimony that the world cannot be transformed and offered to God without the spirit of the beatitudes." (LG, 31) Or putting it in different terms, they serve the "welfare of the entire Body of Christ. (LG, 43)

[76] Cf. *Perfectae caritatis*: "the manifold results of their holiness lends luster to the people of God which is inspired by their example and which gains new members by their apostolate which is as effective as it is hidden." (article 7)

[77] *CSOL*, 375.

this diagram. By giving themselves over completely to Christ's work of redemption, religious have a normative role with respect to both priests and the laity.

Religious make present the only way of following Christ namely through self-surrender and they make it present as a concrete element in the experience in the lives of laity and clergy. Here von Balthasar mentions Paul's injunction: "Those who have wives should live as if they have none . . . those whose life is buying things should live as if they had nothing of their own, and those who have to deal with the world should not become engrossed in it." (I Corinthians 7:29ff.) The existence of the life of the counsels is also a safeguard against a reduction of the Church to consisting simply of those in authority and those in the pews. Von Balthasar saw this latter position as leading to clericalism or laicism, because the moderating influence of the other state of election would not be present in their lives.[78]

The religious way of life centers on the notion of complete surrender as the core of love.[79] In other words, it demonstrates what love truly is. Theologically, the religious state has always been seen as the public sign of those who follow Christ since all love in fact has the inner structure of a vow.

Finally from the perspective of form, this reflection shows the inner appropriation of the form of Christ's own existence as poor, chaste, and obedient before the Father and his will.

(vi). The State of Election is at the Service of the Lay State

The lay state is indeed the "principal state" in the Church both because of the vast numbers involved and because of its secular nature, so that it has a very special place in the mission of Christ which is in fact to the whole world.

---

[78] Hans Urs von Balthasar, *Laicat et Plein Apostolat*, trans., E. Bernimont O.P., (Liege: La Pensée Catholique, 1949), 33.

[79] See Benedict XVI: "My deep personal sharing in the needs and sufferings of others becomes a sharing of my very self with them: if my gift is not to prove a source of humiliation, I must give to others not only something that is my own, but my very self; I must be personally present in my gift." (*Deus caritas est*, 34)

Pointing to this interrelationship brings out the dimension of radical service to the community by those in the State of Election.[80] The Priestly State serves the lay community through teaching, sanctifying, and governing the community.[81] Nevertheless it means, in von Balthasar's terms, that "the certainty of personal mission [does not] preclude the urge "to spend and be spent" to the end for the brethren."[82] Laity can indeed demand this depth of service. Similarly religious serve the laity in numerous ways by their example, by their introduction of the counsels into life situations, to the service provided by religious schools and other institutions.

However, the key point that von Balthasar makes in identifying this relationship is that both groups in the State of Election help the laity to be *Christian* laity. They help laity toward perfection but always through helping them reach goals "proper to themselves."[83] Consequently, von Balthasar considers taking on specifically ecclesiastical roles to be a "burden" on the laity. In this he is in good company. Thomas Aquinas reminds us that "whatever laws are enacted for the special sanctification of certain ones, are binding on them alone; thus clerics who are set aside for the service of God alone are bound to certain obligations to which the laity are not bound" and similarly for the religious. (ST I II q. 98 a. 5) Hence, von Balthasar wants to avoid terms like 'lay apostle,' or 'Catholic Action,' and so on. The lay person's mission is very definitely *in* the world and in and through his "own life and self."[84] Thus, in conclusion, this reflection shows the perfection that the laity achieved in and through their own lives, where the lay person's mission "is of necessity limited to the modest

---

[80] Thus the Second Vatican Council speaks of the Church: "He continually distributes in His body, that is, in the Church, gifts of ministries in which, by His own power, we serve each other unto salvation so that, carrying out the truth in love, we might through all things grow unto Him who is our Head." (LG 7)

[81] Similarly Thomas taught that "the Apostles and their successors are God's vicars in governing the Church, which is built on faith and the Sacraments of faith." ST III q. 64 a. 3.

[82] *CSOL*, 382.

[83] *CSOL*, 383.

[84] *CSOL*, 385.

and more homely one of influencing and illuminating the place destined for him in the world," supported and aided by clergy and religious.⁸⁵

These six interrelationships display the rich interplay of relationships of authority and obedience, of example and service, of speaking and hearing that make the Body of Christ a dynamic presence of the Incarnate Son in the world, receiving precepts and gifts from the Father and offering worship and love to the Father.

But one question remains: where exactly do secular institutes fit into these relationships?

The Position of Secular Institutes

From a theological perspective, secular institutes consist of laity formally living the life of the counsels.⁸⁶ But this is not a life where the "monastic ideal [is] transferred to lay men".⁸⁷ Life in a secular institute is first and foremost a demonstration of the mystery of the Church and the fact that the states of life in the Church "remain mysteriously dialectic," which is what he has already demonstrated above.⁸⁸ The interrelationships of the other states are not 'disturbed' by the historical development of a new state of life with the rise of secular institutes. So the interrelation-ships that we have studied remain as they are. However, from the earliest times—in fact, Christ himself set the example—people have lived the virginal life out of a love of Christ, while they still followed their 'ordinary' secular occupations. Christ himself lived the life of the counsels even while he

---

⁸⁵ *CSOL*, 383.
⁸⁶ The historical questions about the approval of such institutes are answered in Chapter Eight.
⁸⁷ Hans Urs von Balthasar, "A Theology of the Secular Institute," *ET II*, 424.
⁸⁸ "A Theology of the Secular Institute," 430. The Second Vatican Council also recognized the wide ranging possibilities of the life of the counsels: "This practice of the counsels, under the impulse of the Holy Spirit, undertaken by many Christians, either privately or in a Church-approved condition or state of life, gives and must give in the world an outstanding witness and example of this same holiness." (LG 39)

worked for his step-father. This means that the formal state of life in a secular institute is at least plausible.

Theologically, von Balthasar concluded that "if the reshaping of what is worldly by what is Christian can be fundamentally affirmed in a worldly situation, then such giving of form must also be recognized to be possible and real in the life of the counsels."[89] The person called to radically follow Christ through the life of the counsels, in a religious order, is called to live them 'in' the Church alone. In contrast the members of secular institutes are called to live them 'in' the Church *and* in the world.

Here is the new wrinkle! Their vows inform their approach to their secular occupations. The exemplary and relational presence of the person living the life of the counsels fits into the above interrelationships, in the sense that the member of the secular institute is in the position both of a religious and a lay person from the point of view of the relationships. Obviously such a person's canonical situation is more complex but that is not the issue here.

Finally, at this juncture, it is worth noting that the relationships can show the theological situation of the member of the secular institute within the Church. For our purposes, they would be included under the Religious State.

Moving back to the general discussion of the form of Christian existence within the Church: the form of the multiple relationships highlighted above must be *experienced*. This leads us to our next section.

Christian Experience

In thinking about laity in theological terms not only must we consider the objective beauty of the Church, but also what happens when we *experience* such a beautiful form. What does the lay person's experience of the Church look like?

Two constant dimensions of the history of salvation are the objective form of salvation history (and hence of the Church) as well as the subjective operation of faith in the laity. When they are *not* both present, and when the beauty of the Church is *not* actively being sought by the lay person, then "the good

---

[89] "A Theology of the Secular Institute," 437.

loses its attractiveness, the self-evidence of why it must be carried out."⁹⁰ This is to say that the Church and the life of the Christian should both have a certain attractiveness, so that they are engaging and convincing. The Catholic who is selective about elements of the Church that he holds to be part of his life shows a dull and amorphous witness of the form of Christ to the world. In other words, when von Balthasar points to the attractiveness of a person's life he is pointing to the Christian *eros* for us.

The terms that von Balthasar used can take this consideration further. The word 'objective' means "that there is something there for faith to see."⁹¹ In the Scriptures and for the Fathers of the Church, God *is* presenting himself to his creation in a form that manifests his glory. Then, by 'subjective' von Balthasar means the subject's response in faith to what is being objectively presented to him. ⁹² Now, everyone has to know that what they are seeing is not simply a natural phenomenon. This is only the first 'phase' of true seeing, but it is an inescapable element of knowing in faith, and is rooted in "an antecedent knowledge of Being [by which] can man think rationally and will and love freely."⁹³ So man has to first of all be open to being as such. For example, at the level of being, a citizen has to actually be interested in his country's elections and know what they mean for his country. To take another example: for a married couple, the act of seeing the possibilities of their marriage in faith is predicated on the spouses relating to each other in a substantial way in ordinary conversation and so on. These 'ordinary' possibilities of married existence, or 'knowing the being of relationship' lay the groundwork

---

⁹⁰ Ibidem.
⁹¹ *GL I*, 175.
⁹² The vital need for the presence of faith leads me to differ with W.T. Dickens when he contends that someone who does not have faith in Christ "can see the harmony of relations seen by a Christian." See W.T. Dickens, *Hans Urs von Balthasar's Theological Aesthetics*, 75. I would suggest that the form is both a 'harmony of relations' and the 'radiance from its center' at the same time. So that the relations between the elements, let us say in the Scriptures, are only clear in the light of the radiance of the inspiration of the Holy Spirit working in the believer to illuminate his perception of what the Holy Spirit has inspired in the sacred texts.
⁹³ Ibidem.

for the discovery of their Christian depths through the light of faith.

But knowing being is only the beginning. The self-disclosure of God to man is not a dialogue among equals. God's very divinity means that in grace the believer "perceives [the created form of] God['s self-manifestation] by being transported outside of himself; he hears and grasps God in God and through God."[94] This is the *ekstasis* of grace. Man is brought out of himself by the Spirit of God to be able to appreciate the significance of what he is seeing of the signs of God's manifestation.[95] The Spirit of God in the baptized Christian "include[s] in an anticipatory fashion that point of convergence which makes the signs comprehensible . . . [And] it strengthens and deepens the power of sight."[96] (Here 'sign' is a synonym for form.)

The faithful Christian sees things that people who do not cooperate with grace cannot see hence Pierre Rousellot's catch-phrase 'the eyes of faith.'[97] These concepts are essential for appreciating von Balthasar's emphasis on the notion of form as it is used in understanding Christian participation in the plan of salvation.[98]

Now before we examine the experience of the form, there is one fundamental point that has to be made. The work of the Spirit through the eyes of faith does not go against the work of the Spirit *in the Christ-event* itself. So there is never any contradiction between the truth of the Church and the truth being sought by the believer, as if the believer can ever know 'more' than or 'differently' from the Church.

---

[94] *GL VI*, 13.
[95] He recognizes that the subjective conditions for participation in the form are many but they do not 'cancel' the objective reality of Christ and his Church that is presented and more to the point "the fact that Christ 'says nothing to me' in no way prejudices the fact that, in and of himself, Christ says everything to everyone." *GL I*, 464.
[96] Ibidem.
[97] Ibidem.
[98] This is the response to both the great deficiency of Catholic rationalism and the flaw that often appears in Protestant thinking where the 'Christ of faith' and the 'historical Jesus' are separated. To cite von Balthasar: "Nothing expresses more unequivocally the profound failure of these theologies than their deeply anguished, joyless and cheerless tone." See *GL I*, 174.

Now to take one example about the experience of the Christ-form in the writings of John: Jesus Christ's experience of God is the archetype of all human experiences of God. It is both God who is touched, heard and seen in Jesus and it is man who touches, hears and sees God in Jesus Christ. (Cf. 1 John 1:1)[99] In other words, it is God who speaks through the experience of *this* historical man, Jesus Christ. This also means that God has chosen to manifest his grace to the world through the intersubjective relationships of particular human beings with his incarnate self.[100] Again this is a theology of the Church that is rooted in being itself in this case the being of relationships and community. Furthermore, it is man who experiences God through *this* historical man, and according to the *Gospel of John* the incarnate Son permits human beings to participate in this experience. John wrote: "Truly, truly I say to you, we speak of what we know, and bear witness to what we have seen." (John 3:11) (Cf. also John 9:4.) This experience took place within the Church community gathered with John in the Body of Christ—to use an image from Paul. (Romans 12:5) So von Balthasar concluded that in every Christian's experience, "Christ himself is the primary subject" of the experience of God.[101] In other words, von Balthasar works from a specifically Christological ontology.

The understanding of the form of the Body of Christ that preceded this reflection on experience, offers a theology of the complete Christian experience of God in the Church. If experience is taken to be one of the initial dimensions of knowing then an *adequatio*

---

[99] *GL I*, 324.

[100] Intersubjectivity will be explained in Chapter Five. Also note the comment of Karl Rahner S. J., in "The Role of the Layman in the Church," *Theological Investigations VIII*, (New York: Crossroad, 1982) where he says: "The final reason for grace being accorded a quasi-sacramental embodiment in the world is that it must confront man as a free and embodied, and therefore *historical* person as such." 57. (Emphasis added.) Using a more Thomistic lexicon he has identified the heart of the nature of historical encounter and its reason for taking place in this way. The reasoning is ultimately anthropological. This is the way that man experiences.

[101] *GL I*, 264.

intellectus et rem develops which is the traditional scholastic understanding of the act of knowing. The phrase means 'a conforming of the mind to the object'. Then people's minds are helped to conform in grace to God in Christ. The experience of Christ in the mediated manner offered by participation in the Church community gives believers the graced measure of God. Furthermore, because of the unique nature of the relation between man and God in Christ, people can only deal with Christ in accepting the measure of God and man that is in him. The *adequatio* of the mind means that the subject allows himself to be informed by the truth of the object.[102] This is the power of the concept of the Christ-form. Since one lives through one's intellect and will, and these are reformed and informed in Christ, the believer receives a new form of life. The believer participates in the form of Christ's life in the world.

The Christ-Form and the Church

The treatment of Christian experience requires one further reflection on the nature of the Church itself.

The Church is, most emphatically, not an 'extra' element between God and human beings, but rather is formed in the pair of unions between God and human beings in Christ (the hypostatic union of divine and human nature in Jesus Christ) and then the offer of the union between human beings and Christ in his grace. The latter includes the important intersubjective component that will be examined in the theodramatic study. (Chapter Five) [103] However, when speaking of the Church, both John the Evangelist and Paul, whom von Balthasar drew upon to develop his theology never understood the 'time of the Church' and the 'time of Christ' as being simply identical.

---

[102] Cf. *TL I*, 36.

[103] According to Timothy McDonald, Yves Congar O. P. understood that "God communicates his life to human beings according to their mode of being and therefore, whatever is given them of the final reality of divine life is given through the *sacramentum humanitatis Christi*. The Church as institution has not other meaning but to carry on this mediation." *The Ecclesiology of Yves Congar*, (Lanham MD: University Press of America, 1984), 107. Note the similarity between his thought and the thought of von Balthasar on this point.

Mediation is the necessary category to describe the Christian's experience of Christ and of the Church. This is due to the intrinsic mediatory character of created forms.[104]

In general terms, the metaphysics of forms holds that the form mediates or is the expression of its interior depths. Scripturally, the very character of the form of Christ is mediation. The Son mediates the Father to the world. So "to hear the teaching of the Father and learn from it is to come to me." (John 6:45) The Church too is pure mediation: "she can be and intends to be a medium of God's form of revelation in Christ."[105] Now this mediatory character has a further implication for those participating in the Christ-form. The lay person should expect to be faced with this mediation, and to prepare for it when participating in the celebration of the Sacraments, or when making the effort to hear what a Church council or the Holy Father is saying.

Those graced by Christ join the historical Christ-form around the historically present Jesus Christ, and inevitably become mediators as well. In the *Acts of the Apostles*, the Risen Christ says: "you will receive power when the Holy Spirit has come upon you; and you shall be my witnesses both in Jerusalem, and in all Judea and Samaria, and even to the remotest part of the earth." (Acts 1:8) Those who are graced by Christ receive the Spirit of God and so each mediates or becomes transparent to the glory of God in their own particular historical situation as they are now part of the Body of Christ.

In the history of the Church, the first mediators were eyewitnesses to the actions of Jesus of Nazareth in the Holy Spirit. The term 'eyewitness' itself embraces both the subjective and the objective aspects raised earlier and is a total human experience of Christ in faith. In this way, the two features of the aesthetic experience the concrete form and the

---

[104] Using a different terminology, Karl Rahner indicates the presence of the same phenomenon of mediation: "Because salvation comes in the flesh of Christ, and because man has to be made whole in and through out all dimensions of his existence in their mutual interdependence and influence on one another, it follows that grace must be embodied, must be an historical and social reality." "The Role of the Layman . . .." 56.

[105] *GL I*, 556.

informed perception of that form are realized in their unity. For the later generations of believers, their faith is analogous to the faith of Jesus' disciples and Jesus Christ is still the way to the Father even for succeeding generations. Just as seeing, hearing and touching were part of the first generations' experience, so in faith, the experience of the later generations is the same. They meet Christ in the Body of Christ namely the Church. The Church not only reflects the light of Christ it also embodies the form of Christ which it receives from Christ. [106] (Incidentally this means that describing the lay person's form of life requires describing the form of the Church! See below.)[107]

The link between the generation of the eyewitnesses and the next generation lies in the testimony and actions of the eyewitnesses. They are the archetypal participants in "the historical encounter with the God-man (both as promised and as present)."[108] This is the second level of imitation, where the first level is the archetypal relationship between man and God that occurs in Jesus Christ himself.[109] The disciples give glory to God through their witness. Their communication is the transition from the archetypal experience of the disciples to the imitative experience of the succeeding generations.[110]

The six relationships diagrammed above extend what is archetypal—by which von Balthasar means an 'exemplary typology'—for the experience of the generations that follow the time of Christ.[111] This means that in the later history of the Church Christ continues to draw members into aspects of *this* form of

---

[106] See Vatican II: "Christ is the Light of nations. Because this is so, this Sacred Synod gathered together in the Holy Spirit eagerly desires, by proclaiming the Gospel to every creature, to bring the light of Christ to all men, a light brightly visible on the countenance of the Church." (LG 1)
[107] See chapter one of the Dogmatic Constitution on the Church, *Lumen gentium*,
[108] *GL I*, 305.
[109] Aquinas noted the unique mediation that takes place in Christ: "it belongs to Him, as man, to unite men to God, by communicating to men both precepts and gifts, and by offering satisfaction and prayers to God for men. And therefore He is most truly called Mediator, as man." (ST III q. 26 article 2)
[110] Von Balthasar cites Cajetan, Aquinas and Maximus the Confessor in his theology of mediation. Cf. *GL I* p. 308ff.
[111] *GL I*, 350.

experience through the work of the Holy Spirit. The word 'aspects' is important because it brings to the fore the differentiated nature of experience in the community around Christ. Paul's experience was not Peter's and so on. The individual believer's experience will manifest features of the archetypal experience as Christ follows the will of the Father and distributes them to believers. In the words of Paul: "He is the sole author of all ecclesial works, and yet at the same time, through the different charisms and at different levels, he bestows on the members of the Church the grace of being co-workers with him. (II Corinthians 2:7; 4:1)"[112] So faith is nourished by these archetypes which have a proleptic character for Christians who are working out their lives until the Second Coming.

Conclusion

The archetypal experiences really communicate what the relationship to Christ means. Briefly the archetypes have a diachronic extension through history of a synchronic form that contains the experiences of Peter, Mary, John and the multitude. There are also unexpected 'Pauline' appearances of charisms at particular times in history. The archetypal experience ground the six relationships that were considered in this chapter.

The next thing suggested by the category of form focuses more on the specific metaphysical characteristics of form and the way they help us expound the meaning of the statement "to be a Christian is precisely a form."[113] This is the concern of the next chapter.

---

[112] *GL I*, 350.
[113] *GL I*, 28.

Chapter Four: Laity: Fruitful in the World

Introduction
Fruitfulness in the Scriptures
Sin and Fruitfulness
The Christian Form of Life in General
The Qualities of the Lay form of Life in the Church
  (A) The Radiance of Form: The Christian Radiates the Life of Christ and his Church.
  (B) The Proportion and Integrity of Form: The Art of Lay Life
Conclusion: The "Hour of the Laity"

Introduction

The conclusion to von Balthasar's aesthetic study of lay life in the Church lies in a final Scriptural figure that brings out the vitality and depth of the form of Christ and his Church. Most appropriately, it appears also at the end of the series on the *Glory of the Lord*. The figure is the *fruit* of Christ in his Church and its corresponding *fruitfulness* in the re-deemed world as it reflects the glory of the Lord—a fundamentally aesthetic quality of the form of lay life.[1] So to sum the integrated position in which laity find themselves, our author says that they "bear fruit because they themselves are fruit, and they become one single principle of fruitfulness together with the stock."[2] Our first concern will be to trace how this image develops in the scriptures and its metaphysical consequences. The second will be to show some of the consequences of the formal aspects of fruitfulness that von Balthasar noted in his work. A constant feature will be the way in which the theological aesthetic leads by inner

---

[1] Vatican II issued the Decree *Apostolican actuositatem* (AA) on the apostolate of the Laity. In the very first article, the council noted that: "Sacred Scripture clearly shows how spontaneous and fruitful such activity was at the very beginning of the Church (cf. Acts 11:19-21; 18:26; Rom. 16:1-16; Phil. 4:3)." They thus linked spontaneity and fruitfulness to the category of the activity of the lay person.

[2] *GL VII*, 420. Cf. Vatican II: "the laity likewise share in the priestly, prophetic, and royal office of Christ and therefore have their own share in the mission of the whole people of God in the Church and in the world." (AA 2)

necessity into the theodramatic study that starts in the next chapter.³

Fruitfulness in the Scriptures

The power of the image of fruitfulness cannot be understated. Von Balthasar goes so far as to say that the image of the vine in the *Gospel of John* is "the essence of the Church."⁴ The Church is the living planting of the Lord for the fruitfulness of the world to bring it to render glory to God. There are many reasons for this fundamental understanding, but a comment from the renowned ecclesiologist Gérard Philips will suffice.

Philips noted that both the Communists and the Nazis, among others, tried to impose a simplified view of the situation of the Church in the world, where "the Church occupies itself with the things of heaven for those who believe, but the earth belongs to man and the earth is the domain of the organized proletariat."⁵ The same view can be found throughout history as the Church has confronted other political powers and movements. However, the image of the vine (Christ) very clearly roots participation in the Church in this world.⁶ Meanwhile the Communist and Nazi views actually deny the significance of the Incarnation itself!

Another common and flawed view touches on the nature of the Church itself, but from a different angle. In this view the Church is somehow separate from Christ. On the contrary, as von Balthasar notes in his book on Saint Augustine, "existence in Christ

---

³ The Second Vatican Council said that: "[The Laity] exercise the apostolate in fact by their activity directed to the evangelization and sanctification of men and to the penetrating and perfecting of the temporal order through the spirit of the Gospel." (AA 2) They have indicated both what we will learn of as the dramatic dimension of Christian existence and the formal aspect of the transformation of the world by the work of the Laity.
⁴ *GL VII*, 421.
⁵ See G. Philips, *Le Rôle du Laïcat dans l'Église*, (Paris: Casterman, 1954), 57. (My translation.)
⁶ Note Henri de Lubac's comment that; "In everything he does on the supernatural level the Christian acts *ut membrum Ecclesiae, ut pars ecclesiae.*" *Splendor of the Church*, 45. He is citing Cajetan. See also LG 6.

has its authenticity in ecclesial existence."[7] In other words, Christ and the Church are distinguishable but not separable.[8] Separating the two terms in the relation returns the concept of Church to the misunderstanding of the Church, once again, as 'congregational'.

Von Balthasar says that the image of fruitfulness is latent in the first three Gospels where "man is fruitful only by reason of the seed that is given him."[9] Then the image reaches its fullest expression in the *Gospel of John*, where Jesus speaks of himself as the vine: "I am the true vine, and my Father is the vinegrower. . ... Remain in me as I remain in you. Just as the branch cannot bear fruit on its own unless it remains on the vine, so neither can you unless you remain in me." (John 15:1, 4) This is the image used by Vatican II. (LG 6) The very nature of the vine (its ontology) indicates, with suitable allowance for the divine-human nature of Christ, that members of the Church, as fruit, can be fruitful by remaining 'on the vine'.[10] The metaphor that Jesus chose also indicates the form of the Church, and the form to which the individual lay person belongs. Hence, the aesthetic study is by its own nature unfolding into a theodramatic expression, because the vine is not a static image. It grows and it is fruitful.

Furthermore in John's Gospel, the metaphor of "the grain of wheat" (John 12:24) and the various images of water such as the "well of water springing up to eternal life" (John 4:14), and so on, are all metaphors from the mouth of Jesus, and they express his understanding of the work of his Spirit in the New Creation. The 'New Creation' is in fact the perfection of the existing creation a dynamic that is maintained by

---

[7] Hans Urs von Balthasar, *Augustinus: Das Antlitz der Kirche*, (Einsiedeln: Benziger Verlag, 1955), 12. (My translation.)

[8] Cf. Constitution on the Church: "The true vine is Christ who gives life and the power to bear abundant fruit to the branches, that is, to us, who through the Church remain in Christ without whom we can do nothing." (LG 6)

[9] Ibidem.

[10] Note the Second Vatican Council teaching: "The true vine is Christ who gives life and the power to bear abundant fruit to the branches, that is, to us, who through the Church remain in Christ without whom we can do nothing." (LG, 6)

the ontology of the changing of being by Christ.¹¹ So the transformation of the world that starts with Jesus Christ himself, through his Death and Resurrection, becomes fruitful in that the Father glorifies him. (John 14:13) Then in turn, the glory is returned to the Father: "By this is my Father glorified that you bear much fruit and become my disciples." (John 15:8) The Son becomes like the grain of wheat, and his Death is fruitful in drawing others into the fruits of his Death.

What exactly are the fruits of his Death? First and foremost, there is the new life in the Spirit. This is the life by the new principle, the Spirit of God himself. The rebirth in the Spirit is spoken of in the *Prologue of John*: "to those that did accept him he gave power to become children of God." (John 1:12) The inner fruitfulness of the Divine Trinity is now being shared with his creation. So the members of the Church become the friends of Jesus Christ: "You are my friends if you do what I command you." (John 1:14) Then comes the key sentence: "This is my commandment: love one another as I love you." (John 5:12) As children of God, Christians love in the same inexhaustible Spirit as the Son loves the Father. Here is the fruitfulness of the Christian form of life. This is what is distinctive about the Christian life.¹² In bringing these lines of thought together, von Balthasar says that "in the economy of salvation . . . the Spirit tends to take form, to become *Gestalt*."¹³ Here is the point to which the whole of von Balthasar's aesthetic study has been converging. God is re-creating the world, starting with his Son through his Spirit, and extending this transformation to the ends of the earth through the Church. The lay person is a member of this new *Gestalt*¹⁴, this new form in the world. The

---

¹¹ Cf. Vatican II: "By his labor a man ordinarily supports himself and his family, is joined to his fellow men and serves them, and can exercise genuine charity and be a partner in the work of bringing divine creation to perfection." (GS 67)

¹² Hans Urs von Balthasar, "What is distinctively Christian?" *ET, IV*, 37.

¹³ "The Christian Form," *ET, IV*, 59.

¹⁴ See the Second Vatican Council: "The Spirit dwells in the Church and in the hearts of the faithful, as in a temple." (LG, 4) Thomas Aquinas notes the fullness of grace poured out upon the Church: "*constat quod gratia novi testamenti est gratia plenitudinis, inquantum de plenitudine Christi omnes accepimus. Si igitur ad illos de primitiva Ecclesia propter*

form is the form of the presence of Christ through the Holy Spirit.[15] Note how von Balthasar describes the connection of the themes that have been treated so far: "The form of the Church is "come forth from Christ . . . rendered fruitful through his Spirit . . . she ministers to his work for the world through her fruitfulness—which is *his* in her."[16] (Original emphasis.)

Now, the Spirit quickening this new form is the Spirit present at the conception of Jesus. (Luke 1:35) It is the Spirit present at the Baptism of Jesus, (Matthew 3:16) and it is the Spirit breathed on the Apostles at one of his appearances after the Resurrection. (John 20:22) The manifestation of the Spirit "appears as a defining and concretizing movement that gives final definition from above to what has historically already been predetermined."[17] Von Balthasar's perspective on the role of the Spirit in the economy of salvation is beginning to be clear. The Spirit of God defines the particular moment, as it is to be for all time in the history of salvation by filling it with the Spirit of God in Christ. The end of the overflowing of the Spirit into each moment is, as Heinrich Schlier notes: "faith . . . lays hold of δόξα [glory] as its basis; but the only way in which this occurs is for the believer to 'give' God the δόξα, by acknowledging it and yielding himself to it in his confession."[18] Here 'confession' is both by word and deed. Revelation has shown us the full 'circle' of God manifesting his glory in love, so that we are drawn out of ourselves, and then render loving glory to him in turn in his grace.

To appreciate exactly how this Gestalt operates as it gives the life of the lay person its form requires one simple but dramatic theological step: It is life according to the Spirit of God (in Christ through his

---

gratiae plenitudinem missio spiritus sancti fiebat, videtur quod etiam ad omnes fideles fieri debuerit." Super Sent., lib. 1 d. 16 q. 1 a. 2 arg. 2.

[15] Cf. Vatican II: "The temporal order must be renewed in such a way that, without detriment to its own proper laws, it may be brought into conformity with the higher principles of the Christian life and adapted to the shifting circumstances of time, place, and peoples." (AA 7) So the reform of the world is to be specifically Christian!

[16] *TD III*, 361.

[17] "The Christian Form," 59.

[18] Cited by von Balthasar, *GL VII*, 506.

Church), and not according to the world spirit.[19] Von Balthasar chose the phrase 'world spirit' quite deliberately.

The concept has a long history. Saint Paul taught that "We have not received the spirit of the world but the Spirit that is from God, so that we may understand the things freely given us by God." (1 Corinthians 2:12) The phrase reappears in the world of Friedrich Hegel, the brilliant Evangelical philosopher. In his work, it is sometimes not clear whether God is even distinct from the world. It is this distinction that needs to be respected, because the God of the Scriptures radically transcends the world that he is redeeming and sanctifying.

The principle of transcendence just stated helps lead, for example, to a solution to the ongoing problem of the expert lay person and the teaching of the Church. This is a good illustration of a difficulty that many lay Catholics face. Von Balthasar cites the instance of Catholic medical doctors who "take little or no notice of the Roman regulations and pronouncements that affect them."[20] They even may "have a perhaps unspoken objection . . . as long as the [theologians] have not come to know the lay profession from inside."[21] Von Balthasar's response to the problem is to state that first of all, knowing a profession 'from the inside' most often means accepting the dictates of the world spirit which means that worldly professions are not passed on in a value-neutral sense.

As the philosopher and theologian David Schindler has shown, in the case of liberal institutions of higher learning, the issue with the learning that they pass on that they "have within them a "supposed 'empty' [that is value neutral] theory [but in fact it] is already full enough of [a kind of] theology and anthropology that it serves in the end to displace a *communio*-informed freedom and institution."[22] Here in

---

[19] "The Christian Form," 58.
[20] Hans Urs von Balthasar, "The Demands of the Present Day," in *The Laity and the Life of the Counsels: The Church's Mission in the World*, trans., Brian McNeil C.R.V. with D.C. Schindler, (San Francisco: Communio Book, Ignatius Press, 2003), 93.
[21] Ibidem.
[22] David L. Schindler, *Heart of the World, Center of the Church*, (Grand Rapids MI: William B. Eerdmans, 1996), 34.

fact is the answer that von Balthasar is looking for. He wants to articulate the way professions operate in a whole new way. In other words, he seeks institutions of the particular kind—in Schindler's formulation 'a *communio*-informed freedom and institution.' Without this *communio*, institutions and professions contain both implicit and explicit elements of philosophy and theology that have *not* been informed by the wisdom of God in Christ.

Schindler's reference to the concept of *communio*, from theological aesthetics, (introduced in the previous chapter) recalls the *gestalt* brought about by the Spirit which is a Spirit of communion, just as it is the Spirit of eternal communion between the Divine Father and the Divine Son.[23] The lay person's participation in this communion shows the possibilities of being the 'junction' of the work of the Spirit and the work of the secular profession, with all that means in terms of informing and enriching the secular profession and making it much more fruitful.[24] Instead of reducing a profession to being a mere instrument for extending the reach of the world spirit, von Balthasar's approach results in the profession achieving both its natural and its supernatural goals through the cooperation with the Spirit of God, achieved in and through the practitioner of the profession.[25] Moreover the communion of life and love engendered by the Spirit is enlarged through this way of exercising the profession in this place and time.

To be more specific for a moment: von Balthasar understands a dynamic process within the

---

[23] Cf. Vatican II spoke of "the Church, which the Spirit guides in way of all truth and which He unified in communion and in works of ministry." (LG 4)

[24] The Second Vatican Council showed the relation and value of the natural sphere: "All those things which make up the temporal order, namely, the good things of life and the prosperity of the family, culture, economic matters, the arts and professions, the laws of the political community, international relations, and other matters of this kind, as well as their development and progress, not only aid in the attainment of man's ultimate goal but also possess their own intrinsic value." (AA, 7)

[25] The Second Vatican Council proposed the same relationship: "They should not cease to develop earnestly the qualities and talents bestowed on them in accord with these conditions of life, and they should make use of the gifts which they have received from the Holy Spirit." (AA, 4)

communion that involves the Catholic of a particular profession. In his words:

> This [*communio*] has far-reaching implications, for "crisis" means separation (and therefore s struggle and choice), but also decision, settlement, and therefore, in order to produce this, investigation, inquiries, procedure, and, finally, judgment. All these acts are indispensable for discovering the truth in freedom, even in the individual, whose reason must "divide in order to unite" (*intellectus dividens et componens*), and all the more in the community, in which a number of freedoms and points of view have to struggle their way through to a common and correct decision.[26]

Here is the route (investigation, enquiry, procedure, judgment) to breaking down the false dichotomy between the Church and the world in this case within a profession. When the Church is operating as a real *communion*, it stimulates the kind of profound discussion that professionals need to get involved in to imbue the profession with the Spirit of the Church rather than the world spirit. But in fact this kind of discussion can equally be found among mothers who are trying to bring up their children and sustain their families in a Christian way.

Coming at the same point a different way, von Balthasar reminds us of the fact that the great figures, such the saints Ambrose and Augustine, both came from a totally secular training and then after their baptisms, they had to expand and repair that knowledge through the theology that they learned later in life.[27] They saw it as part of their duty as Catholics to bring what they had learned earlier up against the wisdom that they had received from Christ. He became the higher principle of their knowing in actual practice.[28] They recognized that Christ could inform

---

[26] Hans Urs von Balthasar, "Communio: A Program," *Communio*, 33, No: 1, (2006), 156.
[27] Hans Urs von Balthasar, "The Limitations of Catholic Action," in *The Laity and the Life of the Counsels*, 46.
[28] Cf. Vatican II: "Christians should rather rejoice that, following the example of Christ Who worked as an artisan, they are free to give proper exercise to all their earthly activities and to their humane, domestic, professional, social and technical enterprises by gathering them into one vital synthesis with religious values, under whose supreme

and reform (both aesthetic terms!) what they already knew. What was true that was taught by the world spirit was taken up into a larger and more authentic vision of existence through the Spirit of God.

The recognition of the flaws of the world spirit and the way that it disrupts the communion of truth has its echo in the work of Saint Augustine, who explained: "To this Founder of the holy city [Jesus Christ] the citizens of the earthly city prefer their own gods, not knowing that He is the God of gods, not of false, *i.e.*, of impious and proud gods, who, being deprived of his unchangeable and freely communicated light, and so reduced to a kind of poverty-stricken power, eagerly grasp at their own private privileges, and seek divine honors from their deluded subjects."[29] Augustine enlarged the field of the inquiry by listing some of the other results of ignoring the role of the Spirit of God through his use of the scriptural images of the earthly city and the heavenly city (e.g. Psalm 87:3).

These two cities 'converge' in the human spirit, and each individual has to constantly commit to developing his citizenship of the city of God and so receive the fruits of the Spirit. However, the two cities do *not* converge in a theocratic state, so in a secular state the Christian can only "fill the structures of the state with Christian spirit and life, and thus blunt them a little."[30]

The concept of the two cities can be further developed by examining their origins. As Augustine explained: "Accordingly the two cities have been formed by two loves, the earthly one to the love of self, even to the contempt of God; the heavenly one to the love of God even to the contempt of self."[31] This recourse to one of von Balthasar's great inspirations among the fathers, leads from a consideration of sin

---

direction all things are harmonized unto God's glory." (GS 43)

[29] Augustine of Hippo, *City of God*, XI.1. The Second Vatican Council referred to the heavenly city: "The Church in this is mindful that she must bring together the nations for that king to whom they were given as an inheritance, and to whose city they bring gifts and offerings." (LG, 13)

[30] *GL VII*, 502. Von Balthasar notes that the very nature of the Christian message precludes a political theology!

[31] *City of God*, XIV.28.

and form, in terms of the images of the 'cities', to a more abstract reflection on sin and form.

Sin and Form

The subject of the relation between sin and form is an urgent one in von Balthasar's treatment of beauty, even though the references are scarce. The stakes are very high. For example: "man stands before the good and asks himself why *it* must be done and not rather its alternative, evil."[32] The reality in question is the aesthetic form of lay life, and the light that radiates from it. So, for example, it is the proper experience of beauty (understood in the ontological sense being recovered here) that makes Satan's form unattractive. He is not beautiful. He is not a being radiant with the grace of the Creator. His only beauty lies in the fact that he is still a creature of God, despite his denial of God. Returning to the theory of the transcendentals: our author says that "the light of the transcendentals . . . can only shine if it is undivided."[34] The truth of the creature is to acknowledge that he is indeed a creature.[35] If the True is missing, then the light of being is dark, and the fruitfulness of the form diminishes.[36]

For human beings, the core of faith is obedience. This was already the case in the Old Testament, where God gave the imperative: "Be holy, for I am holy." (Leviticus 11:44)[37] Remember that holiness is the glory of God. The holy God is present in Christ. This defines his form: "For in him dwells the

---

[32] *GL I*, 19.
[34] Hans Urs von Balthasar, *Explorations in Theology I*, 107.
[35] In the question on goodness in general, Thomas Aquinas notes that "in order for a thing to be perfect and good it must have a form . . . .. Now the form presupposes [a number of things including that] the form follows an inclination to the end" for which it was made. *ST I*, q. 5 a. 5. Then as he notes further on "evil deprives a thing of some sort of being." So a blind person loses the 'being of sight'. *ST I* q. 5 a. 5. Vatican II refers to the lack of truth in the Evil one: "But often men, deceived by the Evil One, have become vain in their reasonings and have exchanged the truth of God for a lie, serving the creature rather than the Creator." (LG 16) The lack of truth leads to the disorder in the relationship to God.
[36] The Second Vatican Council itself formulated the issue in aesthetic terms: "As deformed by sin, the shape of this world will pass away." (GS 19)
[37] Cited in *GL I*, 220.

fullness of the Deity bodily." (Colossians 2:9) The bodily form of Jesus Christ radiates with the "light of love".[38] Hence, any man who is invited into and participates in this radiance and form, then and only then, becomes "an adequate answer to God's Word."[39] Here faith is structured as the response to the Word of God, and a response that means becoming attuned to God in obedience. In contrast, Satan "transforms *himself* into an angel of light." (RSV 2 Corinthians 11:14) This is the solipsism of self-construction. The significant point is the source of the transformation of the creature. The believer is transformed by the Spirit of Christ.[40]

Once we have reflected on evil's deficient form, there is still the question of the corresponding response to the form. The key lies in an abstract statement of von Balthasar's: "whoever is not capable of seeing and 'reading' the form will, by the same token, fail to perceive the content."[41] Recall the solipsism of the citizen of Augustine's earthly city! By working in this way, von Balthasar is bringing back together two approaches to the form that have diverged historically. These are, first of all, the approach that attends to the concrete historical form so the "evidential force" of the objective reality is the focus, and the second is the approach that focuses on the "light of faith".[42] Von Balthasar brings the two back together, so that the light shines forth 'from the form itself'—a phrase that has occurred previously. The interest here is not so much the history of theology directly but rather how this insight affects the theology of the Laity.

The laity both encounter the form of God's action in the world, and are enlightened by the light ("The great radiance from within") that shines forth

---

[38] *GL I*, 218.
[39] Ibidem.
[40] "The devil refused righteousness." *ST I* q. 63.
[41] *GL I*, 151. Note too Vatican II's teaching that: "All should be persuaded that human life and the task of transmitting it are not realities bound up with this world alone. Hence they cannot be measured or perceived only in terms of it, but always have a bearing on the eternal destiny of men." (GS 51)
[42] *GL I*, 150.

from it (the "species" or form).⁴³ So the heart of lay experience is that "an aesthetic element must be associated with all spiritual perception as with all spiritual striving."⁴⁴ This is very abstract but in fact this formulation recovers the core of the experience of the believer. (Chapter Three) If any single phrase could sum up the work of von Balthasar in this regard it would be that he is the "theologian of the Divine Trinity". The striking feature of his work is that he has recovered the basic character of creation as the created finite image of the Divine Trinity. The result is that salvation is interpreted as drawing creation into the infinite love of the Divine Trinity. The above formulation echoes the beautiful expression found in the writing of Saint Irenaeus.⁴⁵ He wrote of the Son and the Spirit in the economy of salvation as being the two 'hands of the Father'.⁴⁶ The lay person in communion with everyone else is in the hands of the Father with the external concrete sign of his presence in Christ and with the interior presence of the Spirit to enable him or her to perceive what he is actually seeing. The two act in an inseparable whole "with and in one another".⁴⁷

The Christian Form of Life in General

Von Balthasar's 'trilogy' deliberately starts with a reflection on beauty—as is being done here—because for moderns it is the transcendental that is the least appreciated. When this happens then "the witness borne by Being becomes untrustworthy for the person who can no longer read the language of beauty."⁴⁸ For modern laity this means that their values can get

---

[43] *GL I*, 18. Note Vatican II's formulation: "the Church does not only communicate divine life to men but in some way casts the reflected light of that life over the entire earth, most of all by its healing and elevating impact on the dignity of the person, by the way in which it strengthens the seams of human society and imbues the everyday activity of men with a deeper meaning and importance." (GS 40)

[44] *GL I*, 153.

[45] *Adversus Haereses* V. 6.1. Cited in Hans Urs von Balthasar, *Theologic III: The Spirit of Truth*, trans. Graham Harrison, (San Francisco: Ignatius Press, 2005), 167.

[46] See Section III. "The Father's Two Hands", in *TL III*, 165 – 218.

[47] *TL III*, 185.

[48] *GL I*, 19.

turned upside down by their secularized culture if they do not appreciate the beauty of the form of being and the beauty of the form of Christ and his Church.

It is the beauty of being that, for example, leads into the argument about why abortion is wrong. To kill a human being is wrong (the Good). But for people who cannot trust the sense of beauty that is conveyed by young new life in the womb of a mother, they might ignore the wonder and seek the tragic route of convenience instead. The word 'convenience' comes originally from the Latin *convenientia* which in fact means 'harmony'.[49] The harmony referred to was harmony with being. So choosing to live 'near the shops' or choosing a 'suitable time' to do something were both exercises in the harmony of living with one's surroundings. One's actions fit the larger fabric of life. But the word has lost its connection to being and has come to be used completely subjectively so the harmony is now one imposed by me and what suits my short term needs. The category of form reminds us that there is an objective harmony to being and so if a child is growing in the womb then the harmony of being means that the child should have every chance at life.[50] The fact that something is rather than is not means it has been given being by God.[51] This is the good of the person and it cannot be denied for any reason.

---

[49] *American Heritage Dictionary*. Saint Thomas Aquinas uses the argument from fittingness to show how God works. See the extensive analysis of this concept and its parallels with the notion of form in Hans Urs von Balthasar's work in the work by Gilbert Narcisee O.P., *Les Raisons de Dieu: Argument de convenance et Esthétique théologique selon saint Thomas d'Aquin et Hans Urs von Balthasar*, Studia Friburgensia Nouvelle Serie 83, (Friburg: Éditions Universitaires Fribourg Suisse, 1997).

[50] Saint Thomas explains that where "an evil mode, species and order [mean] being less than they ought to be . . . . Therefore they are called evil, because they are out of place and incongruous." *ST I*, q. 5 a. 5.

[51] The way that John Paul II explains the issue in *Veritatis splendor* is: "Reason attests that there are objects of the human act which are by their nature "incapable of being ordered" to God, because they radically contradict the good of the person made in his image." (VS, 80). Amongst other acts this applies to having an abortion. Note the relationship between the concept of order and the concept of form.

Now in philosophical terms a person's life has a form if "he has chosen for his life, a form into which and through which to pour out his life, so his life becomes the soul of the form and the form becomes the expression of his soul".[52] Building on this, and infinitely more rich in possibilities, is the fact that Catholic lay life is beautiful because lay people commit themselves to graced participation in the historical form that is Christ and his Church. This means that "when it is achieved, the Christian form is the most beautiful thing that may be found in the human realm."[53] It speaks of the glory of God in Christ to the world that he loves. The faithful person is being taken into the form of Christ with all that that means for the world. So it is no accident that the lives of the saints are a vital tool in helping people to discover the meaning of life in Christ: "The simple Christian knows [that] . . . he loves his saints among other reasons because the resplendent image of their life is so love-worthy and engaging."[54] The saints are who they are because they are part of the Christ-form in their time and place.

The Christian's beauty lies in the fact that the Christian's life form is manifesting something of the hypo-static union between God and man in Christ. As von Balthasar puts it "it is the end of the Church's life [and also the life of the individual member] . . . to make visible the Son's form to a world that does not believe."[55] Perhaps people will be inspired by the good example of *this* person rather than the poor example of *that* person. The inspiration to follow Christ is due to the presence of the grace of Christ being responded to in the light of faith which is itself a "*lumen increatum, a gratia increata.*"[56]

It is vital to note here that the purpose is *not* necessarily that "there is generated from this something beautiful within the world, some form of 'Christian art'."[57] This would be akin to the celebrity phenomenon that is so much of a fascination today. There are certain 'rules' of packaging a person as a celebrity to whom some given demographic groups will

---

[52] *GL I*, 24.
[53] *GL I*, 28.
[54] Ibidem.
[55] *GL I*, 214.
[56] *GL I*, 215.
[57] *GL IV*, 28.

respond. The celebrity becomes in a superficial sense a 'work of art'. However, by contrast the Christian life form is beautiful because it is open to the transcendent and is radiating the transcendent depths of theform. The merely this-worldly construction such as the packaging of entertainers fails to even approach the phenomenon of the Christian life because "the birth of what is artistically beautiful is subject to inner-worldly conditions and periods of taste which do not apply to what is Christian."[58] What is Christian is that Christ radiates through the Christian who thus lives a beautiful life.[59] What is a beautiful life? Well, here is something from Pope Benedict, in his exhortation to Africa. He said:

> the ability to perceive the light of the mystery of the Trinity shining on the faces of brothers and sisters around us, to be attentive to "our brothers and sisters in faith within the profound unity of the Mystical Body, and therefore as 'those who are a part of me', in order to share their joys and sufferings, to sense their desires and attend to their needs, to offer them deep and genuine friendship"; the ability as well to recognize all that is positive in the other so as to welcome it and prize it as a gift that God gives me through that person, in a way that transcends by far the individual concerned, who thus becomes a channel of divine graces; and finally, the ability "to 'make room' for our brothers and sisters, bearing 'each other's burdens' (*Gal* 6:2) and resisting the selfish temptations which constantly beset us and provoke competition, careerism, distrust and jealousy. (*Africae munus*, 34)

This is not a physical beauty but the beauty of the earthly form as it becomes transcendent. It comes alive

---

[58] Ibidem.
[59] See John Paul II's *Letter to Artists*, where he states that: "This prime epiphany of "God who is Mystery" is both an encouragement and a challenge to Christians, also at the level of artistic creativity. From it has come a flowering of beauty which has drawn its sap precisely from the mystery of the Incarnation. In becoming man, the Son of God has introduced into human history all the evangelical wealth of the true and the good, and with this he has also unveiled a new dimension of beauty, of which the Gospel message is filled to the brim." (art. 5), 4th April 1999.

through the expression of love. This is where the analysis of the dramatic expression of the form will take us.

In his book on Reinhold Schneider, the twentieth century German writer who reflected on the problems of culture in the West, von Balthasar wrote the following: "not all saints are called to penetrate into the external sphere of history: many turn the spokes of the wheel invisibly."[60] Thus he points to the whole realm of prayer to which we shall return below but participation in the spiritual radiance of Christ is one of the powers of the Christian form whose effects might not even be known in the Christian's life-time. Prayer then is the first concrete feature of the life-form of the lay person. Such prayer opens the lay persons to deeper meanings of even the most apparently mundane of actions.

Another possible experience for the Christian is where he or she is "totally open to God's demand, [and] hears in this the demand of history too."[61] Here in concrete terms, we can say that the saint speaks and acts in his time. Following the flow of Schneider's thought, von Balthasar examines at length the impact of saints such as Saint Joan of Arc[62], Bartolomè de las Casas[63] and others to show how God's sphere pushes into history through these people who have made themselves completely disponible to God.

Joan of Arc (1412-1431) and Bartolomé de las Casas (1484-1566) illustrate the demand that God can make on people—"this task (and no other), this particular grace to be used in this way."[64] This is a much more exclusive grace that is only given to a few. But its recipients have changed history!

The Christian forms that lay people build of their lives are the source of Christianity's contributions to many cultures. Culture itself can have a form. Christianity offers grace and light to a culture. Christianity has mediated the grace of Christ into

---

[60] Hans Urs von Balthasar, *Tragedy under Grace: Reinhold Schneider on the Experience of the West*, trans., Brian McNeil C.R.V., (San Francisco: Ignatius Press, 1997), 194. See also his book on *Prayer*, trans. Graham Harrison, (San Francisco: Ignatius Press, 1986).
[61] Ibidem.
[62] *Tragedy under Grace*, 187ff.
[63] *Tragedy under Grace*, 196ff.
[64] *Tragedy under Grace*, 187.

many cultures around the world. This process has a dramatic effect. Christ came as redeemer and so "it is most important to see that the kingdom that has come near from the Father in the person of Jesus cannot be cramped within forms that belong to a human society alienated from God, whether they are profane or sacral forms."[65] These forms born of sinfulness and concupiscence are simply too limited to respect the full scope of being human! The presence of Christ breaks open the cultural forms and heals and makes the culture more human and infused with the beauty, goodness and truth of God himself. From another perspective, the presence of Christian forms allows the culture to develop a critique of forms in the culture, so that forms can be analyzed and remade until they communicate something that beautiful, good and true.[66]

The isolation of a particular culture from the Church means that the culture misses out on these salutary effects, a fact bewailed by both Paul VI[67], and John Paul II[68]. Both were supremely aware of the

---

[65] Hans Urs von Balthasar, "Are there Lay People in the Church?" *New Elucidations*, 173.

[66] See Vatican II: "the Church, in the very fulfillment of her own function, stimulates and advances human and civic culture; by her action, also by her liturgy, she leads them toward interior liberty." (GS 58)

[67] See Paul VI's *Ecclesiam suam*, where he wrote: "One part of this world, as everyone knows, has in recent years detached itself and broken away from the Christian foundations of its culture, although formerly it had been so imbued with Christianity and had drawn from it such strength and vigor that the people of these nations in many cases owe to Christianity all that is best in their own tradition-a fact that is not always fully appreciated." (ES, 13) He is simply describing an historical fact. This is affirmed even by atheists such as Oriana Fallaci in her *La Forza della Ragione*, (Roma: Rizzoli Internazionale, 2004). She says for example, criticizing the attempts to stop all mention of religion in Italian schools: "*dovremmo evitare riferimenti alla religione di cui la nostra cultura è imbevuta, cioè al Cristanesimo.*" (118)

[68] In his words to the International Cinema Conference, John Paul II raised a point that is the philosophical companion to the Christological point made above by Paul VI. Paul VI had emphasized the theological aspect while John Paul II started his address with the corresponding anthropological (philosophical) point, namely that: "Man, the whole man, one and indivisible: a cinema that considers, only some aspects

philosophical and theological underpinnings of the Christian contribution to world cultures.

Here lies the difference between Christianity and *all* other religions. Only in Christianity, can we say that the religious "form does not stand in opposition to infinite light".[69] This fact is crucial in understanding the sheer uniqueness of Christianity, *and* also the sheer uniqueness of being a Christian lay person. The light radiates from the very heart of the form that God has created in this world, Jesus Christ and his Body the Church. Other objects and persons to whom religious significance is attributed, by man, are simply inadequate to mediate the glory of God. But Jesus Christ is unique. In John's Gospel we hear: "The Word became flesh, and made his dwelling among us, and we saw his glory, the glory as of the Father's only Son, full of grace and truth." (John 1:14) The beauty of Jesus Christ qualitatively far surpasses any earthly beauty. Saint Gregory's commentary on Jacob's words ("I have seen God face to face." (Genesis 32:31)) says that "when the eye of the soul turns towards God, it is thrown back by the lightning flash of the infinite."[70] Here is the unique wonder of the form that Christ brings into being. In Jesus' words: "Remain in me, as I remain in you. Just as a branch cannot bear fruit on its own unless it remains on the vine, so neither can you unless you remain in me." (John 15:4) The lay person is participating in something extraordinary, and not in something purely man-made, even if the man-made efforts, "nonetheless often reflect a ray of that Truth which enlightens all men" which was the way that the Second Vatican Council summed the thought on the nature of *non*-Christian religions in general. (NA, 2) But the same could be said of non-Christian cultures as well!

---

of the amazing complexity of the human being inevitably ends up being simplistic and does not provide a useful cultural service." Thursday 2 December 1999. The wholeness of the view of man that is promoted by Christianity inevitably provides a critique for lesser more partial views. See Chapter One on the "Dignity of the Human Person" in *Gaudium et spes* which sets up the anthropological foundation for the entire constitution and gives the document its capacity to critique the many kinds of difficulties faced by man.

[69] *GL I*, 216.

[70] *GL IV*, 394. Von Balthasar is citing Gregory's *In Boeth. De Trin.* 1, 2.

The evident power of aesthetic analysis is why so many pages have been devoted to the aesthetic study of the lay life. As Gilbert Narcisse explains, von Balthasar chose an approach that "corresponds to the most intimate order of the real [itself], that which man perceives and it leads him to a profound philosophical explanation."[71] The beauty of lay life has not been treated consistently through the years. At Vatican II, for instance, the term 'beauty' is only used when referring to the liturgy and liturgical furnishings but not to the form of Catholic life. However the council did apply the notion of 'form' to the Body of Christ. For example, the council said that: "Through Baptism we are formed in the likeness of Christ: 'For in one Spirit we were all baptized into one body.'" (LG 7)

It was John Paul II who specifically applied the term 'beauty' to lay life, starting with the beauty of the life of virtue (where he cites Saint Methodius) (CF, 61), and to the beauty of children dedicating their energies to serving God. (CF, 62)[72]

The theme of the *attractiveness* of the form and the meaning it radiates resurfaces in von Balthasar's work on human life. When a person's life has a form, and is not an amorphous collection of unconnected expressions and activities, then it begins to be 'love-worthy'. This is an ancient insight that goes back to pre-Christian times, because it was known, even then, that ultimately man longs for "transcendence in God as the primordial unity, the primordial beauty."[73] In Catholicism, the transcendent God is the source of the love-worthy attractive fulfilling form.[74] The theme reappears again and again in the Christian centuries,

---

[71] Gilbert Narcisse O.P., *Les Raisons de Dieu*, 244. (My translation.) In the sentence before this one, he also says that von Balthasar's method "does not immediately suggest itself from the Scriptures." I would perhaps suggest that the nature of the Scriptures themselves in relation to the being of Salvation History *does* suggest his method for reasons that were examined in the first chapter.

[72] See also his *Letter to Families*, 22nd February, 1994.

[73] *GL IV*, 321.

[74] Cf. Vatican II: "The laity fulfill this mission of the Church in the world especially by conforming their lives to their faith so that they become the light of the world as well as by practicing honesty in all their dealings so that they attract all to the love of the true and the good and finally to the Church and to Christ." (AA 13)

in the Sacred Scriptures, in the writings of Gregory of Nyssa, and Augustine, and still continues to be a theme in Christian spirituality. The concrete experience—of living a beautiful life and seeing the beauty in the lives of others—of people in history has value. Someone's form of life 'in Christ' draws others to discover that what they are seeking is 'in Christ'. This is a dimension of the ontological openness (introduced in Chapter One) of the Christian, and grounds the concept of the rightly directed *erôs* of the human being.[75]

The concept of *erôs* involves man's historical encounter with the form. There is, first of all, the event of 'beholding' the holy form of life. Then there is the experience of becoming 'enraptured' with the light of Christ radiating from the form of life of the saint, as it is contemplated.[76] This experience contrasts with that of becoming enraptured with *earthly* forms that lack the transcendent element. For example, Reinhold Schneider, whom we have referred to before because of von Balthasar's study of his work, saw this flaw in Hitler's *Mein Kampf*, to which he had to respond that instead "what lies ahead of me is clearly the confrontation with Christ himself."[77] The empty demagoguery and manipulation of power in Hitler's writing needed to be brought face to face with Christ himself. (I do not think that the history of World War II has been mined sufficiently for all that it still has to teach us.)

One sees a similar problem in the emptiness of the modern fascination with the appearance of the body. The whole industry of molding appearance (face lifts, weight loss, cosmetics etc.) has no spiritual core to it at all. We may not be facing dictators in the west but empty commercial demagoguery is in full force. The forms of actors and models dominate the scene and yet few of them have any spiritual depth at all. Advertising and even the development of characters on television is most often related to how the individuals look. The shallow dialog and the trite perspectives on relationships show that this strategy is being followed. Then too fact checking gives the lie to much political speech in our time. Seeking what has not been widely reported shows that we are being treated as recipients

---

[75] Ibidem.
[76] *GL I*, Foreward.
[77] *Tragedy under Grace*, 92.

who should remain passive and just accept the messages being passed to us.

Now looking for some depth that is both human and spiritual: Saint Ignatius of Loyola's *Spiritual Exercises*, following the period of active purgation of the First Week, instruct the retreatant to contemplate the Life of Christ so that—in von Balthasar's words—he is "dispossessed of any self-constructed pattern of life, to enter into the imitation of Christ."[78] This puts aside the *self*-construction of one's life. The solipsism of the modern period receives its strongest challenge from such a conception of life. Most emphatically, the higher principle, Jesus Christ himself, is at work redeeming and sanctifying the human person who believes in him. It is this personal quality, the personal response to the grace of God that appears consistently in von Balthasar's writings.[79] More importantly, it is a consistent element in the Scriptures, but in von Balthasar's judgment the role of the personal response had not been sufficiently appreciated in the history of spirituality, before Ignatius of Loyola. Ignatius returned to examining the Gospels, and thus "a revolution was effected."[80] Provided that it is understood correctly, the role of the 'self' is not diminished in the Christian understanding of lay life.

For the lay person, the personal struggle to be aware of the workings of the world is an important operation of the self. The acceptance of the Christian Life, as a form, acknowledges the choices made by the Christian. It shows the intrinsic respect for being as the Christian becomes the shepherd of being. Furthermore, the light of Christ shines through the words and deeds of the faithful Christian. In this way, Christians contribute to cultures being able to shift their mode, species and order—to use Thomas' terms[81]—towards the good. The other 'side' of the existence of Christian forms means being trained enough to appreciate them when they are present.

---

[78] *GL V*, 103.
[79] See also "The Nature of the Call," in *The Christian State of Life*, 391ff.
[80] *Christian State of Life*, 391.
[81] *ST* I q. 5 a. 5.

Christians learn this skill through their contemplation of Christ.[82]

The Qualities of the Lay Form of Life in the Church

The metaphysical understanding of form, when illuminated and informed by the Scriptures, can teach us something about the qualities of lay life. Traditionally, form has been considered beautiful because of three essential characteristics: radiance, proportion (harmony) and wholeness or integrity.[83] These are found to some degree in all created forms, because they image in some way the beauty of the divine source of all that is. More particularly for us, they characterize the life of the lay person, as it is given form by the mission of Christ to the world, in and through his Church.

(A) <u>The Radiance of Form: The Christian Radiates the Life of Christ and his Church</u>.
Form is fundamentally expressive of interiority.[84] This was made clear in the previous chapter where we related the composer and his work. His idea for a musical piece is expressed in the concrete sensible forms of notes, and timing, and instruments. Von Balthasar called this expressiveness, 'radiance'. Generally, "we are confronted simultaneously with both the figure and that which comes forth from the figure."[85] Theologically, 'radiance' means even more. Just as the forms of God's manifestation, in both the Old Testament and the New Testament manifested *God*, so too does God's new creation in Christ radiate the glory of God into his creation.[86]

---

[82] Cf. Vatican II: "It is, finally, through the gift of the Holy Spirit that man comes by faith to the contemplation and appreciation of the divine plan." (GS 15)
[83] See the history in *GL IV* and *GL V*.
[84] According to Louis Dupré: "With St. Bonaventure [von Balthasar] agrees that the essence of form lies not in its being an object of potential sense perception, but rather in its intrinsic power to express." *Hans Urs von Balthasar: His Life and Work*, ed. David Schindler, (San Francisco: Ignatius Press, 1991). But I think that von Balthasar is drawing from earlier in the history of theology.
[85] *GL I*, 20.
[86] At this point in his presentation, von Balthasar makes a crucial point this figure with its expressive radiance is a "primal phenomenon" and this aspect of being indicates flaws in the work of both Aristotle and Plato. Since Christ is

A number of features of lay life demonstrate their participation in this radiance. To change the metaphor: lay life has its own 'momentum' that starts beyond itself, in the mission of Christ and his Church, and yet bursts out of the life form of the individual lay person. 'Momentum' links the dynamism of the mission (Chapter Five) of the Son to its expression in the fruitful mission of each Christian. In the Old Testament, glory (*kabod*) had the character of a weighty appearance, one that makes an impression. See for instance, the references to the wealth of Abraham (Genesis 13: 2), or the renown of Job (Job 19: 9), as these personages revel in the favor of God. The same term now translated as δοxα (glory) was applied to Jesus Christ in the New Testament. God's glory bursts through in Christ's Death, and Resurrection, and its momentum (in von Balthasar's sense) is fruitful in the Christian community, and in the life of every believer.[87] The point is that the 'momentum' of the Father's initiative in sending the Son, continues in the Church and its members as well as in others, outside of the Church, in whom God's grace is working in the world. The radiance of Christian existence implies that this existence is fruitful.

However, at no point is there any indication of a 'distance' from Christ, in the sense that the Church, and the individual lay person within it, was 'set on its way' by Christ and that now he is 'further away' from his Church, than he was back in the first century. The metaphor of 'momentum' might suggest this understanding if it is read in a physical sense. Instead, von Balthasar has offered a *metaphysics* of momentum containing the two elements of 'sending' (that a suitably biblical concept requires) and then secondly, all the consequent implications of representation of the sender and 'participation'(a notion that pervades the

---

such a 'primal phenomenon', a philosophically undiscoverable gift from God, Aristotle could not make place for such a gift. With Plato the problem is more primarily philosophical since he could not describe the unity of soul and body such that they form a primal phenomenon as well. See *GL I*, 20 and 21.

[87] For his introduction of the relation between glory and momentum see the sections: "The momentum of Time" *GL VII*, 162 – 201, and "The Momentum of the Cross," *GL VII*, 202 – 235.

Scriptures). The participation safeguards any reflection that we do from even tacitly hinting at a 'distance' from Christ. With this proviso in mind, we can pursue the connection between the concept of fruitfulness and 'momentum'.

There are two parts to the image of fruitfulness in the New Testament: (i) God is the planter or owner of the vineyard, for example. (eg. Matthew 20) Thus God establishes the situation of the individual man. (ii) Then produce is expected from the plant or the individual in the situation.[88] So, as an example, the *Parable of the Talents* is a lesson on fruitful activity. (Matthew 25)[89] Then the ultimate conclusion of the fruitful cooperation with grace is that "my Father is glorified, when you bear much fruit." (John 15:8) This is to be understood as a fruitfulness arising out of participation in the fruitfulness of Christ himself.[90] So there is no possibility here of saving oneself by one's own good works. Whatever good one does expresses the goodness of Jesus Christ himself, because "God himself remains the Lord of the Vineyard, the possessor of the fruitfulness."[91]

As a community in Christ, Christians live fruitful lives and, in so doing, they give glory to God. The Spirit of God constitutes the community and fills this new form with vitality. (II Timothy 3: 5) Earlier Karl Barth said that God brings about the acknowledgement of his glorious self-manifestation through the power of his Holy Spirit. The community demonstrates its awareness of the glory of God, in Christ, through giving glory to God in the Holy Spirit. In this way, the community participates in manifesting God's glory, as his community, and renders glory to him.

Individually (here 'individual' means a single personal subject even though the primary subject in the life of the individual is Jesus Christ) and as Church, Christians are radiant by making an impression on the world.[92] The 'movement' of the

---

[88] Cf. Mark 11; Matthew 21; Luke 13 etc.
[89] See his exegesis of the text. *GL VII*, 416.
[90] See *GL VII*, 418.
[91] *GL VII*, 418.
[92] Karl Rahner agrees with this notion because "the Christian . . . has to render present the victory of grace, of love and faith, of the fact that the kingdom of God has arrived." See "The Role of the Layman . . . ." 63.

Church is always centrifugal. As von Balthasar notes: "Even the autarchic abbey does not escape this law, which makes it a city set on a mountain, radiating a light that directs others to their end."[93] To illustrate something of what this might mean, von Balthasar spent much time on one specialized field in which lay people have been making an impression.

He dedicated an entire volume of *The Glory of the Lord* series to the work of lay theologians. For us the content of the volume is not of primary interest, but some characteristics of the lay 'impression' on the world, through the development of theologies, are worth noting. I am not saying that lay people write theologies but I think that von Balthasar's point is that—as we had earlier with the notion of the *communio*-informed discussion—lay people, no matter what their walk of life, and no matter what their occupation, develop a theology of life, whether they ever write it down or not! Now on to what von Balthasar found in the lives of certain people who had a lay style of thought:

(a) First, <u>lay people are fundamentally part of the world</u>:

Each lay person lives and works in a unique historical setting and composes a form of life out of the 'stuff' of that situation. Perhaps 'composes' is too strong. Lay people use their own genius (and also sinfulness) in their response to the historical and personal currents around them in the world.[94] This is the secular character that was emphasized by the Second Vatican Council and John Paul II's *Christifideles laici*. The council, for example, said that "the secular character is properly and particularly that of the lay faithful."

---

[93] Hans Urs von Balthasar, "The Experience of the Church," *Explorations in Theology II*, 29.

[94] Cf. Vatican II: "acting as citizens in the world, whether individually or socially, they will keep the laws proper to each discipline, and labor to equip themselves with a genuine expertise in their various fields. They will gladly work with men seeking the same goals. Acknowledging the demands of faith and endowed with its force, they will unhesitatingly devise new enterprises, where they are appropriate, and put them into action. Laymen should also know that it is generally the function of their well-formed Christian conscience to see that the divine law is inscribed in the life of the earthly city." (GS 43)

(LG, 32) Then to drive home the embeddedness of the laity, they noted that lay people express their faith, hope, and love "through the framework of their secular life." (LG, 35) (Emphasis added.) John Paul II followed the same theme further and expanded the detail that the council had mentioned about the lay participation in the Offices of Christ. In this book, this material will appear in the third part of the book on the truth of existence.

Nothing shows the unique personal quality and historical situation of lay forms of life more clearly than a few examples drawn from von Balthasar's writings. The illustrations also show the dramatic tension in the life of Christians (See Chapter Five) as they exercise their freedom by cooperating in the development of their life form, under the illumination of a deeper truth, the Incarnate Word himself.

Consider the poet Dante Alighieri (1265-1321) for example: when his entire body of work is considered, then in von Balthasar's judgment, no later thinker writing in Latin (apart from Nicholas of Cusa and Thomas Aquinas, he reminds us!) made a greater contribution in the history of human thought. Dante made some distinctly *lay* contributions to Catholic thinking. First of all, there is the force of his personality in his writing.[95] He does not 'disappear' behind his work the way Thomas Aquinas (a cleric) chose to. Instead, Dante wrote about his fulfillment, both as a human being and as a Christian. Dante believed that human beings have an earthly goal as well as a heavenly one.[96] The two goals are not in opposition and neither displaces the other. Here the focus is on being, as transformed by revelation, which is also the keynote of von Balthasar's own understanding of being a lay person.

Then there is Dante's concern throughout his life with his ultimate destiny. According to von Balthasar, Dante's sufferings "enable[d] him to grasp the Christian account of the meaning of existence".[97] Interestingly, even the experience of Dante's exile gave him 'material' for his work. It gave him the intellectual

---

[95] Hans Urs von Balthasar, *The Glory of the Lord III: Studies in Theological Style: Lay Styles*, trans. Andrew Louth, John Saward, Martin Simon and Rowan Williams, (San Francisco: Ignatius Press, 1986), 9 - 104.
[96] *GL III*, 24.
[97] *GL III*, 30.

distance needed when describing the characteristics of Christian existence, in the culture and society of the home land, from which he had been exiled.

Lastly, it was Dante who introduced the question of personal 'fateful' love into theology. Dante's love for Beatrice starts out as earthly love, but uniquely in the history of theology, his love for Beatrice has theological implications. So in von Balthasar's summation, Dante's view was that "he [could] incorporate his finite love into that which is infinite—but at the cost of terrible sufferings, of course, as Dante shows us."[98]

These three lay themes, in Dante's theology, illustrate how the lay Christian truly functions as a Christian, within the relationships and vicissitudes of the world.

Another exponent of a 'lay' theology was Saint John of the Cross (1542-1591).[99] He wished to reform his Carmelite Order even as he himself sought God. His order was in a sense his 'world', but it spoke to a larger world divided by the efforts at reform initiated by Martin Luther (1483-1546). John used many aspects of his own situation in the world as materials for his self-expression. He drew upon the monastic tradition up to his time. He used poetic styles that were taken from the world of poetry, but more significantly he used his own inner experience. (Note the parallel with Dante here!) He described the movements of his spirit under the impulse of God. From the perspective of faith, God was literally working in the world using the soul of John as an instrument.

John's work has a surprisingly modern focus on the personal, the experiential, and the psychological, but it also has a not-so-modern acceptance that 'God alone suffices'. John's life is a striking illustration of the true source of a Christian life form, and how it responds to and uses the particular situation of the saint (in this case) in

---

[98] *GL III*, 32.
[99] John of the Cross was ordained in 1567! So von Balthasar's inclusion of him in a list of 'lay' theologians clearly has something to do with the content and style of his work. The appellation of a theology as a 'lay' theology points to the focus of living in the world rather than starting his theology from a consideration of the Church. See *GL III*, 105-171.

forming his expression of his life.[100] In fact, this is the essence of sanctity. Holiness involves the unity between the knowledge of Christ and the outward expression of one's life. This unity is achieved through a "remorseless power of discrimination" so that one selects only those things that will bring one to God.[101]

Along with Denys the Areopagite (fifth or sixth cent.), von Balthasar noted that "we can only grasp the structure of the Church and make it intelligible if we start from what ought to be, what in fact is, when seen in its existence in Christ and in its direct constitution by Christ."[102] It cannot be emphasized enough, how much ones understanding of the Church must come from its constitution in Christ, and not from the historical results of even very serious human sins. The sin is not *the* Church.

Historically, the mathematician and physicist, Blaise Pascal's life (1623-1662) lies between the medieval tradition and modern attempts at knowledge. He considered his life's work to be the effort to unite Christianity and science. Von Balthasar's analysis of the conversation in Pascal's "Infinity-Nothing" fragment sums up the meaning of Pascal's short text as follows: "the Christian offers a justification by faith by means of the proof that choice and decision are demanded by existence itself . . . and that only the decision for God can be regarded as rational." (Emphasis added.)[103] Von Balthasar's call to wonder at the existence of being finds a kindred spirit here.

How about another example? There is the lay embeddedness in the world, throughout the life of Georges Bernanos (1888 -1948). He specifically chose lay life because, as he put it: "a layman can fight on many levels where the cleric cannot accomplish much."[106] There too, in his detailed analysis of

---

[100] Cf. Vatican II: "In the lives of those who, sharing in our humanity, are however more perfectly transformed into the image of Christ, God vividly manifests His presence and His face to men." (LG 50)
[101] *GL III*, 109.
[102] Hans Urs von Balthasar, "Theology and Sanctity," *ET I*, 184.
[103] *GL III*, 204.
[106] *Bernanos*, 155.

Bernanos' life and work, von Balthasar inserted one of his rare references to the 'priesthood of the laity'.[107]

He opined that Bernanos' deep sense of his responsibility for the soul of his neighbor was exemplified two ways. When Bernanos met someone "he assumed the person into his very soul".[108] Then later on his deathbed, Bernanos expressed his concern for the several people whom he handed over, so to speak, to his confessor. These actions indicated the "perfection of what the priesthood of the laity can be."[109] Thus too, Bernanos most poignantly illustrates the lay manner of fulfilling the commandment to 'love thy neighbor'.

These meager examples from the vast history of lay experience in the Church, indicate the ways that von Balthasar's theology of the laity deepens the understanding of the relationship between the baptized man and his world, that is the world for which Jesus Christ died. However, from the Middle Ages up to our own time, the cultural conception of man's relationship to his world, which structures the assimilation of elements of the world into his life form, has undergone many changes. A significant change for those of us living in the modern period occurred through the rise of humanism at the end of the Middle Ages. This was not the benign development of "free personal individualism and the discovery of the world of nature."[110] Instead, it was to some extent, the start of a movement to locate the meaning of the world in

---

[107] This is a term that comes at least partially from Martin Luther's work. It was a useful term to describe some of the reality of the effects of Baptism. The Second Vatican Council completed the concept by setting it up in contrast to the priesthood of the ordained. Cf. *Lumen gentium*: "Though they differ from one another in essence and not only in degree, the common priesthood of the faithful and the ministerial or hierarchical priesthood are nonetheless interrelated: each of them in its own special way is a participation in the one priesthood of Christ." (LG 10)

[108] Ibidem.

[109] *Bernanos*, 156. This parallels the thought of Vatican II. For example: "They likewise exercise that priesthood in receiving the sacraments, in prayer and thanksgiving, in the witness of a holy life, and by self-denial and active charity." (LG 10)

[110] Hans Urs von Balthasar, *Science, Religion and Christianity*, trans. Hild Graef, (Westminster MD: Newman press, 1958), 19.

man. For von Balthasar, this movement is evident in the works of the great artists of the medieval period such as Leonardo da Vinci, Albrecht Dürer and Michelangelo, to name a few.[111] This trend, which will not be examined in detail here, leads to a confusion of the nature of being itself and man's relation to being as a human being.[112]

Nevertheless despite what we would now consider to be errors in terms of geography and some aspects of science, the Christian world-view in the Middle Ages did in fact provide "a view of the world which had deeply affected not only man's idea of himself and of the cosmos, but also the relation of both to God."[113] Such a world-view allowed man to finds his place within a hierarchy of being, where there are God and the spirits above man and animals and inanimate objects, and so on, below him. The notion of the ontological hierarchy has much to teach man in terms of his relationship to God. In von Balthasar's words, "it communicates God's mysterious words to him."[114] This is metaphysics being informed by revelation! The examples of lay life show how the figures that we considered stayed faithful to this insight. These individuals appreciated how God has illuminated all being, through Christ, and has given each order of being its appropriate role in the history of salvation.[115]

(A final note: the notion of the incorporation of the historically present elements of the world into the life form of an individual, finds a special resonance in the choosing of a spouse. This particular commitment to a new and permanent relationship will be examined in its own chapter. (Chapter Eight))

(b) Second, <u>the life work of lay people is the fruit of their own redeemed creativity</u>.

---

[111] Ibidem.
[112] Ibidem.
[113] *Science, Religion and Christianity*, 21.
[114] *Science, Religion and Christianity*, 25.
[115] The Second Vatican Council worked with this concept of the hierarchy of being. For example: "For by His incarnation the Father's Word assumed, and sanctified through His cross and resurrection, the whole of man, body and soul, and through that totality the whole of nature created by God for man's use." (GS 41)

Each lay person is a unique person, but the key to understanding the meaning of a person's life's work, is the 'redeemed' nature of this person's creativity. John Paul II frequently spoke of 'creativity'. Explaining it to a cultural affairs group, he said: "When we speak of creativity, spontaneously we think of the beautiful. However, the beautiful can begin to exist only when the power of good resides in her nature."[116] He conceived of creativity as involving the relation between the good and its form and this principle also appears in von Balthasar's metaphysics.[117]

In terms of uniqueness, for example, Dante's poetry cannot be confused with that of John of the Cross. The philosopher George Simmel (1858-1918) identified the "law of individuality" underlying their work that points to the origin of the work of art from deep within the individual.[118] Their missions (and we will examine the notion of mission further in Chapter Five) and the forms of their lives were substantially different. In an unprecedented way, Dante knew that he had a mission. In the *Monarchy* he wrote: "I want to demonstrate truths which no one else has dared to attempt."[119] He was setting out on a voyage that was not only his own life directed towards God, but he wanted to speak of this voyage in poetic terms.

Similarly, Saint John of the Cross' mystical poetry grew out of his own heart "where the lover carries the image of his beloved".[120] Even as a student he had the call to mysticism and he wrote a thesis on the structure of Christian mysticism.

Then there is the poet Gerard Manley Hopkins (1854-1889) who was interested in the way in which the individual particulars of creation spoke of the Creator. He had the insight that von Balthasar then drew into a formal description. So, for example, Hopkins wrote of the storm-fowl: "While he is aiming

---

[116] *Address of John Paul II to a Polish Group from the Cultural and Artistic formation Center, Sunday*, 25 January 2004.

[117] The same principle appears in Leo XIII's *Mirae caritatis*: "Everyone is aware that no sooner had 'the goodness and kindness of God our Savior appeared' (Titus 3:4), than there at once burst forth a certain creative force which issued in a new order of things and pulsed through all the veins of society, civil and domestic."

[118] *GL I*, 221.

[119] Cited in *GL III*, 10.

[120] Cited in *GL III*, 125.

only at impressing me his hearer with the meaning in hand, I am looking out meanwhile for his specific, his individual markings and mottlings".[121] Precisely in the individual markings of the bird he could see *this* particular bird as a product of God's creative palette. Lastly, more specifically, the very nature of redemption is that created forms manifest not only being but are also illuminated by the very depths of the ground of being, God himself as Jesus Christ.[122]

Last of all, the creativity of these poets shows the traces of the individual personalities and gifts of these men.

(c) Third, the life of the layperson speaks to the world. The form of an individual's life brings together the 'stuff' of the world, in such a way, as to express the deepest truth of the ground of all being. The author Bernanos was deeply involved with the world of his time and brought Catholicism to bear on his critiques of the Church and the politics of Europe. Dante used the world-view of his time, the historical figures and metaphors that were part of his culture, to describe the form of the whole of reality including Purgatory, Paradise, and Hell. Similarly, the Carmelite reform presented the character of a complete following of Christ through the lens of monastic existence. Although John of the Cross was an exceptional mystic, he was in fact showing that contemplation is a feature of all faith even for non-religious and notably for lay people.[123] Moreover, the contemplation of the Scriptures themselves is crucial to von Balthasar's theological method and to the method of thinking that he is proposing for laity..

Returning to two concepts developed earlier, we can now say that the 'momentum' of the mission of the Son of God in Christ gathers up the lives of individual Christians in such a way that they 'express God's truth' to the world.

---

[121] Cited in *GL III*, 356.
[122] See Vatican II's *Lumen gentium*, 41.
[123] The Second Vatican Council understood the role of contemplation in the reforming of culture. For example: "In this way, the human spirit, being less subjected to material things, can be more easily drawn to the worship and contemplation of the Creator." (GS 57)

(d) Fourth, there is mystery—in the theological sense—in the life of lay people. Now the hiddenness of being is the complementary attribute to the radiance of being. While the form is the manifestation of the depths of being, it does not render that being totally transparent or accessible to us. The being remains innately mysterious. If this is a law of general ontology, then it must be especially true of Christ and the Church as well. So in the case of Jesus Christ, the 'Messianic Secret' that characterizes the *Gospel of Mark* is not simply a literary construction created by Mark the Evangelist, but rather it is a literary feature that indicates something of the actual nature of Jesus Christ himself.[124] In von Balthasar's estimation, the hiddenness of Christ, shown for example in his avoidance of the title 'Messiah', manifests the incomprehensibility of God himself.

Then as a consequence, the Church too is characterized by hiddenness precisely because it originates from the side of Christ. However the Church is not simply the pure Body of Christ. It is also the community's *resistance* to the power of Christ. Both aspects have implications for the lay Christian.

The hiddenness that is a feature of the Christ-form means that the Church is not simply a human institution, with a constitution that can be completely described. According to the Second Vatican Council: "The visible society and the spiritual community . . . are not to be thought of as two realities. On the contrary, they form one complex reality which comes together with a divine and a human element." (LG, 8) Consequently we can say that the theology of the laity, or any other part of ecclesiology, can at best be a selection of themes.

In addition, the theme of hiddenness also presents itself as a limit to the theological enterprise. So Dante's works are marked and limited in a sense by the worldview of his time. Similarly, Blaise Pascal could not avoid the shadow of Jansenism that he had learned in Rouen and Port Royal, and so on.

When we consider the community's hiddenness to include the community's resistance to the work of Christ in the Church, then it gives rise to penance and the confession of sins, exhortation and even correction and ecclesial discipline as parts of a Church member's

---

[124] *GL VII*, 318ff.

life. The innate hiddenness of the Church—its origins hidden in God himself—and the sinfulness of Church members means that some Christians might not even recognize Christ in the Church, even where there is objective evidence to the contrary. One might also miss the form of Christ in the Church because one does not encounter the form of Christ in one's life. Or perhaps the form of Christ that is presented is so distorted as to be unrecognizable.

More generally then, the lay person is uniquely placed to demonstrate an appreciation of all being, since every form to some degree manifests the goodness, beauty, and truth of the Creator. It is this appreciation of all being that can then be brought together with the biblical record of the manifestations of the glory of God.[125] At the point where one values each and every aspect of the world as created, then the doctrines of grace, redemption, and justification can be spoken. In this way, von Balthasar's theology respects "the truth of the world and specifically with its world-relatedness, but at the same time [he leaves] open the possibility, that this truth may include within it some elements of a divine origin."[126] This is the third possible way to conduct the search for truth. The other two are to (i) unknowingly appropriate possible supernatural effects into a philosophy that does not duly credit these effects. This is where the metaphysical approach shows its superiority by allowing metaphysics to be guided by the light of Scripture.[127] Then (ii) a second possibility is to imagine that one can manipulate revealed truth using philosophies that are somehow viewed as 'free' of supernatural effects. In this case metaphysics reminds us of the impossibility of a 'neutral' philosophy.

In conclusion then, these are some of the ecclesial consequences of the radiance of the form at the individual and communitarian levels.

---

[125] Joseph Ratzinger comes to a similar conclusion. Cf. *Introduction to Christianity*, 137ff.

[126] *TL I*, 21.

[127] Joseph Ratzinger also comes to the same conclusion. When he is arguing for the significance of the Fathers of the Church, he says that the Scriptures and the Fathers, go together as word and answer. *Principles of Catholic Theology*, 147.

The next characteristic of the form of Christian life is the proportion or harmony between the different elements that compose the form.

(B) The Proportion and Integrity of Form: The Art of Lay Life

In analyzing Thomas Aquinas' work, von Balthasar showed that Aquinas' treatment of beauty drew on the tradition for categories speaking about the relationships between the elements of a form and their relation to the whole, in other words, the *proportion* of the form. Von Balthasar summed up the relationships as follows: "the parts or aspects . . . are distributed and adapted (*pro-portio*) to one another, but in such a way that the parts do not have their ultimate measure from themselves but from the whole, this is at the same time, both the distributer and the ultimate consumer of its own measuring."[128] Von Balthasar has incorporated the last two features that Aquinas associated with beauty, namely proportion and wholeness. (Cf. ST I q. 5 a. 4)[129]

For our purposes, a successful Christian chooses and orders the elements of life so that the whole is given a beautiful shape by the indwelling of Christ in the person and what they do and think and say. So, for example, von Balthasar found the life of Saint Augustine (who still had to be a faithful Christian despite being a clergyman!) to be beautiful because of the "measure and rhythm" of his experience, and not because of what he wrote on music![130] What von Balthasar found, when he examined the lives of God's chosen, lay and cleric, was that they are moved by the Holy Spirit in ways that shape them and color their experience. Their experience then becomes 'archetypal' for other believers. However, von Balthasar is adamant that

---

[128] *GL I*, 468.

[129] Karl Rahner was aware of the same relationships and their fundamental character. For example, he wrote: "The nature of the Church cannot initially or adequately be described simply by pointing to the relationship which individual members bear one another, because in fact, in order rightly to determine how two elements in a whole are related to one another, one must first understand the nature of the whole itself." "The Role of the Layman . . . ", 65.

[130] Hans Urs von Balthasar, "Revelation and the Beautiful", *Explorations in Theology I*, 101.

grace perfects nature, it does not supplant it. Grace usually does not develop the capacities that a person has not made the effort to develop.[131] It is grace that opens up the final meaning of created being and makes it transparent to the glory of God.

Turning again to the laity named in *The Glory of the Lord III*, the life of each one recapitulates the most fundamental truths, and by doing so is a living demonstration of God's truth shining through, bringing everything together as a single message. The Russian writer Vladimir Soloviev (1853-1900) tried to describe the entire process of God's self-manifestation in the world. He used the resources of the Catholic tradition because Hegel's influence moved him to seek a religious form that transcended national boundaries. This transcendence spoke of the larger transcendence and internal integrity that von Balthasar and Soloviev saw in the Catholic form. In the same way, the priest and poet, John of the Cross, incorporated the whole understanding of monasticism, from the earliest times of the Church, and so was able to show his world the underlying truth—monastic life is a profound way to follow Christ. By its very integrity, the life of the counsels offers a complete following of Christ that cannot be surpassed by other vows.

All of the individuals cited above express what Gerard Manley Hopkins spoke of too namely that Christ works through Christians giving their lives proportion for the glory of the Father.

Lastly, it is worth turning to an example of this phenomenon of radiance and proportion of the Christian form, taken from European political history. Relying on the thought of the noted French historian Raymond Aron, let us examine the situation in France after the Second World War. In 1948, he concluded that "democratic individualism, with its Protestant origins and Christian spirit, is fundamentally incompatible with the message of Stalinism."[132] He considered communism in Europe to be an 'anti-religion' but a religion none the less, and this is significant because "it is correct to say that the religion

---

[131] Also see Aquinas' concept of 'co-creation' *ST 1a* q. 45 a. 8 *Respondeo*.
[132] Raymond Aron, *The Dawn of Universal History: Selected essays from a witness to the twentieth century*, Barbara Bray trans., (New York: Perseus Books – Basic Books, 2003), 234.

of salvation is still the chief enemy of secular religion."[133] In the terminology of this work, the secular religion of communism has the formal elements of 'dogma' and 'discipline' and so "communism . . . derives extraordinary strength from the fact that it poses as a rival church."[134] The 'ecclesial' form of communism has real power, even though it is not the right power. There is more to Aron's thought, but there is enough insight here for us to appreciate that even forms that only have a certain integrity and completeness, have power.[135] These brief comments also indicate the reasons for laity to help to sustain and contribute to the form of the Church, as it makes itself present to the secular society. Only the Church can ultimately guarantee the significant anthropological concepts and values. But it is usually the lay person who actually carries them into the culture. Laity present concepts and values to the society at large. Hopefully these are values learned in the interactions of the *communio* rather than those learned from the world spirit. Aron's insights also indicate to the lay person that caution is needed when faced with alternative total forms in society.

Conclusion: The "Hour of the Laity"[136]

The notion of the 'Hour of the Laity' draws together the themes that have been touched on in this chapter. The concept frequently occurs in the literature and points to a real historical fact about the laity. In earlier times, prior to the Middle Ages, some laity had well defined spheres of influence and were not viewed as diminished because they were not "religious specialists".[137] Similarly, priests had specific functions but "did not form a caste of their own in the

---

[133] *The Dawn of Universal History*, 235.

[134] Ibidem.

[135] Aron's insights demonstrate the nature of the operation of form in the world. However perhaps because of his Jewish background Aron also thought that "in our day and age the religion of salvation is stronger when it is not imprisoned within the structure of a church". (235) Judaism does not have an ecclesial structure.

[136] The title is taken from title of the first chapter of G. Philips, *Le Rôle du Laïcat dans l'Église*, 7-26. (My translation.)

[137] "Demands of the Present Day," 102.

secular sociological sense."[138] The history of the development of the clergy into a caste and the rise of religious specialization because of a corresponding specialization in the field of education during the Enlightenment and Post-Enlightenment is not our interest here.[139] However in the Modern Period, the "caste" system—in von Balthasar' sense so as to avoid any hint of a derogatory view!—developed so strongly that Pope Pius XI had to announce that "unfortunately the clergy no longer suffice for the necessities and requirements of our time . . .. This is why it is necessary for all to become Apostles, so that the world of the Catholic Laity does not stand idly by but is closely united to the Church's hierarchy . . . and is present and involved in the sacred struggle."[140] The reason that the pope gave for calling the laity to the Church's apostolate was that clergy had become isolated from the world. As von Balthasar says: "the more the Church 'specializes' herself in the clergy, the more the layman leaves the responsibility for his apostolate to the clergy."[141] Both the pope and von Balthasar are asking to redress the imbalance in the operation of the Church that has been caused by the 'isolation' (the pope's thinking) or the 'specialization' (von Balthasar's term) of the clergy and the consequent diminution of the apostolic activity of the laity.

This is of course not to say that the Church's only relationship with the secular world is *via* individual laity. The Church herself relates to other institutions in society and should do so.

---

[138] Hans Urs von Balthasar, "The Limitations of Catholic Action," *The Laity and the Life of the Counsels*, 45.
[139] Von Balthasar has examined this history exhaustively in his articles: "The Limitations of Catholic Action," "The Lessons of History" and "The Demands of the Present Day," that can be found in *The Laity and the Life of the Counsels*. See also G, Philips "L'heure des Laïcs" in his *Le Rôle du Laïcat dans L'Église*. There is also a useful chapter in Louis J. Luzbetak, S.V.D., *The Church and Cultures: New Perspectives in Missiological Anthropology*, American Society of Missiology Series No.12, (Maryknoll NY: Orbis Books, 1988) entitled "A Historical Overview of Mission Models," 85-104.
[140] Pope Pius XI to Cardinal Segura y Saens, November 6, 1929, cited in "The Limitations of Catholic Action," 45.
[141] Ibidem.

So the concept of the 'hour' of the laity highlights the specific function of the laity so well expressed by the Second Vatican Council and which taught concerning the apostolate of the laity: "An indication of this manifold and pressing need is the unmistakable work being done today by the Holy Spirit in making the laity ever more conscious of their own responsibility and encouraging them to serve Christ and the Church in all circumstances." (*Apostolicam actuositatem*, AA, 1) The reader will note the threads of the consideration of lay life under the rubric of the Good and hence of action are beginning to be apparent here. (For more see Chapter Five)

The work of the Holy Spirit at the heart of the lay form of life meant that in the past "the Church's theology was founded primarily by laymen. The apologists Justin, Tertullian, Clement and Origen were laymen" and then von Balthasar notes the long list of theologians who were obliged to become clerics: Jerome, Basil, Cyprian etc.[142] Today specialized lay expertise means that: "With a constantly increasing population, continual progress in science and technology, and closer interpersonal relationships, the areas for the lay apostolate have been immensely widened particularly in fields that have been for the most part open to the laity alone." (AA, 1) Von Balthasar was already thinking along the same lines because he said that it is at least conceivable that if laity are truly developing the relationships described earlier—and summed up in the idea of the *communio* of truth—and are making use of them then the official Church would not need "to issue such detailed statements about the social order" because competent laity, rooted in the life of the Church, would be doing serious research into these issues.[143]

Thus our look at the fruitfulness of lay life comes to its conclusion. The fruit of the Holy Spirit in lay persons lives shines through their tasks in the family and in the world at large. In the next chapter we turn to the lay person in action, whose life is a theodrama.

---

[142] For details see von Balthasar's Footnote 18, in "The Lessons of History," 85.
[143] *CSOL*, 359.

Chapter Five: The Drama: Laity on Fire

Introduction
'Fire' in the Scriptures
The Theodramatic Approach
Drama - Setting the Stage
    (i) The Heavens and the Earth
    (ii) Man: Created as elected, called, and sent
    (iii) Sin and Dialogue
Drama - Election, Vocation and Mission in Christ
    (i) Christ the Source of our Election as Theological Persons
    (ii) Von Balthasar's 'Consciousness Christology'
        (a) Dying and Rising with Christ
        (b) The Church
    (iii) Jesus Christ: The Source of our Vocation as Theological Persons
        (a) Is the Lay State the result of a Call?
    (iv) Jesus Christ: The Source of our Mission as Theo-logical Persons
        (a) The Christian as an individual
        (b) The Christian as a member of the Community
Conclusion: The Battle of the Logos

Introduction

The study of the dynamic fruitfulness of the Christ-form (and hence the lay form of life) has prepared us for the theodramatic study promised in the *Introduction*. We need to do that now.

The second transcendental quality of being is that it manifests the good. Von Balthasar's five volume *Theo-drama* examines precisely how being manifests the good. He retrieved the category of drama to correctly describe the human struggle to do good.[144] So the 'theo-drama' is the human struggle before God (*theos*).[145]

---

[144] Take note of the frequency with which the word appears in the words of John Paul II. For example, he referred to "the violent drama of Calvary, the traumatic struggle between darkness and light, between death and life, between hatred and love. The Prince of Peace, born today in Bethlehem, will give his life on Golgotha, so that love may reign on earth." *Urbi et Orbi*, Christmas 2002.

[145] Note that Karol Wojtyła was working in this direction early in his life. See Kenneth L. Schmitz *At the Center of the Human Drama: The Philosophical Anthropology of Karol*

In fact this is a very scriptural insight. The *Gospel of John*, for example, is written in dramatic terms. The author writes about the clash between light and darkness, between good and evil. The Second Vatican Council reflected on the Church in the modern world and explained that "the whole life of men, both individual and social, shows itself to be a struggle, and a dramatic one, between good and evil, between light and darkness." (*Gaudium et spes*, GS, 13) The Christian message explains that human beings find the good in God's doing the good *for* us, and *with* us. The category then has two parts–the divine initiative arising out of the freedom of God and the graced human response in freedom (being on fire).

There was a substantial reason for reviving the category of drama. As von Balthasar explains: "Theater intends to be an interpretation of the world, in its 'unreality' shining a ray of light into the confusion of reality."[146] The dramatic life of the Church (a 'theater' in this metaphor), and of the Christian, shines with the light of Christ (his fire) into the confused and darkened world. The Church resembles a theater because by participating in the theodrama it manifests the 'whole' (that is heaven and earth and the union between God and man in Christ) to confront all of the more partial conceptions of reality—the individual preoccupied with his own life, abstracting himself from the larger community; the government making itself into 'big brother' and ignoring the roles of the smaller communities in society, and so on. The Christian vision is unique and overwhelmingly powerful. In fact, according to von Balthasar, "we have the right to assert that no other, mythical or religio-philosophical anthropology *can* attain a satisfactory idea of man, an idea that integrates all of the elements, but the Christian one."[147] (Emphasis added.) This is how

---

Wojtyła/ Pope John Paul II. (Washington D.C.: CUA Press, 1993).

[146] Hans Urs von Balthasar, *Theodrama – Theological Dramatic Theory I: Prolegomena*, Graham Harrison trans., (San Francisco: Ignatius Press, 1988), 10. After the initial complete reference to a particular volume, the volumes in the series will henceforward be referred to by the abbreviation TD followed by the volume number.

[147] Hans Urs von Balthasar, *Theodrama II: Dramatis Personae: Man in God*, Graham Harrison, (San Francisco: Ignatius Press, 1990), 343.

unique and significant Christianity and specifically the Church are.[148] Furthermore, the lay person is part of making the 'whole' present. The echoes of our consideration of 'form' are immediately apparent!

Lay people participate in doing Christ's good as a part of the theodrama, part of God's transforming of the world.[149] The *doing* is important as we will see in the image of the fire (see below). As Jesus explained: "My teaching is not from myself, it comes from the one who sent me; if anyone is prepared to *do* his [God's] will, he will know whether my teaching is from God." (John 7: 17) (Emphasis added.) So the good is done. It is not merely contemplated. It was Saint Augustine who bluntly observed: "to be called a cobbler, one must repair shoes . . . .. Now, then, are you called a Christian when you perform no distinctively Christian acts?"[150] The context for these actions is always faith because faith identifies one's place in the unfolding drama.

Now the foundations of the drama lie with God and the subsequent coming of the god-man: "Jesus [who] is the man who burns with God's fire."[151] We will

---

[148] One should note here Benedict XVI's teaching in Regensburg, when he said: "the truly divine God is the God who has revealed himself as *logos* and, as *logos*, has acted and continues to act lovingly on our behalf. Certainly, love, as Saint Paul says, "transcends" knowledge and is thereby capable of perceiving more than thought alone (cf. *Eph* 3:19); nonetheless it continues to be love of the God who is *Logos*. Consequently, Christian worship is, again to quote Paul - "λογικη λατρεία", worship in harmony with the eternal Word and with our reason (cf. *Rom* 12:1)." (*Meeting with the Representatives of Science*, University of Regensburg, 12 September 2006) The emphasis on the role of reason and the logos of God leads him to the same conclusion that von Balthasar has given us.

[149] The Platonic notion of participation in evidence here is also the background to the thinking in the *Constitution on the Church in the Modern World*. See, for example, Joseph Ratzinger, *Commentary on the Documents of Vatican II, vol. V*, Herbert Vorgrimler gen. ed., (London: Burns and Oates, 1969), 132.

[150] Saint Augustine, "The Christian Life," *Treatises on Various Subjects*, Roy. J. Deferrari ed., *The Fathers of the Church 16*, (New York: Fathers of the Church Inc., 1952), 9.

[151] Hans Urs von Balthasar, *Theodrama: Theological Dramatic Theory IV: The Action*, trans., Graham Harrison, (San Francisco: Ignatius Press, 1994), 60. After the initial mention of a volumes of this series, each volume will be

examine the underlying significance of this sentence for the theology of the lay person. We will start with the scriptural image of fire.

'Fire' in the Scriptures

Something so wondrous happens with the coming of Jesus Christ that Jesus himself had to resort to the image of fire to explain what he is doing.[152] Significantly, his words come after the *Parable of the Vigilant Servants* (Luke 12:35-48) and its explanation. He then says: "I have come to set the earth on fire, and how I wish it were already blazing." (Luke 12:49) Back when the advent of Jesus was announced by John the Baptist, John had announced: "He will baptize you with the Holy Spirit and with fire." (Matthew 3:11) Then when the Holy Spirit (the Spirit of God) appeared at Pentecost, sent by Christ himself, "there appeared to them tongues as of fire . . .. And they were all filled with the Holy Spirit." (Acts 2:3, 4)

Fire had already been part of the Old Testament theophanies. It signified the glory of the presence of God in the burning bush (Exodus 3:2) and on Sinai (Exodus 2:26). Fire from heaven completed the sacrifice in the *First Book of Kings* (1 Kings 18). As Elijah announced: "The one who answers with fire is God." (1 Kings 18:24) For Isaiah, it was the fire of purification. (Isaiah 6:6) Finally, the action of the Holy Spirit was like fire.

The second aspect of the theme is the testing nature of the fire: "the genuineness of your faith, more precious than gold that is perishable even though tested by fire." (1 Peter 1:7) Lastly, there is the fire of judgment: "anyone who does not remain in me will be thrown out like a branch . . . people will gather them

---

referred to by the abbreviation TD followed by the volume number. See also Aquinas's comment on the nature of Christ: "instead of material fire, there was the spiritual fire of charity in Christ's holocaust." (ST III q. 46 a. 4)

[152] Note Thomas Aquinas' comment on the appropriateness of the appearance of the Holy Spirit in tongues of fire: "to show with what fervor their hearts were to be moved as to preach Christ everywhere, though surrounded by opposition. . . . [And] when we have obtained grace we must look forward to be judged; and this is signified by the fire." (ST III q. 39 a. 6)

and throw them into the fire." (John 15:6) If we apply von Balthasar's approach to Scripture, we conclude that the image of 'fire' captures the presence and action of God, including his testing of his people in their actions, up to the final judgment. These are also the dimensions of the theodrama itself.[153] More formally, one can say that the whole point of theodramatic theory is to describe "the singular divine action" which has many different facets.[154]

The Theodramatic Approach

The proposition that 'Jesus is the man of fire' has its roots in the Scriptures and the Tradition of the Church, and safeguards us from the major Post-Enlightenment flaw that is a view of man, the world, and history, that is "developed primarily from below".[155] Such a mindset has had many deleterious effects on man's view of God, man, and the world but they would take a volume of their own to detail.[156] Suffice it to say that lay people, immersed in a secular Post-Enlightenment culture, are being flooded with 'thinking from below' all of the time. Such thinking trims God down to man's measure and limits the implications of divine and human action which is why we are taking the theodramatic perspective.

The view of man from below can be traced to the early Pre-Enlightenment efforts to develop a 'Universal Philosophical Religion' that was to be 'free' of revelation.[157] For example, Auguste Comte (1798-1857) wrote that Christians "worship an absolute Being, whose power is boundless, so that its wishes necessarily remain arbitrary. Thus, if they were really

---

[153] Hans Urs von Balthasar, *Theodrama: Theological Dramatic Theory I: Prolegomena*, trans., Graham Harrison, (San Francisco: Ignatius Press, 1988), 17.
[154] Ibidem.
[155] Hans Urs von Balthasar, *Theodrama: Theological Dramatic Theory II: Dramatis Personae*, trans. Graham Harrison, (San Francisco: Ignatius Press, 1990), 9.
[156] See Henri de Lubac S.J., *The Drama of Atheist Humanism*, trans., Edith M. Riley, (New York: World Publishing Company, Meridian Books, 1971)
[157] The phrase is Frederik van Leenhof's (1647-1712), but it sums the broader project at the time. See Jonathan I. Israel, *Radical Enlightenment: Philosophy and the Making of Modernity 1650-1750*, (Oxford: Oxford University Press, 2001), 406.

consistent they would have to regard themselves as genuine slaves, subject to the whims of an inscrutable power."[158] As a result he proposed a human-centered philosophy with no role for revelation. And no Jesus as the man of fire!

Philosophical efforts in this direction displace the central place of revelation in man's search for meaning. Lesser displacements might either simply reduce the truth of revelation to a 'spirituality' or alternatively to shifting revelation into an epic story that makes no demands on man. In the case of the laity, the 'spiritual' direction consists of turning it into a "lyrical edifying utterance in the bosom of the Church".[159] This keeps one's religiosity 'in-house', so to speak, and although such discourse serves a legitimate purpose when speaking about religion within the family and the Church community, it cannot be the only form of religious discourse because the Church in fact has a mission to the whole world. On the other hand, the 'epic' direction is more external and precise in the sense that it occurs in dealing with heresies "or the threat of error."[160] The trouble is that both directions are at a remove from the *real living drama* of the ecclesial relationship between God and man in the world.

The effort to abstract us from the act of revelation itself removes us from being "willing to hear right to the end," as constantly open to the revelation that is reaching us through the scriptures and the tradition of the Church.[161] (You will recall that this is the structure of the *communio*-based institution in Chapter Four.) In addition, routine religious practice and thought do serve a practical purpose, but they cannot reduce the interpersonal relationship between God and man to mere routine.

Put differently the category of theodrama calls us to appreciate the *single* drama of God and

---

[158] *The Drama of Atheist Humanism,* 101. Note too Benedict XVI's statement to the Representatives of Science at Regensburg University: "God does not become more divine when we push him away from us in a sheer, impenetrable voluntarism; rather, the truly divine God is the God who has revealed himself as *logos* and, as *logos*, has acted and continues to act lovingly on our behalf." (12 September 2006)
[159] *TD II,* 56.
[160] Ibidem.
[161] "Characteristics of Christianity," 173.

humanity, embodied in Jesus the man of fire, instead of imagining "a multiplicity of independent dramas."[162] This is being said from the perspective of the whole of being. So, for example, Christianity is not like the isolated privatized religion of author and philosopher Henry David Thoreau (1817-1862) and his transcendentalism. The Christian drama is about the *community* of men in Christ (the Church), in the world, for God. But before getting into the Christological issues, there is more to say about God's initiatives in salvation history.

We are now isolating the elements in the statement: "Jesus [who] is the man who burns with God's fire." The first is the stage on which this action occurs.

Drama - Setting the Stage
Von Balthasar's view is that the theme of the divine fire is capable of "recapitulate[ing] everything we have said, by way of introduction," in the first three volumes of the *Theodrama*.[163] The theme sums up the key features of theodramatic study that have to appear in any theology of the laity. These are: (i) God's setting of the world stage for the laity, and then Christ brings the fire. Then, (ii) the inclusion of the laity in Christ, and lastly, (iii) the Christological heart of all lay action.

(i) The Heavens and the Earth
If we consider the individual Christian lay person then he or she lives on a stage that has been set by God, and participates in the Spirit of Christ (the fire of Christ) as a member of the Church. The theory of theodrama is searching for a description of the *entirety* of the theological picture of divine and human action. This is ontology from the perspective of action.[164]

---

[162] *TD IV*, 62.

[163] *TD IV*, 61. Thomas Aquinas noted that "fire enlightens actively." (ST III q. 66 a. 3) He has captured the foundation of divine action in the world through the power of the Holy Spirit. He also notes Jerome's view that "we may understand fire . . . to mean the Holy Ghost." (ST III q. 66 a. 3)

[164] Von Balthasar's theory of human action is similar to that of Karol Wojtyła. As Kenneth Schmitz explains: "he insists that an existential metphysics of actual being (*esse actu*) is required to situate the moral agent in the actual context in which one acts." *At the Center of the Human Drama*, 126. Von Balthasar does an analysis of human action through a

The place to start is with the heavens and the earth as the 'stage' for the drama (the fire) of the lay person's life. This is a consistent element in the theology of the laity who are by definition secular. As John Paul II explained: "The term secular must be understood in light of the act of God the creator and redeemer, who has handed over the world to men and women so that they may participate in the work of creation. (*Christifideles laici*, CL, 15) The word 'secular' comes from the Latin term for worldly or temporal rather than eternal (*saecularis*). This characteristic distinguishes the heavens and the earth but both the heavens and the earth are the stage for the Christian participation in Christ's redemption.[165] In Jesus words: "I have come to set the earth on fire, and how I wish it were already blazing!" (Luke 12:49)

God created the heavens and the earth freely out of love.[166] The *Book of Genesis* posits the beginnings of the stage where the drama will take place. Heaven and earth are always distinct but each has a role.[167] The biblical teaching on heaven as created and resting on the gracious favor of the Creator gives heaven a sense of being 'worldly' yet invisible, and it is the starting point and the finishing point of salvation. By contrast, the pre-biblical religions had divinized the heavens.

---

reflection on the theater as illuminating existence (TD I, 135 - 257) and then through a reflection on the theater as springing from existence itself. (TD I, 259 – 478.)

[165] Note too Benedict XVI's affirmation of the same principle: "The denial of God distorts the freedom of the human person, yet it also devastates creation." (*Address to the Diplomats accredited to the Holy See*, 11 January 2010.)

[166] See also Nicholas J. Healy III, "The World as Gift," *Communio* 32 (Fall 2005)

[167] Cf. *TD II*, 187. The similar idea appears in the work of von Balthasar's friend, Karl Barth, who wrote: "There is in the cosmos an 'above' and a 'below' . . . they only reflect but they do reflect, the true and proper and strict above and below of Creator and creature, of God and man." *Church Dogmatics III/3*, (Edinburgh: T & T Clark, 1950), 421. This text was cited in *TD II*, 177. Then in following on from this section just cited, Karl Barth went on to say something very significant: "We cannot try to get behind this likeness to a true reality that can be detached from it." Barth (and von Balthasar) has shown the importance of the real. Trying to 'get behind' the real, as attempted by Hegel and other idealists is a futile exercise.

Then according to the Scriptures, God created hum-an beings in the image and likeness of God. (Cf. Genesis 1)[168] The patristic understanding of these terms was that human beings are made in the image of God, a character that cannot be lost, while human beings can lose their likeness to God through sin. This likeness is only restored in Christ.[169]

Furthermore, human beings are not simply images of God, but more precisely, they are images of the three-personed God.[170] The three divine persons are eternally constituted by their relations so that within the divine essence there is a differentiation of absolutely unique personhood as Father, or Son, or Spirit, and each person is constituted as a person, open to the others as terms of the processions. Hence at the level of created being, the human as image means that each person is not an interchangeable subjectivity, but a totally unique incommunicable *person* called by name by the unique personal God.[171]

---

[168] It is instructive to pursue the notion of man as the image of God in the writings of Origen. As Henri Crouzel summarizes Origen's theology: "Let us simply say that the likeness will end in unity with Christ, a unity which is not understood in a pantheistic manner, for it respects the 'hypostases' of the angels and of men as Origen makes clear in contradiction of the Stoic 'conflagration.' Henri Crouzel, *Origen*, A. S. Worrall trans., (Edinburgh: T & T Clark, 1989), 98.

[169] To cite one example: Origen explains, when speaking of Moses : "in fact he said, ' He made him in the image of God,' and was silent about the likeness, points to nothing else but this, that man received the honor of God's image in his first creation, the perfection of God's likeness was reserved for him at the consummation." *Origen on First Principles*, G. W. Butterworth trans., (Gloucester MA: Peter Smith, 1973), 245.

[170] Here von Balthasar sees himself in the line of Romano Guardini, Gabriel Marcel and Denis de Rougement. See Hans Urs von Balthasar, "On the Concept of Person," *Communio* 13 (Spring 1986).

[171] Note Maximus the Confessor's comment that "God and man are patterns each to the other." Cited in *TD II*, 202. And see also Ratzinger's comment that the theology of the Trinity uncovers the depths of human existence. It is in the revelation of the divine Trinity that the true meaning of person, the true meaning of unity and plurality, and the true meaning of absolute and relative is uncovered. Joseph Ratzinger, *Introduction to Christianity*, (New York: Crossroad Publishing, 1969). John Paul II wrote: "The sacredness of the human person cannot be obliterated no matter how often it

This is a fundamental point to make as we go about studying the actions of subjects on the stage.

But as always on 'this side' of the analogy of being, "the trace, the image of this primal Life [of the divine Trinity] is hard to see in the realm of naked creatureliness. Dissimilarity predominates, for even the highest creature lacks the most divine attribute: it lacks self-subsistence."[172] However we can still affirm that intersubjectivity is a crucial trait of lay people in operation as we will come to see.

We can learn more from the persons in the Trinity. The eternal 'dialog' within God, where the one uttered and the one uttering are united in love[173], suggests a fundamental openness in *human* being on the interpersonal level, that is grounded in the human's openness to God.[174] We can call this the 'word-dimension' of human being.[175] More specifically, as already indicated, the 'word-dimension' is present because the Son is the efficient, (Cf. John 1: 2) final (Cf. Ephesians 1: 4ff.), and exemplary cause (Cf. Hebrews 1: 3), of this particular human being. So in any attempt to describe created reality, the freedom of creatures and the drama of their life before God, the Son is the foundation of this reality, this drama and the freedom of this individual. And he is the one who becomes the man of fire.

Moreover, Christianity believes that *creation* is redeemed. The *Letter to the Hebrews* relates the orders of creation and redemption: "At various times in the past and in various different ways, God spoke to our ancestors through the prophets, but in our own time, the last days, he has spoken to us through his Son,

---

is devalued and violated because it has its unshakeable foundation in God as Creator and Father." (*Christifideles laici*, CL, 5).

[172] Hans Urs von Balthasar, *Theodrama III: Dramatis Personae*, (San Francisco: Ignatius Press, 1992), 525.
[173] Hans Urs von Balthasar: "The procession of the Second divine hypostasis out of the first is simultaneously interpreted as 'generation' and 'utterance' (since the Son is the Word) . . . and if Love, in turn, is grasped as the Third Hypostasis, proceeding from both the One who generates/utters and from the Word, it becomes clear how profoundly rooted the dialogic principle is in God." *TD II*, 72.
[174] This explains the teaching of the Second Vatican Council that: "By his innermost nature man is a social being." (*Gaudium et spes*, GS, 12)
[175] *TD II*, 73.

the Son he has appointed to inherit *everything* and through whom he made *everything.*" (Hebrews 1:1) (Emphasis added.) The creation that came about out of love by the Father, through the Son, in the Spirit, is redeemed—so Christians have a real freedom, and a real fire in their lives—and will be gathered in to the Father, by the Son, through the Holy Spirit. So, neither Christians nor any other people are faced with a neutral *tabula rasa* of a world on which to make their mark (the western materialist view).[176] The Incarnate Word lived out his Life, Death, and Resurrection, and thus redeemed and sanctified the world and continues to do so. He inaugurates the space in which Christians and others face God in day-to-day life. Christians are Christians *because* they are deliberately participating in Christ's transformation of the world.[177] This is the life of the man on fire! In this way, man as 'the likeness of God' is realizing his nature as likeness. He is becoming part of the word to the world in the drama that Christ brought to its supreme level, the Theo-drama rather than the mere drama of buying an Iphone!

Now what von Balthasar has done is introduce us to the missiological dimension of the metaphysics of existence. The category of mission is the heart of the description of Jesus Christ's life so too it is at the core of the account of Christian existence. It tells us how the individual Christian man or woman becomes a person on fire. Thus the Second Vatican Council would teach that "These faithful are by baptism made one body with Christ and are constituted among the People of God; they are in their own way made sharers in the priestly, prophetical, and kingly functions of Christ; and they carry out for their own part the mission of

---

[176] The concept of the world as a neutral *tabula rasa* is the product of the Enlightenment.
[177] See Second Vatican Council: "the Church, being the salt of the earth and the light of the world (cf. Matthew 5:13-14), is more urgently called upon to save and renew every creature, that all things may be restored in Christ and all men may constitute one family in Him and one people of God." (*Ad gentes*, AG, 1) The purpose of this document is "to rally the forces of all the faithful in order that the people of God, marching along the narrow way of the Cross, may spread everywhere the reign of Christ, Lord and Overseer of the ages (cf. Ecclesiastes 36:19), and may prepare the way for his coming." (AG, 1)

the whole Christian people in the Church and in the world." (LG 31) Sharing in his functions makes them people on fire. But how does this sharing come about?

(ii) Man: Created as elected, called and sent
The 'word-dimension' of creation, the category of mission leads us to the meaning of the terms 'elect,' 'called,' and 'sent.' Now these terms can already be applied to the created human being in a restricted sense. In terms of creation: human beings are created through the Word as inescapably relational and in this sense *elected* for dialogue. Dialogue is essential to the drama of life! God envisioned human beings for dialogue before all eternity. God then *calls* them into existence and gives them a specifically dialogical *mission* building relationships on the world stage by creating them through the Word. But first true dialogue involves freedom. Freedom matters in the playing out of the drama.

Now following von Balthasar's method (Chapter One), human freedom can only be described in two stages: firstly, there are the results of philosophical reflection on freedom, and secondly, there are the theological insights based on revelation.

Philosophically, freedom has long been thought to have a binary structure. There are two moments to freedom: firstly, self-possession, and secondly, the going out of oneself in love (will) and knowledge (intellect). Pre-Christian thinkers such as Plato and Aristotle had already reflected on freedom as autonomous motion. The Fathers of the Church expanded this according to the notion of 'image and likeness'.[178] So von Balthasar's proposal—following Tertullian—is that the image of God in human beings lies in their finite freedom, and the free human being must *choose* God in an act of freedom and so realize his likeness to God.[179] The key point for the rest of this chapter is that the Fathers considered Christ to be the

---

[178] Here I am only offering the conclusions of a study by von Balthasar that involves both examination of the exegetical problems and the theological proposals of the Fathers and the various modern writers on this question. See "Third Excursus: The Image and Likeness of God," *TD II*, 316 – 334.
[179] Note Vatican II: "authentic freedom is an exceptional sign of the divine image within man." (GS 17)

true image of God and the one to bring us to likeness with God.[180] Sharing in his fire has content!

Returning to the two poles of freedom: each one grounds different characteristics of human freedom.

At the pole of the unique self, human beings are present to themselves through the 'light' of being. This 'light' confers the power to understand and to decide, and these are inseparable, since we cannot choose what we do not know. Von Balthasar is consistent with the ontological tradition that includes Vatican II itself.[181] Moreover, human beings develop *themselves* by knowing and deciding, in relation to the whole of being, in what von Balthasar called 'shared being' which means that human beings are not simply a given.[182] Benedict XVI, for example, says that: "Freedom presupposes that in fundamental decisions, every person and every generation is a new beginning." (SS 24) In a sense human beings 'make' themselves. Nevertheless, humanity is only too aware of the basic ambiguity "between the power to mediate a higher truth of existence and the power to obstruct it through intrusive self-affirmation."[183]

The 'going out' of the human being into all being, in knowledge and love, grounds the other pole of freedom (self-possession) and structures it. Here von Balthasar is not speaking of a *self*-intuition, or one's own grasping of one's own essence. Instead a person's self-possession "articulates itself only *in and with* the

---

[180] Note Origen's comment: "the man who is such as God who made him wished him to be, shall receive from God the power to exist forever and endure for all eternity." *Origen on First Principles*, 39.

[181] Cf. Vatican II: "Man judges rightly that by his intellect he surpasses the material universe, for he shares in the light of the divine mind." (GS 15)

[182] Cf. Vatican II: "Man is not wrong when he regards himself as superior to bodily concerns, and as more than a speck of nature or a nameless constituent of the city of man. For by his interior qualities he outstrips the whole sum of mere things. He plunges into the depths of reality whenever he enters into his own heart; God, Who probes the heart, awaits him there; there he discerns his proper destiny beneath the eyes of God." (GS 14)

[183] *TD I*, 295. Cf. Vatican II: "Profound and rapid changes make it more necessary that no one ignoring the trend of events or drugged by laziness, content himself with a merely individualistic morality." (GS 30)

universal opening to all being."[184] (Original emphasis.) The interrelation of the two poles is disturbed by sin but such a disturbance can only be dealt with in the light of revelation. (See below.)[185]

Interestingly the universal openness to all being is aided in its operation by the participation in the *communio* of the Church that we discussed in the previous chapter.

Now another feature of human freedom is that humans learn by experience. He or she encounters others endowed with freedoms that he or she cannot absorb. The other freedoms need to choose to relate to him. This fact is crucial if man is to respond to God's revelation correctly. God's revelation—in which God chooses to relate to man in love—shows that finite freedom is, in fact, only fulfilled in the loving initiative of the infinite freedom of God.[186]

How does von Balthasar explain this last statement? Well, he returns to the ontology of uncreated Being. The divine persons of the Trinity are defined by their relations such that they are "perfectly transparent one to another, *and* they possess a kind of impenetrable 'personal' mystery."[187] (Emphasis added.) This transparency and self-surrender, through which infinite freedom exists, means that the infinite freedom of the divine has the character of a 'letting-be' in von Balthasar's phenomenological lexicon.[188] Each procession of a divine Person is fundamentally an eternal 'letting-be' of the other. The divine Son is truly God because the Father eternally lets this to be so, and similarly for the Holy Spirit, who is eternally let be by the Divine Father and the Divine Son. In loving

---

[184] *TD II*, 211. Cf. Vatican II: "cannot fully find himself except through a sincere gift of himself." (GS 24) Then when it speaks of man's entry into working, the council says: "For when a man works he not only alters things and society, he develops himself as well. He learns much, he cultivates his resources, he goes outside of himself and beyond himself." (GS 35)

[185] See Vatican II: "Since man's freedom has been damaged by sin, only by the aid of God's grace can he bring such a relationship with God into full flower." (GS 17)

[186] Von Balthasar has noted pre- Christian hints of this concept. He refers to the concept of *eudaimonia* in Democritus and the *daimonium* of Socrates. *TD II*, 199.

[187] *TD II*, 258.

[188] See *TL I*.

obedience, the Son only eternally chooses what the Father wills and the Father wills out of love for the Son because there is only one divine will.

The fundamental character of the 'letting-be' in infinite freedom means that when finite freedom encounters it, finite freedom is not dissolved or overwhelmed, but rather it is 'let-be' by God who is the loving Other in the dialog of existence. In fact, this is how finite freedom came to be in the first place. But letting-be characterizes finite freedom as well. The most fundamental feature of created human freedom is that it reaches for what is *perceived* as good. But in freedom, it is not only the will but the intellect that operates, and so knowledge of what is good means that real human freedom is indifferent. In von Balthasar's words, an 'indifferent' person in this sense, "is able to let the Good be."[189] Here again we have the *Ignatian* reminder of the role of indifference, and it is already apparent at the philosophical level of reflection on freedom.[190] Now we did mention sin above . . . .

(iii) Sin and Dialogue

The reason for spending so much time on the nature of human freedom, so crucial in the theodrama, aside from having a properly developed theology of freedom, is to highlight again the dialogal nature of human being. Philosophically we come to be who we potentially can be through a dialogue with the world and particularly with other persons. Human freedom is not reducible to self-possession.[191] In fact, the cutting-off of dialogue can be understood as the basis of sin.

---

[189] Ibidem.

[190] In the statement of the Principle and Foundation, Ignatius wrote: "We should not prefer health to sickness, riches to poverty . . . and so in all things we should desire and choose only those things which best help us attain the end for which we are created." Ignatius of Loyola, *The Spiritual Exercises of St. Ignatius,* Anthony Mottola trans., (New York: Doubleday, Image Books, 1989), 48.

[191] Consider Vatican II's teaching: "Modern atheism often takes on a systematic expression which, in addition to other causes, stretches the desires for human independence to such a point that it poses difficulties against any kind of dependence on God. Those who profess atheism of this sort maintain that it gives man freedom to be an end unto himself, the sole artisan and creator of his own history." (GS 20)

With created freedom comes the possibility of sin. It is sin when the first pole of human freedom, namely self-possession is made into an absolute. As the Second Vatican Council explained, by "refusing to acknowledge God as his source, man has also upset the relationship which should link him to his last end." (GS 13) Attending purely to self-possession means that the indebtedness, the vocation and the mission of the human being lose their structure. Because divine self-giving created the two poles of human freedom, ignoring the structure of finite freedom means that the dynamism of the search for the good (the Christian *eros*) is reduced to a power over a good. When this happens then the human person himself becomes the source of the norm of what is good.[192] The human person is then caught in a contradiction that affects the relationship with God by claiming—or at least acting as if—man himself is an alternative absolute entity. The same contradiction arises in human relationships if a person falls into the illusion of being absolute in a relationship.

Now it is this structure of human freedom that is transformed in Jesus Christ.

Drama: Election, Vocation and Mission in Christ[193]

(i) Christ the Source of our Election as Theological Persons

In the 'fire' brought to the earth by Christ, active Christians become part of the 'blaze' as the theodrama is played out. In the previous section, the relational structure within which finite freedom is created and sustained by infinite freedom and for which it will always be indebted, forms finite freedom as both a given (election) and yet calls it (vocation) out of itself (mission). So, finite freedom already has a mission by its openness to God.[194] Then, when

---

[192] This is the moving towards the will to power as conceived by Friedrich Nietzsche. Cf. *TD IV*, 163.

[193] John Paul II taught that "the Gospel parable [Matthew 20:1 – 2] sets before our eyes the Lord's vast vineyard and the multitude of persons, both men and women who are called and sent forth by him to labor in it." (*Christfideles laici, CL*, 1)

[194] See Vatican II: "out of this religious mission itself come a function, a light and an energy which can serve to structure

Christians decide, through grace, to follow in the self-surrender of the Son to the Father, in the Holy Spirit, they approach the goal of freedom through the mediation of Jesus Christ, and in him they share in the life of the Trinity.[195] Only in this way is it clear that the finite freedom is in a constant search for God as such, and is not simply in a search for self-fulfillment. Both 'poles' of finite freedom are operant as the believer becomes more of a self-possessed individual (coming to his or her God-given identity), in direct proportion to going out of himself in graced self-surrender as part of the loving relationship of Jesus Christ to the Father in the Holy Spirit.

The presence of Christ on the world stage trans-formed the structure of freedom. But how do von Balthasar and the tradition of the Church explain this? He takes the explanation offered by Paul in the New Testament. In the *Letter to the Corinthians*, Paul wrote citing the *Book of Genesis*: "So, too, it is written, 'the first man Adam, became a living being,' the last Adam a life-giving spirit." (1 Corinthians 15:45)[196] More formally, the 'Adam-principle'—to borrow von Balthasar's term—is taken up into and transcended by the second principle that of Christ himself.[197] As the author of the *Second Letter of Peter* wrote: "His divine power has bestowed on us everything that makes for life and devotion, through the knowledge of him who called us by his own glory and power. Through these . . . you may come to share in the divine nature." (2 Peter1: 3, 4)[198] Before this happened man was not able to understand himself. This fact sets a real limit on the capacities of political and social theories to help man understand himself, unless they are rooted in Christian anthropology, unless they are part of the exchange of the *communio*. This exchange is part of the drama of life. Regarding the mission of the Church and

---

and consolidate the human community according to the divine law." (GS 42)

[195] See too Vatican II's teaching that "The followers of Christ are called by God, not because of their works, but according to His own purpose and grace. They are justified in the Lord Jesus, because in the baptism of faith they truly become sons of God and sharers in the divine nature. In this way they are really made holy." (LG 39)

[196] Cited in *TD III*, 35.

[197] *TD III*, 34.

[198] Cited in *TD III*, 35.

its members, the Second Vatican Council taught that "out of this religious mission itself come a function, a light and an energy which can serve to structure and consolidate the human community according to the divine law." (GS, 42) There is that fire again! So the Church and its members learn from Christ in whose Spirit they live and form community (*communio*).

Given that Christ is the Incarnate Son, the previous paragraph then means that "Christianity will be the only fully satisfactory unfolding of what has been implied in the first experience of Being on the part of the awakening human spirit."[199] Human beings were created to go out into Being, in loving understanding. The life of the Christian is realized as the infinite freedom of God accompanies the finite freedom of the human being and shows it the true object of its search. Once again the unique quality of Christianity is evident!

Pausing at this point to review what this means for the laity: it is apparent that in grace laypeople receive an experience and understanding of freedom that is not merely the possibility of doing *something*. The popular western idea of freedom as the selfish license to do something diminishes the rich Christian notion of freedom as coming to self-possession through reaching out in love.[200] Thus the

---

[199] Hans Urs von Balthasar, "Movement toward God," *Explorations in Theology III: Creator Spirit*, Brian McNeil C.R.V., (San Francisco: Ignatius Press, 1993), 17.

[200] In the psychological studies of Luigi Rulla S.J. et al, the psychological components of self-transcendence and their contribution to personal consistency are well documented. See Luigi Rulla S.J., Sr. Joyce Ridick S.S.C. and Franco Imoda S.J., *Entering and Leaving Vocation: Instrapsychic Dynamics*, (Rome: Gregorian University Press, 1976), 13. There is a striking parallel here with the teaching of John Paul II in his chapter on 'Man in the Dimension of Gift' in *Man and Woman He created Them: A Theology of the Body*, Michael Waldstein ed., trans., (Boston: Pauline Books and Media, 2006), 178-203. Note too John Paul II's comment on the lesser perspectives on freedom: "All too often freedom is confused with the instinct for individual or collective interest or with the instinct for combat and domination, whatever be the ideological colors with which they are covered. Obviously these instincts exist and are operative, but no truly human economy will be possible unless they are taken up, directed and dominated by the deepest powers in man which decide the true culture of peoples." (RD, 55)

Christian has to actually learn about freedom and how to exercise it from Jesus Christ himself.[201] In fact the Second Vatican Council stated that: "[Christians] must follow in His footsteps and conform themselves to His image seeking the will of the Father in all things." (LG 40) They have indicated the aesthetic dimension of Christian existence as it comes into its active expressive form through participation in the theodrama. Thirdly, the comments emphasize the need for conversion both to Christianity and then within Christianity to becoming more and more a follower of Christ.

Lastly, the Christian exercise of freedom has a special quality. The lay person prays: "may your will be done on earth as it is in heaven." (Matthew 6:10) This means that in following the will of the Father, the Christian is 'playing a role,' in von Balthasar's sense. But this is not a role that the Christian is writing for himself—many elements of the role are already 'scripted' in the scriptures, the tradition and the socio-historical situation of the individual. He or she is only going to learn about this role through the *communio* of the Church. So that at this point, with creation and redemption already in progress, "much has already been decided . . . the relation between God and the world, man's specific constitution, matters of Christology and ecclesiology and the doctrine of the Last Things."[202]

This is why von Balthasar cited the philosopher Maurice Blondel's understanding of the situation of the Christian in his *L'Action*. Blondel said: "It is not simply a case of doing all the good one wants to do, and deciding to do it in an act of free good will. The important and hard thing is to do it in the right manner, in a spirit of humility and calm, sensing the

---

[201] See John Paul II's comment: "Jesus Christ meets the man of every age, including our own, with the same words: "You will know the truth, and the truth will make you free." These words contain both a fundamental requirement and a warning: the requirement of an honest relationship with regard to truth as a condition for authentic freedom, and the warning to avoid every kind of illusory freedom, every superficial unilateral freedom, every freedom that fails to enter into the whole truth about man and the world." (RD, 35)

[202] Hans Urs von Balthasar, *Theodrama II: Dramatis Personae: Man in God*, 188.

presence of another will by which one has to take one's bearings."²⁰³ This illustration concludes the reflection on the theological understanding of freedom.

The next topic to be considered is how the individual participates in Christ's mission or catches Christ's fire.

(ii) Von Balthasar's 'Consciousness Christology'

As a way to explain the new situation of the Christian in Christ, von Balthasar offered what he called his "Consciousness Christology"²⁰⁴ which centers on Christ's awareness of his mission.

The Jesus of the *Gospel of John* knows that he has been sent by the Father through the Holy Spirit.²⁰⁵ But Jesus Christ's consciousness as a personal human subject (his "I" consciousness) is identical with his consciousness of his mission.²⁰⁶ The scripture texts such as: "the Father loves the Son and shows him everything he does," (John 5:20) cannot be reduced to referring only to Christ's pre-existence as the Son. It is possible—and necessary—to interpret them as applying to Jesus' experience on earth as well. Hence, Jesus does not discover anything new at his Baptism or on Mount Tabor or in the Temple. This would contradict the perfect coincidence of his person and his mission with its Trinitarian root in the relationship of the Father and the Son. (The mission is

---

²⁰³ Maurice Blondel, *L'Action*, (1893) cited in *Theodrama IV: The Action*, Graham Harrison trans., (San Francisco: Ignatius Press, 1994), 151.

²⁰⁴ *TD III*, 201.

²⁰⁵ In von Balthasar's view, the New Testament forms a unity that gets its form from Jesus Christ. The individual books offer successive theologies yet they are always written from within the Spirit of Christ. The Gospel of John is the 'vanishing point' that is "the point to which we are always traveling – though all of the theologies . . . remain open both forwards (into the mediation of the Church, which can never come to its end) and upwards (to God)." *GL VII*, 10.

²⁰⁶ Von Balthasar illustrates this identification of personhood and mission by referring to John 16: 32 which says that: "The time will come . . . when you will be scattered . . . leaving me alone. Yet I am not alone because the Father is with me." The forsakenness of the Son is a central part of the mission. The intimate union of father and Son remains "even when it appears in the mode of God's turning away from him." *TD III*, 450. Cf. also *TD III*, 230.

rooted in the divine procession.)[207] In Christ and uniquely in Christ is the identity—to cite Theodor Haecker: "between the sublime actor and the role he has to play."[208] Von Balthasar adopted the theatrical terms to clarify the relation between Christ's person and his mission. Three things can be said about this relation.

First of all, Jesus Christ is the perfect dramatic character. By playing his role, he "either attains his true face or (in analytic drama) unveils his hidden face."[209] Von Balthasar's point here is that 'being' and 'seeming', which are constant problems that humans face (highlighted in the discussion of being 'image' and 'likeness') are united in Christ because he does the will of the Father. In this von Balthasar not only stays within the Christian tradition but also shows the fundamental inadequacy of two weak philosophical attempts to identify the basis for the human role—that is to answer the question: "who am I?"

The two flawed positions are (i) the Stoic one where the human individual is simply a part (an emanation) of the whole, and (ii) the Neo-Platonist position, where the individual has an identity ever in front of him to be striven after.[210] In both of these, the role of the person amounts to an alienation of self. Responding to these positions, Thomas Aquinas "waged a fierce battle, as a Christian fighting for the individual".[211] The solution that von Balthasar developed, following Aquinas and the Jewish philosopher Martin Buber, is that the individual is addressed through the Word-Spirit, and hence the individual is "constituted as an 'I' and is able to grasp God as his true 'thou'."[212] Given the work of the Word-

---

[207] Hans Urs von Balthasar noted that: "Thomas Aquinas describes this identity [between actor and role] by saying that in Christ the *processio* within the godhead, which constitutes the Son as the father's dialogue partner, is identical, in God's going from himself toward the world, with the *missio*, the sending of the Son to mankind. (This mission is completed by the sending of the Spirit into the world, proceeding from both the Father and the Son." *TD I*, 646. He refers to *ST I* q.43 a. 1 – 8.
[208] *TD I*, 646.
[209] *TD III*, 201.
[210] Cf. *TD I*, 545.
[211] *TD I*, 549.
[212] *TD I*, 641.

Spirit in this process, the individual (the lay person) can only come to understand himself within the context of the community of the Church.

Secondly, only in Christ is there a complete identity between the actor and the role because: "The Son's mission is the economic form of his eternal procession from the Father."[213] However, other individuals experience a great personal struggle in this regard. The identity in Christ comes about because his mission to the world is intimately linked to his divine personhood. In following Christ, the lay person is called to bring his person, and the role to which he has been called, into ever greater alignment.[214]

Thirdly, because he is who he is, Jesus Christ gives the entire *drama* of salvation its meaning. On the stage, the lead character develops the roles of the other actors precisely through *playing* the lead. The person of the Logos "constitutes the final proportional between the two [divine and created being] and hence must be the concrete '*analogia entis*' itself" for the rest of the actors.[215] Here von Balthasar is arguing from the transformation of Being itself by Christ. As the lead, Christ is "*the* person in an absolute sense" in relation to the Father through the Spirit.[216] As concrete *analogia entis*, the Life, Death and Resurrection of Christ restructures the 'world-stage' as the place of dialogue for human beings with God and each other.[217]

---

[213] *TD III*, 200. Von Balthasar refers to ST I 43 art.1.

[214] Note Vatican II's teaching that: "all Christ's faithful, whatever be the conditions, duties and circumstances of their lives-and indeed through all these, will daily increase in holiness, if they receive all things with faith from the hand of their heavenly Father and if they cooperate with the divine will." (LG 41)

[215] *TD III*, 222.

[216] *TD III*, 509. (His emphasis.) Yves Congar started from the Scriptures and the principles noted by Thomas Aquinas of the higher order influencing the lower: "All things will be gathered under Christ, as their one head: a single hierarchical total order, consequent on the perfect dominance of the higher principle over the lower elements, and finally on perfect dominance of the higher principle of the *Pneuma*, the gift that belongs to the messianic era." *Lay People in the Church*, 69.

[217] Von Balthasar reviews the history of the theory of dialogue. *TD I*, 625 – 643. Note that Yves Congar has an identical view with respect to the role of Christ as the Son

On the one hand, Christ transforms the relation of all humanity to God. God speaks through the experience of *this* man and man experiences God through *this* man.[218] As fully divine and fully human, Jesus Christ is the fullest relationship possible between the "world-stage" and God: "I have given them the glory you gave me so that they may be one as we are one." (John 17:22)

On the other hand, Christ changes people's intersubjectivity as well. As people join the Church, they do not 'dissolve' into one amorphous personality but are rather graced "from above." (Ephesians 4:10). They are in a sense entering the consciousness of Christ by Christ's grace. As individual persons, they *know* that Christ died for them, they *believe* it and they *act* upon it, most especially in the celebration of Eucharist.[219] It is the graced knowing, believing and acting of individuals that includes them in the work of Christ.[220] Such a change transforms their whole

---

incarnate: "When God accomplishes his purpose in respect of creation, not only from the height of the Godhead but by becoming man, he then ceases to exert his power only as God and exerts it also as man; and the manhood thus joined to him for the fulfilling of his purpose becomes the universal and supreme cause of all that depends on the design of grace." Yves Congar, *Jesus Christ, Notre Mediator, Notre Seigneur*, 144, cited by Timothy Macdonald, *The Ecclesiology of Yves Congar: Foundational Themes*, (New York: University Press of America, 1984), 96.

[218] Cf. Yves Congar: "Jesus Christ is the reality of the fellowship-Temple, which is none other than his fellowship-Body (John 2:21)." Yves Congar, *Lay People in the Church*, 54. See also John Paul II: "The Lord himself renews his invitation to all the Lay faithful to come closer to him every day, and with the recognition that what is his is also their own (Philippians 2:5), they ought to associate themselves with him in his saving mission." (CL, 2)

[219] Cf. also Yves Congar. Christ "is the head of the Church, but the head of all creation as well." Yves Congar, *Lay People in the Church*, 58. Note also Vatican II's words when speaking of the lay faithful: "Taking part in the Eucharistic sacrifice, which is the fount and apex of the whole Christian life, they offer the Divine Victim to God, and offer themselves along with it." (LG 11)

[220] The connection between the action of Christ and the community which calls itself the Church of Christ rests on the faith of sinners but primarily on Mary's consent.

intersubjective world.²²¹ In fact, it is only when the human intersubjectivity becomes transparent to the I-Thou relation with God, and is borne by it, that the depths of intersubjectivity between persons are plumbed through grace.

The Christology offered here is neither an 'ascending' nor a 'descending' Christology, instead it is an *integrating* Christology.²²² It offers a substantial answer to the long ideological struggle that started early in the last century to identify 'ascending' and 'descending' Christologies and to give ascendency to one or the other.

Individuals, in the drama of Christ, then are *new* persons in Christ so they become 'theological persons' in von Balthasar's lexicon.²²³ The fundamental nature of this category is reiterated in John Paul II's statement that the mystery of Christ "constitutes the Christian's most basic features." (CL, 9) Similarly von Balthasar defined 'theological persons' as being 'in' Christ and his mission. Such a conception of person is the human analog to the form of Christ resting on the Son's being sent by the Father and having the absolute all-encompassing mission of bringing creation back to the Father.

As people are drawn into the perfect personal relationship between the Son, and the Father, in the Spirit, the restoration of the intersubjectivity that is the original created image of God takes place. As Yves Congar O.P. tells us, "man's integrity is seen also to be an effect of the triumph of the Spirit which raised Jesus from the dead, which has to restore the world and in man, from one end to the other, the integrity of the vestiges or image of God which are in them."²²⁴ The

---

[221] Vatican II simply notes that: "Celebrating the Eucharistic sacrifice therefore, we are most closely united to the Church in heaven in communion with and venerating the memory first of all of the glorious ever-Virgin Mary, of Blessed Joseph and the blessed apostles and martyrs and of all the saints." (LG 50)

[222] See Marc Ouellet, "Foundations of Christian Ethics," *Communio* 17 (Fall, 1990), 381.

[223] In my view this term is the beginning of the answer to the criticism posed by Thomas G. Dalzell, S.M., who complains of the "lack of social drama in Balthasar's theological dramatics." See his article with this title in *Theological Studies* 60 (1999).

[224] Yves Congar, *Lay People in the Church*, 60.

Christian individual is becoming a person not simply in a philosophical sense but in a theological sense as well.

The concept of 'theological personhood' grounds von Balthasar's theology of the Christian life. But how exactly does 'theological personhood' come about?

(a) Dying and Rising with Christ

Saint Paul wrote to the Romans: "You have been taught that when we were baptized in Christ Jesus we were baptized into his death, in other words when we were baptized we went into the tomb with him and joined him in death, so that as Christ was raised from the dead by the Father's glory, we too might live a new life." (Romans 6:3, 4) This part of the *Letter to the Romans* immediately raises the question, what does joining Jesus in his Death and Resurrection mean?

Christians (a term not used by Paul) are understood as living 'in Christ' (*en Christoi*) in the Pauline writings.[225] Paul understood himself and his fellow believers as having been expropriated by Christ precisely through his Death and Resurrection. To understand this more deeply we need to start from the nature of Christ's mission. The understanding of tragedy in the theater provides a starting point for our reflection.

Firstly, a human hero can only bear his own tragedy in the face of an unforgiving fate, but the divine Son faced the *whole* tragedy of humanity out of obedience to the Father. In von Balthasar's Trinitarian theology, the locus of the world is 'between' the Father and the Son.[226] In other words, all that the world is

---

[225] Von Balthasar does not offer an exhaustive list. Cf. Galations 2:19 – 20. There is also the reciprocity of the texts 'we in Christ' and 'Christ in us'.

[226] I use the term 'shorthand' because von Balthasar used the Trinitarian formulation as the summary of the argument. One has to consider the shorthand form as founded on all of the more nuanced statements that lead up to it since he really does hold to the notion of analogy with the 'ever greater dissimilarity' as defined by Lateran IV. In fact, he offers a lengthy philosophical analysis of self-possession and relationality so that their Trinitarian and incarnational features are highlighted but only if creation is understood as

(even in terms of sin) only exists in the Son, precisely because he is the One who receives being eternally from the generous Father. Consequently, the alienation of the world can only be resolved between the Father, and the Son, in the Spirit, so: "The entire act of judgment remains contained within the love of the Father who gives up (John 3: 16) and the love of the Son who places himself at his disposal."[227]

To bear the human tragedy, Jesus Christ had to be a conscious human subject. Each conscious subject is *quodammodo omnia* –in Thomas' terms– which means that, at least in principle, the subject is open to the whole of being. Thus, "every man, insofar as he possesses complete human nature, has access through love and understanding to all that is felt.[228] Nevertheless, as O'Donnell sums it: "Jesus is real man only as assumed man."[229] This is the key difference between Christ and a human hero, and then the Son's assumption of human nature also becomes the basis for the Christian's election in Christ.

Secondly, in human tragedy, there is usually a way of being reconciled to some degree. In the divine-human drama, it is the pure grace of the forgiving Father that reconciles the world completely with God. The reconciliation was realized in the Life, Death and Resurrection of Christ, in other words in the fulfillment of his mission.

Jesus' dying as the bearer of humankind meant that he freely accepted the guilt of humankind and bore the wrath of God. Now affirming God's wrath is not an anthropomorphism. With Rabbi Abraham Heschel, von Balthasar believed that the "'pathos' on God's part . . . [is] identical with God's ethos" and just as Jesus revealed the pathos of God (his love, his anger) throughout his life, he revealed it supremely in his Death.[231] The union of natures in Jesus Christ made him the arena of conflict between the wrath of God and the human being threatened with death from

---

taking place through the Word. Cf. *TD II*, 200 – 213 and 238 – 242. And then philosophy finds its completion in theology.
[227] *GL VII*, 225.
[228] *TD III*, 272.
[229] John O'Donnell, *Hans Urs von Balthasar*, (England: Geoffrey Chapman, 1992), 48.
[231] *TD IV*, 344. He uses Abraham J. Heschel's *The Prophets*, (New York, Evanston: Harper and Row, 1955).

his sin.[232] Christ's Death is a representative action based on the personal choice of the Son who was incarnated into the situation of the sinner.

So for example, Anselm's theory of satisfaction both grasped the unity of God's righteousness and his love, and the inner logic of the new relationship with God, being achieved by an act within the world. Clearly, the Passion and Resurrection of Christ are not merely a 'visual aid' that God is using to instruct us.[233]

Christ completed his mission in giving up his Spirit in death. The Spirit is both the Spirit of the Father offering his Son and the Spirit of the incarnate Son who is sacrificed and glorified.[234] It is this same Spirit that is given to human beings to set them on fire. The Spirit embraces the whole economy of Jesus' life and thus human beings are drawn into *his* Life, Death, and Resurrection. Thus: "If in union with Christ, we have imitated his death, we shall also imitate him in his resurrection." (Romans 6:5) This is the fire he brings upon the earth. Von Balthasar emphasized that what takes place in humanity is prior to humanity's embracing it in faith. He reminds us that "the whole of human nature is co-crucified and co-risen (Cyril)," and also of Gregory of Nazianzen's maxim that: "What has not been assumed has not been redeemed."[235]

It must be noted that for Christians, the passage from death to resurrection is not immediate but rather eschatological. The existence of death and resurrection means rather that, "wherever we may be, we carry with us in our body the death of Jesus, so that the life of Jesus too may be seen in our body." (2 Corinthians 4:10)

So, Christians join the mission of Christ and find their missions in the Spirit. But Christ's disciples do not have the same relation to the Father as he does, rather he makes them "coheirs" with him, though the Spirit. (Romans 8:29) The Spirit of Christ is their fire! Von Balthasar completed his presentation of the 'economic Trinity' with this action of the sending of the

---

[232] He cites K. Barth, *Church Dogmatics* II/1, 396. Cited on *TD IV*, 346.
[233] *TD III*, 117.
[234] He has noted Thomas' distinction that Jesus always enjoyed the *gratia capitis* but it only operated through his Passion. (See *ST III* q. 48) *TD IV*, 390.
[235] *TD III*, 238.

Spirit. We can conclude that Christ's disciples join him in his role of revealing the goodness of God, not just by word but in action as well. This is the fire in action. More precisely, turning to Paul's experience, we could say of the Christian: God "chose to reveal his Son" in him. (Galatians 1:16) He showed his power in him. (2 Corinthians 12:9) With the result that he had "Christ's truth in [him]," (2 Corinthians 11:10) and he lived with the life of Christ. (Galatians 2:19, 20) But Paul was not operating independently rather all of this happened to Paul because he was part of the Church of Jesus Christ.

(b) The Church

The analysis of the I-Thou address in the section on dialogue (above) showed that the human community is crucial to the individual. But the Church does not depend on the merely created capacity for relationships—it is not only a sociological entity. Instead, the Church is based on the redeemed participation of the creature in the relationships of the Divine Trinity. This is a common theme in efforts to present a theology of the laity. So for example, regarding *Christifideles laici*—in the words of Robert W. Olivier: "the relationship of the Church to the Holy Trinity formed the theological and ecclesiological basis upon which the Synod [1987] and Pope John Paul established their reflections on the vocation of the Laity."[236]

The same insight is found in the *Letters of John*. The Johannine community could write: "What we have seen and heard, we are telling you, so that you too may be in union with us, as we are in union with the Father and with his Son Jesus Christ." (1 John 1: 3) More precisely, because Christ is the one who unites us and brings us into the union with the Father, it must be said that the "*subject* of the Church

---

[236] Robert W. Olivier, *The Vocation of the Laity to Evangelization*, (Rome: Editrice Pontificia Universitas Gregoriana, 1997), 21.

is Christ." (Emphasis added.)[237] He is the Head of the Body, the Church. (cf. Colossians 1: 18)[238]

Paul's 'Head-Body' metaphor also emphasizes the fundamental relationship of working together and suffering together, that constitutes the Church and makes it unique among the institutions of the world.[239] Von Balthasar cites Aquinas' phrase in this regard– Christ and the Church form "a single mystic person."[240] This is crucial for appreciating how Christians take on the fire of Christ as well as the starting point for all kinds of theological reflections such as the way in which the Church reads the Scriptures, for example. Hence the study of the Church simply in terms of its parts, or its history, or certain individual members, leaves one without a real understanding of the Church itself.

Christ's headship illuminates our understanding of another Christological concept that will be useful for lay theology, namely *kenosis*. The Church flows from the Cross and Resurrection of Christ.[241] It results from the kenosis (the self-emptying) of Christ as the Head. Von Balthasar is following Aquinas' distinction in this formulation. (ST II q. 48) Thus he based his explanation of the constitution of the Church on the action of Christ alone, 'while we were yet sinners,' and not on the action of the members of the Church. Christ possessed the grace as Head of the Church, from the moment of

---

[237] Von Balthasar cited Thomas' notion of *quasi unam personam* as the relationship between Christ and the Church where the "Head (who possesses the *gratia capitis* for the whole Body) can 'merit for the members.'" *TD III*, 343.

[238] John Paul II called Christ the True Vine (John 15:1). And then in the same article he also says of the Church "she herself is the vine." (*CL*, 8.)

[239] Cf. I Corinthians 12:12 – 30; Ephesians 1:22, 23.

[240] *TD III*, 242. Cf. *ST III* q.19 a. 4. See also Bonnet's emphatic "neither can this interplay of ecclesial relationships . . . be called the 'subject' of the Church; this subject is made up (*coalescit*) of human and divine elements." Pier Antonio Bonnet, "The *Christifidelis* restored to His role as Human Protagonist in the Church." Renè Latourelle ed., *Vatican II Assessment and Perspectives Vol I*, (New York: Paulist Press, 1988).

[241] Cf. The Second Vatican Council: "By communicating his Spirit Christ mystically constitutes as his body those brothers of his who are called from every nation." (LG, 7)

conception, but it only functioned in human history through the Passion.²⁴²

The power of the Cross, pouring out in time, can be traced back to the eternal timeless "*kenosis*" of the Father in the begetting of the Son. Von Balthasar did apply the term *kenosis* to the Father but put it in parentheses. His explanation was that: "the Father strips himself, without remainder, of his Godhead and hands it over the Son; he 'imparts' to the Son all that is his . . .. The Father must not be thought to exist 'prior' to this self-surrender (in the Arian sense); he *is* this movement of self-giving that holds nothing back."²⁴³ (His emphasis.)

The eternal self-emptying of the Father grounds all subsequent *kenoses*, from the gifting of creatures with freedom, to the covenant with Israel, and hence the whole of the Old Testament. Most particularly, the eternal generation of the Son is the ground of the mission of the Son in time. (Cf. Philippians 2:6ff.) Within this mission, the *kenosis* of Christ on the cross forms the basis for "all [that] we mean by separation, pain and alienation in the world and all we can envisage in terms of loving self-giving, interpersonal relationship and blessedness."²⁴⁵ It is Christ's *kenosis* that gives the Church its character as Church.

Lastly, the *kenosis* of Christ grounds the mission of Christians, since "in your minds you must be the same as Christ Jesus."(Philippians 2:5) This leads in turn to the kenotic structure of Christian life. The lay person pours himself out in service to his fellows for the love of Christ. The developing ontology of the lay person is beginning to gain its interior movement and direction. One can see practical examples of this outpouring in love in one's family, one's care for society and so on.

The kenotic axis at the center of the catching-up of creation into redemption, the operation of the Church, and the defining of the theological person, shows the irreplaceable centrality of the action of Christ.²⁴⁶ He is the lead actor in the drama!

---

²⁴² Cf. Vatican II: "By communicating his Spirit, Christ mysteriously constitutes as his body those brothers of his who are called from every nation." (*LG*, 7)
²⁴³ *TD IV*, 325.
²⁴⁵ *TD IV*, 325.
²⁴⁶ Marc Ouellet, "Foundations of Christian Ethics," 380.

With Christ a new meaning of human togetherness—again we have a change in ontology due to Christ— develops. Participation in the Trinitarian relations, through Christ, means that human togetherness now has an intrinsic value far beyond what it meant before. Human community is not simply a human plurality that differs from divine unity. God who is superlative personhood as unique, individual, and unimaginable is defined by this very same personhood as opposition, cooperation, and surrender, which in turn are the characteristics of the Christian community that it realizing itself. God manifests himself as self-giving and self-surrender in reciprocal love, and in Christ this surrender, self-giving, and love are mediated by the community. Thus, participation in the Christian community becomes the fullest realization of individual theological personhood. It is also the only place where the individual can learn what self-surrender in love really means because it is the place where the full meaning of humanity is being demonstrated day in and day out. Then as well, some human beings who are successful in allowing their lives to be expanded by this meaning—in other words, saints—are always present in the community.

Furthermore within the intersubjective relationships borne in Christ, the Christian individual is both image and likeness, fully individual and fully 'community bearer,' within a community of reciprocal relations.[248] Christians are Christians precisely within an 'ensemble'—to return to the dramatic lexicon. These relationships are part of the fire of Christ.

The Church exists because of what God has done in Christ.[249] But what Christ has done has

---

[248] Similarly Karl Rahner S.J. starts from the intrinsic social nature of the human person and God's offer of salvation to the whole person that is including his social and interpersonal aspect, although his methodology is very different! *Foundations of Christian Faith*, (London: Darton, Longman and Todd, 1978), 343.

[249] Von Balthasar summed up the soteriology of the New testament in five motifs: "(1)The Son himself, through God the Father, for the world's salvation. (2) The Sinless One 'changes places' with sinners . . . (3) Man is thus set free (ransomed, redeemed, released). (4) More than this, however, he is initiated into the divine life of the Trinity. (5) consequently, the whole process is shown to be the result of an initiative on the part of divine love." *TD IV*, 317.

"abiding actuality" because of the work of the Spirit. This is the theological foundation for the 'common matrix' (to use Osborne's phrase) shared by all the members of the Church.[250]

Communion with the Father, and the Son, in the Holy Spirit, is accomplished most especially in the Eucharist. It is the experience of the mediation that was mentioned above: "The blessing cup is a communion with the blood of Christ." (Romans 10:16) The Eucharist is not primarily a means of creating "brotherly fellowship," rather it is the communion with the Father, and the Son, in the Spirit, and it transforms a person into a theological person – *homo ecclesiasticus*—a man or woman of the Church.[251] This is someone who is aflame with the fire of Jesus Christ.

(iii) Jesus Christ: The Source of our Vocation as Theological Persons

Our third Christian characteristic is the fact that we have a vocation. Von Balthasar's most detailed treatment of the call is to be found in the *Christian State of Life*.[252] There he gives us his commentary on the concept of vocation in the *Spiritual Exercises*. Von Balthasar's fundamental proposition is that "the 'where' of the Christian is the stand he takes in [the Father's] will as it is revealed to him again and again in the call that comes through the Word of truth that is the Son."[253] This statement describes exactly how the Christian is a theological person with regard to vocation. The will of the Father becomes the will of the Christian through Christ, hence the Christian can say: "I know that his commandment [which is the expression of his will] is everlasting life." (John 12: 50)

Von Balthasar is emphatic that the call is fundamental to the life of every Christian and it is a concrete call. It is also a temporal occurrence. It happens in time. People are called at a point in their

---

[250] Cf. Kenan B. Osborne, *Ministry: Lay Ministry in the Catholic Church*, (New York: Paulist Press, 1993), 534.
[251] *TD III*, 452. Henri de Lubac had the same thought in his *Splendor of the Church*: "In the original sense of the term, the ecclesiastic—*vir eclesiasticus*—is a churchman . . . .. He is a man in the Church; better a man of the Church." *Splendor of the Church*, 241.
[252] Hans Urs von Balthasar, "The Call," *CSOL*, 391 – 504.
[253] *CSOL*, 391.

history.²⁵⁴ At the philosophical level, in other words, at the level of reflection on Being, the analysis of the I – Thou address showed that people *actually have to be addressed* to become aware of their indebtedness, subjectivity and mission. So at the natural level, human personhood and spiritual life develop from the child being addressed by its mother as a 'thou.' From this address, the child gradually learns that it owes itself to another and not simply in a biological sense. It owes its freedom to another as well. The subjectivity of the child deepens as it encounters other subjects and has to 'leave them room.' Lastly, the I–Thou address calls for a response where: "What I have been given is to be transformed and freely given back."²⁵⁵

Then on the supernatural level, unlike Jesus Christ, people often do not have "an inbuilt awareness of their election."²⁵⁶ Vocation is something even sought in prayer: "May he enlighten the eyes of your mind so that you can see what hope his call holds for you." (Ephesians 1:18) The call of God is, of course, pure grace. It is also unexpected, but even Paul could look back and finally know that he was elect in his mother's womb. (Galatians 1:15)

Secondly, a vocation is 'located' in the will of the Father. This concept gave the *Spiritual Exercises* of Ignatius their novelty over and against the prevailing notion of the stepwise advancement towards God.²⁵⁷

Much of what has been said above applies also to those with vocations to religious and priestly life, but there are clues in the *Christian State of Life* to the nature of a secular vocation. Starting from the story of the artisan Bezalel who was chosen by God to build the Tabernacle in the *Book of Exodus* (Exodus 31: 2 – 6), von Balthasar argued that there is "no abyss between the secular orders and the grace of redemption."²⁵⁸ God's wisdom can enter anyone who is open to it for the good of the Church and the world. It is already glimpsed in the natural sciences, and it is also seen in any skill exercised by someone who is not closed to the ultimate theological possibilities. Von Balthasar's conclusion is that, "this grace-filled

---

[254] Please note his comments on the baptism of infants. *TD II*, 263.
[255] *TD III*, 458.
[256] *TD III*, 263.
[257] *CSOL*, 391.
[258] *CSOL*, 422.

perfecting and appropriating of secular skills by God can manifest itself in a variety of forms and degrees. It can be a restrained, as it were, indirect irradiation of a person's lifework on earth by the blessing grace, as for instance, in the case of a pure scientist; it can be the external employment of one in a secular profession to accomplish the work of God's kingdom as in the case of a doctor, lawyer or journalist; but it can also be an interior laying claim to an individual's whole natural ability as it was in the case of Bezalel."[259]

There is also a historical reason why this recognition of the lay vocation (using 'vocation' in an analogical sense) is crucial. In von Balthasar's view, the specialization of areas of knowledge that took place after the Renaissance isolated the clergy. They are now specialists in the field of religion over against the laity who are specialists in their fields of expertise.[260]

Finally, and most disturbingly perhaps, the call does not necessarily coincide with one's natural aptitudes. Moses haltingly asked: "Who am I that I should go to Pharoah?" (Exodus 3: 11) But the call does coincide with one's *divine* election in the foreknowledge of God. Ignatius' prayer was "Take, O Lord, and receive all my liberty, my memory, my understanding, my entire will, all that I have and possess."[261] There is however an important consideration in von Balthasar's reflection on the question of vocation, as it applies to the lay person, just how specific is the calling?

(a) Is the Lay State the result of a Call?

Up to now, the term 'vocation' has been used without further qualification, but there is another consideration. Does the lay state involve a *specific* vocation? This is important because of the nature of the elements involved in the Christian form of lay life.

As a starting point, there is an important passage in The *Christian State of Life* that is worth citing in full, to avoid confusion about what von Balthasar is suggesting: "The choice of human ways of

---

[259] *CSOL*, 424,
[260] Hans Urs von Balthasar, *Laicat et Plein Apostolat*, E. Bernimont O. P. trans., (Liege: La Penseė Catholique, 1949), 18.
[261] Ignatius Loyola, *The Spiritual Exercises of St. Ignatius*, 104.

life within the purely natural orders and 'vocations'—the choice of a career in medicine or architecture, for instance, but also the choice of the married state and of a particular spouse—cannot be regarded as objects of divine election and vocation in the same way as can the forms of [God's] election to religious and clerical life."[262] This way of stating things respects the distinction between the orders of creation and grace. It is the fact that the choices of a lay person take place *within* the natural order that means that the 'general state' of the baptized faithful is actually distinguishable from the state of election to religious and priestly life.

What might sound harsh, and he acknowledges it as such,[263] is his comment that "what is properly designated as the call of God is always far removed from a sphere in which the call is not heard."[264] For von Balthasar, the 'sphere in which the call [to the State of Election] is not heard' is the general state of the baptized.

The closest that von Balthasar comes to a *particular* lay 'call' is to say that some elements in a lay person's life are *analogous* to the call to the religious or the clerical life.[265] For laity there are 'inspirations', and 'encounters', and other 'natural determinants', that are analogous to divine calls but they come from the Providence of God.[266] Drawing once again on Saint Paul, these elements are in concord with "the mystery of his will, according to his kind intention which he purposed in him." (Ephesians 1:9) They are in accord with his grace. From the perspective of Divine Providence, Paul wrote in the *Letter to the Romans*, "we know that in all things God works for the good of those who love him, who have been called according to his purpose." (Romans 8:28)

How does this proposition relate to John Paul II's point in *Christifideles laici*, for example? John Paul said that the People of God is "moved by this faith [as] it tries to discern authentic signs of God's presence and purpose in the events, the needs, and the longings

---

[262] *CSOL*, 418.
[263] *CSOL*, 421.
[264] *CSOL*, 419.
[265] *CSOL*, 419. Note that John Paul II recognizes a general call to conversion and reconciliation as well as a "special' vocation to the religious life. Cf. *Redemptionis donum*, 3.
[266] *CSOL*, 420.

which it shares with other people of our time." (CL, 3) Then also, the faithful lay person faces all of the elements of the world as the products of Divine Providence. In fact, John Paul II had the same vision of the role of Divine Providence. He expressed it at his first audience: "Man who is the image of God, must—as Saint Thomas again teaches—in some way be led by Providence: but within the proportions of his life."[267] John Paul II picked up the theme of response to God's Providence and building a "unity of life," which again looks towards the aesthetic dimension of the lay Christian life. (CL, 59) This unity comes from being unified through attention to God's plan.

The Pope does distinguish between a 'call' and an 'analogous call' in the same way as von Balthasar. However, he does note that the call to be a priest (as an example of the State of Election, for our purposes) is 'distinctive'.[268] The vocation's distinctiveness rests on the priest's distinctive participation in the priesthood of Christ. The distinctiveness of the religious vocation has already been mentioned. In other speeches, John Paul II did refer to the *general* call to Marriage, for example.[269]

Returning to the experience of Bezalel, in the *Book of Exodus*: God "filled him with the Spirit of God in wisdom, in understanding, in knowledge, and in all kinds of craftsmanship." (Exodus 31:3) For von Balthasar, this gift of God for the building of the Tabernacle "corresponds" to the New Testament concept of *charism*, which "can be the perfecting by grace and the appropriating for the service of God of man's natural talents and abilities."[270] So von Balthasar is not offering a description of the lay state that *separates* the orders of grace and nature. He knows that they are intimately intertwined, but the call to be a priest or religious is clearly distinguishable from the 'call' of a lay person, let us say, to marry *this* person. Hence the latter (lay) is an analog of the former (priest).

---

[267] John Paul II, Audience, 25th October, 1978. Text from *Osservatore Romano*, 2 November 1978, 5.
[268] See John Paul II, *Letter to Priests*, Holy Thursday 1996.
[269] See for example, John Paul II, *Address to the Young People of Slovakia*, June 30, 1995.
[270] *Christian State of Life*, 422. The example of Bezalel is also used in *Bernanos: An Ecclesial Existence*, 154.

The third aspect of life in Christ is the mission that accompanies the vocation can be carried out in the strength of Christ.

(iv) Jesus Christ: The Source of our Mission as Theological persons

As the Son who is eternally begotten by the Father, and sent from the Father in time, Jesus Christ is the perfect unity of person and mission. His is the absolute mission that encompasses all other missions.[271] The mission of Jesus Christ totally defines the notion of mission for all time. The mission of the Christian can be presented in two ways that acknowledge the individual and the community aspects of Christian mission. They are distinguished here purely for heuristic purposes.

a) The Christian as an Individual

The Sacrament of Baptism begins the process of someone becoming a theological person in Christ (on fire in the scriptural lexicon!) The personal profession of faith in Christ and the response to the grace of Baptism is a conscious individual action. This follows from the 'consciousness Christology' that is the hallmark of von Balthasar's work. Now just as the persons of the Trinity don't 'dissolve' into each other, analogously the Christian individual does not 'dissolve' into the person of Christ, in the sense of disappearing. Instead he or she remains a unique and responsible—and accountable—individual.

In their freedom, Christians are given a personally specific mission in Christ as an offer from the sovereign freedom of the Father. Those participating in Christ receive true dramatic roles (with actions that count in the history of salvation) in the history of the world. This analysis corrects certain historical views that might have diminished the role exercised by groups of Christians in the Church. Perhaps the laity has been undervalued over against clerics for example. Yves Congar O.P., to cite one, held that there in-deed is "a tendency towards a clerical

---

[271] Note that Yves Congar is in agreement here with the idea of the higher principle (of the work of the Spirit after the Resurrection) within which the lower elements find their perfection. Yves Congar, *Lay People in the Church*, 60.

view of the Church."[272] However, the identification of the prevailing views of the Church in any particular period is a complex question.

Certainly things are more complex than Piero Bonnet's claim that the Second Vatican Council 'restored the laity to their role as protagonist' in the Church.[273] Conversely von Balthasar's exercise identifies laity active in different historical periods, who exercised their lay character.[274] They really were actors in the sense that they made something present in the stream of history by their actions. They made the revelation of God's goodness in Christ present. Yves Congar O.P. expressed exactly the same thought: "each individual layman must be a witness to the Resurrection and Life of the Lord Jesus, and a sign of the living God." (LG 38) Congar called this process the 'Christofinalization' of the world.[275] A person's individual mission may or may not be highly visible, well known or hidden, social or individual. It may well bear some analogy with figures from the New Testament such as Mary, Paul, Peter, Mary of Bethany etc.

Christians primarily accomplish this mission through their disponibility (Remember Saint Ignatius!) towards the mission.[276] The Christian mission is characterized by obedience as was the mission of Christ himself. Jesus was obedient to the Spirit of God, and this is the Spirit that he shares with his followers. The result of the movement of the Spirit of Jesus Christ is a solidarity which is transformed from the foundation of a common nature, such as one would find in a clan, to a solidarity *in Christ*, which is both somatic and pneumatic, in which "the power of Jesus himself is infused into the believer's mind and being."[277]

The theater metaphor suggests some features of the disponibility that we are considering. For example, an actor is trained to make the gestures and the actions appropriate to his role. Turning from drama to theo-drama, the physical (somatic) dimension of Christian living cannot but be seen

---

[272] Piero Antonio Bonet: "The Christifidelis restored to his role as human protagonist in the Church," 545.
[273] Ibidem.
[274] See *GL III*, for example.
[275] *Lay People in the Church*, 209.
[276] *TD I*, 288.
[277] *TD IV*, 407.

behind this example. In theo-drama there are both moral strictures to identify disordered uses of the body and relationships and there is the chance to actually be the Good Samaritan who lifts the body of the mugging victim onto his donkey. In other words, there is a conforming of one's body to one's role. (See Saint Francis' efforts to regulate Brother Ass. This is not only for saints but for the rest of us too!)[278] Simultaneously one's mind and heart are disponible too: "Learn from me for I am meek and humble of heart." (Matthew 11: 29) (Pneumatic).

In addition, actors are trained to observe. They observe others so that they know how people express themselves, and hence they play their own role better. The Christian is turned towards the Christian community and the lives of the saints, to observe them, since the person of Christ is active in them all making them who they are. Lastly, the actor needs imagination. He has to use his imagination to get into the role. But all technique is ultimately surpassed by inspiration (on fire!) This is a term that lays itself open to the movement of the Spirit.

But the Spirit sent by Jesus Christ is not a 'free-lance' spirit going in all kinds of directions. Christians live out the tension between their created selves and who they can become in the one Spirit of Christ. Another way to express the dichotomy borrows the conception of Thomas Aquinas where human beings exist as a tension between their essence and their existence, and for that reason the human's state of being is one of becoming, of striving for self-realization in the direction of the mission. Even in this striving, von Balthasar sees an image of God. In its very incompleteness, the human life is somehow a "parable" of the fulfilled God.[279]

Just how close is the Christian to his God-given role? In the theater, actors on stage can distinguish between their "I" and their role. Generally, people experience a dichotomy between the core of their being, which is not ready at hand, and the role (mission) that they live in society. According to Plato,

---

[278] Johannes Jörgensen, *Francis of Assisi*, (New York NY: Image Books, 1955).
[279] Hans Urs von Balthasar, "Characteristics of Christianity," *Explorations in Theology I*, (San Francisco: Ignatius Press, 1989), 164.

the individual chooses his role in pre-existence. In the plays of the playwright Calderon, the bonding of the individual, and his role as a Christian in the world, already occur in the mind of God.[280] In the theater, if the actor truly enters the role then he is no longer playing himself.[281] However, something of himself slips through, as it does supremely in Christ and, by derivation, in those who follow Christ right up to the Pauline experience of: "Not I but Christ in me." (Galatians 2:20)

Finally, Christians can refuse their call. Attaining theological personhood depends lovingly accepting the call. Refusal, in von Balthasar's view, does not remove person-hood from the person but makes it "unrecognizable" in the drama of salvation.[282] They have a role but they do not pick it up.

b) The Christian: Bearer of Community[283]

Now there are consequences to a life on fire: the Christian's mission means that he or she leads a 'deprivatised' life. The Christian's interpersonal side as *imago Trinitatis* is opened in Christ. By joining the Son's relationship to the Father in the Spirit, Christians become *bearers* of community. This means that Christians are necessarily ecclesial and so work to develop the larger culture—which is the meaning of a community— too.[284]

The foundation of ecclesial existence, that is existence in Christ, is that Christians join the priesthood of believers.[285] The key aspect of this priesthood is acting on behalf of human beings

---

[280] *TD I*, 252.
[281] *TD II*, 256.
[282] *TD II*, 266.
[283] Compare this with John Paul II's "Mission to Communion" in *Christifideles laici*, 32.
[284] John Paul II mentioned two temptations in this regard (i) One is becoming occupied with the Church at the expense of family, professional and societal obligations and (ii) the other is legitimizing the 'unwarranted' separation of faith and life. *CL*, 2.
[285] Note Vatican II's words: "The baptized, by regeneration and the anointing of the Holy Spirit, are consecrated as a spiritual house and a holy priesthood, in order that through all those works which are those of the Christian man they may offer spiritual sacrifices and proclaim the power of Him who has called them out of darkness into His marvelous light." (LG 10)

through self-sacrifice. (Cf. Hebrews 5:1) In terms of freedom, Christians are the vehicles to open up other people's freedom in Christ.[286] To the degree that Christians enter into the mission of Christ, they open up an 'area' through building relationships where others can develop their own freedom to act. This can range from telling people the truth, to giving someone a roof over their heads, to the greatest level of help of all and that is in the offering of friendship and support to them to be persons.[287] Participants in Christ can mediate Christ's aid to others in their moving towards their goal within the infinite divine freedom.[288]

Christians are part of a very real communion—the communion of saints in Christ—and in it we can pray and serve and suffer for the rest of humanity, and in fact as far as the benefits of Christ's Death and Resurrection extend. They truly have a universal mission in Christ. Von Balthasar cites Origen's analogy between the People of God and the Eucharist, when he says that Christians can serve as sustenance for the Body of Christ (the community), to the degree that they are included in Christ.[289] Christians form part of a continuum where they play a part in the salvation of others (a secondary share in Christ's *pro nobis*), yet without forgetting that they are still

---

[286] Note Vatican II once again: "since they are tightly bound up in all types of temporal affairs it is their special task to order and to throw light upon these affairs in such a way that they may come into being and then continually increase according to Christ to the praise of the Creator and the Redeemer." (LG 31)

[287] Vatican II thought along similar lines: "In order that the exercise of charity on this scale may be unexceptionable in appearance as well as in fact, it is altogether necessary that one should consider in one's neighbor the image of God in which he has been created, and also Christ the Lord to Whom is really offered whatever is given to a needy person. It is imperative also that the freedom and dignity of the person being helped be respected with the utmost consideration, that the purity of one's charitable intentions be not stained by seeking one's own advantage or by striving for domination, and especially that the demands of justice be satisfied lest the giving of what is due in justice be represented as the offering of a charitable gift." (AA 8)

[288] Note Karl Rahner's comment: "Within the Church, he cooperates in rendering this grace historically tangible." Karl Rahner, "Notes on the Lay Apostolate," 324.

[289] *TD III*, 527.

responsible for their own lives and are moving towards their own death and judgment.

The Christian's power (fire) as theological persons in Christ enters into their role and influence in society. Christians, like Christ himself, express truth and values as best they can in each of the passing moments of life. Thus Christians are precisely "infusing lasting values into the changes and chances of life."[290]

Moreover, Christians have to struggle against the sinful dimension of the world. Jesus himself understood that he was at war. He could only enter the strong man's house "once he has tied him up." (Matthew 12:29) (There is a very real enemy who was not even able to be clearly indicated in the Old Covenant.[291]) As a result the disciple too is in a battle with temptations and demons. This battle (drama) has been marginalized in the history of Christian thought, and so the dramatic aspect of dogmatic theology has sometimes been lost as well.

The Christian struggle against evil happens within the Church because, as Saint Augustine knew so well, the two *civitates* (cities) meet in each and every heart.[292]

Further, beyond being in the Church, in their mission, Christians also stand *for* the Church. This is particularly the case where they are the only Christians who are present in a given situation. The communal nature of a Christian's being means that Christians always stand in *persona ecclesia*, with or without a commission.[293] A tragic situation arises when a part of the Church falls into liberalism—for example transposing a belief in American exceptionalism into the sphere of theology—then the

---

[290] *TD IV*, 100.
[291] Cf. TD II, 166. He also lists John 15: 20ff.; I Thessalonians 5: 8; II Corinthians 6: 7; 10: 3 – 6; Romans 6: 13ff.; 23; 13: 12; Philippians 2: 25; Colossians 4: 10; I Timothy 1: 18; II Timothy 2ff. See *TD II*, 165. footnote 68.
[292] *TD II*, 167.
[293] Cf. Karl Rahner: "By the very nature of being a member of the mystical Body of Christ, he is also an active cooperator in the fulfillment of her mission and mandate." This is found in "Notes on the Lay Apostolate," 326. But note also his reminder that "the official apostolic mission is *not* a Lay apostolate." 332. In both points he agrees with von Balthasar.

individual has to witness to a Church that offers no clear appeal. Situations like this occurred in the lives of Athanasius, Maximus the Confessor, Kierkegaard and Pope Martin, to name a few.[294]

Nevertheless, the community dimension of Christian life does not mean that the Christian represents Church authority. What Christians represent is the *role* of the Church, which is to address the world, to love it, and to train it, in true freedom through Christ.

Lastly, Christians are "created in Christ for good works." (Ephesians 2:10) Good works are done because "heaven is open to us through God's kindness."[295] With Paul, von Balthasar see works as pure grace. The one who is actually doing the good is Christ. Christians adopt this standpoint—standing with Christ—and they are consequently empowered by him. (Mark 3:14) They have become full theological persons, because of their union with him, and so the Christian is always at least potentially ready to do good out of love. The *Letter to the Corinthians* sings the praises of the being of love: "If I speak with the tongues of men and of angels, but do not have love, I have become a noisy gong or a clanging cymbal." (I Corinthians 13: 1) The degree of readiness needs to be openness to the point of death as Christ was.

Conclusion: The Battle of the Logos

This conclusion is rather in the nature of an unscientific postscript, because despite the many comments on theological anthropology that have to be made to introduce the notion of the Christian on fire as elect, called, and sent in Christ, the range of applications of these principles is very wide indeed. Culling some of the more general comments from von Balthasar's work on the working out of the Christian life, one can say the following. . . .

The theo-dramatic study starts with the ontological 'stage' that God created for the great historical drama with mankind. The key dramatic moments in the history of salvation are realized on this stage. But so that man is truly involved in his salvation, his *nature* as elect, called, and sent is redeemed and sanctified in Christ. This happened

---

[294] *TD III*, 454.
[295] *TD IV*, 420.

when Christ lived, died, and rose in history. What happens to the individual lay person is that he is 'put on stage' in the drama between man and God. But what is the life like 'on stage'?

To start with: in this situation Christian existence definitely becomes "paradoxical".[296] The Christian has been reconciled to God, in Christ, and yet his opposition to God continues. However, they have a whole new perspective on life and even on their own opposition to God, precisely because they have been redeemed in Christ. So the Christian knows that through all of his decisions and actions, he is still a "sinner and a failure and feeling this to his very bones"[297] Attached to this identification of who he is, is the constant need to do penance in his life, because of the unanswerable question about when he will have done enough penance for his sins and for the sins of humanity? The Christian is before God, both as an individual, and as a member of the community, at the same time.

Furthermore, the tragedy of human existence continues after Christ. As von Balthasar explains it: "the realms of the old Adam and the new, of the murderer and the one murdered but making superabundant atonement for this deed—these realms are at least coextensive."[298] The struggle, interiorly and externally, in the larger society, is permanently present as the core of existence 'on stage'. This is the "Battle of the Logos."[299] The lay person is welcomed into this battle as an active participant and does not leave it. There can be no "flight from the Cross."[300]

In this battle, the lay person makes gestures of existence on the world stage, so as to advance the cause of Christ. These are gestures, first of all in favor of 'Being as a whole.'[301] So they require man's use of his 'intelligent freedom'.[302] These are gestures that are on fire namely they affirm the actual good of beings and relationships, a good that became apparent in the life of the Logos, and is inserted into situations by the

---

[296] Hans Urs von Balthasar, "Tragedy and Christian Faith," *ET III*, 403.
[297] Ibidem.
[298] Ibidem.
[299] *TD IV*, 67.
[300] "Tragedy and Christian Faith," *ET III*, 409.
[301] *TD IV*, 111.
[302] Ibidem. See too Benedict XVI's *Caritas in veritate*.

positive decisions and actions of the Christian individual, and also by the Church. Looking to the scriptural precedent: "Whoever speaks, is to do so as one who is speaking the utterances of God; whoever serves is to do so as one who is serving by the strength which God supplies; so that in all things God may be glorified through Jesus Christ, to whom belongs the glory and dominion forever and ever. Amen." (1 Peter 4:11)

Then, in relationships, the Christian is to make gestures to help the one, to whom he relates, to convert more and more towards what is absolutely true and good to spread the reign of fire upon the earth. Such relationships have to radiate both of justice and mercy. The relationship is seen within the overall context of existence for which Christ has died. Such a Christian perspective helps one avoid the pitfalls of imagining that there is "cheap grace", where one lets the values of another person slide and yet imagines that he receives grace.[303] Grace was bought at the price of the Cross.

Thirdly, the Christian makes gestures of love that in its finest and richest sense means "a love that can stand in the face of the judgment of eternity."[304] To simply present von Balthasar's theology of love would require a volume of its own, but please let two comments suffice. They are taken from his massive study on Georges Bernanos.

The first comment reflects on the nature of real love as opposed to the flawed loves of Bernanos's flawed characters, who love as an expression of the self. Von Balthasar writes: "The situation changes totally, however, when it is a question, not of sinner encountering sinner, but of a sinner standing before a saint as a mirror in which the latter can recognize himself."[305] There is more to explore but we will do this in Chapter Seven.

Von Balthasar's other comment on love, from the writings of Bernanos, is the following: summing up the insight about false love in the novel *Monsieur Ouine*, he says: "The eloquent symbol for the dream character of the whole trilogy is homosexuality, a theme with an oblique, shadowy presence . . .

---

[303] *TD IV*, 113.
[304] *TD IV*, 114.
[305] *Bernanos*, 530.

homosexuality as the perversion of love into self-love, . . . for a love-partner of the same sex is but a duplication and a mirror of the self."[306] These words have to be left without further comment, but by sheer contrast, they illustrate the meaning of the gesture of true love.

But most of all and this is the final gesture that von Balthasar lists: the supreme Christian gesture to his fellows, and to society, is always to show "that there *is* an absolute light" through one's words and deeds.[307] (Original emphasis.) In six words, he has indicated the heart of the battle that lies before the Christian. To bring the absolute into conversations, and into business transactions, and family relationships, and the decision about which party to choose, is the heart of the Christian struggle. To conclude then, von Balthasar gives us this thought: "In the midst of a finitude that can only yield finite things, there springs up the apparently deluded attempt to embrace the infinite, a hope that takes all energies captive and is prepared to endure all manner of renunciations, as in the pre-Christian Quest of the Holy Grail."[308]

---

[306] *Bernanos*, 150.
[307] *TD IV*, 114.
[308] *TD IV*, 115.

Chapter Six "The Word is the Goad"

Introduction
Man rooted in the Cosmos
Man as spirit and body
Man and Woman
    (a) Some Definitions: The Trinity and 'Gender'
    (b) The Ordering of the Mystery of Salvation through 'Gender'.
    (c) The First Part of the 'Feminine' Dyad: Receptivity
        (i) A Proper Understanding of the Notion of 'Feeling'
        (ii) The Christian *Fiat* within culture.
    (d) The Second Part of the 'Feminine' Dyad: Creative Expression
The Individual and Community
Conclusion

Introduction

The chapter title comes from a line by von Balthasar in his essay describing the relationship between the divine Word and history.[1] The full sentence reads as follows: "The Word is the goad of human civilization."[2] Only describing the nature of the presence of the Word in human history in such a forceful way can both present the true state of affairs on the one hand, and on the other, counter the pernicious view that being a 'lay person' in the Church is just another membership among so many. Instead, as has been noted before, "the ordinary believer . . . [is] sent to live the life of the Word" in the world.[3] In other words such a 'membership' is ontological. The being of the Christian himself is transformed. The divine Word develops *human* civilization and takes it to its proper

---

[1] Hans Urs von Balthasar, "The Word and History," *ET I*, 27ff.
[2] "The Word and History," 39. Vatican II has the same teaching: "The Lord is the goal of human history, the focal point of the longings of history and of civilization, the center of the human race, the joy of every heart and the answer to all its yearnings." (LG 45)
[3] Hans Urs von Balthasar, "The Implications of the Life of the Word," *ET I*, 62.

conclusion.⁴ This chapter is concerned with the Christian's need to act in the Theodrama.

A recurring theme in von Balthasar's works is a warning against mere activism. Regarding the building of civilization, the Scriptures, for instance, are not programmatic. As von Balthasar insists: "to be consistently Christian means to be consistently human, if only because no other religion demands and shows such reverence for one's neighbor as well as the body as does the religion of the Incarnate, of Christ and his dual commandment."⁵ It is the transformation of the human, in all of its aspects, that is the fruit of the coming of Christ.⁶ So this chapter will examine some of the more concrete changes wrought in man and his understanding of himself, by the incarnation of the divine Word.

Von Balthasar noted that, philosophically, there are specific "tensions" that describe human existence, and each of these have been transformed in the existence of the Word.⁷ These are the dimensions of (i) man as rooted in the cosmos; (ii) man as spirit and body; (iii) human beings gendered as man and woman, and finally; (iv) man as individual and community.⁸ These are the four main tensions in the existence of the individual in any civilization, and they have all been redeemed and sanctified in the Word, leading to the founding of a new culture.⁹ Here culture

---

⁴ Vatican II refers to Jesus Christ: "Who was crucified and rose again to break the strangle hold of personified evil, so that the world might be fashioned anew according to God's design and reach its fulfillment." (GS 2)
⁵ Hans Urs von Balthasar, *Test Everything: Hold fast to what is good*, trans., Maria Shrady, (San Francisco: Ignatius Press, 1989), 52.
⁶ See Vatican II's teaching: "The council brings to mankind light kindled from the Gospel, and puts at its disposal those saving resources which the Church herself, under the guidance of the Holy Spirit, receives from her Founder. For the human person deserves to be preserved; human society deserves to be renewed. Hence the focal point of our total presentation will be man himself, whole and entire, body and soul, heart and conscience, mind and will." (GS 3)
⁷ *TD II*, 398.
⁸ See *TD II*, 346ff., 355ff., 365ff., and 382ff. respectively
⁹ Von Balthasar has the same philosophical understanding of culture as Vatican II which said: "The word 'culture' in its general sense indicates everything whereby man develops and perfects his many bodily and spiritual qualities; he

"is understood not as a closed system alongside other cultures but as the culture resting on the Word of God and its workings within history, and so [it is] the center to which every culture is polarized, whether positively or negatively."[10] Leaving aside the difficulty that the baptized have in aligning their life with their mission until the next chapter, this chapter examines the four human dimensions that lie at the foundations of the new Christian culture brought by Christ.[11] But these can only be appreciated in the drama of actual existence because man lives in the alienated state "to a large extent in the *natura lapsa* yet . . . able to participate proleptically (*spe, non re*) in the ultimate state" of man in glory.[12] The latter point is just a hint of the eschatological propositions that will have to be made to complete the sketch of man in this life. (See Chapter Seven)

Now we can look at the theology of the human tensions—if I may express it that way. The theology adds some detail to the metaphysics of human being in Christ.

---

strives by his knowledge and his labor, to bring the world itself under his control." (GS 53)

[10] "The Word and History," 43. The Second Vatican Council came to the same understanding building on the anthropology of the Old Testament. It said: "When man develops the earth by the work of his hands or with the aid of technology, in order that it might bear fruit and become a dwelling worthy of the whole human family and when he consciously takes part in the life of social groups, he carries out the design of God manifested at the beginning of time, that he should subdue the earth, perfect creation and develop himself. At the same time he obeys the commandment of Christ that he place himself at the service of his brethren." (GS 57)

[11] Note that John Paul II writes that: "The liberation and salvation brought by the kingdom of God came to the human person both in his physical and spiritual dimensions." (RM, 14) The four dimensions listed by von Balthasar cover these two areas.

[12] *TD II*, 236. Note too Vatican II's teaching that: "Already the final age of the world has come upon us and the renovation of the world is irrevocably decreed and is already anticipated in some kind of a real way; for the Church already on this earth is signed with a sanctity which is real although imperfect." (LG 48)

Man rooted in the Cosmos

Von Balthasar's choice of the word 'cosmos' expresses the locus of man within the whole of being. With the Life, Death and Resurrection of Christ, some wondrous changes took place in man's relation to the cosmos. Prior to the coming of Christ, in various ancient cultures, there was a substantially valid understanding of man as being part of the cosmos, a concept that included the divine realm (*theion*), and then he was also seen as part of the *polis* (community) that mediated the divine *nomos* or law to him.[13] The same understanding saw man as a microcosm of the cosmos itself, in the sense that he is both material and spiritual. The revelation in Christ gave rise to "the releasing of man from a *theion* that is bound to the cosmos and so [was] initiated an irreversible 'history of liberation'."[14] This has several consequences for lay life.

First of all, for example, as illustrated in the thought of Hildegard of Bingen in the Middle Ages, the world is "homininform" which means that it is ordered to man.[15] This concept is a recovery of parts of the ancient insights that we have just reviewed, but now it regards man as being in a world that is separated from the divine being, who far transcends the world. Yet divine being then chose to freely enter the world in Christ. As von Balthasar explains, in Christ "God has unite[d] history and cosmos in himself."[16] Then as a result, man's freedom has been redeemed and sanctified by the infinite freedom of God, but this means that as man determines himself, he is to operate in terms of virtue.[17] Hence man retains his

---

[13] See *TD II*, 351 for example.

[14] *TD III*, 28. The relationship of finite freedom to infinite freedom was studied in the previous chapter.

[15] *TD II*, 354. Benedict XVI uses a different term to refer to the same reality, namely 'human ecology'. For example, he said: "May the light and strength of Jesus help us to respect human ecology, in the knowledge that natural ecology will likewise benefit, since the book of nature is one and indivisible." (*Address of His Holiness to the Diplomatic Corps*, January 11, 2010).

[16] Ibidem.

[17] See John Paul II: "The acting subject personally assimilates the truth contained in the law. He appropriates this truth of his being and makes it his own by his acts and the corresponding virtues." (VS, 52)

position within the cradle of the world (ancient component), even as he is elevated in freedom through Christ (Christian component).

The second consequence for a theology of the laity lies in the shift in man's relationship to the world's institutions.[18] Von Balthasar tantalizes us with the suggestion that the "richer realm" achieved by the aforementioned liberation in Christ "holds out a promise."[19] The promise is for the removal of certain kinds of limits on becoming human, so that no earthly institution can ever again "appropriate [this realm] for its own ends."[20] Man is freed from the potential absolutism of man-made institutions. Note John Paul II's teaching on the institution of work, for example, where he says that: "In the modern period, from the beginning of the industrial age, the Christian truth about work had to oppose the various trends of *materialistic and economistic* thought." (LE 7) These trends ignore the human being doing the work and his or her need to make a living. In addition, the Christian opposition is not fully realized in the things of this world. There is a spiritual dimension to our existence. It takes on the character of a continuing struggle by the one who lives in this world in Christ.[22] This is the eschatological dimension of the presence of the Kingdom of God that is "fighting to assert itself in this world."[23] The struggle is founded in the choice to live in Christ, or to live "following the ruler of the power of the air, the spirit that is now at work in the

---

[18] See also *Gaudium et Spes.*

[19] *TD II*, 398.

[20] Ibidem. Vatican II taught that "The Lord is the goal of human history, the focal point of the longings of history and of civilization, the center of the human race, the joy of every heart and the answer to all its yearnings." (GS 41)

[22] Blondel had also recognized the inherent limitations that are present in philosophy when faced with the truth of Christ: "It follows that even in the heart of a Christian society, even when one has before one's eyes the whole organism of Christian dogmas and Christian precepts, one must continue to respect the limits of philosophical investigation." Maurice Blondel, *The Letter on Apologetics & History and Dogma*, trans. Alexander Dru and Illtyd Trethowan, (Grand Rapids MI: Eerdmans Publishing, 1964), 165.

[23] *TD III*, 53.

disobedient." (Ephesians 2:2)[24] Paul is referring to the struggle *for* the world. The Christian has been drawn into this battle and cannot leave it.

Thirdly, man's new way of being rooted in the world in Christ means that it falls to the Christian to make the best possible response to the problem of integralism. As von Balthasar explains it, the word means the way of thinking that "claims for the Church the means used by those who do not belong to it."[25] Von Balthasar is not advocating cutting oneself off from the world and from the various media and organizations that it possesses, but these can only be valued and used in a way that is "governed by a 'so far as' determined by the Spirit—the Spirit of Jesus Christ."[26] Christ as the goad, the driving force, is operative once again!

The life 'determined by the Spirit'[27] leads to the next feature of this new relationship to the world, which is the 'swordlike life' of the Christian which is "shining and sharp . . . clear-cut so that the truth is reflected."[28] This is, of course, the truth of Jesus

---

[24] See *TD III*, 53. See John Paul II: "Paul's admonition urges us to be watchful, warning us that in the judgments of our conscience the possibility of error is always present. Conscience is not an infallible judge; it can make mistakes. However, error of conscience can be the result of an invincible ignorance, an ignorance of which the subject is not aware and which he is unable to overcome by himself." (VS, 62)

[25] "The Experience of the Church," *ET II*, 14. Similarly de Lubac regards this as a temptation whereas "truly faithful servants . . . may have to mortify much in themselves." *Splendor of the Church*, 279.

[26] Ibidem. The issue of integralism is complex. See Yves Congar's history of the issue in his chapter six entitled "In the World and not of the World," *Lay People in the Church*, 379ff. Note Congar's opinion: "there has been secular world and a fully Lay life only since the time that social and political life has been laicized, and especially since the inauguration of a mechanized civilization which, born outside the Church, has never been consecrated and regulated by her." (393)

[27] Following Thomas Aquinas, Congar refers to "God's holy and hallowing will". *Lay People . . .*, 405.

[28] "The Experience of the Church," *ET II*, 15. Note that Congar too identifies the two dynamics of lay existence as involving "two principal demands, corresponding respectively to an aspect of detachment or transcendence and one of engagement or immanence." *Lay People . . .*, 412. The Second

Christ who represents man's true relationship to the world. The reader will note here the opening towards the theo-*logic*-al study from the perspective of truth that is being indicated at this point. (That study will be presented in Chapter Eight.) The significance of this 'swordlike life' is extensive, but let us look at just one global statement from one of von Balthasar's spiritual writings. He wrote: "a member of the Church lives in and for an ecclesial mission [and] is praying for the necessary grace to fulfill it: for purity and courage for clarity and trust, for understanding and selflessness—for everything needed by a person who, through his life and example, would like to be an apostle of Christ."[29] This is a description of the overall consciousness of the Christian. It offers us a 'consciousness anthropology' to parallel the 'consciousness Christology' that we have already studied.

Even though the list can be extended, one final point is the specifically eschatological one, and that is that Christians have to make judgments concerning the different aspects of the world.[30] They measure things against the standards of Christ, because the end-times are upon us and these 'little' measurements *anticipate* the judgment of the world by Christ when he comes as Judge.[31]

The next tension in human existence that is transformed by Christ is the nature of man as spirit and body.

Man as spirit and body

As spirit and body, man is a microcosm of the cosmos itself. He experiences himself as a series of

---

Vatican Council similarly explains: "While helping the world and receiving many benefits from it, the Church has a single intention: that God's kingdom may come, and that the salvation of the whole human race may come to pass." (GS 45)

[29] Hans Urs von Balthasar, *The Threefold Garland: The World's Salvation in Mary's Prayer*, trans. Erasmo Leiva-Merikakis, (San Francisco: Ignatius Press, 1982), 123.

[30] The Word and History," 37.

[31] Vatican II taught that "With the help of the Holy Spirit, it is the task of the entire People of God, especially pastors and theologians, to hear, distinguish and interpret the many voices of our age, and to judge them in the light of the divine word, so that revealed truth can always be more deeply penetrated, better understood and set forth to greater advantage." (GS 44)

polarities where he is "obliged to engage in reciprocity, always seeking complementarity and peace in the other pole."[32] Man experiences himself as spirit and body. Without examining the historical data on this polarity that is amply supplied by von Balthasar, we place the focus on Christ's trans-formation of the polarity.[33]

The polarity of spirit and body that characterizes man is heightened through Christ in the following sense—von Balthasar argues that: "Jesus Christ can only enter the human sphere at the one pole [as a body], in order from that vantage point, to go on to fulfill the other pole [the spirit]" in love.[34] He deduces this from the 'direction' of the Incarnation, in which the divine Son (God is Spirit. (John 4:24)) takes on flesh. (John 1:14) But the enfleshing of the divine Word does not stop there, the 'descent' of the Word continues on the Cross, the descent into Hell, and finally, into sacramental food for all.

At the same time, the descent is an *ascent* of the flesh into the divine Spirit. The new rhythm of the life of the believer is that of life in the Spirit of God. This is life that is "understood in a wholly primary sense as reverence's act of worship and is lived in this way."[35] The reverential aspect of life starts with the reverence for being alluded to already, and then develops into a 'liturgical' sense of life, where every good act is an act of worship of God.[36] There are two interesting scriptural parallels for this 'liturgical' view of Christian life in the *Letter to the Hebrews*, and the *Book of Revelation*.[37]

---

[32] *TD II*, 355. Von Balthasar mentions that the notion of polarities as a method of organizing anthropological data is due to the work of his mentor Erich Przywara S.J.
[33] *TD II*, 355-364.
[34] *TD II*, 411.
[35] Hans Urs von Balthasar, "Liturgy and Awe," *ET II*, 470. See also Joseph Ratzinger's (now Benedict XVI) "The Cross as Worship and Sacrifice" in *Introduction to Christianity*, 215ff.
[36] There is a similarity here to the Vatican II perspective on life through the lens of worship: When man seeks wisdom then: "In this way, the human spirit, being less subjected to material things, can be more easily drawn to the worship and contemplation of the Creator." (GS 57)
[37] The Second Vatican Council said of the family: "if it appears as the domestic *sanctuary* of the Church by reason of the mutual affection of its members and the prayer that

The contradiction of this worshipful life, in the Spirit of God, is the activism that is "the heresy of the West".[38] Von Balthasar has done some reflection on the practical means needed to discover the will of God and counter this heresy.[39] The Life, Death and Resurrection of Christ, have redeemed the world in both its physical and spiritual aspects, but the individual believer still has to act to find the will of God.[40] This involves seeing, hearing, and reading, on the part of the laity.[41] Without going through the natural phenomenology of these activities, it can be said that the intellectual senses "have received a priori a fulfillment in this supernaturally elevated world in which God has revealed himself . . . [a]nd at the same time . . . a wholly new sensitivity for the modes in which the divine appears in the world, a sensitivity that is only the result of the 'infusion' of grace."[42] The believer is elevated spiritually, but has to *use* the spiritual abilities to 'read' the mediated appearance of the divine in the Church and in the world.

The effort to develop the spiritual senses is some-thing that has atrophied in the modern West. So the believer has to learn again how to read the Scriptures, but to read them with awe. This is the appropriate respectful approach to a beautiful form! In von Balthasar's view the problem is that books

---

they offer to God in common," then it is fulfilling its mission. (AA, 11) Similarly in his encyclical on human work, John Paul II wrote: "Let the Christian who listens to the word of the living God, uniting work with prayer, know the place that his work has not only in *earthly progress,* but also in *the development of the kingdom of God,* to which we are all called through the power of the Holy Spirit and through the word of the Gospel." (LE, 27) (His emphasis.)

[38] Hans Urs von Balthasar, "Seeing, Hearing, and Reading," *ET II,* 496.

[39] Here he runs along the same lines as Vatican II. The council taught that "The intellectual nature of the human person is perfected by wisdom and needs to be, for wisdom gently attracts the mind of man to a quest and a love for what is true and good." (GS 15)

[40] See John Paul II: "It is [Christ] who opens up to the faithful the book of the Scriptures and, by fully revealing the Father's will, teaches the truth about moral action." (VS, 8)

[41] "Seeing, Hearing and Reading," *ET II,* 473ff.

[42] "Seeing, Hearing and Reading," 478. For a substantial treatment of the theology of the spiritual senses in the Catholic tradition see *GL I,* 365ff.

themselves have simply become a means of escape, and entertainment. This diminished approach to texts means that people might not value spiritual reading either. The development of the 'new senses' should help believers to approach other spiritual reading with a sense of awe, because they will then 'see' the real object, 'behind' the text, which is the manifestation of God himself.

To start with, from the phenomenological perspective, seeing, and hearing, involve a mutual relationship between the one seeing and hearing and the one being seen and heard. The 'new' act of seeing and hearing in Christ contains a mutuality that can only be illustrated from the Scriptures. And so, to start with seeing . . .

Seeing has long been held as the most noble of the senses. In von Balthasar's analysis of the redemption of the act of seeing, he turns to the *Gospel of John* where John wrote: "And the Word became flesh, and made his dwelling among us and we saw his glory." (John 1:14) Yet this seeing is both a seeing and a not seeing at the same time, because at one and the same time: "No one has seen God" (John 1:18), and yet there is a seeing in faith (John 5:37-38) which involves the grace of Christ to bring the believer to see Christ as *the* Christ. In the mutuality of seeing and being seen, the seeing of the believer is carried within the seeing of Christ.

The faculty of hearing is part of an even more complex process for the believer. There is the divine injunction: "This is my Beloved Son . . . .. Listen to him." (Matthew 17:5) The Church is a hearing Church that listens to Christ, and then speaks his word to the world.[43] In the field of hearing, von Balthasar believes that there are two heresies that the West is heir to, namely, "the actualism of the pure word and the activism of pure activity."[44] Since the theme of activism is the subtext for the whole chapter, it can be put aside for the moment. The 'actualism' of the word is our immediate concern here. The problem with actualism is that it avoids the way that the word leads

---

[43] See the Second Vatican Council teaching: "in order that love, as good seed may grow and bring forth fruit in the soul, each one of the faithful must willingly hear the Word of God and accept his will, and must complete what God has begun by their own actions with the help of God's grace." (LG, 42)
[44] "Seeing, Hearing, and Reading," 484.

beyond itself to the objective reality (the manifestation of the divine in the world) to which it refers. It takes serious re-training of the ability to hear so as to be able to overcome the "roar of civilization."[45] It is the proper development of the senses, through the grace of Christ, that will 'make space' for the civilization that Christ comes to bring. Those who belong to it are 'keeping' the Word. As Jesus noted: "Blessed are those who hear the word of God and observe it." (Luke 11:28)

The next anthropological tension that is transformed in Christ, is the gendered nature of human beings. This deserves a much more detailed presentation, since von Balthasar himself devoted so much time to it.

Man and Woman

Von Balthasar argued that being itself is the root of 'gender'. 'Gender' is in inverted commas because we still have to define its meaning. But the commas will be retained to indicate that we are working throughout with von Balthasar's definitions. The commas also serve to indicate that von Balthasar did not simply adopt the cultural and biological connotations of the terms, but argued for an ontological meaning of 'feminine' and 'masculine' that embraces the biological and should then inform the cultural. For him, the biological and authentic cultural and religious notions of gender express this intrinsic 'gendering' of the human being which is now able to be experienced as redeemed and sanctified.

Von Balthasar's description of the nature of gender starts by grounding created 'gender' in the nature of the Trinitarian God. So then the ordering of ontological un-created 'gender' exists within the Trinity. This order is the basis for the 'gendering' of all being, created in the image of the God. And thirdly, this line of reasoning grounds the stance of Christians vis-à-vis God and the world as 'feminine'.[46] This should not be surprising since Mary is the epitome of the lay person and so she illustrates the principles being proposed here. According to the Second Vatican

---

[45] "Seeing, Hearing, and Reading," 490.
[46] It is important to note that Henri de Lubac would characterize this 'trait' of Christianity, its receptivity, as obedience. See *Splendor of the Church*, 257-267. It has both a passive dimension (257) and an expressive active dimension (261).

Council: "She is our mother in the order of grace." (LG 60) The bulk of this chapter will be concerned with the latter point. It is a further specification of the notion of the theological person that was developed in the previous chapter.

Characterizing created being in this way—that is as spiritually 'feminine' with respect to God— then adds to our picture of being Christian. It has immense consequences for the lay person's relations within the Church, in marriage, in society, and as the member of a culture. So the starting point of our discussion is the Trinitarian basis for any notion of gendering.

a. <u>Some Definitions: The Trinity and 'Gender'</u>.

At the outset it must be made clear that von Balthasar is not guilty of anthropomorphism. His proposal is that "ultimately the divine unity of action and letting-be—whose complimentarity is shown in love—is translated into binary gendering in the world."[47] He has respected the analogy of being. John Paul II noted the same divine complementarity: "'God is love.' (I John 1) and in himself he lives a mystery of personal loving communion." (*Familiaris consortio*, FC, 11). In other words, (i) there are the characteristics of 'action' and 'letting-be' in God. This is the notion of 'uttering and being uttered' that was presented in the previous chapter; (ii) These characteristics are complementary in divine love; (iii) These characteristics of 'action' and 'letting-be' are then fundamental to the concept of 'gendering' in created being.[48] Von Balthasar arrived at these conclusions as follows:

Firstly, the Trinitarian God created the world. For our purposes, von Balthasar's citation of Aquinas is sufficient: "God the Father creates the creature through his Word which is the Son and through his love which is the Holy Spirit." (*ST I* q. 45)[49] The more

---

[47] My translation. Hans Urs von Balthasar, *Theodramatik IV Das Endspiel*, (Einsiedln: Johannes Verlag, 1983), 80.

[48] John Paul II used an identical starting point in his treatment of the 'image and likeness' in *Mulieris dignitatem*, MD, 6 – 8. He went on to say "we must . . . seek in God the absolute model of all 'generation' among human beings." (MD, 8)

[49] Cited in *TD IV*, 54. The intimate relation between the Trinity and the nature of the creation that it grounds must be emphasized: "the doctrine of the Trinity is the final underlying guarantee of Western, transcendental philosophy:

complex question is the way in which creation images God.

Second, the world is made in the *image* of the Trinity. To arrive at the nature of this imaging, we have to make some statements about the intra-trinitarian relations.[50] (Please note that this section is simply stating what von Balthasar says and what his sources are for saying it.) To start with, for von Balthasar, the description of God as *actus purus* is to distinguish God from creatures who have potentiality.[51] Then drawing on Bonaventure, within each relationship in the divine Trinity, each divine person demonstrates 'a form of passivity'[52], a 'letting-be' in each relationship.[53] This particular formulation is illustrated by the correlation between the paternity of the Father and the filiation of the Son, for example.[54] So in Bonaventure's words, for example, "the Son is a passive generative potency as appropriate to being begotten."[55] In other words, there is a complementarity between the 'letting-be'[56] of the Father and the 'receiving'[57] of the Son.

Lastly, the act of 'letting-be' and 'receiving' is fundamental to the notion of the absolute love of the divine persons, and since God's goodness

---

for only a triune God can render credible a world outside himself as true and good and yet in its free independence united with him which is most free and independent." *GL IV*, 376.

[50] Manfred Hauke starts from the relation between God and the world. Then "God's transcendence and immanence [are] prototypes of the polarity of man and woman." *Women in the Priesthood – A Systematic Analysis in the Light of the Order of Creation and Redemption*, trans. David Kipp, (San Francisco: Ignatius Press, 1988), 141.

[51] *"Wo die Gotheit as actus pururs beschrieben wird, is das Unterscheidende der Kreatur ihre Potentialität."* TD IV, 74.

[52] "eine Form von Passivität." *TD IV*, 74.

[53] *"Wo dagegen nach der imago trinitatis in der Kreatur gefragt wird, muß aufallen, daß innerhalb des trinitarishen Geshehens eine Form von Passivität einer Person der Aktivität einer andern Person gegenübergestellt wird."* TD IV, 75.

[54] Bonaventure Quart. I 183. See TD IV, 75. Footnote 1. In the same text von Balthasar also offers numerous footnote references to the works of Adrienne von Speyr to whom he is indebted in this section.

[55] Cited in *TD IV*, 75.

[56] *"Sein-konnen-lassen,"* TD IV, 75.

[57] *"Sich-entspringen-lassen-Können,"* TD IV, 75.

characterizes the goodness of all created being, then created being images the intra-trinitarian relations. Therefore, created human being mirrors the 'letting-be' and 'receiving' within the Trinity, with the constant reminder that the 'mirroring' occurs within the analogy of being and its reminder of the 'ever greater difference' between God and created being. But no matter how great the dissimilarity, the similarity remains, and there is a dynamic of 'letting-be' and 'receiving' in loving fruitfulness, in male and female beings, as complimentary beings.[58]

Turning back to the Trinity: von Balthasar identified the character of the Divine Father, with respect to the Divine Son, as 'supra-masculine', while the Son in being begotten is 'supra-feminine'.[59] Also the Father and the Son are 'supra-masculine', with respect to the Spirit, in the active spiration of the Holy Spirit. Then, as the recipient of the filiation of the Son and the passive spiration of the Spirit, the Father demonstrates a 'supra-feminine' character. John Paul II also argued that if the Old Testament applies masculine and feminine terms to God, then this is an indirect confirmation of the fact that men and women are created in the image of God. Thus: "If there is a likeness between Creator and creatures, it is understandable that the Bible would refer to God using expressions that attribute to him 'masculine' and 'feminine' qualities." (MD 8)

This means that, for the two authors, if 'active' and 'passive' are defined as above, then both the Father, Son, and Spirit manifest active and passive

---

[58] In *Christian State of Life*, von Balthasar offers a slightly different approach: firstly God's being as Trinity is infinitely fruitful and interpersonal, "Let us create . . .." (Genesis 1:26) The image of God must share this fruitfulness too and so "human beings were created for fecundity" in a specific complementary fashion. (226)

John Paul II wrote that: "All 'generating' among creatures finds its primary model in that generating which in God is completely divine, this is spiritual. All 'generating' in the created world is to be likened to this absolute and uncreated model. Thus every element of human generation which is proper to man, and every element which is proper to woman, namely human 'fatherhood' and 'motherhood,' bears within itself a likeness to, or an analogy to the divine 'generating'." (MD, 8)

[59] *TD IV*, 80.

characteristics in their respective relations.⁶⁰ Furthermore, they possess both 'supra-masculinity' and 'supra-femininity' in an "unsymmetrical" way.⁶¹ This asymmetry is to be expected from the differences between the Divine persons.⁶² In the realm of the human creature, each individual is an image of God by possessing both 'masculinity' and 'femininity' in an asymmetrical way. The asymmetry, at the ontological level, gives rise to either biologically masculine or biologically feminine human beings, who are also endowed with 'masculine' and 'feminine' spiritual characteristics. The scope of the relations between 'masculine' and 'feminine' is not limited to sexual relationships but rather embraces *all* human relationships, since they are all part of being and are contoured by the gendered nature of being itself.⁶³

To differentiate these terms more fully, we can refer again to the intra-Trinitarian relationships themselves. The 'supra-femininity' of the Son can be defined as at once receptive, and creatively generative, and so has a dyadic structure. While on the other hand, the 'supra-masculinity' of the Father can be defined as simply generative, in keeping with the nature of the Father as the origin, and which is inherently monadic in nature. By analogy then, for von Balthasar, being 'masculine' in act is monadic and purely generative, and parallels but is not limited to, the existence of masculinity at the biological level.⁶⁴

---

⁶⁰ Von Balthasar cites the caution of the Fourth Lateran Council: "One cannot say that he gave a part of his substance and retained a part for himself, since the substance of the Father is indivisible, being entirely simple. Nor can one say that in generating the Father transferred his substance. . . .." (DS, 805)

⁶¹ David Schindler, "Catholic Theology, Gender and the Future of Western Civilization," *Communio* 20 (Summer, 1993), 207.

⁶² "The irreducible opposition in the paternal, filial, spiritual relationship and behavior is the basis for the unity of nature and the equality of the 'personal' relationships." Hans Urs von Balthasar, "The Marian Principle," *Elucidations*, (London: S.P.C.K., 1975), 67.

⁶³ John Paul II noted that: "God inscribed in the humanity of man and woman the vocation, and thus the capacity and **responsibility**, of love and communion." (FC, 11) (Emphasis added.)

⁶⁴ *TD IV*, 80. Von Balthasar was careful to remark that the male cannot simply be equated with the heavenly principle

Then continuing the analogy: being 'feminine' is intrinsically receptive, but with a receptivity that gives itself over into creative generativity.[65] (The commas indicate that the terms are being defined here. Their meanings are not simply being drawn from the cultural context, even though there are some obvious parallels that suggest the underlying ontological definition.)[66]

There are two analogies for the dyadic nature of the 'feminine': One is found in the existence of the Divine Son, who both eternally receives all that he is from the Divine Father, and is the appropriated as the agent of creation. The other is to be found in the existence of Mary. In a sermon, von Balthasar said that: "What Heaven sends cannot attain perfection without the cooperation of the earth, the matrix-*materia-mater*, which in turn cannot utter a full, unreserved and vulnerable 'Yes' by its own power but only through the power of the Spirit of God." [67] (Emphasis added.) Thus the emphasis on the *graced* condition of Mary shows that she is not the unaided pattern for spiritual femininity. From now on Mary will be the archetype of the 'feminine' Christian in what follows. The description of the 'feminine' parallels, but

---

and female with the earthly principle or nature. (*TD III*, 286) This view is found in Plato (*Timeus* 90e, 91a; *Laws* 5,939c) and Aristotle (*Physics* I.9, 192 A 13-14) *TD II*, 367.

[65] It can be stated that John Paul II's usage of 'fatherhood' and 'motherhood' parallels the usage of 'masculine and feminine' in von Balthasar. Cf. MD, 8.

[66] "The more apparent anatomical differences between males and females, are as one contemporary writer puts it, 'not mere accidentals or mere attachments . . . [instead the] differences in the body are revelations of differences in the depths of their being." William E. May, "Marriage and the complementarity of Male and Female," *Anthropotes* VIII (1) June 1992, 45. The contemporary wuthor that he refers to is Robert E. Joyce in his *New Dynamics in Sexual Love*, 34, the work he co-wrote with Mary Rosera Joyce.

Note also Scheeben's use of the man-woman analogy, von Balthasar sums it this way: "it is not the relations of persons separated from their physical aspect that are decisive; decisive, rather, are precisely the 'physical' relationships which 'carry' the personal relationships ontologically." *GL I*, 111.

[67] "Heaven and Earth," in *You Crown the Year with your Goodness – Radio Sermons*, trans. Graham Harrison, (San Francisco: Ignatius Press, 1989), 195.

is not limited to, the existence of the feminine at the biological level.

But to make the issue clear, these capacities of 'masculine' and 'feminine' are part of *each individual* human being. Thus a biologically male human being can be spiritually 'masculine' and 'feminine' and a biologically female human being can be spiritually 'masculine' and 'feminine'.[68] This is in no way a proposal for androgyny, since the characteristics are spiritual *and* present asymmetrically. To use Sister Prudence Allen's summary: "The combination of the three factors of male, masculine, and feminine in a male individual will always differ from the combination of the three factors of female, masculine and feminine in a female individual."[69] In other words, the human biological male and female contain within them-selves the 'masculine' and the 'feminine' at an ontological level. Thus each individual mirrors the asymmetrical 'gendering' in the Divine Trinity, even down to the cellular level.[70]

It must also be emphasized that von Balthasar is not offering the definitive description of male and female by this approach. He follows the method that was used in dealing with scriptural terms, where statements about one term shed light on another. But he is aware that in all cases one is "attempting to describe a mystery."[71] His attempts are an asymptotic

---

[68] William E. May cites from Robert E. Joyce's Human Sexual Ecology: A Philosophy and Ethics of Man and Woman, when he says that "I would define a man as a human being who both gives in a receiving way and receives in a giving way, but is so structured in his being that he is emphatically inclined towards giving in a receiving way." (67-69) May agrees with this conclusion but arrives at it from an analysis of the presentation of the nature of the human being in Genesis 2. Cf. William E. May, "Marriage and the complementarity of Male and Female," *Anthropotes* VIII (1) June 1992.

[69] Prudence Allen, "Integral Sexual Complementarity and the Theology of Communion," *Communio: Internationa Catholic Review* 17 (1990), 533. This view is cited favorably by both William E. May in Marriage and the complementarity of Male and Female," (50) and David Schindler in "Catholic Theology, Gender, and the Future of Western Civilization," *Communio* 20 (Summer, 1993), 203.

[70] "Masculinity and femininity are . . . structural principles." M. Hauke, *Women in the Priesthood*, 119.

[71] *TD II*, 366.

approach to the richness of gender, particularly in its spiritual sense.

In conclusion: the 'feminine' will be considered as dyadic in nature, because it is both receptive and creatively generative. The point to note is the continuity between the two moments. What is 'creatively generated' is in continuity with 'what is received'. So in the Incarnation, the Christ was born of a woman to have human nature, but he is still the Son of God.[72] Mary then brought up Christ in a way consistent with the Jewish tradition that was born of obedience to the same God. But she did it in her inimitable personal way.

Now turning to being masculine: by contrast, being 'masculine' is monadic in nature, since it is purely generative[73], i.e. as a principle with a single moment as compared with the double moment of the 'feminine'. Furthermore, there is a relativity, and indeed a complementarity, between the 'masculine' and the 'feminine', in that they only come to fullness of realization in loving relation to one another. It is this complementarity which is the ontological key to the communion between God and humanity in the history of salvation.

(b) The Ordering of the Mystery of Salvation in a 'gendered' fashion

The 'gendered' complementarity in the history of salvation has a number of different facets.

To start with, creation itself is ontologically 'feminine' with respect to God. Then in the Incarnation, God's union with humanity comes about through a woman. Her offspring was masculine, namely Jesus Christ. He brought salvation to a 'feminine' creation. And lastly, summing up the theological position, von Balthasar wrote that "the final relationship between the triune God and man [is the

---

[72] John Paul II: "The dogma of the divine motherhood of Mary was for the Council of Ephesus and is for the Church like a seal upon the dogma of the Incarnation, in which the Word truly assumes human nature into the unity of his person, without canceling that nature." *Redemptoris mater, RM*, 4.

[73] "The masculine element . . . pushes forward into things in order to change them by implanting and imposing a something of its own." Hans Urs von Balthasar, "Women Priests?" *New Elucidations*, 189.

locus] in which the relationship of male and female must be also perfected."⁷⁴ Note that the description of the place of gender within the whole understanding of Being is the result of Christian thought itself.⁷⁵

Now these points can be explained as follows: given the nature of the 'supra-masculine' Father and the role of the Son who is sent, the one received as the Word of God by creation, had to be necessarily masculine⁷⁶ to make the Father (the *arche*) present. Thus: "To have seen me is to have seen the Father." (John 14:9)⁷⁷ Creation then receives not only its being from God, but also its redemption and is 'feminine' in this reception.

The 'femininity' of redeemed creation is most easily understood through Mary herself. Not only is she the created feminine counterpart to Christ, but another counterpart developed around her the "woman-in-community", namely the Church.⁷⁸ In fact, the very 'feminine' nature of the Church with respect to Christ is "the ultimate realization of the creature's relationship to God."⁷⁹ The Church as the Virgin, Bride

---

[74] Hans Urs von Balthasar, "The Marian Principle," 67.
[75] *TD II*, 368.
[76] The masculinity of Christ is irrelevant for Karl Rahner S.J. For example he disagrees that the 'masculine' ordained priesthood follows from the masculinity of Christ. Rahner follows Haye van der Meer's view that many of Christ's actions were simply directed by his culture. Karl Rahner, "Women and the Priesthood," *The Content of Faith*, (New York, NY: Crossroad, 1992), 424-433. He thus ignores the fact that Christ did many things contrary to his culture.
[77] This is an approach to the question at the level of Being. "Sexual differentiation is a much more deeply rooted aspect of human existence than are political and cultural superimpositions." Manfred Hauke, *Women in the Priesthood*, 250.
[78] *TD III*, 290. See also Manfred Hauke, "The Image of Marriage as a Central Symbol," in *Women in the Priesthood*, 252ff. Note the teaching of Vatican II: "because she belongs to the offspring of Adam she is one with all those who are to be saved. She is 'the mother of the members of Christ . . . having cooperated by charity that faithful might be born in the Church, who are members of that Head.' Wherefore she is hailed as a pre-eminent and singular member of the Church, and as its type and excellent exemplar in faith and charity." (LG 53)
[79] Hans Urs von Balthasar, "A Word on *Humane Vitae*," 443.

and Mother has a long history in the tradition.⁸⁰ Given that the members of the Church are part of this 'woman-in-community,' there is a graced 'femininity' (this fits the nature of the human spirit as it is understood in the great Christian spiritual writers) that comes about in the Christian individual. This has a number of consequences.

(c) <u>The First Part of the 'Feminine' Dyad: Receptivity</u>

If being spiritually 'feminine' is understood as having a dyadic structure in the created order (as receptive and then creatively generative), then the 'feminine' character of the Christian response to God has its archetype in the exclamation of Mary: "I am the handmaid of the Lord . . . let what you have said be done to me." (Luke 1:38) As was argued earlier, Mary's experience is archetypal, since she is Mother of God and Mother of the Church.⁸¹

The nature of her existence as the archetype rests precisely on the fact that she has received the Word, and so—in von Balthasar's inimitable summary—"Mary opens up countless possibilities of saying 'Yes' for all who come after her . . .. For the Christian is a man who says 'Yes'."⁸² Mary received the Word, who is the formal and final exemplar for the whole of creation, and through his grace, in her, all of these possibilities open up.⁸³

---

⁸⁰ See the virginal Church of II Corinthians 11:2; the Church as Spouse in Ephesians 5:25-33; and as mother in Galatians in Galatians 4:26 and Revelations 12. Cf. Hans Urs von Balthasar, "The All-Embracing Motherhood of the Church," *The Office of Peter and the Structure of the Church*, (San Francisco: Ignatius Press, 1986), 183-226.

⁸¹ "In the Incarnation [the Church] encounters Christ and Mary indissolubly joined: he who is the church's Lord and Head and she who, uttering the first fiat of the New Covenant, pre-figures the church's condition as spouse and mother." (RM, 1)

⁸² *You Crown the Year with your Goodness*, 24.

⁸³ "In the relation of mother and son there is the most intimate, the most concrete encounter of all between divine and human history." *A Theology of History*, 60. Speaking of the Word, Aquinas says: "the Word of God, Who is His eternal concept, is the exemplar likeness of all creatures. And therefore as creatures are established in their proper species, though movably, by the participation of this likeness, so by the non-participated and personal union of the Word with a creature, it was fitting that the creature

Christ fulfilled every aspect of the Law through his obedience to his mother, and he did it in such a superabundant way that was completed on the Cross.[84] Bearing in mind the theatrical language used in the previous chapter to enlarge the theoretical discourse, von Balthasar could then say of Christ, who is the formal exemplar of the world and its redemption: "Every worldly dramatic production [the life of every lay Christian] must take its bearings from, and be judged by, the ideal nature of this coincidence of freedom and obedience [in Christ] or of self-being and consciously acknowledged dependence."[85] Similarly, in the graced mutualities examined in the first human tension, the Word appears to be growing in the self until it becomes clear that the opposite is the case, and in fact, the individual is discovered to be contained and growing in the Word.

In conclusion then: turning back to the human 'side' of the relationship, von Balthasar is at pains to emphasize that the "isolated acts of faith and love" are not the issue in following Christ. The issue is that human beings become primarily "ontologically resonant to God and for God."[86] This is the starting point for von Balthasar's theology of feeling which again has to be properly understood in a theology of the laity.

(i) <u>A Proper Understanding of the Notion of 'Feeling'</u>.

Another of von Balthasar's insights is a proper understanding of the concept of 'feeling' that does not somehow look on feeling as a separate faculty. (The inverted commas indicate that the concern is with von Balthasar's understanding and not the common cultural understanding of 'feeling'.) To explain his point, von Balthasar starts from a quotation of Thomas Aquinas in which the human capacity "acquires direct knowledge of the thing to which it cleaves, in so far as it takes complacency in it. Hence

---

should be restored in order to its eternal and unchangeable perfection." (ST III q. 3) Hence the Word is the formal and the final exemplar.

[84] *A Theology of History*, 60. Cf. Vatican II: "Let them follow the example of Christ, who by His obedience even unto death, opened to all men the blessed way of the liberty of the children of God." (LG 37)

[85] *TD II*, 268.

[86] *GL I*, 245.

it is written (Wisdom 1:1) 'Think of the Lord in goodness,'" (*ST I II* q.15 a. 1)[87] For von Balthasar, this conception of a total capacity embraces the whole human being and hence involves both the intellect and will, as Thomas had shown through the reference to their integrated operation above.[88] So 'feeling' is not somehow isolated from the intellect and the will, but instead, identifies the total human disposition rather than an isolated emotional state that is distinct from the intellect and will.[89]

Now we can apply this insight to von Balthasar's conception of Christian 'attunement': He holds that the action of the Spirit of Christ transforms the ontic disposition of the human being into a faculty that delights in the revelation of God's own self, leading to 'complacency'—in Thomas' sense—or 'joy' (von Balthasar) at Being that has been transformed by the Holy Spirit.[90] But the Christian has to become attuned to this revelation—the ontic and the experiential are intimately connected.[91] They mutually inform one another, so that the objective revelation of God becomes normative for the Christian in faith, as

---

[87] Cited in *GL I*, 244.

[88] Joseph Ratzinger (now Benedict XVI) came to the same conclusion. See his "The Truth of Christianity," in *Truth and Tolerance: Christian Belief and World Religions*, trans., Henry Taylor, (San Francisco: Ignatius Press, 2004), 143.

[89] John Paul II wrote: "Deprived of what Revelation offers, reason has taken side-tracks which expose it to the danger of losing sight of its final goal. Deprived of reason, faith has stressed feeling and experience, and so run the risk of no longer being a universal proposition." (FR, 48) More importantly the Second Vatican Council noted that: "Human dignity requires man to act through conscious and free choice, as motivated and prompted personally from within, and not through blind internal impulse or merely external pressure. Man achieves such dignity when he frees himself from all subservience to his feelings, and in a free choice of the good, pursues his own end by effectively and assiduously marshaling the appropriate means." (GS, 17)

[90] Cf. the teaching of Vatican II, when speaking of the development of the human being: "Apart from this message nothing will avail to fill up the heart of man: 'Thou hast made us for Thyself,' O Lord, 'and our hearts are restless till they rest in Thee.'" (GS 21)

[91] Note how von Balthasar chose closely related terms: he speaks of the initial created resonance of the human being to God and the graced attunement to God in and through his Son. Cf. *GL I*, 247.

he or she becomes "now fully subordinate to it, determined by it, and animated by it."[92]

For illustrative examples of this attunement in the writings of lay theologians, von Balthasar cites, by way of example, Blaise Pascal's (1663-1623) understanding of God's continuous grace, as analogous to the continuous begetting of the Son by the Father. Pascal says that in response the human being "must continually make new efforts to acquire this continual newness of grace."[93] This is the Christian *fiat* to grace. Similarly in John of the Cross's (1542-1591) writings: "all the things of God and the soul become one in participant transformation . . . and the soul appears . . . to be God more than a soul."[94] In both instances, the 'feminine' receptivity of the believer is highly active, but it is graced activity. God is elevating, and expanding, and leading the human agent under the goad of Christ.[95] So there is no opposition between contemplation and action. They are both components of genuine lay activity, as they realize the respective receptive and creatively expressive aspects of the 'feminine dyad.

(ii) <u>The Christian *Fiat* within culture</u>

The 'feminine' dyad suggests that the Christian always starts with wonder: "wonder at being is not only the beginning of thought, but also the permanent element (ἀρχή) in which it moves."[96] This is also the Christian response to beauty! Wonder at this gushing and totally gratuitous existence of Being, that need not be, grounds the Christian contribution to human culture.

Human beings start with awe at what is, and then its meaning must be allowed to unveil itself out of

---

[92] *GL I*, 247.
[93] Blaise Pascal, *Letter 4* (5 November 1648) cited in *GL III*, 175.
[94] John of the Cross, O.C.D., *Ascent of Mount Carmel* ii, 5, 7. Von Balthasar's translation cited in *GL III*. 108.
[95] Cf. Vatican II: "For Adam, the first man, was a figure of Him Who was to come,(20) namely Christ the Lord. Christ, the final Adam, by the revelation of the mystery of the Father and His love, fully reveals man to man himself and makes his supreme calling clear. It is not surprising, then, that in Him all the aforementioned truths find their root and attain their crown." (GS 22)
[96] *GL V*, 614.

what is. This is to approach being "as God's children" do.⁹⁷ There are four stages in his analysis of reflection in wonder. Briefly these are (i) "I find myself in a limitless world and part of a wonderfully rich community of life." (ii) "All that exists participates in this Being that I see and am part of." (iii) "Yet this Being is not the source of all that is." And finally, (iv) "this Being is grounded in God."⁹⁸ Von Balthasar was amazed at how little philosophers have had to say about the wonder of human reproduction, for example.⁹⁹

In sum then, the Christian serves the culture by wondering, that is finding objects of nature and human artifacts in the culture that develop the subject as a subject through contemplation.¹⁰⁰ Von Balthasar noted that there have been whole historical periods when objects have *not* been recognized as having depth. They were not seen as manifesting the glory of God, radiating from the heart of existence. Art, religions and philosophies can all suffer from this serious flaw, when they are not being faithful to reality.¹⁰¹

---

⁹⁷ Hans Urs von Balthasar, *Unless You become like this Child*, (San Francisco: Ignatius Press, 1991), 43.
⁹⁸ GL V, 615.
⁹⁹ GL V, 615.
¹⁰⁰ The same problem with perception in the modern period was noted by the Second Vatican Council: "For while the mass and the diversity of cultural factors are increasing, there is a decrease in each man's faculty of perceiving and unifying these things, so that the image of "universal man" is being lost sight of more and more. Nevertheless it remains each man's duty to retain an understanding of the whole human person in which the values of intellect, will, conscience and fraternity are preeminent. These values are all rooted in God the Creator and have been wonderfully restored and elevated in Christ." (GS, 61) Referring to the close relation between nature and culture, the Second Vatican Council said that: "Wherever human life is involved . . . , nature and culture are quite intimately connected one with the other." (GS 53)
¹⁰¹ When the Second Vatican Council spoke about finding the truth in being it said that: "when man gives himself to the various disciplines of philosophy, history and of mathematical and natural science, and when he cultivates the arts, he can do very much to elevate the human family to a more sublime understanding of truth, goodness, and beauty, and to the formation of considered opinions which have universal value." (GS 57)

These few spare comments show the vast range of the analysis of ontology that can be found in the work of Hans Urs von Balthasar. But there is more! The receptivity of the first moment of 'femininity', then passes over into the second moment, which is the taking of what has been received into creative expression.

(d) <u>The Second Part of the 'Feminine' Dyad: Creative Expression</u>

The second part of the 'feminine' operation of the Christian is that of creative expression. The starting point of the theological explanation is, as always, the fact that the mission of the Son is *the* global, all embracing, divine expression in the world. We are concerned with a missiological ontology. However, "what Christ brings with him is not primarily his historical environment but the world of creation and redemption as a whole. His form imparts to the things of the world the right distance (from himself and each other) and the right proximity (to him and each other)."[102] These aspects are, in fact, the key to *every* relationship to any aspect of the world. Thus the finite world is not transcended as much as it is taken up and transformed and given a new relationship to the divine in Christ.[103] It becomes the 'monstrance' of the presence of God, to use one of von Balthasar's images.[104]

There is a parable in the New Testament that applies to this process of transformation. The explanation of the *Parable of the Talents* (Matthew 25:14-30), that von Balthasar offers, indicates that God opens up a 'space' in which his servants can operate. This is a gratuitous act of his infinite freedom.[105] More significantly for the reflection on

---

[102] *GL I*, 419.

[103] Cf. Vatican II's teaching: "Indeed, the mystery of the Christian faith furnishes them with an excellent stimulant and aid to fulfill this duty more courageously and especially to uncover the full meaning of this activity, one which gives to human culture its eminent place in the integral vocation of man." (GS 57)

[104] *GL I*, 420.

[105] John Paul II was aware of this dynamic as well. Speaking of the Synod that he called to discuss the theology of the Laity, he said "The basic meaning of this Synod . . . is the faithful's hearkening to the call of Christ . . . to take an

activism in this chapter, in this parable "what [God] gives them is wealth, which they can use wisely or fritter away."[106] The nature of the 'space' created is clarified by the distinction that von Balthasar makes between clerical and lay theology. To illustrate this point, we must consider that clerical theology is official, in the sense of dealing within the space of the Church, while lay theology addresses things like 'the mystery of the eternal love between man and woman,' (Dante) and the notion of 'pure faith' in Saint John of the Cross.[107] This is how specifically lay theology uses the 'space' that God opens up.

These brief comments bring us to the final anthropological tension . . .

The Individual and the Community

Historically, the individual and the community have always had an organic relationship.[108] From the purely philosophical perspective, the "individual grows into the community", and the individual grows within the community.[109] The latter point means that there has always been the understanding of a kind of 'macro-ego' associated with the community. This 'macro-ego' is the "essential incarnation" of the "state organism".[110] It is this ego that informs the world-view

---

active and conscientious and responsible part in the mission of the Church in the great moment in history." (CL, 3) The apostolic exhortation *Christifideles laici* uses the parable in article 31.
[106] *TD II*, 273.
[107] See *GL III*. Yves Congar also highlighted this difference. According to his commentator Timothy MacDonald: "theology properly so-called is pre-eminently a clerical, priestly learning for inasmuch as they have the priestly charism and celebrate and celebrate the Sacraments, priests have to a greater degree a living contract with the realities of tradition. In [Congar's] opinion, Lay activity in matters of religious thought should be expressed 'in the immense field that lies between the Church' dogmatic problems and man's actual problems'." *The Ecclesiology of Yves Congar*, 136.
[108] See also Joseph Cardinal Ratzinger, trans. Henry Taylor, *Pilgrim Fellowship of Faith: The Church as Communion*, (San Francisco: Ignatius Press, 2005). Cf. Vatican II: "The well-being of the individual person and of human and Christian society is intimately linked with the healthy condition of that community produced by marriage and family." (GS 47)
[109] *TD II*, 385.
[110] *TD II*, 386.

of the individual. This is the most ancient view of the community.

This feature of natural anthropology is taken up and transformed in the Incarnation of the Divine Son. As von Balthasar explained: "the God-man is able to permeate the world he shares with others from within."[111] Thus individual men can become part of the Body of Christ. He or she can join the *communio eucharistica* that is fed by Christ's own giving of himself in Eucharist. Through this communion, the individual "bear[s] the burden of his brothers", in Christ.[112] The tension of the individual and the community is transformed, and the individual develops in individuality as a theological person (previous chapter) as he operates within the Body of Christ.

The communitarian conception of life means that Christ is so much more than the supreme example from the perspective of the individual, and so much more than a mere leader of the community from the perspective of the group. This sentence also summarizes the Pauline teaching that, on the one hand, means as Paul explains: "I live, no longer I, but Christ lives in me" (Galatians 2:20) Then on the other hand, Paul understood that: "so we though many, are one body in Christ and individually parts of one another." (Romans 12:5) Paul describes the Christian community as a people drawn into a community by the operation of the divine Spirit of Christ, so that they extend the love of Christ through living out of their lives for the Kingdom of God.

Evidently, the transformation of the ancient notion of community is completed in the existence of the Church—the Body of Christ. The pouring out of the Life of Christ "is completed by becoming ecclesial, and even cosmic."[113] The Christian notion of civilization is fundamentally ecclesial, but this does not work itself out in terms of "a vanishing of the world, [or] a hyperspiritualization, or a turning away from history, or from earthly work and culture, but [it is] rather a point of departure for the Christian's

---

[111] *TD II*, 410.
[112] Ibidem. Note the Pauline principle: "None of us lives for himself and no one of us dies for himself." (Romans 12:7)
[113] *TD II*, 412.

mission into the world *as it is.*" (His emphasis.)[114] There has to be a profound humility with regard to the world. It is the eschatological existence of the Church community that gives it this perspective, the perspective of participating in Christ's mission to *this* world. (Here we have only alluded to the eschatological issues because they will require a chapter of their own. (Chapter Seven))

The view just expressed can be described as the *Christocentric view* of the world.

It is worth noting too that this perspective means that the clerical and religious states only exist to further this mission, that is "in order better to go into [the mission] with Christ, to be a leaven for the Church and the world."[115] Here again the rider is that the Church community, and everyone in it, joins Christ "*en route*" to the eschatological fulfillment of the world in Heaven.[116] This fact and the understanding of life on the basis of the Cross of Christ are interrelated. (Chapter Seven) The understanding of life, based on its fulfillment in the Cross and Resurrection, is the living of life in "*the presence of* the event" of the Cross and Resurrection, rather than a "religion of divine and human truths."[117] Not that von Balthasar is denying their place, but reducing Christianity to the level of a "doctrinal lecture" makes of it a mere gnosis.[118] This critique properly responds to the activism that von Balthasar constantly opposes.

Re-examining *gnosis* is relevant today because of the effects of the Enlightenment that are still being felt. However, Saint Irenaeus (2nd. Cent.) had already noted the impact of gnosis in his century and he wrote defending Paul's critique of *gnosis* (eg. 1 Timothy 6:20; 1 Corinthians 8:1). Irenaeus explained this Pauline text: it is "not that [Paul] meant to inveigh against a true knowledge of God, for in that case he would have accused himself; but, because he knew that some,

---

[114] Hans Urs von Balthasar, "A Theology of the Secular Institute," *ET II*, 432
[115] Ibidem.
[116] Hans Urs von Balthasar, "The Faith of the Simple Ones," *Explorations in Theology III: Creator Spirit*, trans. Brian McNeil C.R.V., (San Francisco: Ignatius Press, 1993), 68.
[117] Ibidem. John Paul II wrote: "The mission [of the Christian] follows this same path and leads to the foot of the cross." (RM, 88)
[118] Ibidem.

puffed up by the pretence of knowledge, fall away from the love of God, and imagine that they themselves are perfect, for this reason that they set forth an imperfect Creator."[119] The shift away from love rooted in the great event of the Death and Resurrection grounds Paul's and Irenaeus' objections. It was Clement of Alexandria (150-215) who argued for a true *gnosis* based on faith.[120] This theme was also taken up in John Paul II's work when he picked two sentences from Saint Augustine to use as chapter headings in his encyclical *Fides et ratio*, and to explain the profound inescapable connection between reason and faith. The pope used the sentences "*credo ut intellegam,*" and "*intellego ut credam,*" from Augustine's *de Trinitate*, to show how the rational process actually works, because it is only complete when illuminated by faith.[121]

With regards to activism, in von Balthasar's understanding, the term means working with the blueprint that one has worked out oneself, rather than being led into understanding the blueprint by the work of the Spirit. Obviously using one's reason is vital but it has to participate in a genuine *credo ut intellegam*.

Another feature of the redeemed and sanctified experience of the individual in the community goes right to the heart of the meaning of community, as it touches the transformed mutuality of persons. Due to sinfulness, the self-surrender that human beings were created for (as the image of God), and which is fundamental to community falls far short of this goal. Complete self-surrender is only achieved in Christ and his Spirit. The self-emptying that is at the heart of Christ's Life, Death, and Resurrection, grounds the possibility of true mutuality in the lay person. The true mutuality in Christ means that the lay person lives a life of readiness that wants to *allow* "the encounter of two freedoms".[122] Von Balthasar describes this readiness as "childlike", in the sense that there is a trusting "naïveté" that can never be limited for self-defense.[123] Laity cannot limit the extent of their love on the pretext that it might not be accepted! It is this

---

[119] Irenaeus of Lyons, *Adversus Haereses II*, 26, 1.
[120] Clement of Alexandria, *Stromata* VI – VIII.
[121] See chapters two and three of *Fides et ratio*. Also see Augustine of Hippo, *De Praedestinatione Sanctorum*, 2, 5: PL 44, 963., cited in FR, 79
[122] "Spirit and Institution," 216.
[123] Ibidem.

rhythm of giving and receiving in the new Christian mutuality, that "becomes a concrete metaphor of [the] Trinitarian life within God".[124]

It is the working at the mutuality of Christian interpersonal relations that "fashion[s] [Christians] into individual persons."[125] The developed nature of the individual is crucial to the Christian nature of community. Christian community is not a community where one can hide or expect someone else to pick up one's burden. It is instead a community that "continue[s] in particularity, for this is how Christ's path began, proceeded—and ended."[126] Christ is not just the model but the higher order principle—the goad—of the life of the lay person, and thus he joins in the building of civilization.

Conclusion

Under the goad of Christ, the lay person is filled with the Spirit of Christ and empowered to be a member of the Church and a disciple of Christ in the world. The four tensions that characterize the life of the lay person have received their new Christian expansion through the Life, Death and Resurrection of Christ, that is to transform human civilization. The four redeemed and sanctified tensions of (i) man's relationship to the world; (ii) man as spirit and body; (iii) man as male and female; and (iv) man as individual within the community, form the basis of the new civilization grounded in Christ.

To close, some illustrations can be drawn from von Balthasar's studies of prominent laity to show how they have contributed to the new civilization. The way in which the first tension of (i) man's relationship to the world, can be lived out in a Christian mode, is illustrated by an extract from a lecture given by Georges Bernanos (1888-1948), in Switzerland, after the Second World War. He said that: "This world no longer protects anyone or offers anyone security. It no longer defends anyone; rather, it is the world that needs defending, it is we who must save the world."[127] So for the lay man Bernanos, it meant speaking to the

---

[124] *TD II*, 415. See the same understanding of the new meaning of community in Joseph Ratzinger, *Introduction to Christianity*, 127ff.
[125] *TD III*, 450.
[126] *TD III*, 447.
[127] *Bernanos: An Ecclesial Existence*, 246.

world about the specific nature of man. In von Balthasar's words: "Only where man understands himself by reference to God are human dignity and culture possible: [citing Bernanos] 'A civilization disappears with the kind of man, the type of humanity that has issued from it.'"[128] He knew the meaning of the life in Christ, and that meaning profoundly contradicts the activist strain in western culture.

The second tension which is (ii) man's existence as body and spirit comes up, for example, in the work of the playwright Bertolt Brecht (1898-1956). In reviewing Brecht's writings, von Balthasar explained that Brecht frequently noted that "the fact that Christians are caught up in a capitalist ideology and praxis—which Brecht demonstrates in many passages—means that they fail vis-à-vis their own program (which is that of the *Sermon on the Mount*) at the decisive moment."[129] The spiritual and the bodily material dimensions are related to the point where the spiritual informs and leads the temporal to its proper goal.

The most extensive analysis in this chapter was devoted to the notion of (iii) the gendering in human existence. Not only is man only present as a gendered individual, but the drama of salvation itself is ordered in gendered terms. The nineteenth century Russian philosopher, Vladimir Soloviev's (1853-1900) work was unusual in the sense that it was articulated "more painstakingly than [that] by Newman and [was] deployed against the rigidly retrogressive Eastern Church."[130] Soloviev's theology explained—in von Balthasar's words that show the 'masculine' and 'feminine' tensions—that "after the appearance of Christianity, the Divine itself, incarnate now forevermore, stands over against man as a firm foundation, as the element in which our life exists; what is sought is a humanity to answer this divinity."[131] Soloviev had grasped the gendered ordering of the tension in the unfolding of salvation. The community has the 'feminine' role in response to the 'masculine' action of God himself.

---

[128] *Bernanos: An Ecclesial Existence*, 222.
[129] Hans Urs von Balthasar, "Bertolt Brecht: The Question about the Good," *ET III*, 416.
[130] *GL III*, 283.
[131] *GL III*, 287.

The final tension of human existence is (iv) the tension between the individual and the community, that has been transformed by Christ. As with the other anthropological tensions, there are many different dimensions to be considered, but just to illustrate one of them, we will refer to the writings of the German playwright Reinholt Schneider (1903-1958). Schneider grasped his own role of service to the post-war nation of Germany as posing a challenge to the young people of the recovering nation. Von Balthasar described Schneider's "urgent appeals to young people [that] make the demand that they bear witness to a responsibility vis-à-vis history by sharing in bearing and expiating the guilt, contributing their help to the process of clarification and purification in such a way that the past can take its place in the new reality as something good, something cleansed and sifted."[132] Schneider grasped the real level of mutuality within a community, even across the generations, even as it discovered its duty precisely because of the horrors of the Second World War.

Jesus Christ is the goad that drives the Christian and the whole community towards ever richer and more profound manifestations of love and care, as it expresses externally more and more of the character of being the Body of Christ nourished by the Eucharistic Bread. The spiritual 'more and more' feeds the temporal. The 'masculine' and the 'feminine' reach more and more for their development in mutual relationships in the Church, in the world and very specially in the Sacrament of Marriage.

There are still three central temporal features of life in Christ that have deliberately been set aside, namely finitude, suffering and death. They too are part of the Theodrama because Christ is the goad in the

---

[132] Hans Urs von Balthasar, *Tragedy under Grace: Reinhold Schneider on the Experience of the West*, trans. Brian Hans Urs von Balthasar, "The Word and History," *ET I*, 27ff.
[132] *Bernanos: An Ecclesial Existence*, 222.
[132] Hans Urs von Balthasar, "Bertolt Brecht: The Question about the Good," *ET III*, 416.
[132] *GL III*, 283.
[132] *GL III*, 287.
[132] Hans Urs von Balthasar, *Tragedy under Grace: Reinhold Schneider on the Experience of the West*, transMcNeil C.R.V., (San Francisco: Ignatius Press, 1997), 160.

unfolding of these human experiences! They form the focus of the next chapter.

Chapter Seven The Drama of Life: Finitude, Suffering and Death

Introduction
The Metaphysics of Catholic Experience
The *theologia crucis* of Lay Life
The Experience of Finitude
Suffering
Death
Conclusion: The Community of the Cross

Introduction

This final chapter of the theodramatic analysis of a lay person's life in the Church considers the question: what is the source of the individual's understanding of, and response to, experiences of finitude, suffering, and death? This is a significant question because according to von Balthasar, "a genuinely human figure, developing over the course of a lifetime, is not something [merely] given."[1]

Von Balthasar's answer is a complex one. He starts by establishing the ontological context of the lay person from both the philosophical and the theological perspective. In this way, he could recover principles that had been lost through the rise of modern western individualism. The foundation of his answer lies in the fact that the horizon of the meaning and the response to finitude, suffering, and death, points towards hope and fulfillment as the new possibilities of transcendence opened by Christ.[2] This truth is the redeemed 'new creation'—so to speak—of the more general philosophical proposition that "things are always more than themselves, and their constantly self-surpassing transcendence open ultimately onto an idea that is not the things themselves, but God and

---

[1] *TD II*, 37. See Vatican II's teaching that: "The word "culture" in its general sense indicates everything whereby man develops and perfects his many bodily and spiritual qualities." (GS 53) So they also used an anthropology that included the process of development in its ontology.

[2] Note the Second Vatican Council's teaching: "Among the trials of this life they find strength in hope, convinced that "the sufferings of the present time are not worthy to be compared with the glory to come that will be revealed in us" (Rom. 8:18)." (AA, 4)

their measure in God."³ The embrace of these situations inevitably involves dramatic actions and decisions by the individual.

Now as was mentioned earlier, the spiritual structure of human being is 'feminine' because it involves both receptivity and a corresponding creative expression. It involves the genuine embrace of experience and then a creative Christian response to it. In David Schindler's summation these two moments of life are united because "man's decision works . . . to help bring Being to decision, that is to realize actuality. This is the essence of all creativity."⁴ The individual realizes himself in act. He expresses who he is in act. The lay person becomes the authentic expression of who he is as finite, suffering, and dying, through what he chooses to do when he meets these experiences.⁵

As always the believer's "decision works within God's decision," to give expression to the transcendence of this world that happens in Christ.⁶ It must immediately be said that transcending the world 'brings along' the world, as it were, to this new realm in Christ.⁷ The world is not left behind, but is taken up

---

³ *TL I*, 59. The philosophical transcendence was mentioned by Vatican II when it said: "There are, indeed, close links between earthly things and those elements of man's condition which transcend the world." (GS 76)

⁴ David C. Schindler, *Hans Urs von Balthasar and the Dramatic Structure of Truth: A Philosophical Investigation*, (New York: Fordham University Press, 2004), 94. In his Letter to Artists, Pope John Paul II cited Nicholas of Cusa: "Nicholas of Cusa made clear: "Creative art, which it is the soul's good fortune to entertain, is not to be identified with that essential art which is God himself, but is only a communication of it and a share in it". The last phrase mentioning 'communication' and 'share' goes in the same direction as von Balthasar's description of spiritual 'femininity'.

⁵ Cf. Benedict XVI's statement about Boethius and his being condemned to death: "It is precisely because of his tragic end that he can also speak from the heart of his own experience to contemporary man, and especially to the multitudes who suffer the same fate because of the injustice inherent in so much of 'human justice'." *General Audience*, 12 March 2008.

⁶ Ibidem.

⁷ Cf. Vatican II's teaching: "men are not deterred by the Christian message from building up the world, or impelled to neglect the welfare of their fellows, but that they are rather more stringently bound to do these very things." (GS 34)

and transformed by the grace and truth of Christ. So in some way, the lay person's world is 'brought along' in the decision to face finitude, suffering and death. What this could mean appears below.

Finally, this chapter aims to begin setting out the theme of the next chapter, which is about "the unveiledness of being, truth, [as it] . . . becomes an amazing participation in the sphere of divine truth itself through God's ever-new meting out of truth."[8] The opening up of the meaning of being through the authentic grasp of the experiences of finitude, suffering, and death, is an expression of truth realized in the act of grasping experiences and not denying them. Incidentally, this is the foundation for the theological response to agnostic attempts to solve the 'problems' of finitude, suffering and death. (It is also the root to presenting the nature of the states of life in the Church that will be considered in Chapter Eight.)

Now the ontological limitations of human being that are the sources of the experiences of finitude, suffering, and death, are the result of Original Sin. Von Balthasar noted that a way to conceive of these three characteristics, in a theological fashion, is to start with the fact that "as a creature, man is finite. But because God [gives] him the power of submitting his spirit to the grace of mission, and of letting his body be enveloped by his spirit, his finiteness [is] open to God."[9] This is the fundamental ontological principle at the heart of the believer's response.

But how does one understand a particular trait as the effect of Original Sin? For example, regarding finitude, von Balthasar explains: "Once [man] freed himself from God, however, and had made a goal of what had been a means, his finiteness appeared in all its nakedness. Earthly life, when it is no longer hidden in eternal life, becomes hopelessly immured in its own

---

[8] Ibidem.
[9] *CSOL*, 103. Note Aquinas' very specific summary of the situation: "like [the] defects of those who are born with them, or which children suffer from, are the effects and the punishments of original sin, . . . ; and they remain even after baptism, . . . : and that they are not equally in all, is due to the diversity of nature, which is left to itself, ... Nevertheless, they are directed by Divine providence, to the salvation of men, either of those who suffer, or of others who are admonished by their means—and also to the glory of God." (*ST I*, q.87 a.7)

finiteness."[10] It is only the life 'hidden in eternal life' that demonstrates how the limits of finite experience find their meaning and are opened out to God.[11]

Pre-Christian notions of the individual considered him as a mere "personless" subjectivity.[12] Christianity demonstrates that the 'subjectivity' is a person and has personality.[13] This is relevant because many modern philosophies and attempts by parapsychology, for example, to try to penetrate the experiences of suffering and death have gone in this direction. They lose the concept of the person. There will be more about this question below.

Lastly, the Christian response to finitude, suffering, and death, is an inextricable part of belonging to a community—the Body of Christ—and the Church's mission of responding to the individual's tragedy can, in fact, *only* be understood in terms of the community for whom Jesus Christ died.[14] The concept of community—the *communio* of which we spoke earlier— will be a constant theme of this chapter. The final section of the chapter then gathers the elements of the community dimension of existence together.

---

[10] Ibidem. Cf. Vatican II: "Thinking they have found serenity in an interpretation of reality everywhere proposed these days, many look forward to a genuine and total emancipation of humanity wrought solely by human effort; they are convinced that the future rule of man over the earth will satisfy every desire of his heart." (GS 10)

[11] See Schindler, *The Dramatic Structure of Truth*, 255-265. Cf. Vatican II: "Through Christ and in Christ, the riddles of sorrow and death grow meaningful. Apart from His Gospel, they overwhelm us." (GS 22) And then again: "The Church also maintains that beneath all changes there are many realities which do not change and which have their ultimate foundation in Christ, Who is the same yesterday and today, yes and forever." (GS 10)

[12] *TD IV*, 119.

[13] Cf. John Paul II's explanation of the Yahwist tradition in *Genesis*: "In relatively few sentences, the ancient text portrays man as a person with the subjectivity that characterizes him." *General Audience*, 12 October 1979.

[14] See also Nicholas J. Healy, *The Eschatology of Hans Urs von Balthasar: Being as Communion*, Oxford Theological Monographs, J. Day et al eds., (Oxford: Oxford University Press, 2005).

The Metaphysics of Experience

Sketching the description of the Christian approach to finitude, suffering, and death does not 'close the door on metaphysics,' to borrow a concept from Joseph Ratzinger (Benedict XVI).[15] The crucial features of the understanding of finitude, suffering, and death—as revelatory events in the life of the lay person—come from metaphysics, when it is illuminated and purified by revelation.

To start with, these experiences remind the individual that he was created even though he might not have been. He is held in existence by a loving God. The individual is transient, and yet von Balthasar says (citing Max Scheler) that "'in every act, the conscious person transcends the given insofar as that given represents a 'limit' on the part of the body—which is 'given' him along with the experience', but he also understands that the 'space' within which such acts are realized is always his own restricted time."[16] The person has to respond to the experience in time. Applying this concept to Jesus Christ: he has already assumed finitude, suffering, and death, since he assumed real human nature. Furthermore, his actions to save us were realized within his time.

However the situation of the individual is more complex still, because the individual only knows himself, and comes to himself, in a myriad of I-thou relationships realized within the common continuum of time. So while his actions are *his*, they are also *ours*—borne by the community— in a very real sense, so that "in the 'I-thou' and the 'I-we' relationship, the individual's responsibility (for his action and conduct in the face of death) plays a part in the like responsibility of others in the face of death."[17] So the challenges of finitude, suffering, and death, raise the question of the presence of a co-responsibility of members of the community for discovering meaning and making a response.[18]

---

[15] See Johann Auer, Joseph Ratzinger, *Dogmatic Theology 9: Eschatology: Death and Eternal Life*, (Washington D.C.: Catholic University of America Press, 1988), 69ff.
[16] *TD IV*, 96.
[17] *TD IV*, 100.
[18] Cf. Vatican II: "That is why this community [of the Church] realizes that it is truly linked with mankind and its history by the deepest of bonds." (GS 1)

On the one hand, by his actions, the individual is expressing values into the community of life with consequences that he cannot even imagine. On the other, he is also living in a tension between caring for himself and caring for others that continues until the end of life.

Considering the individual now: the receptive moment of being human means that finitude, suffering, and death, are first and foremost, to be truly *received*.[19] They are not avoidable despite the many ways that modern man has found to deny them.[20] Instead they are to be embraced. The Christological foundation of this understanding is that Christ's "taking on of finitude . . . [was achieved in a way that meant it] should not be nullified, but brought to fulfillment in God: not disincarnated, but made spiritual in the Resurrection."[21] The 'taking on' by the individual, who dies with Christ, means that he *becomes* in the sense of becoming more like Christ, the true man.[22] Finally, "the point where personal and social ethics meet is reason, which aspires to the sovereign norm of an absolute good."[23] The individual has to use his reason to see the highest good. Now the absolute good has been manifested for us on the Cross, so we are looking to a *theologia crucis* in the reflections that follow.

Karl Barth (1886-1968), von Balthasar's respected friend and dialog partner, introduced the notion of the theology of the Cross. He said that the meaning of the challenges of worldly existence, when responded to in the Spirit of Christ, involve "a *theologiae gloriae*, celebrating what Jesus Christ in his Resurrection, received for us, and what he is for us as the Risen One, [but it] would have no meaning unless

---

[19] Aquinas already knew of the nature of finite human existence: "we ourselves suffer many things against our will from natural necessity—as, for instance, death, old age, and like ills." (*ST I*, q.41 a.2)

[20] John Paul II taught that: "When the *prevailing* tendency is to value life only to the extent that it brings pleasure and well-being, suffering seems like an unbearable setback, something from which one must be freed at all costs." (EV, 64) (Emphasis added.)

[21] *GL VII*, 403.

[22] *TD II*, 11.

[23] *TD IV*, 101.

it also contained in itself the *theologia crucis*."[24] It is the Cross of Jesus Christ—and only the Cross of Jesus Christ—that opens up the meaning and the possibilities of the Christian's experience of finitude, suffering, and death.[25] The hermeneutic of the life of the Catholic lay person, living to give glory to God, 'contains in itself' and presents to the world, a theology of the Cross.

Pre-Christian attempts to penetrate suffering and death sought answers in the direction of the transmigration of souls and the post-Christian attempts sought answers from parapsychology. Neither direction of thought does justice to the true meaning of suffering and death.[26] Such efforts deny the nature of being itself, and short-circuit the gift that pre-Christian metaphysical ideas can offer, when purified by the experience of the Scriptures. This is the method that is being recovered by von Balthasar and presented in detail in Chapter One.

Thus von Balthasar—and the Catholic tradition—avoid both the pantheistic notion of the individual being absorbed into God, as well as the idea that the human being somehow exists alongside God.[27] Both notions confuse the concept of the nature of created being and its relation to uncreated being! As was argued earlier, human freedom is borne by the divine infinite freedom. But human freedom is still a

---

[24] Karl Barth, *Kirchliche Dogmatik IV/1*, (Zollikon, 1953), 622 cited in Hans Urs von Balthasar, *Mysterium Paschale: The Mystery of Easter*, trans. Aidan Nichols O.P., (Edinburgh: T&T Clark, 1990), 82. Here Barth is indicating the meaning of salvation as it is achieved by the Incarnation, Death and Resurrection of Christ. It is to be enabled to glorify God through his Son.

[25] Note John Paul's comment that "The Church never ceases to relive his death on the Cross and his Resurrection, which constitute the content of the Church's daily life." (*Redemptor hominis*, 20) Cf. Vatican II: "if anyone wants to know how this unhappy situation can be overcome, Christians will tell him that all human activity, constantly imperiled by man's pride and deranged self-love, must be purified and perfected by the power of Christ's cross and resurrection." (GS 37)

[26] Cf. Vatican II: "He taught us by example that we too must shoulder that cross which the world and the flesh inflict upon those who search after peace and justice." (GS 38)

[27] Hans Urs von Balthasar, *Theodrama: Theological Dramatic Theory V: The Last Act*, trans., Graham Harrison, (San Francisco: Ignatius Press, 1998), 385.

genuine freedom, so it has a personal center and reaches out into the world before returning to itself. Human freedom engages the world, and in the process it experiences the constraints of finitude, and often endures suffering with its constant reminders of being a being-unto-death. It is this act of the grasping of the nettle of life that shows the truth of Christianity, against the Gnostic perspective, that would "leave behind the earthly Jesus and understand the Risen Jesus as an idea with exclusive reference to the present tense, so doing without any hope in a future Resurrection."[28] It is precisely the humiliation that comes from responding to the present life that in fact bears so many similarities to the earthly life of Jesus, and so Jesus as 'the Way' is both found and followed. (Cf. John 14:6) [29]Also the attempts to avoid the Cross and 'live in the Resurrection,' so to speak, are illusory.

It was not for nothing that von Balthasar noted in his analysis of Blaise Pascal's work (1623-1662), the French mathematician, physicist and philosopher, that Pascal—one of von Balthasar's exemplary lay thinkers—sought a "return [for meaning] to the life of Jesus and through the undistorted facts of that life to the mystery of the suffering love of God."[30] The lay person's fundamental expectation is that he or she will learn this 'suffering love' from Christ and embrace it as the only possible 'style' of lay life.[31]

A final point: in this chapter, a consideration of some of the limits that are experienced in human life must start with the theology of the Cross, leading to a consideration of finitude and suffering and then that

---

[28] GL *VII*, 183.

[29] John Paul II noted that "He must, so to speak, enter him with all his own self; he must 'appropriate' and assimilate the whole of the reality of the Incarnation and Redemption in order to find himself." (VS, 8)

[30] *GL III*, 177. Saint Theresa Benedicta of the Cross O.C.D., (Edith Stein) cites Saint John of the Cross where he says: "Sustain always the desire to imitate Christ in all things and to bring your life into conformity with his. You must always study his life in order to imitate it and behave always as he would." *The Collected Works of Edith Stein VI: The Science of the Cross*, trans., Josephine Koeppel O.C.D., (Washington D.C.: ICS Publications, 2002), 48.

[31] Cf. Vatican II: "By suffering for us He not only provided us with an example for our imitation, He blazed a trail, and if we follow it, life and death are made holy and take on a new meaning." (GS 22)

then leads to the believer's understanding of death. These issues palpably fall within the domain of the theology of the laity, because lay life specifically involves the "reflection on the reality and the conditions of the possibility of an authentic human existence."[32] In each case, the consideration of a particular experience draws it within the horizon of the meaning of death, and within the horizon of the Death of Christ himself. In von Balthasar's words, "the wisdom that comes with the death agony sits in judgment on all the partial wisdom of life."[33] Turning then to the cross that everyman bears . . .

The *Theologia Crucis* of Lay Life

When reflecting on the question of Christ's Cross in lay life, von Balthasar mentions the theologian Dom Odo Casel (1886-1948), who wrote: "The word at Galatians 2:9 'I have been crucified *with* Christ,' has a wonderful depth. It expresses the total contemporaneity of the Master and the pupil: both hang together on the same Cross."[34] (Emphasis added.) Christ himself alone achieved the Sacrifice of the Cross, but at the same time, he makes this mystery present for his Church in the central act of worship of the Church, and to its members as well, namely in the celebration of the Holy Eucharist.[35]

The core of all of Jesus' affirmations about those chosen to follow him—those who "take up their cross and follow" (Matthew 10:38 and parallel texts)—is the truly exorbitant claim that he makes of his followers. For example, a significant scriptural text notes that the Good Samaritan pays for the injured man, "without awaiting anything in return."[36] However, considering the Christian himself, he works with Christ *only* as long as he concentrates on the

---

[32] *GL III*, 24.
[33] *Bernanos*, 502.
[34] Hans Urs von Balthasar, "The Mass, A Sacrifice of the Church?" *ET III*, 198. He is citing Odo Casel's *Das christliche Kultmysterium* (1960).
[35] Cf. Vatican II: "As often as the sacrifice of the cross in which Christ our Passover was sacrificed, is celebrated on the altar, the work of our redemption is carried on, and, in the sacrament of the eucharistic bread, the unity of all believers who form one body in Christ is both expressed and brought about." (LG 3)
[36] *GL VII*, 141.

transformation of the culture, but "if the success of these efforts is the standard, [then] they fall away from the path of Christ."[37] The Cross is, once again, the measure of experience because the Son of God has become man and died for us![38]

Through Baptism, Catholic laity participate in the mystery of the Cross, which is the supreme expression of the self-emptying (*kenosis*) of God in Christ for the world. The Cross is the spiritual foundation of the kenotic life of the Catholic lay person who pours himself out for the service of his fellows and the world at large.[39] This is the *second* moment of Christian life. The exact meaning of the lay person's participation in the Cross begins to unfold in the grace and truth of each of the events in the Life of Christ that the lay person receives in the *first* moment of his life. (The 'contemporaneity' mentioned by Odo Casel above!) The meaning culminates in the events that Christ himself associated with his Death on the Cross and, of course, with his Resurrection from the Dead.

During the events of the last evening with his disciples, besides the offering at the Last Supper of the Eucharistic Bread and Wine, Jesus Christ also washed the feet of his disciples. (John 13:12) This act is "the typical service performed by slaves, [and] is the image of the death on the Cross, which is precisely that: a slave's death (W. Thüsing)."[40] However, as von Balthasar goes on to explain, this was not all that was happening. Jesus was not simply *copying* the action of a slave. The deeper meaning of the act of the washing the feet of the disciples is the fact that it takes place during the celebration of the first Eucharist. The action of washing the feet of the disciples was an illustration of Jesus' pouring out of himself in love, in offering himself to the divine Father, that is

---

[37] "Discernment of Spirits," *ET IV*, 350.
[38] The *Constitution on the Church and the World* notes that: "while earthly progress must be carefully distinguished from the growth of Christ's kingdom, to the extent that the former can contribute to the better ordering of human society, it is of vital concern to the Kingdom of God." (GS, 39)
[39] See Rino Fisichella, *Hans Urs von Balthasar: Amore e Credibilità Christiana*, (Rome: Città Nouva Editrice, 1981), especially his section on kenotic existence 269-276.
[40] Citation from Oscar Cullmann, *Die Erhöhing und Verherrlichung Jesu im Johannesevangelium* (1959), in "The Mass: A Sacrifice of the Church," 219.

represented in the Last Supper and fulfilled on the Cross.

The fundamental point here is that the rendering of Christ's offering of himself takes place because of the perfect harmony between his person and his mission. Such harmony belongs to Jesus alone.[41] His consciousness "coincides with his universal trinitarian mission" precisely because he is the incarnate person of the Divine Son.[42] There is no need to explore this Christological point here, because the real issue is that for everyone else—lay people included—the harmony between one's person and one's mission has to develop over time. This is precisely because of the incompleteness of human existence.[43] Every Christian "cannot make a total response, overnight, to what this new name [of Christian] means, he must grow into it."[44] This 'growing' involves a myriad of real activities and choices on the part of the individual. It also involves a real letting-go of previous meanings and undergoing a real conversion to the staurological perspective on life. (See Footnote 57.) The constant in all lay activity is the assimilation of "our own 'I' more and more completely to our God-given mission".[45] Lastly, the lay Catholic discovers his identity from the mission that he has received from heaven and not from any earthly institution.

Von Balthasar does not illustrate this point, but for example, a lay person training as a medical doctor cannot simply take on everything that he is taught by the medical school. Any unethical action

---

[41] See *GL VII*, 160.

[42] *TD III*, 271.

[43] See Ben Quash, "Drama and the Ends of Modernity," *Balthasar at the End of Modernity*, 156.

[44] *TD III*, 267. The conclusions drawn by von Balthasar also explain the requirement of an appropriate education. As the Second Vatican Council explained: "children and young people must be helped, with the aid of the latest advances in psychology and the arts and science of teaching, to develop harmoniously their physical, moral and intellectual endowments so that they may gradually acquire a mature sense of responsibility in striving endlessly to form their own lives properly and in pursuing true freedom as they surmount the vicissitudes of life with courage and constancy." *Gravissimum educationis*, 1.

[45] *TD III*, 271.

such as the practice of abortion cannot be part of how he visualizes himself functioning as a doctor.[46]

The lay person's route to the coincidence of his person and his mission lies in the 'forsaking' spoken of by Jesus Christ, and that is involved in taking up one's cross. Jesus said: "If anyone comes to me without hating his father and mother, wife and children, brothers and sisters, and even his own life, he cannot be my disciple." (Luke 14:26)[47] The text indicates that there is a situational immediacy, as well as a set of familial and other relationships that serve as the locus of a person's discovery of his or her mission. But as von Balthasar concludes: a *new* hierarchy in personal relationships is imposed by the individual's relationship to Jesus Christ. Then the proximity of mission and personal identity develops as "we discover God by obeying him, our fellow men by serving them, and ourselves, whom we only encounter in such service and obedience."[48] Von Balthasar has identified the unity of the dynamic between the external world and the spiritual world, where we only come to ourselves through obedience and service to the world at large.[49] This is the Christian's response to

---

[46] John Paul II explains: "the value of life can today undergo a kind of "eclipse", even though conscience does not cease to point to it as a sacred and inviolable value, as is evident in the tendency to disguise certain crimes against life in its early or final stages by using innocuous medical terms which distract attention from the fact that what is involved is the right to life of an actual human person." *Evangelium vitae*, 11.

[47] See Aquinas' treatment of this text: "A thing ought to be loved more, if others ought to be hated on its account. Now we ought to hate our neighbor for God's sake, if, to wit, he leads us astray from God, according to Luke 14:26: "If any man come to Me and hate not his father, and mother, and wife, end children, and brethren, and sisters . . . he cannot be My disciple." Therefore we ought to love God, out of charity, more than our neighbor." (*ST II*, q.25 a.1)

[48] Ibidem. Note the French philosopher Fénelon's comment: "It is Catholicism alone which teaches, fundamentally this evangelical poverty." Cited in Henri de Lubac S.J.'s *Splendor of the Church*, 258.

[49] See Vatican II teaching: "Human activity, to be sure, takes its significance from its relationship to man. Just as it proceeds from man, so it is ordered toward man. For when a man works he not only alters things and society, he develops *himself* as well." (GS, 35) (Emphasis added.) See also Rino Fisichella, *Hans Urs von Balthasar:Amore e Credibilità*

the being of the world. The wonder of the discovery of the subject through relation to the object—taking this word in its widest possible sense—was already part of von Balthasar's phenomenological reflections on truth long before he wrote the *Theodrama*. Much earlier, in a work on phenomenology, he said that the subject "awakens in the act of service, and henceforth it will awaken to itself in the measure that it serves in an attitude of self-forgetfulness."[50] In the case being considered here, the graced growth of the subject works in the redeemed and sanctified form of this created dynamic of service.

From the perspective of sanctification, this conclusion can be recast as follows: "the duty of the layman, after his own sanctification, is the portrayal of what is holy in the realm of the profane, the realization of the Kingdom of God in the kingdom of this world."[51] But the 'portrayal' of what is holy is situated *within* the lay Christian's dramatic interaction with the world. However, "it can only come about only through Cross, tribulation, persecution, and martyrdom."[52] Von Balthasar has a properly theological answer to the question of why human experience only finds its meaning within a range of human experience that includes so many 'negative' experiences. The God, who was crucified for us, has taken on the whole range of human experience to show the vastness of eternal life that extends immeasurably far beyond this life. The Christian then "cannot restrict himself to anything less" in terms of what his experience will be, if he is going to serve God and the world.[53] If the Christian is to be a true disciple then he cannot choose to avoid certain experiences when they prove to be onerous or even dangerous. In this chapter, the Christian response to the experiences of finitude, suffering, and death, shows the Christian glorifying God in the other experiences of injustice, persecution, and martyrdom.

God's sanctification of the lay man means that the lay man can love with the love of Christ, in *all* kinds of situations, precisely because "the Cross—'for us'—is substantial love, the uttermost implementation

---

Christiana, (Rome: Città Nouva Editrice, 1981), especially his section on obedience, 262-268.
[50] *TL I*, 71.
[51] "The Layman and the Church," *ET II*, 327.
[52] Ibidem.
[53] "The Characteristics of Christianity," *ET I*, 176.

of the commandment to love."⁵⁴ In other words, for the Christian believer to love is to love to the point of death itself.⁵⁵ This is the life of the one who is called to live as 'the grain of wheat' in order to bring God's fruitfulness to the world. (Cf. John 12:23-36)⁵⁶ This is the life of Christian martyrdom—suffering for faith in Christ, or more generally, suffering for daily responding to the world in faith.

As always, "all human anguish remains comprehended within God's redeeming anguish" on the Cross.⁵⁷ So as we work through some of the features of the human situation, the particular experience of finitude or suffering and the final experience of death will receive its light from the Cross of Christ himself. But there is still more to the *theologia crucis* . . .

The last step in the argument that we have been following, is that the Cross can be said to achieve a new "vantage point" for the meaning of the world in "the Resurrection of the Crucified One."⁵⁸ It is the Resurrection that grounds the *theologia comprehensorum* for the believer.⁵⁹ This overarching theology of the meaning of the life, here and now, is only completed in the Resurrection of Jesus Christ that opens up the world to all of the elements of the end-times in Christ. As Paul explained: "you were . . . put to death to the Law through the body of Christ, so that you might belong to another, to the one who was raised from the dead in order that we might bear fruit

---

⁵⁴ *TD III*, 128.

⁵⁵ Here Aquinas notes the limits of the one who does not accept going to death for his faith. He refers to Satan's words to the Lord God in the *Book of Job*: "Skin for skin! All that a man has he will give for his life. But now put forth your hand and touch his bone and his flesh, and surely he will blaspheme." (Job 2:4) See *ST II* q.124 a.4.

⁵⁶ See Aquinas' explanation of the effects of Christ's Passion: "Christ's Passion is applied to us even through faith that we may share in its fruits, according to Romans 3:25: 'Whom God has proposed to be a propitiation, through faith in his blood.' But the faith through which we are cleansed from sin is not 'lifeless faith,' which can exist even with sin, but 'faith living' through charity; that thus Christ's Passion may be applied to us, not only as to our minds, but also as to our hearts. And even in this way sins are forgiven through the power of the Passion of Christ." *ST III*, q. 49 a. 1.

⁵⁷ *Bernanos*, 502.

⁵⁸ *TD V*, 373.

⁵⁹ Ibidem.

for God." (Romans 7:4)[60] In the Resurrection, a new 'space' opened up in which the world of the Cross becomes a medium of true inner freedom in which "the Risen Lord makes himself known as and when he wishes."[61] There is a new freedom for the disciple in the midst of the experiences of finitude, suffering, and death.

For us, the difficulty lies in the distance between the new realm of freedom in the Risen One, and "the organism that expresses it."[62] The human organism is constantly tired, or hungry, and suffers from illness, and psychological troubles. These physiological and psychological experiences do not automatically lie within this new freedom in Christ, so ordinarily humanity only responds to the new freedom in the most partial way. However, the expressions of freedom such as they are, are nevertheless the expressions of the unique personality of the one who has risen in Christ, and "this personality will manifest itself in ever new ways that spring from its inexhaustible depths, yet specifically and ambivalently within the medium of the world of communication shared by all."[63] It is this growth that will come to bear and even transcend the particular troubles but does not replace them. Often the suffering remains until the end. For example, Saint John Vianney (1786-1859) suffered from hernias to the end of his life. John Paul II had Parkinson's Disease in the later years of his life!

The new and inexhaustible depths of the possibilities of the 'person in Christ' can be glimpsed in the life of someone like Saint John Vianney. Fr. George Rutler describes one of Vianney's visions of the Blessed Virgin. He narrates that Vianney's housekeeper walked in on him, while he was speaking with the Blessed Virgin. The housekeeper later said: "'May I tell you Father, what I thought? I thought it was the Blessed Virgin.' The Curé grinned a little: 'And you were not wrong.'"[64]

To conclude this swift overview of some of the fundamentals of the theology of Christian existence, one more point must be remembered and that is that

---

[60] Cited in *GL VII*, 408.
[61] *TD V*, 381.
[62] *TD V*, 381.
[63] *TD V*, 381.
[64] George William Rutler, *The Curé d'Ars Today*, (San Francisco: Ignatius Press, 1988), 206.

overshadowing the whole vision of man in Christ is the horrible prospect of the Antichrist. The existence of the Antichrist is one of the elements of the end times and he occasioned some reflection by Vladimir Soloviev, the Russian writer (1853 -1900). I refer to him because von Balthasar chose him as an exemplary lay thinker, and obviously his writings struck a chord with von Balthasar himself.

In Soloviev's *Third Conversation,* his conceived of the Antichrist as follows: "Christ divided men in terms of good and evil; [the Antichrist] shall unite them through the benefits of salvation, which are necessary to good and evil alike."[65] This is the manifesto of the Antichrist. The purpose of mentioning the Antichrist is that he is the one who "will blur the edges of the apocalyptic rift between morality and the Cross, between cultural progress and the Resurrection of the Dead."[66] These are von Balthasar's words, but they indicate the point at issue. It is precisely that the stark nature of the consequences of the Death and Resurrection of Christ means that they cannot be 'blurred'. They cannot be reduced to social programs, for example, even those with great motives. The presence of Christ and his grace poses a never-ending challenge to the world, and it is not simply a moral challenge. There is no merely social, psychological, or scientific 'answer' to the subject of finitude and its consequences.

To return to Soloviev once more: his words strike a powerful chord even today: "In earlier times, Christianity was comprehensible to one, incomprehensible to another, but only our age has succeeded in making it repellent and mortally boring."[67] A moralization has crept into some parts of Christianity such that Soloviev's words do still ring true. Von Balthasar's estimation of the nature of true Christianity is that "Christianity, after all is not moral rearmament; it demands a yes or a no."[68] It is a

---

[65] *GL III,* 351.
[66] *GL III,* 351. See *Catechism of the Catholic Church,* 675.
[67] *GL III,* 350.
[68] Ibidem. This necessary distinction that von Balthasar makes emphasizes the conversion that necessary for the following of Christ. The approach to Christianity is not asymptotic. The conversion means taking on Christ and leaving the 'old man' behind. As von Balthasar explains: "'conversion is not the "complementing' of something already

decisive choice before the God who loves us. In a similar vein, Benedict XVI too has reminded us that: "For the Church, charity is not a kind of welfare activity, which could equally well be left to others, but is part of her nature an indispensable expression of her every being." (*Deus caritas est*, 25) The Church's expression of love—which means the expression of love by the lay person as well—has its own character *because* it is the expression of the Church.

The expression of love when colliding with the walls of finitude, of suffering and death is what the lay person is called to do. One of the false teachings of the Antichrist bypasses this persisting paradox of life, the paradox of the 'germ of wheat' (John 12:24). Instead, the Gospel tells us that the Christian experience of finitude, suffering, and death continues to be the occasion to manifest the love of God in Christ.

So to start with: the experience of finitude for the believing man . . .

The Experience of Finitude

The philosophical and theological concept of finitude was presented in the *Introduction*. Here we examine some of the experiences of naked finitude that the Christian comes up against.

From a philosophical point of view, the contingencies of life, "the weight of heredity, instincts, the milieu; education or lack of education," and so on, all play their part in modifying the exercise of our freedom.[69] This is true even though "our freedom is 'laid up' in God's Word; thus, so is our true 'I'."[70] Our "I", in phenomenological parlance, still has to develop through the choices that we make. Furthermore, people are always also under the influence of other people's exercise of their freedom as well, and this can also aid or limit people's development.[71] These are

---

possessed but rather a total 'turning around' in which what is fragmentary is *left behind*; it will be found again but only within the totality, on the far side of a hiatus." *TD III*, 421. (Author's emphasis.) See the whole section entitled 'Coming near' and Conversion, *TD III*, 418-422.

[69] *TD II*, 37.
[70] *TD V*, 389.
[71] To this list John Paul II adds: "There are situations of acute poverty, anxiety or frustration in which the struggle to make ends meet, the presence of unbearable pain, or instances of violence, especially against women, make the

some of the determinisms of life, but it is still true that human beings are free if they should choose to exercise their freedom. The very nature of freedom itself means that no matter what the determining factors in life, "it is only by responding to the personal and impersonal challenges of the world around him that man's freedom is provoked and summoned to realize itself."[72] Thus the human being is given an unfinished life as part of a drama that has to be played out.

However, something more about the structure of finite freedom must be kept in mind, and that is that it "is constantly on the lookout for a solution, a redemption . . . but can never anticipate or construct it from his /[her] own resources, nor does he [/she] even have an intimation of it."[73] This explains the desperate medical searches to extend life, and the searches for a merely natural meaning that mark modern western culture. The essentially pagan searches for pharmaceutical highs, or longevity, or for public prominence, are natural efforts to answer the inescapable limit in finite freedom. They are all attempts at self-redemption, and they all contain the false idea that man will, by his own power, transcend his existence to attain fulfillment. Christian thinking is completely contrary in the sense that it leads us to

---

choice to defend and promote life so demanding as sometimes to reach the point of heroism." (*Evangelium vitae*, EV, 11.) Cf. Benedict XVI's *Spe salvi*: "where freedom is concerned, we must remember that human freedom always requires a convergence of various freedoms. Yet this convergence cannot succeed unless it is determined by a common intrinsic criterion of measurement," (SS 23) He has the same philosophy of the interrelation of individual freedoms.

[72] Ibidem. The basic meaning of freedom was stated by Aquinas as follows: "Now spiritual freedom or servitude may be considered in man in two ways: first, with respect to his internal
actions; secondly, with respect to his external actions." (ST II q.184 a. 4) See also, as an illustration of this fact, for example, the main theme of Viktor Frankl's *Man's Search for Meaning*, (New York: Simon and Shuster, 1984).

[73] *TD IV*, 75. It was John Paul II who noted that: "The divine origin of this spirit of life [in man] explains the perennial dissatisfaction which man feels throughout his days on earth." (EV, 35.)

fulfillment through Christ—the Way (John 14:6)—in the very midst of our lives.

Now even if, in a very real sense, human existence is hopeless in terms of its own structure, man will still strive to achieve "things of ultimate value."[74] So the frail finite person is caught in a situation of tremendous pathos. It is only the Christological fact that all human nature has been taken onto the Cross that changes this structure in terms of its possibilities. It is in this sense that von Balthasar could speak of the believer being "fettered" in terms of his relation to God.[75] The believer is tied—*re-ligio*—to God, in Christ, if he is genuinely seeking real fulfillment.

One instance of naked finitude is best expressed in the words of Georges Bernanos himself: "the solidarity of all of Christendom has not been kept in the face of major, intolerable scandals."[76] This is despite the fact that in Christ there is in fact a realized *solidarity* of mankind. Going back to Bernanos, the solidarity comes about because, as he says: "Redeemed humanity has been made a partaker in divinity."[77] So humanity is joined together in a profound *spiritual* bond through the power of the Holy Spirit, the Spirit of God himself. The question then becomes are men and women going to act from this spiritual horizon so that they are completely supporting and extending this solidarity? Consequently many peoples sentiments that they are alone or do not owe anybody anything, or 'every man for himself', are all in fact denials of the common spiritual communion of man borne by the Spirit of God.[78]

---

[74] *TD IV*, 76.
[75] *TD IV*, 206.
[76] *Bernanos*, 507. This is a citation from Bernanos' play *Le Chemin de la Croix-des-Ames* (1948).
[77] Ibidem. Note also Aquinas' comment: "the salvation of the human race, accomplished by the Incarnate Son, and by the gift of the Holy Ghost." (*ST I*, q.32 a.1.) It is a true solidarity of humanity! See also Aquinas' explanation that "in Christ each nature is united to the other in person; and by reason of this union the Divine Nature is said to be incarnate and the human nature deified." (*ST III*, q.16 a.5)
[78] Cf. Benoît-Dominique de la Soujeole, O.P. "The Universal Call to Holiness," in Matthew L. Lamb, Matthew Levering, eds., *Vatican II: Renewal within Tradition*, (Oxford: Oxford University Press, 2008), 44. As Vatican II explained it:

Bernanos realized that individualized sentiments were part of the words of the biblical Pharisees, for "what do the Pharisees care, since they have paid their tithes and observed the Sabbath?"[79] The lay person does not aim to become a Pharisee. In fact the communion of prayer and spiritual benefits that God has instituted cannot be denied. The lay person is not alone, and is being supported and uplifted by his brothers and sisters in the Spirit of Christ, and furthermore he or she is expected to lend the same service in turn. This principle is the foundation of Hans Urs von Balthasar's theology of finitude, suffering and death.[80]

The character of the attitude of the individual believer can be expressed in terms of 'receptivity', or more biblically in terms of 'poverty'. Theologically, this kind of poverty is put forward in the *Sermon on the Mount* (Matthew 5). Each provision of the sermon indicates how much the believer—hence every lay person—depends on God. The French lay man, Charles Péguy (1873-1914) the poet and essayist wrote of the dilemma that this situation imposes on man: "You bring everything to God, you relate everything to God. From all sides you reach out to God, you wound him. Therefore you can no longer move yourselves. The least of your sins shares the guilt of the Roman spear it reaches personally to the flesh of Christ."[81] Péguy noted that the human situation can only be resolved in the infinity of God's grace. It can be understood only in the *misere* of the descent of God into Hell. It is only in prayer that the apparently impossible situations in which man finds himself can even begin to be grasped.

"United in Christ, they are led by the Holy Spirit in their journey to the Kingdom of their Father and they have welcomed the news of salvation which is meant for every man. That is why this community realizes that it is truly linked with mankind and its history by the deepest of bonds." (GS 1)

[79] Ibidem.

[80] Cf. Vatican II: "Freedom acquires new strength, by contrast, when a man consents to the unavoidable requirements of social life, takes on the manifold demands of human partnership, and commits himself to the service of the human community." (GS 31)

[81] Here von Balthasar is citing from Péguy's *Oeuvres en Prose 1909-1914*. See *GL III*, 457.

Man learns from the saints how to do this because the saint will 'conduct' him to Christ.[82]

The general structure of the layman's receptive poverty ('femininity') has a number of consequences. As noted already, the first result is that he or she *accepts* the burden of finitude. The real acknowledgement of the 'determinisms' of life allows the individual to begin to develop his freedom. So for example: "a man and a woman who hope to have a child are compelled to submit to natural laws that are not subject to their freedom."[83] Going further: lay acceptance then consists in ratifying the structure of reality through the submission of one's intellect and will to the demands of the 'external' determinism. The acceptance takes place within the Church in all three of its dimensions—its kerygmatic, sacramental and charitable life.[84] The Christian's posture of service is understood in the light of Jesus himself. It is the lived expression of the service of the One, who 'came not to be served but to serve' and who expressed this fact at the Last Supper and indeed throughout his Life. (Cf. Matthew 20:28) This logic of service, as the authentic response to finitude, can be discovered in all of the believer's responses to the determinisms of life. However, this is not only service *qua* service, but also

---

[82] Cf. Vatican II: "They are warned by the Apostle to live "as becomes saints", and to put on "as God's chosen ones, holy and beloved a heart of mercy, kindness, humility, meekness, patience", and to possess the fruit of the Spirit in holiness." (LG 40)

[83] *TL I*, 71.

[84] According to Benedict XVI: "The Church's deepest nature is expressed in her three-fold responsibility: of proclaiming the word of God (*kerygma-martyria*), celebrating the sacraments (*leitourgia*), and exercising the ministry of charity (*diakonia*). These duties presuppose each other and are inseparable. For the Church, charity is not a kind of welfare activity which could equally well be left to others, but is a part of her nature, an indispensable expression of her very being." (*Deus caritas est*, 25a) Note also that Henri de Lubac S.J. describes the same experience in terms of the experience of the individual in the Church: "we owe it above all for the deaths she brings us, which man himself is incapable of, and without which he would be condemned to stay himself indefinitely, going round and round in the miserable circle of his own finitude." *Splendor of the Church*, 277.

because it is only in *love* itself that the Christian's development of his life finds "its ultimate meaning".[85]

This service, at least at the level of being, takes place even before the subject awakens as a subject. It is exactly the service that develops the subject as a subject.[86] The complexity increases as the relationship between two individuals is considered. For von Balthasar, when viewed from the phenomenological perspective, each individual can only develop through 'I-Thou' relationships (discussed earlier) that involve each recognizing the other as 'Thou'. Then the two develop further when functioning as a union of subjectivities as a 'we'. This is the "'we' conduct of these persons, no longer in opposition but working alongside one another and cooperating in common activity."[87] Phenomenological analysis uncovers the fact that the subject's development only happens through the 'I-Thou' and 'we' relations, exercised in love. The phenomenological 'law'—if it may be called that—is a factor of human finitude, imaging the infinite relation between the Divine Father and the Divine Son, who are not independent subjectivities. Lay people need to realize the 'law' in life, since they love both God and neighbor.[88]

So it appears that the aspect of finitude must feature in any consideration of lay life. It is

---

[85] Hans Urs von Balthasar, "*Summa Summarum,*" *ET III*, 375.
[86] See Chart 1 in Luigi Rulla S.J. et al, *Psychological Structure and Vocation: A Study of the motivations for entering and leaving the religious life*, (Dublin: Villa Books, 1979), 36. Kenneth Schmitz cites Karol Wojtyła's *Acting Person* where he speaks of the "'inner norm' concerned with safeguarding the self-determination of the person." *The Center of the Human Drama*, 87.
[87] Hans Urs von Balthasar, "The Holy Spirit as Love," *ET III*, 126.
[88] See Aquinas: "Charity signifies not only the love of God, but also a certain friendship with Him; which implies, besides love, a certain mutual return of love, together with mutual communion, as stated in Ethic. viii, 2. That this belongs to charity is evident from 1 John 4:16: 'He that abides in charity, abides in God, and God in him,' and from 1 Corinthians 1:9, where it is written: 'God is faithful, by Whom you are called unto the fellowship of His Son.' Now this fellowship of man with God, which consists in a certain familiar colloquy with Him, is begun here, in this life, by grace, but will be perfected in the future life, by glory; each of which things we hold by faith and hope." *ST II*, q.65 a.2.

inescapably part of the social dimension of life and because of the fascination with individualism in the west there is a need to emphasize this point. H. Richard Niebuhr, for instance, when explaining the relation between the individual Christian and the larger culture writes that "our individual decisions are not individualistic."[89] Von Balthasar goes along with him on this in emphasizing the social context of life and the co-responsibility that it engenders. As he notes, Jesus always "takes other people along with him," in every event of his life.[90] The disciple does the same.

In addition, the believer's social dimension is also inescapably ecclesial. Von Balthasar repeatedly reminds us where the source of the integrity of the existence of the lay person is to be found. The lay person is within a 'sphere of realization' of his freedom, by being situated in the world, and as such "this sphere . . . is absolutely the center of the Church."[91] This is a very strong statement to make. He knows that the early Church did not conceive of things quite in this way because of its greater emphasis on monasticism and eschatology. The Church-world reality today obliges the Church to avoid the more one-sided nature of the earlier views.

Recognizing the role of the Church leads to two actual fundamental determinisms located within the Church itself. One arises because of the hierarchical nature of the Church. The hierarchy is a given and it is fundamental to the working out of lay life because "without its mediation [the lay person] would have not access to the source of salvation."[92] Then again the priesthood is there to serve the laity which is why the relationship between the clergy, laity, and religious, was laid out in such detail earlier. It must be reiterated: "for this period, the final time before the judgment, the ministry is the casing that protects life."[93] The official ministry of the Church is a determining structural element in the authentic lay life.

---

[89] H. Richard Niebuhr, *Christ and Culture*, (New York: Harper and Row, 1951), 245.
[90] "*Summa Summarum*," *ET III*, 374.
[91] "The Layman and the Church," *ET II*, 326.
[92] "The Layman and the Church," *ET II*, 325.
[93] Ibidem.

Then there is also the determinism imposed by Church doctrine. The doctrine of the Church comes from the Scriptures and the tradition of the Church, and then, built on this foundation, "the meaning of truth and Sacrament is attained only where the truth of the life of Christ is displayed in life, in the millionfold variation of Christian existence."[94]

These determinations of lay life come about because the role of the official Church applies without limit to individual believers. However, according to von Balthasar, at the same time Catholics "cannot also demand of [the Church] that she live out for them as a whole the infallible way of holiness."[95] The Church through the service of the Word, the liturgy, and the works of mercy, demands the holiness of the individual. But there is no reciprocal entitlement on the part of the individual to always see a holy Church and be exempted from the demands of the official Church, if the holy Church is not seen. This one-directional relation with truth leads to what von Balthasar terms the 'ecclesial loneliness' of the individual in the Church. Indeed, the experience of 'ecclesial loneliness' is part of the growth of the Christian toward Christ. There are echoes here, once again, of the experience of isolation that was experienced by his mentor Henri de Lubac S.J.[96]

Now since all of these experiences can be occasions for the love of God (in Christ) to express himself (the love of God is a person!) precisely within the experiences of finitude (of being 'determined' in some way), the finite human being must actively seek the love that is being shown. In von Balthasar's words, "the truth that affirms the human person and takes possession of him requires that one be ready to be taken hold of and to give up control over oneself to another (Luke 1:38)."[97] Then in a sentence that cannot be paraphrased and so is worth citing in its entirety: "The act with which God loves us and definitively draws near to us, affirming us and at the same time bringing us into being, by his own action, is his Son."[98]

---

[94] *ET II*, 326.
[95] Hans Urs von Balthasar, "Loneliness in the Church," *ET IV*, 283.
[96] Hans Urs von Balthasar, *The Theology of Henri de Lubac: An Overview*, (San Francisco: Ignatius Press, 1991).
[97] *GL VII*, 400.
[98] *GL VII*, 401.

It is in the life of the divine Son, that we share, that the ultimate drama of life takes place—man is boundlessly loved by God no matter what is taking place in his life.

Suffering

Von Balthasar said to the world of the twentieth century, a world that should not be surprised, because "the world's suffering exceeds our human powers of comprehension."[99] But what point was von Balthasar trying to make? He—and the tradition—teach that the world is made because of love, and it is sustained in existence through love. The disruption of this ordering of the world by human sinfulness is the source of suffering. God permits suffering to educate man, "mak[ing] us aware of the seriousness of life and death and of man's final goal."[100] To understand what this means we need to turn to the exegesis of the *Book of Job* that our author offers us.

In von Balthasar's exegesis, he turns to where the sufferings of Job become unendurable. There is a profound meaning here. Much of the relationship between God and the world is beyond man's control, and "God reacts to man's behavior in a way that cannot be anticipated from the vantage point of finitude."[101] Man's sufferings, if anything, lead to a rebellion on the part of man. They do not bring man to God *unless* they can in fact be seen, through the revelation of Christ, as a participation in the *theologia crucis*. As, the philosopher Paul Claudel (1868-1955) wrote: "The Son of God did not come to do away with suffering but rather to suffer with us; not to abolish the Cross, but to stretch himself upon it."[102] So the fundamental dimension of the response to suffering is that the Christian is expected to embrace it. So: "Even in the midst of the night of suffering we should not allow ourselves to be separated from the underlying joy

---

[99] *TD IV*, 193.
[100] *TD IV*, 192.
[101] *TD IV*, 193.
[102] Cited *TD IV*, 195. Note too John Paul II's thought that: "The truth revealed in Christ about God the 'Father of mercies,'(II Corinthians 1:3) enables us to 'see' him as particularly close to man, especially when man is suffering, when he is under threat at the very heart of his existence and dignity." *Dives in misericordia*, 12.

of being privileged to suffer."¹⁰³ This is not a simple tolerance or even endurance, but an embrace of the new reality brought about in Christ. This reality contains one final element. Following the data of revelation from the Ascension to the end of the Bible, indicates that the Church too will have to suffer, because "you will be hated by all nations." (Matthew 24:9)

Now there is also suffering within the relationships in the Church: the lay man's suffering is the suffering of having to act as an individual, sometimes even without the support of the community, either the Church community or the local society. In such a situation, the "Church is concentrated in this individual."¹⁰⁴ This brings about a tragic dimension in the real world situation of individual Christian. For example, the individual can find himself testifying to the Church of Christ when even the Christians around him are doing nothing. Von Balthasar lists figures such as Saint Athanasius (c.293-373), Maximus the Confessor (c.58-662), even Søren Kirkegaard (1813-1855), who all found themselves in this 'isolated' position in the Church, to the point of risking their lives.¹⁰⁵

Some of the reasons for the 'isolation' of the individual in the Church are that, for one thing, some clergy might have "made a pact with anti-Christian power structures".¹⁰⁶ He does not illustrate this point, but this was the situation in which Saint Vincent de Paul for example found himself in seventeenth century France. Saint John Vianney too found himself in the same situation in the nineteenth century. Or there might even be the pressures of "a system of terror within the Church".¹⁰⁷ Again he does not offer examples, but here he is probably pointing to a more than general knowledge of the events of Church history. One perhaps obvious instance was the ecclesiastical oppression in the life of his mentor, Henri de Lubac S.J. (1896-19991). This experience impacted von Balthasar's own understanding of the

---

¹⁰³ *TD V*, 338.
¹⁰⁴ *TD III*, 453.
¹⁰⁵ Cf. *TD III*, 454
¹⁰⁶ *TD III*, 454.
¹⁰⁷ Ibidem.

Church.[108] The third example of an isolating factor, again drawn from the history of the Church, is when many of the members of the Church "are caught in a net of ideological slogans that has entangled both the hierarchy and a large proportion of the Catholic people too."[109] Once again, he does not offer illustrations!

In each case the individual has to represent the Church despite the lack of support even from within the Church itself. The individual has to "bear witness to the authentic Church of Christ in the face of an environment that mistakenly imagines it is of the Church."[110] He points to many illustrations of this dramatic test in a Christian's life that are found in the work of the playwright Reinhold Schneider (1903-1958).[111] Each play highlights the dramatic dimensions of the individual's Christian duty. To cite Schneider himself: "Faith addresses the indivisible man. This is why it is so senseless to make a distinction between the statesman as politician and the statesman as Christian, between the Christian as soldier and as the one who kneels at the communion rails."[112] Schneider's project was to analyze the lives of some of the great figures of modern history, but any further treatment of them would take us too far afield.

The recurring point in this reflection on the isolated individual is the need to identify the foundations of the isolation. It is not the isolation of the renegade that is the concern here. In fact, von Balthasar is emphatic that the key to appreciating the actual quality of the life of isolated individuals depends on their humble obedience. So, for example, he asks: "Was not Savonarola [1452-1498] right . . . against the curial administration of the Borgia Pope, and yet wrong through a dark and obstinate fanaticism."[114] Henri de Lubac S.J. himself noted that "the man of the Church does not stop short at mere obedience he loves obedience himself, and will never be satisfied with

---

[108] See the Introduction in *The Theology of Henri de Lubac: An Overview*, trans. Michael M. Waldstein, (San Francisco: Ignatius Press, 1991). See also de Lubac's own discrete allusions to his difficulties in his chapter entitled "*Ecclesia mater*," in his *Splendor of the Church*, 237ff.
[109] *TD III*, 454.
[110] *TD III*, 455.
[111] Ibidem.
[112] *Tragedy under Grace*, 11.
[114] "Tragedy and Christian Faith," 408.

obeying 'of necessity and without love'."[115] Here he is citing Thomas á Kempis' *Imitation of Christ*.[116]

The Christians suffering was described in detail by Georges Bernanos, and he concluded that in the face of this suffering, the Christian "knows no trace of morbidity."[117] Instead everything chosen by the Christian is "a work and an expression of joy."[118] This joy can even emerge in the meaning of Jesus' descent into Hell! There is the underlying theological virtue of hope in every one of the considerations on suffering.

Now we can examine the nature of death.

Death

At the level of being, to quote Kierkegaard: "Between man and truth lies death—that is why we are all more or less afraid."[119] The experience of death is an experience of a different order from the other two that we have considered. Death is the great "interpreter of life".[120]

To begin to sketch the theology of death: patristic scholar that he is, von Balthasar started by noting that Saint Ambrose "distinguishes 'three kinds of death'."[121] These are the death due to sin, the death of the believer as he dies with Christ, and the end "of this life and work."[122] Once again it is clear that the Death of Christ is to be the foundation of the believer's grasp of the meaning of death. The death due to sin is not our concern here. However, the grasp of the meaning of the end of this mortal life has much to do

---

[115] *Splendor of the Church*, 258.
[116] Cf. Thomas à Kempis, *The Imitation of Christ: A New Reading of the 1441 Autograph*, William C. Creasy trans., (Atlanta: Mercer University Press, 2007).
[117] Hans Urs von Balthasar, "Bernanos: Hell and Joy," *ET III*, 467.
[118] Ibidem.
[119] Cited by D.C. Schindler, *The Dramatic Structure of Truth*, 264.
[120] Cited by D.C. Schindler, *The Dramatic Structure of Truth*, 316. Cf. Benedict XVI's words: "For believers the day of death, and even more the day of martyrdom, is not the end of all; rather, it is the "transit" towards immortal life. It is the day of definitive birth, in Latin, *dies natalis*. The link that exists then between the *"dies natalis"* of Christ and the *dies natalis* of St Stephen is understood." *Feast of Saint Stephen, Angelus*, 26 December 2006.
[121] *TD V*, 332.
[122] Ibidem. Citing the words of Saint Ambrose himself.

with the 'death' in Baptism, as will be made clear below!

Man's finitude is the final and most dominating sign of his mortality and it too is a given. In fact "this, more clearly than anything else, shows him that his very existence is a gift."[123] Furthermore, man dies because he is estranged from God. It is the Second Adam, who achieves the unity of all mankind in new life, because "the last Adam [is] a life-giving spirit." (I Corinthians 15:45)

Now von Balthasar has some detailed considerations of the notion of 'natural death'.[124] Because it rarely simply occurs without medical technology being involved, "what the idea of 'natural death' has in view is 'mastery' of death."[125] The problem is that this view can be traced back to the philosophical schools of Stoicism and Epicureanism. This is not the Christian view. In addition, in the post-Modern period, there is the denial of the tension between the concepts of 'our death' (that is as the member of the race) and 'my death' (the death of an individual). In the post-Modern period, the latter notion is being suppressed. Apparently, the latter view means that "it should be enough for him to have made some small contribution to the race's destiny".[126] So what is the Christian answer to the question of death? It must obviously start with Jesus Christ himself.

Most directly, Jesus raised people from the dead and demonstrated his life-giving Spirit, and he often did this by touching. In our time, the glorified and Risen Lord's "'touching' is made concrete in the Church's sacraments".[127] This 'touching' starts with the individual's dying and rising with Christ in the Sacrament of Baptism. The Church is the concrete *place* of Christ's visitation of the dying, just as Mary (the proto-Church) was present at her Son's death. In this event von Balthasar finds the foundation and the meaning of the Church's care for the dying, because the dying person is not alone, and "can look to the grace granted to the Mother and to her mediation of all

---

[123] *TD IV*, 95.
[124] *TD IV*, 126.
[125] *TD IV*, 127
[126] *TD IV*, 128.
[127] *TD V*, 344.

graces."[128] There is a profound internal link between the dying individual and the community in Christ.

So what are the implications for the lay person in this understanding of death? The short answer is the Christian lives a life "marked by the Cross".[129] Thus, the answer to the mystery of death relies on something that goes beyond death itself—Jesus Christ who rose from the dead. For von Balthasar, this means that "'resurrection from the dead' demonstrates the eternity-content and eternal existence of an existence that is lived and died in bodily terms and is unique in each case."[130] First and foremost, understanding death involves the recognition that in poetic terms, death "is the *tear* that actually elicits the wiping away."[131] He is basing his conclusion on the *Book of Revelation*: "He will wipe every tear from their eyes, and there shall be no more death or mourning, wailing or pain, (for) the old order has passed away." (Revelation 21:4) In other words, God allows that the glory of the risen life be prepared for by his people's experience of dying.

Secondly, the transcendent meaning of the Cross means that the Christian lives with the daily recognition that—in Jesus' words— "whoever does not take his cross and follow after me is not worthy of me." (Matthew 10:38) Thus "man's being is bound for death, it is always dying."[132] Only in grasping this fact is the meaning of finite existence illuminated by the transcendent meaning of the Cross.[133] Finite existence is given its true bounds of meaning by the Cross, so that each and every word and deed can be chosen in the light of approaching death, resurrection, and judgment.

To conclude these few comments, our author offers us a powerful quotation, taken from the French philosopher and playwright, Paul Claudel that leaves us with a final thought: "The universe lacks God and God puts himself into the hands of each of us, so that

---

[128] *TD V*, 345.
[129] *TD V*, 339.
[130] *TD IV*, 134.
[131] *TD IV*, 135.
[132] *TD IV*, 122.
[133] See John Paul II's explanation that "Death has justice done to it at the price of the death of the one who was without sin and who alone was able—by means of his own death—to inflict death upon death." *Dives in misericordia*, 81. See I Corinthians 15:54-55.

we can give him to the universe."[134] From this perspective, the way the Christian brings the transcendent meaning of life, as it is illuminated by God, into the world, is through his personal choices for or against allowing God to be glorified in Christ in the life of each individual.

Conclusion: The Community of Saints

Having made a few brief comments about the nature of finitude, suffering and death from the perspective of the Christian lay person, there is one final feature of the Christian reality that inevitably accompanies these considerations and it has been hinted at several times. That topic is the fact of the ever-present community in Christ, the Body of Christ. Western cultures have a fascination with the existence of the isolated individual. There are constant attempts to raise the notion of the 'individual' to the level of an ideal, as some kind of glorious concept of the human being, to the exclusion of other dimensions of being human. Consequently, it is important to spend time on the concept of Christian being-in-community as essential, and not accidental, to the enduring and growing through finitude, suffering and death.

To start with: "the Church is the genuine inter-personal community; each ministry within her is unique, and through the cooperation of these ministries 'the whole body, joined and knit together . . . makes bodily growth and upbuilds itself in love.' (Ephesians 4:16)"[135] Now, as was suggested in each of the sections above, the different elements of the believer's life—finitude, suffering and death—are definitely the experience of the individual, and yet they gain their full meaning and are ministered to, within the interpersonal communion of the Church. In this communion of grace and truth the human being and the Church develop through the ordinary events of human life being brought within the horizon of the Cross![136] The *kerygma*, *leiturgia*, and reaching out in

---

[134] *TD IV*, 416

[135] *TD III*, 428.

[136] See Ben Quash, "Drama and the Ends of Modernity," *Balthasar at the End of Modernity*, 163. He speaks of the 'betrayal of time' by von Balthasar. I think that this is an erroneous conception of Hans Urs von Balthasar's understanding of the time of the Church. Von Balthasar does not 'freeze' time as he describes the development of the

charity, comprise the great dynamics of the Church. All three can help develop the Christian's graced grasp of the Cross, as well as to aid those who are in danger of death.

As von Balthasar puts it: "the encounter with the Lord in one's brother takes place, not in an isolated I-Thou relationship, but in the embrace of both by the global reality of the Lord."[137] The two or more believers who face finitude, or suffering, or death, are living from a common principle of life, the Spirit of Christ himself. Then according to Paul: "whoever is joined to the Lord becomes one spirit with him." (1 Corinthians 6:17) Hence, on the one hand, Christians and laity, in particular, need to look to this life for their salvation, and on the other hand, they cannot, for example, "be yoked with those who are different, with unbelievers." (2 Corinthians 6:14)[138] The Church is an "intimate fellowship" where the experiences of finitude, suffering, and death can open out into the fellowship with Christ and one's Christian brothers and sisters.[139] The whole section at the beginning of the *Second Letter* to the Corinthian community has been entitled "Thanksgiving" because it extols Paul's understanding of life in the community formed by Jesus Christ. In this community, God is "blessed", because in the community, the Father's "compassion" and "encouragement" flow. (2 Corinthians 1:3) Paul goes on to explain that the community is flooded by the "God of all encouragement, who encourages us in our every affliction, so that we may be able to encourage those who are in any affliction with the encouragement with which we ourselves are encouraged by God." (2 Corinthians 1:4) Here is a concept of community stretching far beyond a simple association of persons. It is a community of

---

Lay person bringing his person closer to his mission. Note also that Schindler has argued for two concepts in von Balthasar's thought: 'truth as community' and the 'fruitfulness' of community. These are evident in the Christian community's experiencing of finitude, suffering and death in its members. See *The Dramatic Structure of Truth*, 251-254.

[137] *GL VII*, 458. See also *Hans Urs von Balthasar:Amore e Credibilità Christiana*, the section on love, 276-285.

[138] See *GL VII*, 461.

[139] Ibidem.

intimate horizontal and vertical communication sharing the compassion and encouragement of the divine Father.[140]

Regarding suffering, Paul continues: "Christ's sufferings overflow to us." (2 Corinthians 1:5) There is an interplay between suffering and the encouragement of those who live in the Spirit of Christ so that those who suffer do so "for your encouragement and salvation." (2 Corinthians 1:6) And then "if we are encouraged, it is for your encouragement." (2 Corinthians 1:6) If the community is formed by the Spirit of Christ, then it lives in the theological virtue of hope: "Our hope for you is firm." (2 Corinthians 1:7) The hope is specifically for those who suffer that they will also "share in the encouragement." (2 Corinthians 1:7)

Von Balthasar explained that participating in the life in the Spirit of Christ as the "communion that goes directly from the vertical to the horizontal".[141] The divine Spirit (vertical) becomes the glorified presence of Jesus Christ that indwells the members of the community (horizontal).[142] Then because of this community, generated by the Spirit of God in Christ, specifically with respect to the suffering of the members: "If [one] part suffers, all the parts suffer with it; if one part is honored, all the parts share its joy." (1 Corinthians 12:26) Here Paul is referring to the parts or the members of the community of the Spirit.

This is the picture of the Catholic community when it is fully functioning. The works of grace and charity in the community are not isolated moments for the individual. They are expressions of the inner powers of a community that beats with the heart of

---

[140] See John Paul II's note: "The authentic sense of faith of the people of God perceives this truth, as is shown by various expressions of personal and community piety." *Dives in misericordia*, 126.

[141] *GL VII*, 463. The distinctive nature of the Christian community was described by Aquinas as follows: "The incarnate Son of God is the common Savior of all, not by a generic or specific community, such as is attributed to the nature separated from the individuals, but by a community of cause, whereby the incarnate Son of God is the universal cause of human salvation." *ST III* q.4 a.4.

[142] This is a fundamental point in the Christology of von Balthasar as the mission of Christ continues in the world bringing its own light to the world. See Lucy Gardner, David Moss, Ben Quash, Graham Ward, *Balthasar at the End of Modernity*, (Edinburgh: T&T Clark, 1999) especially 46ff.

Christ himself. The experiences of finitude, suffering, and death, that appear to isolate the individual and crush him into a situation of sheer endurance, are in fact the historical 'set-ups' for the manifestation of the drama of love, that is played out between the divine Incarnate Son and the divine Father in the divine Spirit. Then as John wrote: "No one has greater love than this, to lay down one's life for one's friend." (John 15:14) The divine love makes friends of the members of the community who are bearing with each other and caring for each other. As von Balthasar concludes: "the 'friends' become such in the creative event of this love."[143] The laity are constituted as who they are and who they claim to be, by their acts of charity, in cooperation with grace.

In the words of Georges Bernanos: "who cannot give more than he receives begins to decompose."[144] This could be the motto of the lay person-in-act.

—

This concludes our survey of some themes in the theodramatic study of lay life. The final study in this volume is the theo-*logic*-al study of the laity in the Catholic Church.

---

[143] *GL VII*, 455.
[144] *Bernanos*, 532. Von Balthasar is citing from *Les Grands Cimitiéres sous la lune* (1938)

Chapter 8 Being Brought Home to the Mansions of the Father

Introduction
The Truth of Being
The Three Lay Christian Forms of Life
    Membership of a Secular Institute
    The Ecclesial Form of Marriage
    The Ecclesial State of Virginity
Conclusion: Final Vision

Introduction

    This final chapter on the theology of the Laity, in von Balthasar's work, has a theological reason for being positioned where it is and formulated as it is. The concluding chapter must offer not simply any theo-*logic*-al study of the Laity, but the *terminus ad quem* of the preceding theological description of the events of lay life, namely, the manifestation of Truth. This is where the title of the chapter comes from.[145] It is crucial to keep in mind that "the path of discipleship of Christ, leading to the Father, leads simultaneously in two directions: vertically upward and horizontally into the world in the proclamation of salvation to all nations and in the transformation of the world according to the Christian commandment of love."[146] The two 'directions' in the ecclesial forms of life are the 'vertical' relationship with the Father that gives the horizon of meaning to the local 'horizontal' events in the particular life of the history of the individual, the Church and the world.

    From a philosophical perspective, von Balthasar sums up the tradition concerning the transcendentals as follows: "a being *appears*, it has an epiphany; in that it is beautiful and makes us marvel. In appearing it *gives* itself, it delivers itself to us: it is good. In giving itself up, it *speaks* itself, it unveils

---

[145] See Hans Urs von Balthasar, *Theologic III: The Spirit of Truth*, trans. Graham Harrison, (San Francisco: Ignatius Press, 2005), 437.
[146] Ibidem. Here von Balthasar himself refers to *Gaudium et spes* especially 40-45, 77-93 in footnote 8.

itself: it is true."[147] (His emphasis.) So the metaphysical concepts, introduced in the preceding chapters, converge in the direction of this chapter. Theologically, the perspectives on lay life that have been developed can be seen in their unity in the reflection on the truth of lay life. Drawing on the unveiling of the lay person's truth, it follows that this involves *self*-expression. The redeemed and sanctified self is living-out a particular form of life in the Church.

The concept of the self-expression of the individual *in ecclesia* is grounded as follows: in metaphysical terms, the appearing, giving, and delivering of itself and speaking of itself, continues the scriptural narrative of the Incarnation and the events that followed.

The above metaphysical statement could be said to be a formulation of a line from the *Prologue* of the *Gospel of John* in metaphysical terms. For example, where John states: "the Word [himself] became flesh, and dwelt among us, and we saw his glory, glory as of the only begotten from the Father, full of grace and truth." (John 1:14) Once again, the *Gospel of John* is the 'vanishing point' of the New Testament. Then the ultimate horizon of the meaning (truth) of the lay person can be said to develop one's life to the point where: "When all things are subjected to him [Jesus Christ], then the Son himself also will be subjected to the One who subjected all things to him, so that God may be all in all." (1 Corinthians 15:28). This is the eschatological reference point of all lay life, which at the same time is profoundly rooted in the world. It is both 'vertical' and 'horizontal' at the same time. The reader is aware that being a lay person is a form of "being in action," a "moving idea" within history, as the lay person participates in the form, (does not merely imitate or parallel) through being given a fullness of form of life, in the Life of Christ in the New Testament.[148]

In ecclesial terms, as Schindler has noted, von Balthasar's understanding of the drama of life turns on the individual's decisions (truth), because the

---

[147] Hans Urs von Balthasar, *Hans Urs von Balthasar: His Life and Work*, ed. David Schindler, (San Francisco: Ignatius Press, 1991), 4.
[148] D.C. Schindler, *Hans Urs von Balthasar and the Dramatic Structure of Truth*, 74.

"drama is 'an action of ultimate significance that takes place *within* a finite framework'", (Emphasis added.) and so is manifest in the 'finite' forms of lay life in the Church.[149] The paradox of the 'vertical' infinite truth, being manifest in the 'horizontal' finite concrete moment, is grounded in the fact of the Incarnation of the divine Word itself, and his 'mere' words and gestures allow us to 'see the Father'. (Cf. John 14:9)

In a work called *Our Task*—for our purposes it might have been called 'Our Lay Task'—Hans Urs von Balthasar identifies three theological principles of the finite concrete manifestation of truth.[150] They are: (i) that Laity "carry the 'light' of Christ into the 'darkness' and can heal and reconcile to the true Logos a secularized mentality."[151] (ii) But then he poses the following question to the Laity: "Are they deeply enough rooted in the mysteries of the Catholic faith to *bear living witness* to the unity and interconnectedness of the mysteries?"[152] (Emphasis added.) And finally, (iii) he says that "any program for an inclusively Catholic and apostolic life should surely be constructed out of the *wholeness* of the Creed."[153] (Emphasis added.) Von Balthasar's descriptions of the truth of the ecclesial forms of life are the focus of this chapter.

In each case, the descriptions draw on the principles that we have just listed, so that they safeguard the dramatic expression of truth rather than mere knowledge of the truth. In this way, the

---

[149] *Dramatic Structure of Truth*, 315. Schindler is citing *TD 4*, 88, with a modification to the translation.

[150] Hans Urs von Balthasar, *Our Task: A Report and a Plan*, trans. Dr. John Saward, (San Francisco: A Communio Book, Ignatius Press, 1994). The work is immediately concerned with the establishment of the Secular Institute known as the Community of Saint John however some of the principles apply to all Christian life in the Church.

[151] *Our Task*, 127. A very Johannine formulation but for von Balthasar and the Patristic tradition, the *Gospel of John* is the overarching theological 'umbrella' for the rest of the rest of the New Testament corpus.

[152] *Our Task*, 121. The forgoing theology has been drawn from the mysteries of the faith of the Church.

[153] Ibidem. The unity and all embracing nature of the faith must be represented in the life of the lay person. It is almost redundant at this point to note that he does not envisage a program for a form of life to consist in a set of steps that are ever completed in this life!

descriptions can embrace the whole of a human being's existence, "from its biological roots up to the very heights of grace and life in the Holy Spirit."[154] Put in terms of the transcendentals, the *beauty* of the ecclesial form of life that makes the manifestation of truth possible expresses the *good*-ness of the gift of the spirit-filled self, and then the truth of the self-expression is "where the relation implied by the other two transcendentals is consummated in a fruitful way, and thus it ensures that the whole crystallizes in a mysterious unity."[155] (Schindler) The integrity of the expression of truth comes from the individual, in an ecclesial form of life, participating in the unity of Christ and his Church. The lay forms of ecclesial life are graced so as to have awesome possibilities for expressing the presence of the life of Christ.

Considering the three forms of ecclesial life comprises the final study that von Balthasar suggested in the introduction, namely the theo-*logic*-al study. In this case, it is the study of the truth of lay *existence*. Now as Schindler sums it up, the truth of a lay person's life "is intellectually grasped only in being concretely lived."[156] The lay person comes to understand himself, the Church, and Christ, by a daily *fulfilling* of the particular form of life. Avoiding the demands of the form of life, and its route to a fruitful life, and real freedom, means a life of "certain barrenness."[157]

Last but not least, the reflection on the three forms of Christian life will allow us to finally see the aesthetic, the theo-dramatic and the theo-logical studies in their totality. In the consideration of the three states, the circumincession of the transcendentals is glimpsed within the exercise of lay life. There is a dramatic expressive 'direction' to lived lay life, and as such it has a mission. It is to be a convincing expression of the truth of life in Christ to others.

But first the four aspects of the philosophical reflection on being and truth must be considered,

---

[154] *GL 1*, 27.
[155] D.C. Schindler, *Dramatic Structure of Truth*, 369. See also Hans Urs von Balthasar,
[156] D.C. Schindler, *Hans Urs von Balthasar and the Dramatic Structure of Truth*, 253.
[157] *GL I*, 28.

before the theological issue of truth and ecclesial being is examined.[158]

The Truth of Being

The three volumes of von Balthasar's *Theologik* consider the relationship between the structure of created truth and the structure of uncreated truth.[159] He returns to one of the earliest perspectives on truth, and that is that "truth is not only a property of consciousness, it is above all a transcendental qualification of being itself."[160]

An analysis of the three states in terms of truth must consider the general metaphysical features of the relation between being and truth. Watch how the ecclesial being of the Christian can manifest truth! Von Balthasar makes four points:

(i) <u>The unveiling of the truth of being (through the form of life) only takes place in love</u>.

Each of the ecclesial forms of life involves human relationships. Philosophically, the truth in the relationship of two human beings, for example, is where the unveiling of the essence of one, within the loving knowing of the other, is such that the first comes to know himself, and be known, in the second. Loving the Church means the individual discovers the truth of his existence from the Church.

Moreover, the essence of the first person is not immediately available to be plundered by passersby. Similarly the experience of the Church and ecclesial forms of life, are not fully knowable to those who are not committed to them in love. Von Balthasar also speaks of truths that cannot be unveiled to people who

---

[158] These four points offer the barest introduction to the great reflection on being and truth in von Balthasar's *Theologic I: Truth of the World*.
[159] *TL I*, vii.
[160] Hans Urs von Balthasar, *Phénoménologie de la Vérité: Vérité du Monde*, (Paris: Beauschene et Fils, 1952), 7. (The French text that became *TL I*.) In this choice he agrees with John Paul II who similarly held that "being is not constituted in and by consciousness; quite the contrary, it constitutes both consciousness and the reality of human action as conscious." John Paul II, "Person: Subject and Community," cited by Kenneth L. Schmitz, *At the Center of the Human Drama*, (Washington D.C.: Catholic University of America Press, 1993), 130.

are unworthy, because in fact, truths can be "destroyed by their destination."[161] In other words, where there is no love the truth of being (or of a form of ecclesial life) is stifled. For the lay person, if there is no love then even the merest notion of ecclesial Marriage, Virginity and membership in Secular Institute, will appear empty, that is, not as a loving gift from God in his Church with all kinds of loving possibilities.[162]

For our purposes, at the theological level, living the lay forms of life with love also demonstrates the loving relationship in Christ and his Church, that manifests the deepest truth of being that has been redeemed and sanctified. Without love, these forms simply cannot develop into the manifestation of God's glory which is their potential.[163]

The lived-out ecclesial form of life manifests truth from deep within itself so that . . .

(ii) <u>The unfolding of the truth of being (the form of life) is mysterious</u>

The individual's concrete living-out of an ecclesial form of life has mysterious depths to it. Von Balthasar explained what he means by 'mystery' through a metaphor: "The palace of a king is not necessarily invisible even though only a few people are permitted to visit it," yet the palace is a mysterious place.[164] Knowing what is going on the palace depends on how much one is immersed in the workings of the palace, and one still never knows everything! Now just as the people directly involved with the king may visit his palace, so the people in relationships are the only ones who actually discover the truth of each other and the truth of being (or the Church) itself.

If truth is only uncovered through relationships, then part of the truth of ecclesial life includes

---

[161] *TL I*, 107.
[162] According to Aquinas: "for the received is in the receiver according to the mode of the receiver." *ST I* q.84 a.1.
[163] Cf. The Second Vatican Council: "[Christ] reveals to us that "God is love" (1 John 4:8) and at the same time teaches that the fundamental law of human perfection, and consequently of the transformation of the world, is the new commandment of love." (GS, 38)
[164] Hans Urs von Balthasar, *Theo-logic I: Truth of the World*, Adrian J. Walker trans., (San Franciso: Ignatius Press, 2000), 102.

the truth that unfolds within the relationships to the other States of Life in the Church. (Chapter Three) The individual's own truth is only uncovered by participation in a form of ecclesial life with its relation to all of the others. In practice, this means actually relating to the Pope, bishops, priests and religious and the Laity. Each and every relationship always has an over plus of meaning that is not fathomed instantly—like the life of the palace. There is always more!

The mysterious nature of being does not rest on the concept of being as irrational. Instead *our reason is faced with a reality whose truth cannot be grasped in a single moment.* Only a constant and profound relation with being (an ecclesial form of life) allows openness to the mystery of being (the Church and Christ himself).

Consequently the married life, the virginal life, or life in a secular institute, means trusting, first of all, that objectively such a life is by its very nature mysterious, because the ecclesial form of life images some aspect of the infinite depths of the creator God! So it is simply not realistic to consider that there are three (or n) rules of the form of life to be mastered, and then the particular form of life has been exhausted.

The mysterious quality of the form of life means that each form of life involves some kind of active waiting on the unveiling of further truth. The individual is always in the situation of either, moving towards a deeper understanding of his situation within the form of life through the action of living it out, or he is drifting towards understanding it less when he does not accept the truth that is unveiled, in the drama of faithfully living the form of life.[165] Neither Marriage nor any of the other forms of life are conceivable as a goal to be achieved and surpassed. They are all mysteries to be endlessly participated in. So for example, even the consideration of divorce starts with the denial of this essential feature of the meaning of Marriage! It shows that the persons involved have not sought, and

---

[165] Note David C. Schindler's comment that is the project of his work, *Hans Urs von Balthasar and the Dramatic Structure of Truth*, Perspectives in Continental Philosophy series, John D. Caputo series editor, (New York: Fordham University, 2004). He says: "the reciprocal relation that constitutes the heart of truth will avoid some version of a reduction to immediacy only if it is understood dramatically." (6)

in fact, are choosing to stop seeking the fuller meaning (truth) of ecclesial Marriage, and the demands that it makes on them.

The mysterious nature of an ecclesial form of life then demands faith.

(iii) <u>There is a direct proportion between knowledge and faith in the relation to being (the form of life)</u>.

The loving relation of two people, for example, contains the possibility of growth in knowledge due to the faith each has in the other. Theologically, faith and knowledge are directly proportional as well. To the degree that someone lives out his ecclesial form of life *in faith*, in the Church, through grace, he will come to know what he needs to know, and be what he needs to be.

One further term is needed here. We can say that the form of lay life is authentic "to the degree that it receives its form entirely from the content that molds it."(Treitler)[166] The content is the presence of the Word of God through the Spirit of God.

The possibility of an authentic form of life for a Lay person develops because the divine Son has sent the Holy Spirit and "the Spirit will lead you to all truth." (John 16:13)[167] The Holy Spirit is both 'subjective' and 'objective'. On the one hand the Spirit is the love between the Father and the Son (Immanent Trinity) and so is 'subjective' in von Balthasar's parlance, and 'leads *you* to truth' (Economic Trinity).[168] Then the Father and the Son in the Spirit are the true subjects in relationship. But at the same time, the Spirit is the product of their love and so is 'objective' in von Balthasar's language (Immanent Trinity) and "is the ground of everything 'institutional' in the economy of salvation." (Economic Trinity)[169] Approaching the institutions or ecclesial forms of life

---

[166] Wolfgang Treitler, "Foundations of Authentic Theology," *Hans Urs von Balthasar: His Life and His Work*, 170.

[167] The cooperation of the Son and the Spirit in the work of Redemption is dealt with in more detail in "Die Beiden Hände des Vaters," *Theologik III – Der Geist der Wahrheit*, (Einsiedeln: Johannes Verlag, 1987), 153ff. (*TL III*)

[168] *TL III*, 340.

[169] John O'Donnell, "The Logic of Divine Glory," *The Beauty of Christ – An Introduction to the Theology of Hans Urs von Balthasar*, eds. Bede McGregor O.P. and Thomas Norris, (Edinburgh: T&T Clark, 1994), 169.

in faith means that the Spirit of God is known to work through them and allows the Spirit to speak the truth of existence (and salvation) to the world through this particular person or relationship or community.

Approaching the forms of life in faith means each person becomes the authentic person he is called to be and such a person will come to know more about true Marriage or true participation in the other forms of life and how each draws its members to full personhood and full expression of the truth of Christ.

The committed faithful individual comes to love, know and believe in the Church more too. The heart of any form of Christian life is of course the incarnate divine Word and these forms of life bring Christ's imaging of authentic life before God into their historical situation so that Saint Paul could say: "it is no longer I who live, but Christ lives in me; and the life which I now live in the flesh I live by faith in the Son of God, who loved me and gave himself up for me." (Galatians 2:20)[170]

Lastly, it is love that brings the form of life to life.

(iv) Love has its way of bringing the truth about

Philosophically, one persons love for another produces the ideal image of the beloved in the lover. From the perspective of the divinely instituted ecclesial form, the form and the individual participating in it can be said to 'co-enable' each other. The individual becomes who he or she is called to be and the form is realized in a concrete instance in *this* person's life to advance the mission of the Church in Christ.

Mother Church lovingly presents and models the forms of life in the concrete so that a particular individual can answer his call into one of them in the Church. [171] Relying on von Balthasar's treatment of the 'mother's smile' where the mother is the Church, then it can be said that "insofar as he gives himself, the child perceives I give myself."[172] The 'child' (the individual in the form of life) comes to comprehend his existence and himself within the form of Lay life borne

---

[170] Jacques Maritain said of Christian art that: "the definition of Christian art is to be found in its
[171] Also see Henri de Lubac's chapter "*Ecclesia mater*," in *Splendor of the Church*, 237-278.
[172] "Movement towards God," *ET III*, 15.

by the Church who is his loving Mother in faith as he gives himself fully over to the form of life.

When the Church who offers a particular form of life, people who love see the image they have of the ones they love as the objective representation of the ones they love.[173] This is the image that the beloved can bring to fulfillment. The real depth of a person's being (and being called) surfaces due to the love of the other. Theologically Marriage, Virginity and being in a secular institute are about love.

The fact that the beloved only finds his true image in the eyes of the one who loves him means that in the case of being loved by Christ in his Church the individual discovers a tension in his life. To cite Schindler: "A dramatic conception of truth . . . is encounter."[174] The individual must embrace the tension of seeking out and encountering Christ in his Church and within her the form of life to which he is called and then the "truth in a more comprehensive sense [is] as the whole that emerges in the encounter of mutual dynamisms" between Church (Christ) and individual believer—to return to Schindler once again![175] The encounter with the structure of the form of life in the Church is a constant dynamic encounter with Christ in his Church that brings forth a new whole—the newly structured (in-formed) individual manifesting the form of life in and for Christ and his Church.[176]

To conclude, it can be said that these four metaphysical statements about truth and being that even in the bare paragraphs above show concord with the scriptural revelations on being. Such considerations would however take us far from our objective. The metaphysical statements will be useful in examining some details of the forms of Lay life. Stating them early makes the reader aware of the

---

[173] Ibidem.
[174] Schindler has realized the character of the manifestation of truth that von Balthasar has developed. See his *Hans Urs von Balthasar and the Dramatic Structure of Truth*, 6.
[175] *Dramatic Structure of Truth*, 6.
[176] The same dynamism is evident in the analogy of the palace used above. The one who is permitted into the palace is changed by the entry into the palace in many ways not least because a whole network of relationships are constituted with the people in the palace that were not present before he entered the palace.

possibilities of the dynamic expression of truth through the form of ecclesial life that the individual takes on. They will be applied in the consideration of the forms of ecclesial life once the forms of life have been seen in terms of beauty (Chapters Two to Four) and act (Chapters Five to Seven).

The Three Lay Christian Forms of Life

The three forms of lay life in the Church that receive the most attention from von Balthasar are Marriage, the Virginal State and membership of a secular institute. These are the 'once and for all' forms of life offered to the individual by the Church.

Von Balthasar's reflections start by considering the scriptural data on the original state of humanity even though it is only accessible in a rudimentary way.[177] This starting point is consistent with both von Balthasar's and the Biblical notion of human beings as created in the image of God. The Fall and Redemption through Christ mean that the restoration—and indeed the overwhelming expansion—of the nature if this capacity to be an image is only possible through Jesus Christ.

The theologians of the 'great age'[178] to use his phrase for the medieval period came to the consensus that "in man's original state, virginity[179] and bodily[180] (we do not say 'sexual') fecundity could have coexisted."[181] The two terms 'virginity' and 'fecundity' are the key to the points that follow. They are in parentheses since von Balthasar has expanded the meaning of these terms from their normal colloquial fields of meaning as 'meaning one who has never had sexual intercourse' and 'fruitful or fertile' resp-

---

[177] Hans Urs von Balthasar, in his chapter entitled "From Original State to final State, *CSOL*, 67ff. According to von Balthasar, "in the last analysis, it is from man's original state, from the state in which God conceived, intended and created him that every later state must take its origin and meaning." *CSOL*, 84.

[178] *CSOL*, 95.

[179] "Jungfräulichkeit" in *Christlicher Stand*, (Einsiedeln: Johannes Verlag, 1977), 78.

[180] "leibliche", Ibidem.

[181] *CSOL*, 98. The particular theologians von Balthasar refers to are William of Auxerre (95), Thomas Aquinas (97), and then earlier writers such as Gregory of Nyssa (98), John chrysostom (99), Maximus the confessor, (100).

ectively.¹⁸² The expansion is necessary because of his identification of intra-divine correlates for these terms.

The first form of ecclesial life that occupied a great deal of von Balthasar's time and thought is life in a secular institute.

Membership of a Secular Institute

The Apostolic Constitution *Provida mater* (February 2, 1947) issued by Pius XII recognized a form of canonical association in the Church that was distinct from religious congregations yet still bound by the evangelical counsels. The proclamation announced that they would be called 'Secular Institutes'.¹⁸³ Their purpose was to be the same as that which had been identified earlier by the Congregation of Bishops, namely that of "faithfully practicing in the world the evangelical counsels and of working with greater liberty at works of charity."¹⁸⁴ The proclamation also praised the ability of these institutes to penetrate the world.

The proclamation offered an historical note in its reference to the fact that such associations had already been developing in the Church in the early part of the nineteenth century.¹⁸⁵ It was *Provida mater* that gave them the first canonical recognition. The possibility of forming such associations was unknown to von Balthasar at the time when Adrienne von Speyr was thinking of a community of Catholics who would live the life of the counsels in the world but who first "ought to leave the world for a period of recollection and spiritual formation and then return to the world at full strength."¹⁸⁶ It was the initiative of Adrienne von

---

[182] See *Websters New World Dictionary on Power CD*, (Dallas TX: Zane Publishing, 1994).
[183] Catholic Church, *The States of Perfection*, arranged by the Benedictine Monks of Solesmes, Mother E. O'Gorman R.S.C.J. trans., (Boston MA: St. Paul Editions, 1967), 349.
[184] Decree of the Congregation of Bishops and Regulars, August 11, 1889. See Footnote 624a in *The States of Perfection*, 350.
[185] *The States of Perfection*, 349. Von Balthasar also footnotes the text of Jean Beyer, Les Institutes Seculier (1954) as sources on the nature of the opposition to secular institutes by the older orders. See Hans Urs von Balthasar, "A Theology of the Secular Institute," *ET II*,42.
[186] Ardrienne von Speyr, *Erde und Himmel: Ein Tagebuch*, (Einsied-eln: Johannes Verlag, undated) entry number 95

Speyr and Hans Urs von Balthasar that gave rise to the Community of Saint John.

In this section, the links to the thought and work of Adrienne von Speyr will be put aside. Von Balthasar paid a detailed tribute to Adrienne von Speyr and has listed the numerous instances of her influence on his thought in the volume entitled *Our Task: A Report and a Plan*. This section here will simply examine the main areas of the theology of Lay life as they have been developed in the earlier chapters of this book. The ecclesial context comes first . . .

The Secular institute within the Church

To start with, the creation of Secular Institutes provides an answer to some less than adequate historical developments in the Church. Von Balthasar bewailed the fact that the structure of the Church has developed in a way that excluded the competent Lay person prior to the Second Vatican Council. This was apparently due to some developments in the Middle Ages.[187] For the medical doctor or the architect to follow the evangelical counsels (prior to *Provida mater*), it was usually necessary for them to renounce their occupation. Now with the provisions of Pius XII Lay people are in a position to be the instruments of the evangelical counsels within their own particular secular occupations.

Amongst other things the presence of Secular Institutes remedies the reduction of the Church to a bipolar entity composed of those in authority and those in the parish community.[188] In this distorted view of the Church, the state of the evangelical counsels and its contribution to the complete nature of the Church as the Body of Christ is simply set aside. Yet another positive consequence of the more general entry into the life of the counsels is that the commitment to the counsels puts the religious priest and the religious Lay person in a secular institute on an equal footing. Thus there is a discourse between two people committed to the counsels different from that taking place between teacher and pupil. Both participate in a

---

(June 9, 1941) cited in Hans Urs von Balthasar, *Our Task: A Report and a Plan*, 47.

[187] See "La Leçon de L'Histoire," *Laïcat et Plein Apostolat*, 34-47.

[188] Such a theory is found in the work of Cardinal Mercier, M. Thils etc.

structure that indicates their common mission. Such a possibility of conversation could be the touchstone of a reconciliation of the secular and the theological sciences.

When we turn to the ecclesial relations shown earlier (Chapter Three) we find that the member of the Secular Institute fulfills all of the intra-ecclesial relationships of religious that were shown earlier. They manifest the truth of Christ as poor, chaste and obedient and they do this for the rest of the Church that is to priests, to Laity and to the world.

These considerations lead to some further comments on the form of life in a Secular Institute.

The Theological Form of the Life of a Member of a Secular Institute

The form of life of a member of a Secular Institute is defined by the evangelical counsels. The member follows Christ in a life that involves a unified life of the counsels and a corresponding life in the world. In this way each individual member lives out the principle stated in Chapter Three, namely that the evangelical state is the norm for the lay state. The theology of the counsels starts from the Original State

The Roots of the Original State

The epitome of love is the relation between the Father and the Son in the Holy Spirit. Within this loving relation, the Son is "obedient", "poor" and "pure" with respect to the Father.[189] The Son absolutely accepts his mission from the Father—this is his divine 'obedience', in von Balthasar's terms.[190] The Son is exclusive in that he accepts no other callings but that of the Father and this is his poverty in the face of the Father. The Son is thus pure in his following of the call and hence fruitful (fecund) eternally. The Son's poverty and purity both have obedience (the Ignatian element again!) as their higher ordering principle. That is to say that the whole bounty of his mission (divine fecundity)

---

[189] *CSOL*, 77.
[190] "The application of the concept of obedience to the divine person is, of course, a figure of speech—an anthropomorphism. But, in the final analysis, all human speech is anthropomorphic, and this figure has been made definitive and proper by the Incarnation of the Son (Philippians 2:7)." *CSOL*, 78.

flows from this divine obedience which is an exclusive acceptance of what the Father wills (divine poverty).

Now there are divine intra-Trinitarian analogs within the divine relations for the human existence as obedient, poor and chaste in the Church, the redeemed community of humanity. Hence the principle of dramatic action is fulfilled: "it is ultimately only meaningful when seen against the background of a given absolute meaning."(Schindler).[191] Here is the heart of the dramatic expression of truth for the Religious State in the redeemed humanity. The analogical relation between the divine and creation is only possible because human beings were created as God wanted them to be and the Divine Son was the formal end of this creation.[192]

Furthermore, the fundamental all-embracing nature of poverty, chastity and obedience in the primeval human state meant that there was a primeval *unity* in the states of life (virginity and marriage) even if it is "no longer comprehensible to fallen man."[193] Various theories have been offered to explain how the unity might have come about.[194] The issue here is not the complex attempts of the scholastics but rather that "in Paradise, virginity meant, not the renunciation, but the fulfilling of love, which was the form of perfect fecundity."[195] So too by analogy with the purity and fruitfulness of the Son, the person called to the ecclesial virginal state is living a life of spiritual fecundity drawing on Christ's fecundity.

By way of explanation of the original state, it can be said that the relation between virginity and fecundity resulted from the fact that: "Man's body and its powers stood in the same relationship to his soul as did his natural powers to the supernatural powers of loving faith."[196] It is precisely the nature of love as

---

[191] *TD I*, 74.

[192] Von Balthasar summarizes the situation this way: "It is understandable that the world was created on the model of the Son; that 'all things were created through him and unto him'; . . . (Colossians 1:16-17), because the filial mode of God's eternal love is the most proper, the most exemplarary one for the right relationship between God and creature." *CSOL*, 79.

[193] *CSOL*, 98.

[194] Theories analyzed at *CSOL*, 95-103.

[195] *CSOL*, 94.

[196] *CSOL*, 93.

centered in the spirit that makes the identification of virginity and fecundity in the original state possible. Again the archetype for this understanding is the relation between the Father and the Son in the Holy Spirit. It is the purity (the intra-divine analog of consecrated human virginity) of the Son with respect to the Father that makes the Son eternally fruitful, "so fruitful that the mutual love of Father and Son produces the person of the Holy Spirit."[197] This is the intra-divine fruitfulness that finds its analog in the unity of virginity and fruitfulness in the original human state.

But the relationship of the Father and the Son in the Spirit does not remain within itself, complete and fulfilled as it is. This relationship becomes the archetype (Chapter Two) for the relationship between human beings and God. The existence of such an archetype has two consequences: (i) even in the Order of Creation, "human perfection is not in itself self-sufficient and purposeful: it stands in the service of the glorification of the love within the Trinity."[198] Here is the "significant horizon" of dramatic action noted by Schindler.[199] (ii) After the Fall this perfection is achieved by Christ, who is the Goad (Chapter Six) in those who share in his grace in his form of earthly life. His form of earthly life constitutes the only form of relation to God and within that all embracing form of life it is the only form for the virginal life, married life and for membership of a secular institute in the Church.

In other words, there is a fundamental ontological link between the *form* of the original human state where human beings were created according to God's plan and the *form* of Christianity. The original created humanity is restored in Christ. So: "Man's original state, then was the perfect synthesis of the Christian state of life whether in the world or in the way of the evangelical counsels, in which the state of the counsels expressed the inner attitude and disposition, [and] the worldly state the outer counterpart and fulfillment."[200] The spiritual

---

[197] *CSOL*, 77.
[198] *CSOL*, 82.
[199] D.C. Schindler, *Hans Urs von Balthasar and the Dramatic Structure of Truth*, 315.
[200] *CSOL*, 121.

interior disposition is the higher principle and measure of the use the body, mind and spirit. Now Christ and Mary manifested this unity. (As always Mary does this through the merits of Christ.)[201] It can also be said of Mary she lived out the close connection between the virginal state and fecundity in the plan of salvation since she lived both to the full.[202] The fruitfulness of the ecclesial virginal state is how it expresses the life of service to the Kingdom as Mary and indeed Christ himself did.

The formal element of each individual's virginity is the marriage between Christ and his Church. By being chaste within the structure of the Secular Institute, the member will be fruitful spiritually and in an incarnate fashion within the relationships of the community and beyond as well. A pertinent comment of von Balthasar relates to the efforts to find substitutes for the loneliness that do arise from being faithful to this vow—one must not turn the community into "a family business."[203] There are not to be special relationships that become exclusive of other members in the community.

The third counsel is poverty and it has already been mentioned as a counsel relating to the need for possessions after the Fall. In a Secular Institute, the member under-stands spiritual poverty as self-emptying and self-surrender. This attitude is mirrored in a lifestyle that involves no hoarding and having the minimum necessary for living as a member of the community and working in a profession. Following the Pauline notion of gift, everything is viewed as given for the benefit of the whole Church community. It is the

---

[201] According to von Balthasar, "Mary does not simply echo the paradisal synthesis, but has her own indisputable place in the all-embracing Christological synthesis." *CSOL*, 206.

[202] This is the point at which James Helft's article picks up the notion of the close relation between the virginal state and motherhood in Mary. He does not mention that this unity is the nature of the original human state before the Fall. He also missed the fact that this original human nature finds its archetype in the intra-trinitarian relations. These are crucial to including Mariology in soteriology rather than making it a separate discipline. These two steps have been included in the presentation above. Cf. James Helft, "Marian Themes in the Writings of Hans Urs von Balthasar", *Communio* 7 Summer 1980, 133.

[203] *Our Task*, 141.

greater whole that dictates the role of the individual parts.

There is a fundamental truth to the life of the counsels. Such a life clearly show the fundamental truth of the Son's relation to the Father and so belonging to a Secular Institute takes on the transcendent role of realizing the love between the Father and the Son in Spirit within the created world.

Theological Persons in a Secular Institute

One of the themes in the theodramatic study was the theme of becoming a theological person. Von Balthasar says quite simply that "the chief concern of the Church ought to be the preservation of the robust, free, strong Christian personality."[204] The terminology of the 'Christian personality' emphasizes the completeness of the Christian being in the world as a theological person. The concept of Christian personality has the sense of the Christian *habitus* that lies behind all of von Balthasar's thought on the operation of the person. As Jacques Maritain explained when he wrote of the Christian artist and art: "The whole soul of the artist affects and controls his work, but it should only affect and control it by the artistic habit. . . . A Christian work would have the artist, as artist, free."[205] It is a Christian who does the work but does not work in a programmatic fashion to 'show' Christianity. In the language of forms there is to be a true radiance of the heart of the form. Then and only then can the Christian shoulder great responsibility as a participant in the mission of Christ to the world. Given the argument of Chapter Five that human freedom can only be fully realized in Christ, the member of a Secular Institute gives themselves totally to God who calls them in Christ. The precise form of this giving is dictated by the evangelical counsels. In other words, they draw the secular life into a life that is a following of Christ.

To expand on the nature of life in the Church one must examine two fundamental theological tensions that together define life in the Church. There is a tension in a person's life between eschatology and

---

[204] "A Theology of the Secular Institute," 423.
[205] Jacques Maritain, trans., J.F. Scanlan, "Christian Art," *Art and Scholasticism with other Essays*, (Kessinger Publishing), 54.

Incarnation. Then there is also a tension between general and particular vocation.

In the first tension the Christian is 'in the world but not of the world'. (Cf. John 15:19) The Christian's life is positively in the world since this is the world for which Christ died and the world is being drawn into the Kingdom of God. So on the one hand Christians belong to something fundamentally new in the world through the Incarnate Christ. In this sense the life of the counsels in a Secular Institute are the radical expression of following Christ. On the other hand the old world continues and it is where Christians live and work and they are all called to introduce the spirit of the counsels.

The second tension which completes the first and brings us closer to a theology of the Secular Institute in the relation between a general and a particular vocation. Chapter Three has already indicated some of the differences between these two qualitatively different kinds of vocations. All Christians have a general vocation. They have been called from the world to join the mission of Christ. The point to be repeated here is that the person who has a particular vocation from Christ "to a closer following" receives an objectively better life than that of a general vocation.[206] This comparative applies to the individual concerned. He or she will serve the Church's mission better *because* he or she has entered the State of Election at God's call.[207]

Given these two tensions, the nature of the member of the Secular Institute as a theological person can now be made clearer.

In the tensions between eschatology and Incarnation, the life of the counsels is firstly "the spirit of the whole and not a thing for specialists."[208] The 'whole' is the radical following of Christ. But more than this, the life of the individual member of the institute radicalizes the spirit of the whole Church and serves the Church in its mission by doing this. The fourth Rule for the Women's branch of the Community of Saint John, for example, states that "the professions they practice should give each member the opportunity to cooperate, according to her capacity, in the building

---

[206] "A Theology of the Secular Institute," 434.
[207] *Our Task*, 130.
[208] "A Theology of the Secular Institute," 435.

up of God's Kingdom in the world."²⁰⁹ God's Kingdom is the whole of God's project and the chosen individual carries the light of the counsels into their profession as their part of the project.

The special intimacy of the working of the Spirit in the soul of the chosen Christian is highlighted by the name that Adrienne von Speyr and Hans Urs von Balthasar chose for the community: the Community of Saint John. John is the *realsymbol* for the members of the Secular Institute. Saint John was exemplary in attaining theological person-hood as he was drawn into the work of Christ and so was highly relevant for the new community who hoped to follow the same path. As von Balthasar explained in the plan for the community, John was the one loved by Jesus in a special way.²¹⁰ This constituted a unique call to love Christ in a special way as a response. In responding to this call John could contemplate the mystery of Christ and offer true teaching on Christ, Mary and Peter—the *Gospel* and the *Letters*. In this way von Balthasar recalled the constellation of people around Christ that became the incarnate presence of the mystery of salvation. (Chapter Two)²¹¹ This is again an instance of the whole Church mentioned above.

Furthermore Saint John symbolized the fulfillment of the life of the counsels. The theology of the *Gospel of John* and in the *First, Second* and *Third Letters of John* is spacious enough to embrace the entire Scriptures and the Tradition and so contributes to presenting the true image of Christ. This imaging is the link to the counsels. If John could express—under inspiration—the true meaning of Christ then he was living the life of the counsels! In addition, John was entrusted with caring for Mary.

The handing over of Mary to John (John 19:26) means that one can explain the theological complex around John as follows: "The Mary-John community, established in the Petrine Church, has its origin in the Cross."²¹² Such a complex shows the fundamental way

---

[209] *Our Task*, 169. Bear in mind that *Our Task* is not a rule for all secular institutes. It is the rule that von Balthasar worked out with Adrienne von Speyr for the Community of Saint John in Basle.
[210] *Our Task*, 117ff.
[211] See also the chapter "The Apostolic Foursome," in *The Office of Peter and the Structure of the Church*, 304ff.
[212] *Our Task*, 125.

in which God's truth comes into the world namely through the relationships around the Cross. These real relationships around the Cross and with the Crucified One are the final sign of God's love. This is the truth already prepared for in the relation between Being and Truth.

In the case of the Community of Saint John, as for John himself, the Cross of Christ is the source of the obedience of the community and its poverty. Members are obedient with Christ's obedience to the Father. They are poor as the Son was in receiving everything from the Father. In this way they make present the truth of the inner-Trinitarian mystery in an incarnate sense. Their virginity is the touchstone for the fruitfulness of their lives.

So their professional life is never a closed self-contained world with its sole end located in this world. Members do their secular professions to carry the evangelical counsels into the world. For example, von Balthasar explains that "teachers of secular subjects, to the best of their ability, may well be offering a substitute for the lack of, or the deficiencies in, religious instruction."[213] Von Balthasar's conviction here is that the Church truly has something to offer to the secular professions—von Balthasar spoke of the contribution of the Church as "a power supply from the innermost resources of the Church."[214] For example, the doctor can stand in for the priest by bringing a proper understanding of the human being and of life into his consulting room. The priest does not exercise his ministry in the doctor's consulting room. Thus the truth of God is manifest in the particular situation through the member of the Secular Institute when they do they their work with love.

The Member of the Secular Institute is 'Feminine'.

Members of a Secular Institute are also 'feminine' in the sense found in Chapter Six. If the counsels themselves are "the concrete and comprehensible realization of belief (reinforced by love and hope) in the grace of God that overcomes the world and is our salvation" then God has offered to those he calls the means to love him through a life of

---

[213] *Our Task*, 173.
[214] Ibidem.

the evangelical counsels.[215] To those called to this life, these are the better means to show him love and so constitute a moral demand on the one called. In other words, given the 'feminine' nature of faith, the counsels are concretely 'feminine'. In different terms there is a very specific dying that takes place in one who follows Christ. (The first moment.) This comes about through active cooperation with the received grace of God. It is only through this process of self-surrender that a member will be freed to speak of the Kingdom. (The second moment.)

The true capacity to be 'feminine' in the life of the counsels is only present when the individual genuinely knows what he or she is renouncing. In von Balthasar's words: "Only one who loves the richness of life, one for whom domestic blessings constitute an opportunity and a means for self-expression, only one who posses the courage of self-responsibility, only one who is capable of genuine personal love, can have a real understanding of what is involved."[216] If this capacity is present and chosen for a higher good then another facet of Christian 'femininity' comes to light, the first moment of graced receptivity is specifically open to a higher good.

Von Balthasar has noted three characteristics of this higher good: (i) it is graced offer by God. In other words it is not something attainable by the human being on his own. (ii) It opposes the sinfulness of the world. This is important because a human being is not capable of dividing the world into a sinful sphere and a purely creaturely sphere. (iii) It contains the offer of a hope for the future which is the ground for a renunciation in the present.[217] This line of reasoning means that for example, a professional person who lives the life of the evangelical counsels would practice his or her profession purely for the love of God and neigh-bor.

To repeat a point that has already been made: von Balthasar saw obedience as the key to the other two counsels.[218] Committing one's will to the higher

---

[215] Hans Urs von Balthasar, "On the Evangelical Counsels," *Elucidations*, (London: S.P.C.K., 1975), 150.
[216] "On the Evangelical Counsels," 151.
[217] "On the Evangelical Counsels," 153.
[218] He cites Aquinas in support of this argument: "the vow of obedience includes the other vows, but not vice versa: for a religious, though bound by vow to observe continence and

good which is the will of God overflows in true poverty and true virginity for the sake of Kingdom. There is however the concern about obedience as mere pliancy rather than the freely thought out and willed consigning of one's freedom. Von Balthasar mentioned Bernanos, Guardini and Peguy with their concerns in this regard.[219] Once obedience is the mature commitment of one's freedom then it is not a constraint of liberty.[220]

At this point, obedience and poverty and chastity transform the committed individual into someone who is truly spiritually 'feminine' with respect to God. Von Balthasar also uses the term 'transparent'.[221] This transparency is with respect to all of the mediations of the will of God through the Church, the rule of the community and the instructions of the person's superiors. Looking at a different dimension of transparency, each individual will require prudence to see that their professions never interfere with the fundamental transparency of their lives to the Kingdom.

Here the step from the notion of transparency to the notion of the truth of authentic being is self-evident even if it is not always realized in practice!

The Ecclesial Form of Marriage

Let us start from von Balthasar's words that "Marriage is that indissoluble reality which confronts with an iron hand all existence's tendencies to disintegrate, and it compels the faltering person to grow, beyond himself, into real love by modeling his life on the form enjoined" by Christ in his Church.[222] This statement echoes the metaphysical statements on truth that were laid out above. The individual who is married is accepting the form of life that will bring him or her to fullness as a person who loves another in

---

poverty, yet these also come under obedience, as well as many other things besides the keeping of continence and poverty." *ST II II* q.186 a.8

[219] "A Theology of the Secular Institute," 423.

[220] Cf. ST II II q.88 a.4: "Even as one's liberty is not lessened by one being unable to sin, so too, the necessity resulting from a will firmly fixed to good does not lessen the liberty, as instanced in God and the Blessed." Cited in *Our Task*, 132.

[221] *Our Task*, 132.

[222] *GL I*, 27.

Christ for the Church but behind all of this lies a profound human unity of male and female.

The fundamental concept of Marriage is unity. The original unity is the one divine Trinity itself. Superlative love and fidelity are characteristic of such unity. Marriage in the grace of Christ roots Marriage in the Trinity "more deeply . . . than did the marriage of Paradise."[223] However unity underlies the narrative of Eve's being made from the rib of Adam as well. God's fruitfulness in bringing Eve forth from Adam is "a direct physical image of the origin from the Father's substance of the eternal Son."[224] There are three important points to be drawn from this statement for the understanding of Marriage. The first is that the unity of relationship between male and female images the Divine Trinity and this is prior to the male and female choosing to do such which is to say that this image lies at the ontological level.[225] And second, it indicates the supernatural origin and goal of human being.[226] Then lastly, "the communal oneness of Adam and Eve was thus the oneness of Adam's flesh."[227] The male Adam and the female Eve were successively brought into existence from oneness and they are created to reach oneness again, "that is why a man leaves his father and mother and joins himself to his wife, and they become one body." (Genesis 2:24) The spouses receive each other physically and spiritually which is the first moment of the 'femininity' of each of the spouses. The second moment consists in the generative fruitfulness both physically as biological

---

[223] *CSOL*, 233.
[224] *CSOL*, 227.
[225] Cf. Vatican II: "By its very nature the institution of Marriage and married love is ordered to the procreation and education of the offspring." (GS, 48) John Paul II noted that: "Sexuality . . . is by no means something merely biological, but concerns the innermost being of the human person as such." (FC, 11)
[226] Cf. Vatican II: "Authentic married love is caught up into divine love and is directed and enriched by the redemptive power of Christ . . . with the result that spouses are effectively led to God." (GS, 48)
[227] *CSOL*, 227. Note also John Paul II's insight that, in Schmitz' words "man as male comes to a new self-awareness and self-realization only with the coming into being of man as female." Cited by Kenneth L. Schmitz, *At the Center of the Human Drama-The Philosophical Anthropology of Karol Wojtyla/Pope John Paul II*, 102.

parents and spiritually as the family into which their infant is born.

For von Balthasar, there was more to God's act of bringing Eve out of Adam. The couple as male and female have received their fecundity in the order of creation. Male and female human beings are created from one (Adam) unlike animals that are created in gendered pairs. The gendering of human beings belongs to both man's spiritual and biological nature. Nevertheless human fruitfulness is still a fruitfulness received from God. As Eve says after conceiving Cain: "I have acquired a man with the help of God." (Genesis 4:1) What the couple have received from God is a participation in the "mystery of the Father's self-giving to the Son, in which the Father empties himself of his own godhead in order to bestow it on the Son who is eternally of the same nature as he."[228] So even after the Fall sexual union continued to be the sign of the promise of God's fruitfulness and gave it meaning. In the Old Testament, marriage was the normal human state of life and sterility was considered a curse since fruitfulness comes from God.[229]

In the New Testament in Jesus Christ, the great Christian synthesis of the elements of nuptiality lies in the *Letter to the Ephesians* where they are taken up into Christ's saving action. Through Christ the relation of male and female has a reference point above itself. This is Schindler's 'meaning that embraces the whole immanent order' where the entirety of the lives of the male and the female are drawn into the union.[230] Then the notion of theological personhood achieves its full scope as body, mind and spirit transcend themselves in response to the demands of the union: "Give way to one another in obedience to Christ. As the Church submits to Christ so should wives submit to their husbands . . . .. Husbands love your wives, as Christ loved the Church." (Ephesians 5:21-25) The nuptial relationship of husband and wife

---

[228] *CSOL*, 228. John Paul II notes the totality of the self-giving in the human image. "The total physical self-giving would be a lie if it were not the sign and fruit of a total personal self-giving, in which the whole person including the temporal dimension is present." (FC, 11)

[229] See Aquinas: God "who is the Author of the institution of marriage." *ST II*, q.100 a.8.

[230] D.C. Schindler, *Hans Urs von Balthasar and the Dramatic Structure of Truth*, 315.

functions in obedience to Christ. The mystery of the relationship between husband and wife is shown to be unlimited by the reference to Christ's relation to the Church.[231] The order of redemption has opened a whole new horizon to this relationship unlike the limited and even selfish horizons of non-ecclesial unions.[232] The transcendent horizon of Marriage can only be understood within the relationship between Christ and his Church. It is this synthesis in Christ that echoes the central concept of theological personhood namely the coming to personhood by finding a form of life that is contained in the mission of Christ to the world and manifests it historically.

Returning to the four aspects of the relation between being and truth: Marriage is a human relationship of love that reaches its true fullness of freedom and truth only when joined to the loving relationship between Christ and his Church.[233] Marriage is also mysterious because it takes place between a male and a female who are mysterious in themselves but in Christ Marriage too is "a great mystery" (Ephesians 5:32) and so is never able to be exhausted or quantified. Thirdly, the approach to Marriage in faith is the doorway to knowing the true image of Marriage as it is presented by the Church to the couple. Finally, it is the love of the spouses for each other in Christ that brings each spouse to hold the true image of their spouse in Christ and shows it to the spouse. Further the union of the spouses in Christ makes the relation between Christ and the Church present for everyone to see—provided they in turn look with love.

The further specification of human act in gender adds an additional qualification to the third relation of being and truth. (above) The fruitfulness of the couple brings a very concrete 'image' of the couple

---

[231] Note Schindler's summation: "the form of marriage is nothing but freedom." *Dramatic Structure of Truth*, 332.

[232] This connection comes "from the spring of divine love and [is] modeled on Christ's own union with the Church." (GS, 48)

[233] This connection also emphasizes the positive nature of marriage itself which has not always been easy to find in Church expressions. Von Balthasar listed the more problematic locations of such teaching in "On the Evangelical Counsels," *Elucidations*, (London: S.P.C.K., 1975), 136.

into the world in the form of a new son or daughter. The daughter of the married couple born of the sexual act is seen in faith as the gift of God and the expression through them of the fruitfulness of God. Von Balthasar saw the sexual union as the best human image of the union of Father and Son in the love of the Spirit.[234]

Marriage and Form

The notion of 'form' was examined in detail in the Chapter Two. The focus here is the nature of the form of Marriage as a unity of faith, hope and love.

The love in Marriage has a particular form given to it by the death of Christ and his mission to the world. In other words marital love involves more than just the male and female spouse as individuals. Hence von Balthasar could refer to Marriage as a 'bracket' that goes beyond and at the same time contains all tendencies to individualism and the need to satisfy personal needs.[235] Marriage does this because it is a true theological form and expression of the work of Christ through the Holy Spirit in the world for the glory of the Father.[236] This is the source of its radiance as a theological form.

The living realization of this form taps the wellsprings of the Holy Spirit. In this way the form of Marriage defines freedom, faithfulness and love. For Christians, perfect love is the Son's love for us. Christ's freedom and faithfulness are contained within this love. The crucial point is that "God first loved us." (1 John 4:10) The *a priori* understanding of Marriage comes from Christ because ecclesial Marriage is not a mere natural relationship with an additional 'spiritual' component added. Christ's relation to his Church is the higher principle that gives the union of the man and the woman its proportion. With this in mind, the next step in von Balthasar's argument is clear—

---

[234] John O'Donnell, *Hans Urs von Balthasar*, (England: Geoffrey Chapman, 1992), 164.
[235] *GL I*, 55.
[236] Cf. Vatican II: "All their works, prayers and apostolic undertakings, family and married life, daily work, relaxation of mind and body, if they are accomplished in the Spirit—indeed even the hardships of life if patiently borne—all these become spiritual sacrifices acceptable to God through Jesus Christ (Cf. Peter 2:5)." (LG, 24)

Marriage is the act of a Christian. Specifically it is an action with respect to God.[237] It is an act of hope!

In faith, hope and love, the spouses make a commitment of fidelity to each other which because of its character of faith, hope and love is at the same time a commitment of fidelity to God. "The acts of faith of the two marriage partners meet in God," just as the life-forms of Christians discussed earlier meet in God in the sense that their life-missions are part of the mission of the Son for the Father in the Holy Spirit.[238] The eternal faithfulness of the Son is the tree onto which the faithfulness of the spouses is grafted. God is the basis of the unity of the spouses, as well as witness to this union and the pledge of their faithfulness.

God is the basis of the nuptial unity in that the spouses receive each other from God as a graced gift. Their self-surrender to each other takes place in different interconnected ways: in the vows and in physical union. In the vows, the couple is joined in a faithfulness that comes from God who gives the gift of his own faithfulness. They are limitless because God's faithfulness is limitless. In physical union the couple who have given up their right to dispose of their lives now give up their individual right to dispose of their own bodies: "The wife has no rights over her body; it is the husband who has them. In the same way, the husband has no rights over his body; the wife has them." (1 Corinthians 7:4) They now have a common destiny which they work out together.

For von Balthasar, the married couple has in fact entered the primal unity of created human beings since they now are one flesh, echoing the one flesh of Adam and Eve, where Eve came forth from Adam. Marriage has brought them to this created unity which is their original created purpose. The unity each individual had prior to the Marriage is not a true unity

---

[237] Note Kenneth L. Schmitz' *At the center of the Human Drama*. In reviewing John Paul II's play *The Jeweller's Shop*, Schmitz says: "Love is less a matter of time than of eternity. It is not an adventure of the passing moment, since it is shot through with that vertical axis that 'cuts across every marriage'." (16) Also John Paul II: "Marital Love reflects God's love for his people." *The Theology of Marriage and Celibacy*, 171ff.
[238] *CSOL*, 245.

because: "It is not good that man should be alone." (Genesis 2:18)

To conclude: the unity of the two spouses in God indicates that the distinction of the two ends of Marriage is purely for pedagogical purposes. Distinguishing mutual self-surrender and procreation is not longer possible since Christian Marriage is sacramental meaning that it is fundamentally open to God and his fruitfulness. The birth of a child is not accidental but is God's gift. The believing spouses approach their sexual union with an attitude that is spiritual. They know of the boundless generosity of God and more particularly that it is God's generosity. Hence they approach physical union with hope and with acceptance of whatever comes about. Von Balthasar sees the family as the image of the Trinity in the sense that the Holy Spirit is the personal love of the Father and the Son which is revealed on the Cross. The spouses share in the Cross by their physical giving of themselves as Christ gave himself physically for our salvation.

Reflecting back on the philosophical conclusions about being and truth, the form of Marriage as the unity in one flesh is the most profound human relationship especially when it occurs to express the deep spiritual self-surrender to one another in Christ.[239] The mystery of self-surrender is unbounded because it is the imaging of the surrender of the Son to the Father in the Trinity. And Christ's own incarnation as a virgin indicated that real self-surrender lies "in the spiritual gift of self."[240] There is no possibility of such a relation ever becoming predictable as long as true self-surrender continues in Marriage. The form of Marriage is also characterized by the direct proportion of faith and knowledge. When the couple live in faith, their life together gives glimpses of the ideal of the union of Christ and his Church. In this way the couple's love gives concrete realization to the truth of Christ and the Church in their concrete historical situation.[241]

---

[239] The most complete example of such a close harmony between spiritual self-surrender and bodily fruitfulness is Mary herself. *CSOL*, 204.

[240] *CSOL*, 225.

[241] Cf. Vatican II: "They [the married couple] stand as witnesses and cooperators of the fruitfulness of mother Church as a sign of, and a share in that love with which

The Transcendent Horizon of Marriage

Marriage has always been so much more than a natural community. Precisely because all that is natural in Marriage has an origin that is supernatural, Marriage has a supernatural end.[242] In the Old Testament, in the *Book of Malachi* for example, faithfulness to the covenant is the horizon within which faithfulness to Marriage is to be understood.[243] Citing Malachi: "It is because God stands as witness between you and the wife of your youth." (Malachi 1:14) Malachi was speaking of Marriage to foreign wives and he made the connection between faithfulness to one's wife and faithfulness to God. Old Testament Marriage remained a shadow of the original union because the union of Paradise had been marred by divorce: "For I hate divorce says . . . the God of Israel." (Malachi 2:16)

In the New Testament, Marriage continues and yet is made new. For von Balthasar the newness lies in the birth of Christ himself. He is born of a virgin by the Holy Spirit. This is the highest manifestation within creation of the Son coming forth from the Father in the Holy Spirit and not from a marriage reduced by the Fall. Henceforth, the source of Christian marriage lies much more deeply in the interior life of the Trinity, now that Christ has opened the source of this life to the world.

Then as Eve is brought forth from Adam by the power of the God so is the Church brought forth from Christ. It is the union between Christ and the Church that is the 'measure' of the union between husband

---

Christ loved his Bride and gave himself for her." (LG, 41) Note too the statement of Aquinas' thought that "By sacrament we are to understand not only indivisibility, but all those things that result from marriage being a sign of Christ's union with the Church." *Supp.* q.49 a.2.

[242] Note the comment of Yves Congar O.P.: "Marriage is the sole example in the Christian economy of a natural institution, in itself and as such, being taken into the order of grace and made sacred." *Lay People in the Church*, 192. Furthermore in the words of John Paul II: "The only 'place' in which this self-giving in its whole truth is made possible is Marriage, the covenant of conjugal love . . . willed by God himself, which only in this light manifests its true meaning." FC, 11.

[243] *CSOL*, 231.

and wife.²⁴⁴ For von Balthasar the notion of 'measure' refers to the relation between the higher principle and that which is formed according to the higher principle.²⁴⁵ What has happened is that the union of Christ with his Church opens natural marriage to the fruitfulness of Christ's Eucharistic love. Christian Marriage receives its whole perfection from the Cross of Christ and so it is much more than a natural union in love.²⁴⁶

So finally: In the Church, the lay state is perfected in the Sacrament of Marriage.²⁴⁷ Marriage is undertaken according to the election of God and so is in no way inferior to the State of Election spoken of earlier. The two states (of Marriage and the State of Election) are in fact interconnected and the lay married couple is served in the Church by the States of Election.²⁴⁸ The ecclesial nature of Marriage reflects the character of being as manifesting truth when Marriage demonstrates the union between Christ and his Church. The Church is loved by God in Christ and this ideal is brought to reality in the couple who would not know the ideal if God had not revealed it and blessed it and made it possible.

Another possible state of life for a lay person is the virginal state in the Church.

The Ecclesial State of Virginity²⁴⁹

---

²⁴⁴ *CSOL*, 233.
²⁴⁵ Cf. *GL I*, 34ff.
²⁴⁶ Cf. John Paul II: "In [Christ's sacrifice on the Cross] there is entirely revealed that plan which has imprinted on the humanity of man and woman since their creation, the marriage of baptized persons thus becomes a real symbol of that new and eternal covenant sanctioned in the blood of Christ." (FC, 13) And also Yves Congar's comment: "The state of being husband and wife, inspired by true love and a consent that is free and heartfelt, is very properly a state of 'sacrifice'; it is therefore a priestly state." *Lay People in the Church*, 194.
²⁴⁷ *CSOL*, 248-249.
²⁴⁸ See Chapter Three, Interrelationship vi. Also note that according to Yves Congar O.P., "The Laity are the *pleroma* of the hierarchical priesthood." *Lay People in the Church*, 313.
²⁴⁹ Cf. John Paul II: "Christian revelation recognizes two specific ways of realizing the vocation of the human person, in its entirety, to love: marriage and virginity or celibacy. Either one is in its own proper form and actuation of the

Preliminary considerations

The State of Virginity refers primarily to a Christian who takes a once and for all vow to this state in the Church. A person who is not yet committed to Marriage and who has not been called into the State of Election is still bound to the life of the commandments (The General State) but is not in the virginal state in any complete sense since it is not being taken on in response to a call. Von Balthasar identified the uncommitted person as being in "a state of waiting" that is still regulated by the Commandments and which must be understood to be positive in its own right since it essentially corresponds to the will of God for this individual at this time.

The "state of waiting" is considered the exception since it is not ordinarily a permanent state of life like the Sacrament of Marriage and the State of Election.[250] In the case of someone who makes a personal commitment to Virginity, von Balthasar describes this as a 'true state of virginity' if the person is committed to the full meaning of virginity but in terms of the theology of the States of Life (Chapter Three) such a state is "a borderline case".[251]

The introduction of a more precise understanding is necessary here. In his presentation of Marriage, von Balthasar notes a principle that has a more general application. He speaks of "the form that has chosen [the couple of male and female], because they have chosen it, the form to which they have committed themselves in their act as persons."[252] He is indicating that the objective reality of the form of Marriage in the Church is the occasion of the exercise of the freedom of the man and the woman and it is the form of Marriage that 'co-enables' their freedom to be exercised. This principle also applies in its own ways to the one who is called to the State of Virginity in the Church and to the one who is called to live in a Secular Institute.

Lastly, the presentation of ecclesial virginity helps lay the groundwork for the understanding of the vows in a secular institute.

---

most profound truth of man, of his being 'created in the image of God." (FC, 9)

[250] *CSOL*, 242.
[251] *CSOL*, 237.
[252] *GL I*, 28. See also Schindler's comments, *Dramatic Structure of Truth*, 331-2.

The consideration of virginity starts from a reflection on the primal state of man.

Virginity in the New Testament
In the Old Testament, virginity was at best a promise. In the New Testament, the theological form of virginity is a partial representation of the virginity of Christ on the Cross. This latter mystery means that Christ's Death and Resurrection brought Christ's poverty, chastity and obedience to a divine outpouring of fruitfulness. From this fruitfulness flows the fruitfulness of the Church (Christ's Body) and its ecclesial forms of life.[253]

Now on the one hand the virginity of Christ on the Cross and those who take up their cross in similar ways involve a renunciation of biological fruitfulness so as to allow the greater fruitfulness of God to shine through in a religious community or through making the single vow of Virginity.[254] This illustrates the radiant quality of a true theological form where the depths of being in fact become illuminated by the glory of God in the Risen Lord. But von Balthasar is making another point here as well: ecclesial virginity is a 'partial' state.

The key to Virginity in von Balthasar's theology (and that of Ignatius of Loyola before him) is still obedience to the divine call in Christ. For this reason virginity is a 'partial' state.[255] Nevertheless to be an authentic response to the call of God in Christ, it needs to be accompanied by poverty as well as obedience.[256]

---

[253] Cf. John Paul II: "In virginity or celibacy, the human being is awaiting, also in a bodily way, the eschatological marriage of Christ with the Church, giving himself or herself completely to the Church in the hope that Christ may give himself to the Church of eternal life." (FC, 16). There is a similar teaching in "Marriage and Continence complement each other." *The Theology of Marriage and Celibacy*, 109ff.

[254] John Paul II also emphasizes the real sign value of virginity lies in its permanence as a vow until death. (FC, 16)

[255] *CSOL*, 236.

[256] Von Balthasar criticized the Catholic Action movement because it did not take advantage of the spiritual resources of the evangelical counsels. Cf. Hans Urs von Balthasar, *Laïcat et Plein Apostolat*, E. Bernimont O.P., trans., (Liege: La Pensée Catholique, 1949), 32.

It is the *complete* Religious State with its life of the counsels that is the true spiritual model for Marriage. When virginity is accompanied by a life of poverty and obedience, *then* it is itself a complete theological form. It is complete in the sense that it is a complete following of Christ. The counsels are not simply one form of following Christ among many! They are the form either directly or analogously for all of the authentic forms of life in the Church. So then living the life of virginity in the Church does in fact achieve a full form together with a poverty governed by a higher principle (obedience) namely the life of Christ hence it has the radiance and proportion of a true theological form.

On the other hand when the virginal life is a temporary personal choice or one that is only convenient for achieving certain goals, then "one who chooses it is deceived if he thinks himself a Christian, for he has not attained even that degree of self-giving that is demanded by the indissoluble 'yes' of Christian Marriage."[257] Among other things, the virginal state is a crucial sign of the profound value of unconditional self-giving.[258] This is giving as the Son gave himself. Theological persons whether they have publicly vowed to Virginity or to Marriage are called to give in this way so as to join the mission of the Son to the world at the behest of the Father.

The 'Femininity' of Ecclesial Virginity

The State of Virginity is also spiritually 'feminine' and can best be illustrated by looking to Mary. Besides Jesus Christ, the premier example of the virginal state as a vocation is Mary herself. She realized the fruitfulness of virginity in giving birth to the Son of God as part of fulfilling her virginal vocation: "She is a virgin so that she may become mother."[259] She demonstrated total receptivity to the Spirit of God (the first moment of femininity) and so was able to bring forth the Son of God into the world. (The second moment.)

---

[257] *CSOL*, 235.
[258] Cf. John Paul II: "Virginity or celibacy for the sake of the Kingdom of God not only does not contradict the dignity of Marriage but presupposes it and confirms it." (FC, 16)
[259] *CSOL*, 205.

Turning again to the connections between truth and being, 'femininity' clearly demonstrates the four relations mentioned above. The 'femininity' of faith comes about precisely within a relationship of love. It is because the Christian is loved and so graced that the Christian develops the 'feminine' spiritual capacity to live in the State of Virginity in the first place. The first moment of 'femininity', namely receptivity comes about in obedience to the will of God.[260] There is a mysterious identity through grace between the freedom of the called individual and obedience. Just as there is identity between the nature of Christ and his mission so there is an identity in the Christian between his (her) new redeemed essence when "Christ lives in me" and his (her) mission. This is the coming to knowledge through faith mentioned above. And the moment of creative expressiveness that arises out of this grace will be an expression of God's truth in the world.

The Ecclesial form of Virginity

The whole concept of the states of life is justified in the theology of ecclesial Virginity. This comes about since there are only two[261] possible ways of achieving the complete Christian self-surrender: in the State of Election, the Christian gives up himself "body and soul to God" and in Marriage, the Christian gives himself "body and soul to his [or her] spouse" but always in faith.[262] This is simply another way of restating the third ecclesial relationship found in Chapter Three namely that the interrelationship between the priestly and evangelical states is the model for the Lay State. Both dimensions of the State of Election involve the commitment to celibacy.

The Virginal state also demonstrates the kind of spiritual self-surrender that is crucial to Marriage.[263] "In the married state, the Christian by his sacramental "yes", gives his body and soul to his

---

[260] Cf. Vatican II: "Sanctity . . . is cultivated by all who act under God's spirit and [obey] the Father's voice." (LG,41)
[261] Of course I am putting the grace of martyrdom aside here.
[262] CSOL, 238. Von Balthasar cited Suarez' *De statu perfectionis* bk.III, chapter 2, section 4 on the traditional support for this division. Cf. *CSOL*, 239.
[263] Cf. John Paul II, "Celibacy for the Kingdom affirms Marriage." *The Theology of Marriage and Celibacy*, 128ff.

spouse—but always in God, out of a belief in God, and with confidence in God's bountiful fidelity."[264] Christ gave his body over to God throughout his Life and at his Death. It is the giving that rests on the receiving of the other in God that makes the analogy between the one who is celibate (Christ or a member in the State of Election) and one who is married. Once again love has its way of making Christ's truth present.

The fourth ecclesial relationship in Chapter Three was that of the Evangelical State as the norm for the Lay State. It is evident from the previous paragraph on self-surrender how this can be so. More generally the State of the Evangelical Counsels is a state entered in a complete response to the will of God. Now the will of God is the higher principle of all lay life whether it is expressed through the laws of the natural order (created by God) or whether it is through the revelation of divine law. Going to the revelation of the Gospel, each of the counsels presents a spiritual principle to one of the areas of a lay person's life.

Very briefly: the spirituality of poverty teaches the lay person the correct stance with respect to the things of the world.[265] Celibacy can help people to understand that no one is simply a sex object. Then obedience reminds us that we are all under obedience starting with the obedience to the natural law. Married spouses have to understand that they are obedient to each other. The nature of the life of the evangelical counsels as a source of meaning for both the Lay State and the State of the Priesthood was examined more fully in Chapter Three.

Finally, in conclusion, this brief description illustrates the four aspects of the manifestation of truth in being. First, through their relationship to Christ in love Christian virgins join the mystery of the self-surrender of the Son to the Father so as to participate in his fruitfulness. The fruitfulness of the divine relations pours itself out in the Virginal State within the Church. Second, the Virginal State within the Church demonstrates its own mystery as it exposes the depths of the individual committed to the ecclesial State of Virginity which is mysterious in itself since it shows the mystery of Christ's virginal life and

---

[264] Ibidem, 238.
[265] For von Balthasar's notes on the Patristic notions of private ownership see *CSOL*, 105-119.

that too is grounded in the inner life of the Son within the divine Trinity. Third, it requires faith to enter into the mystery of the life of ecclesial virginity and there arises a corresponding knowledge of what this can mean as the individual pursues the form of the virginal life. It is through the surrender in faith that the individual at the most fundamental level knows Christ through allowing Christ's virginal image to form within him (her): 'Not I but Christ in me.'

Fourth, the individual sees the form of life as it is lovingly presented by the Church who accepts the called individual into the virginal state in the Church. The Church sees many aspects of the ideal form of individual Christian through the form of the virginal state. At the same time the individual discovers his own identity as individual, as Christian, as member of the Body of Christ through seeing the ideal of virginal life presented by the Church. Thus in conclusion, the virginal Christian becomes part of the truth of Christ, the personal Word of God spoken to the world for its salvation.

Conclusion: The Final Vision

With the truth of God made manifest to the whole of Creation through the life of the Lay member of the Church, this work has only one final phase. What is von Balthasar's answer to the question: where is all of this leading?

Von Balthasar would answer by citing Ignatius of Antioch: "A living water murmurs within me; in the depths of my being it summons me. Go to the Father."[266] The reference to the 'depths of my being' was well chosen, it grasps von Balthasar's project that being is the reality in which God the Father manifested himself in Creation and then through redemption in his Son. It is the transformation of created being through Christ that opens up the way to a theology of the lay person.

This theology reflects on the properties of the life of the lay person because there in his being are the trans-formed aspects of existence, act and form in Christ. By the *analogia entis*, they are analogous to the existence, act and form of the divine Trinity. So the One who is the Good, Truth and Beauty is drawing the

---

[266] *Ad Romanum* 7.2. Cited in *TL III*, 399.

individual in Christ into one community with God. This is the end of "our long wandering."[267] The Christian is on the way to the mansions of the Father.

Such a theology means that the life of the lay person is not a private project. It is the joining of a human being lovingly gathered in to the Father through Christ in the Spirit. The infinite love of the Father and Son has set the whole panorama of salvation in play: "He will make his home among them; they shall be his people, and he will be their God; his name is God-with-them. He will wipe away all tears from their eyes; there will be no more death and no more mourning or sadness. The world of the past is gone." (Revelation 21:3, 4)[268]

---

[267] *TL III*, 399.
[268] Cited in *TL III*, 399.

Selected Bibliography

I have not listed Church documents. Papal writings in book form have been listed.

1. Works by Hans Urs von Balthasar

Von Balthasar, Hans Urs von, "Are there Lay People in the Church?" *New Elucidations,* San Francisco: Ignatius Press, 1986.

_____.*Augustinus: Das Antlitz der Kirche in Menschen der Kirche: In Zeugnis und Urkunde,* Einsiedeln: Benziger Verlag, 1955.

_____.*Bernanos: An Ecclesial Existence,* trans. Erasmo Leiva-Merikakis, San Francisco: Communio Books – Ignatius Press, 1996.

_____."Bernanos: Hell and Joy," *Explorations in Theology III: Creator Spirit,* trans. Brian McNeil C. R. V., San Francisco: Ignatius Press, 1993.

_____."Beyond Contemplation and Action? "*Explorations in Theology IV: Spirit and Institution,* San Francisco: Ignatius Press, 1995.

_____."Casta Meretrix," *Explorations in Theology II: Spouse of the Word,* San Francisco: Ignatius Press, 1991.

_____."Characteristics of Christianity," *Explorations in Theology I,* San Francisco: Ignatius Press, 1989.

_____.*The Christian State of Life,* trans. Sister Mary Frances McCarthy, San Francisco: Ignatius Press, 1983. "The Christian Form," *Explorations in Theology IV: Spirit and Institution,* San Francisco: Ignatius Press, 1995.

_____."The Church as the Presence of Christ," *New Elucidations,* trans., Sister Theresilde Skerry, San Francisco: Ignatius Press, 1986.

_____."Communio," *Communio* 1981 XXX

_____."The Contemporary Experience of the Church," *Explorations in Theology II: Spouse of the Word,* San Francisco: Ignatius Press, 1991.

_____."Encountering God in the World," *Explorations in Theology III: Creator Spirit,* trans. Brian McNeil C. R. V., San Francisco: Ignatius Press, 1993.

_____.*Epilog,* Einsiedeln: Johannesverlag, 1987.

_____."On the Evangelical Counsels," *Elucidations,* London: S.P.C.K., 1975.

_____."The Faith of the Simple Ones," *Explorations in Theology III: Creator Spirit*, trans. Brian McNeil C.R.V., San Francisco: Ignatius Press, 1993.

_____."Forgetfulness of God and Christians," *Explorations in Theology III: Creator Spirit*, trans. Brian McNeil C. R. V., San Francisco: Ignatius Press, 1993.

_____.*The Glory of the Lord – A Theological Aesthetics II: Studies in Theological Style: Clerical Styles*, Andrew Louth, Francis McDonagh and Brian McNeil C.R.V. trans., San Francisco: Ignatius Press, 1984.

_____.*The Glory of the Lord – A Theological Aesthetics IV: The Realm of Metaphysics in Antiquity*, trans.,Brian Mc Neil C. R. V., Andrew Louth, John Saward, Rowan Williams and Oliver Davies, San Francisco: Ignatius Press, 1989.

_____.*The Glory of the Lord - A Theological Aesthetics V: The Realm of Metaphysics in the Modern Age*, Oliver Davies, Andrew Louth, John Sayward and Martin Simon trans., San Francisco: Ignatius Press, 1991.

_____.*The Glory of the Lord – A Theological Aesthetics VI: Theology: The Old Covenant*, trans. Brian McNeil C. R. V. and Erasmo Leiva-Merikakis, ed. John Riches, San Francisco: Ignatius Press, 1991.

_____.*The Glory of the Lord – A Theological Aesthetics VII: Theology: The New Covenant*, trans. Brian McNeil C. R. V., ed. John Riches, San Francisco: Ignatius Press, 1989.

_____."The Implications of the Word," A. V. Littledale with Alexander Dru trans., *Explorations in Theology I: The Word made Flesh*, San Francisco: Ignatius Press, 1989.

_____.*Christlicher Stand*, Einsiedeln: Johannes Verlag, 1977.

_____.*Laicat et Plein Apostolat*, trans., E. Bernimont O.P., Liege: La Pensée Catholique, 1949.

_____.*The Laity and the Life of the Counsels: The Church's Mission in the World*, trans. Brian McNeil C.R.V. with D.C. Schindler, San Francisco: Communio Book with Ignatius Press, 2003.

_____."The Layman and the Church," in *Explorations in Theology II: Spouse of the Word*, San Francisco: Ignatius Press, 1991.

_____."Liturgy and Awe," *Explorations in Theology II: Spouse of the Word*, San Francisco: Ignatius Press, 1991.

_____."The Marian Principle," *Elucidations*, London: S.P.C.K., 1975.

_____."The Mass, A Sacrifice of the Church?" *Explorations in Theology III: Creator Spirit*, Brian McNeil C.R.V., San Francisco: Ignatius Press, 1993.

_____."Movement toward God," *Explorations in Theology III: Creator Spirit*, Brian McNeil C.R.V., San Francisco: Ignatius Press, 1993.

_____.*Office of Peter and the Structure of the Church*, Andrée Emery trans., San Francisco: Ignatius Press, 1986.

_____."Office in the Church," *Explorations in Theology II: Spouse of the Word*, San Francisco: Ignatius Press, 1991.

_____."On the Concept of Person," *Communio* 13 (Spring 1986).

_____.*Origen: Spirit and Fire: A Thematic Anthology of his Writings*, trans. Robert Daly, S. J., Washington D. C.: Catholic University of America Press, 1984.

_____.*Our Task: A Report and a Plan*, trans. Dr. John Saward, San Francisco: A Communio Book, Ignatius Press, 1994.

_____.*Phénoménologie de la Vérité: Vérité du Monde*, Paris: Beauschene et Fils, 1952.

_____."Philosophy, Christianity and Monasticism," in *Explorations in Theology II: Spouse of the Word*, San Francisco: Ignatius Press, 1991.

_____."The Place of Theology," *Explorations in Theology I: The Word made Flesh*," San Francisco: Ignatius Press, 1989.

_____.*Prayer*, trans. Graham Harrison, San Francisco: Ignatius Press, 1986.

_____."Revelation and the Beautiful", *Explorations in Theology I: The Word made Flesh*," San Francisco: Ignatius Press, 1989.

_____.*Science, Religion and Christianity*, trans. Hildi Graef, Westminster MD: Newman press, 1958.

_____."Secular Piety," *Explorations in Theology III: Creator Spirit*, trans. Brian McNeil C. R. V., San Francisco: Ignatius Press, 1993.

_____."Seeing, Hearing, and Reading," *Explorations*

_____ in *Theology II*, San Francisco: Ignatius Press, 1991.

_____."Spirituality," *Explorations in Theology I*, San Francisco: Ignatius Press, 1989.

_____."Summa Summarum," *Explorations in Theology III: Creator Spirit*, trans. Brian McNeil C. R. V., San Francisco: Ignatius Press, 1993.

_____.*Test Everything: Hold fast to what is good*, trans., Maria Shrady, San Francisco: Ignatius Press, 1989.

_____.*Theodrama— Theological Dramatic Theory I: Prolegomena*, (San Francisco: Ignatius Press, 1988)

_____.*Theodrama— Dramatis Personae II: Man in God*, San Francisco: Ignatius Press, 1990.

_____.*Theodrama—Theological Dramatic Theory III: Dramatis Personae*, trans. Graham Harrison, San Francisco: Ignatius Press, 1992.

_____.*Theodrama—Theological Dramatic Theory IV: The Action*, trans., Graham Harrison, San Francisco: Ignatius Press, 1994.

_____.*Theodramatik IV Das Endspiel*, Einsiedln: Johannes Verlag, 1983.

_____.*Theologic I: The Truth of the World*, Adrian Walker trans., San Francisco: Ignatius Press, 2000.

_____.*Theologic III: The Spirit of Truth*, trans. Graham Harrison, (San Francisco: Ignatius Press, 2005)

_____.*A Theological Anthropology*, New York: Sheed and Ward, 1967.

_____."Theology and Sanctity," *Explorations in Theology I*, San Francisco: Ignatius Press, 1989.

_____.*The Theology of Henri de Lubac: An Overview*, San Francisco: Ignatius Press, 1991.

_____.*Theology of History*, San Francisco: Ignatius Press, 1991.

_____."A Theology of the Secular Institute," *Explorations in Theology II*, San Francisco: Ignatius Press, 1991.

_____.*The Threefold Garland: The World's Salvation in Mary's Prayer*, trans. Erasmo Leiva-Merikakis, San Francisco: Ignatius Press, 1982.

_____.*Tragedy under Grace: Reinhold Schneider on

the Experience of the West, trans. Brian McNeil C.R.V., San Francisco: Ignatius Press, 1997.
_____."Two Modes of Faith," *Explorations in Theology IV: Spouse of the Word*, San Francisco: Ignatius Press, 1991.
_____.*Unless You become like this Child*, San Francisco: Ignatius Press, 1991.
_____."Who is man?" *Explorations in Theology IV: Spouse of the Word*, San Francisco: Ignatius Press, 1991.
_____."Who is the Church?" *Explorations in Theology II*, San Francisco: Ignatius Press, 1991.
_____."The Word and History," *Explorations in Theology I: The Word made Flesh*, San Francisco: Ignatius Press, 1989.
_____."Women Priests?" in *New Elucidations*, trans. Sister Mary Teresilde Skerry, San Francisco: Ignatius Press, 1986.
_____."A Word on *Humane Vitae*," *New Elucidations*, San Francisco: Ignatius Press, 1986.
_____."The Word, Scripture and Tradition," *Explorations in Theology I: The Word made Flesh*, San Francisco: Ignatius Press, 1989.
_____.*You Crown the Year with your Goodness – Radio Sermons*, trans. Graham Harrison, San Francisco: Ignatius Press, 1989.

2. Secondary Literature on Hans Urs von Balthasar

Bieler, Martin, "Meta-Anthropology and Christology: On the Philosophy of Hans Urs von Balthasar," *Communio* 20 (Spring, 1993).
Bramwell, Bevil, "Hans Urs von Balthasar's Theology of Scripture, *New Blackfriars*, vol. 86 no. 1003 May 2003.
Capol, Cornelia, *Hans Urs von Balthasar: Bibliography* Einsiedeln: Johannes Verlag, 1990.
Dalzell, S.M., Thomas G., "The lack of social drama in Balthasar's theological dramatics," *Theological Studies* 60 (1999).
Fisichella, Rino, *Hans Urs von Balthasar: Dinamica dell' Amore e Credibilità* del Cristianesimo
Goodall, Lawrence D., "Hans Urs von Balthasar: A respectful critique," *Pro Ecclesia* vol VIII.

Healy III, Nicholas J., *The Eschatology of Hans Urs von Balthasar: Being as Communion*, Oxford Theological Monographs, J. Day et al eds., Oxford: Oxford University Press, 2005.
_____ "The World as Gift," *Communio* 32 (Fall 2005).
Henrici, S.J., Peter, "The Philosophy of Hans Urs von Balthasar," *Von Balthasar: His Life and Work*, David L. Schindler ed., San Francisco: Communio Books, Ignatius Press, 1991.
Leahy, Brendan, *The Marian Profile: In the Ecclesiology of Hans Urs von Balthasar*, New York: New City Press, 2000.
Mongrain, Kevin, *The Systematic Thought of Hans Urs von Balthasar – An Irenaen Retrieval*, (New York: Crossroad Publishing, 2002).
Narcisee O.P., Gilbert, *Les Raisons de Dieu: Argument de convenance et Esthétique théologique selon saint Thomas d'Aquin et Hans Urs von Balthasar*, Studia Friburgensia Nouvelle Serie 83, Friburg: Éditions Universitaires Fribourg Suisse, 1997.
Oakes, Edward T., *Pattern of Redemption: The Theology of Hans Urs von Balthasar*, New York: Continuum, 1994.
O'Donnell, John, *Hans Urs von Balthasar*, England: Geoffrey Chapman, 1992.
Quash, Ben, *Balthasar at the End of Modernity*, London: T. & T. Clark Publishers, 2001.
Schindler, David L., *Hans Urs von Balthasar and the Dramatic Structure of Truth: A Philosophical Investigation*, in the Perspectives in Continental Philosophy Series, New York: Fordham University Press, 2004.
Servais, Jacques, "The lay vocation in the world according to H.U. von Balthasar," *Communio* 23 (Winter 1996).

3. Other Works
   à Kempis, Thomas, *The Imitation of Christ: A New Reading of the 1441 Autograph*, William C. Creasy trans., Atlanta: Mercer University Press, 2007.
   Allen, Prudence, "Integral Sexual Complementarity and the Theology of Communion," *Communio: International Catholic Review* 17 (1990).
   Aron, Raymond, *The Dawn of Universal History:*

Selected essays from a witness to the twentieth century, Barbara Bray trans., New York: Perseus Books – Basic Books, 2003.

Augustine, "The Christian Life," *Treatises on Various Subjects*, Roy. J. Deferrari ed., *The Fathers of the Church 16*, New York: Fathers of the Church Inc., 1952.

Saint Augustine: Concerning the City of God against the Pagans, Henry Bettenson trans., London: England, 1984.

Aumann, Jordan, *Christian Spirituality in the Catholic Tradition*, San Francisco: Ignatius Press, 2001.

Barth, Karl, *Church Dogmatics III/3*, Edinburgh: T & T Clark, 1950.

Blair, H. A., *Studia Patristica XVII*, part one, ed. Elizabeth A Livingstone, Oxford: Pergamon Press, 1992.

Blondel, Maurice, *The Letter on Apologetics and History and Dogma*, trans. Alexander Dru and Illtyd Trethowan, Grand Rapids MI: William B. Eerdmans, 1994.

Brown, Raymond S.S., *Priest and Bishop – Biblical Reflections*, New York: Paulist Press, 1970.

Bultmann, Rudolf, *Jesus Christ and Mythology*, New York: Prentice-Hall, 1997.

Calvin, John, *Institutes of the Christian Religion 1 & 2*, ed. John T. McNeill in the *Library of Christian Classics XX & XXI*, gen.eds. John Baillie, John T. McNeill, Henry P. van Dusen, Philadelphia: Westminster Press, 1960.

The Church, *The Council of Trent*, ed. and trans. J. Waterworth, London: Dolman, 1848.

_____, *The States of Perfection*, arranged by the Benedictine Monks of Solesmes, Mother E. O'Gorman R.S.C.J. trans., Boston MA: St. Paul Editions, 1967.

Congar O.P., Yves, *Laypeople in the Church*, Westminster MD: Newman Press, 1963.

_____*Sacerdoce et Laïcat*, Paris: Les Éditions du Cerf, 1962.

Crouzel, Henri, *Origen*, A. S. Worrall trans., Edinburgh: T & T Clark, 1989.

de Lubac S.J. Henri, *The Drama of Atheist Humanism*, trans., Edith M. Riley, New York: World Publishing Company, Meridian Books, 1971.

_____, *Splendor of the Church*, San Francisco: Ignatius Press, 1999.

_____, *Medieval Exegesis Vol: 1 The Four Senses of Scripture*, Mark Sebanc trans, Michigan: Eerdmans, 1998.

_____, *Medieval Exegesis Vol: 2 The Four Senses of Scripture*, trans. E. M. Macierowski, Grand Rapids MI: William B. Eerdmans, 2000.

Douglas, J. D. org. ed., *The New Bible Dictionary*, London: Inter-Varsity Press, 1962.

Fallaci, Oriana, *La Forza della Ragione*, Roma: Rizzoli Internazionale, 2004.

Farkasfalvy, Denis, "A Heritage in Search of Heirs: The Future of Ancient Christian Exegesis," *Communio* 25 (Fall 1998).

Frankl, Viktor, *Man's Search for Meaning*, New York: Simon and Shuster, 1984.

Hastings, Adrian ed., *The Oxford Companion to Christian Thought*, Oxford; Oxford University Press, 2000.

Hauke, Manfred, *Women in the Priesthood: A Systematic Analysis in the Light of Creation and Redemption*, San Francisco: Ignatius Press, 1988.

Hibbert, O. P., Giles, "Mystery and Metaphysics in the Trinitarian Theology of Saint Thomas," *Irish Theological Quarterly* 31 (1964).

ICEL, *The Rites of the Catholic Church as revised by the Second Vatican Council, IA – Initiation*, New York: Pueblo Publishing, 1976.

Ignatius, *The Spiritual Exercises of St. Ignatius*, trans. Anthony Mottola, New York: Doubleday, 1964.

Israel, Jonathan I., *Radical Enlightenment: Philosophy and the Making of Modernity 1650-1750*, Oxford: Oxford University Press, 2002.

John Paul II, *Man and Woman He created Them: A Theology of the Body*, Michael Waldstein ed., trans., Boston: Pauline Books and Media, 2006.

_____, *Theology of Marriage and Celibacy: Catechesis on Marriage and Celibacy in the Light of the Resurrection of the Body*, Pauline Books & Media, November 1986.

Jörgensen, Johannes, *Francis of Assisi*, New York NY: Image Books, 1955.

Judt, Tony, *Postwar: A History of Europe Since 1945*, New York: Penguin Press, 2005.

Kähler, Martin, *The So-Called Historical Jesus and the*

Historical Biblical Christ, Minneapolis MN: Fortress Press, 1964.
Kereszty O. Cist., Roch, Jesus Christ: Fundamentals of Christology, New York: Communio Book – Alba House, 1991.
Kramer, Hilton, The Triumph of Modernism: The Art World 1985-2005, New York: Ivan R. Dee, 2006.
Lamb, Matthew L., Matthew Levering, eds., Vatican II: Renewal within Tradition, Oxford: Oxford University Press, 2008.
Latourelle, René, ed., Vatican II Assessment and Perspectives Vol I, New York: Paulist Press, 1988.
Léonard, Emile G., Bibliothèque des Centres d'Études supérieures spécialisés VI. La Laïcité, Paris: Presses Universitaires de France, 1960.
Luzbetak, S.V.D., Louis, J., The Church and Cultures: New Perspectives in Missiological Anthropology, American Society of Missiology Series No.12, Maryknoll NY: Orbis Books, 1988.
Maritain, Jacques, trans., J.F. Scanlan, "Christian Art," Art and Scholasticism with other Essays, Kessinger Publishing.
May, William E., "Marriage and the complementarity of Male and Female," Anthropotes VIII (1) June 1992.
McDonald, Timothy, The Ecclesiology of Yves Congar, Lanham MD: University Press of America, 1984.
Newman, John Henry, Essay on the Development of Christian Doctrine, Notre Dame IN: University of Notre Dame Press, 1989.
Niebuhr, H. Richard, Christ and Culture, New York: Harper and Row, 1951.
Nolan O.P., Albert, Jesus before Christianity, Maryknoll NY: Orbis Books, 2001.
Olivier, Robert W., The Vocation of the Laity to Evangelization, Rome: Editrice Pontificia Universitas Gregoriana, 1997.
O'Malley, John W., The First Jesuits, Cambridge: Harvard University Press, 1993.
O'Meara, O.P., Thomas, "Theology of Ministry," New York: Paulist Press, 1983.
Origen, Origen on First Principles, G. W. Butterworth trans., Gloucester MA: Peter Smith, 1973.
Osborne O.F.M., Kenan, Ministry: Lay Ministry in the

Roman Catholic Church, (New York: Paulist Press, 1993).
Ouellet, Marc, "Foundations of Christian Ethics," Communio 17 (Fall, 1990).
Philips, G., Le Rôle du Laïcat dans l'Église, Paris: Casterman, 1954.
Pieper, Joseph, Leisure: The Basis of Culture, Gerald Malsbary trans., South Bend IN: Saint Augustine's Press, 1998.
Rademacher, William J., Lay Ministry – A Theological and Spiritual Handbook, New York: Crossroad, 1963.
Rahner S.J., Karl, Theological Investigations II: Man in the Church, Karl-Heinz Kruger trans., New York NY: Crossroads, 1963.
_____.The Content of Faith, New York, NY: Crossroad, 1992.
_____."The Development of Dogma," Theological Investigations I, New York: Crossroad, 1982.
_____.Foundations of Christian Faith, London: Darton, Longman and Todd, 1978.
_____."The Role of the Layman in the Church," Theological Investigations VIII, New York: Crossroad, 1982.
_____.Encyclopedia of Theology: A Concise Sacramentum Mundi, ed. Karl Rahner S.J., (London: Burns and Oates, 1975)
Ratzinger, Joseph, Commentary on the Documents of Vatican II, vol. V, Herbert Vorgrimler gen. ed., W.J. O'Hara trans., London: Burns and Oates, 1969.
_____.Dogmatic Theology 9: Eschatology: Death and Eternal Life, (Washington D.C.: Catholic University of America Press, 1988). Series by Johann Auer and Joseph Ratzinger.
_____.Introduction to Christianity, San Francisco: Ignatius Press, 1990. ,
_____.Pilgrim Fellowship of Faith: The Church as Communion, trans. Henry Taylor, San Francisco: Ignatius Press, 2005.
_____.Principles of Catholic Theology: Building Stones for a Fundamental Theology, trans. Sister Mary Frances McCarthy S. N. D., San Francisco: Ignatius Press, 1987.
_____.Truth and Tolerance: Christian Belief and

World Religions, trans., Henry Taylor, San Francisco: Ignatius Press, 2004.

Riches, John, *A Century of New Testament Study*, Valley Forge PA: Trinity Press, International, 1993.

Riley-Smith, Jonathan, *The Crusades, Christianity and Islam*, New York: Columbia University Press, 2008.

Rulla S.J., Luigi, Sr. Joyce Ridick S.S.C. and Franco Imoda S.J., *Entering and Leaving Vocation: Instrapsychic Dynamics*, (Rome: Gregorian University Press, 1976).

Rutler, George William, *The Curé d'Ars Today*, San Francisco: Ignatius Press, 1988.

Schillebeeckx O.P., Edward, *Jesus: An Experiment in Christology*, New York NY: Crossroads, 1981.

Schindler, David L., "Catholic Theology, Gender and the Future of Western Civilization," *Communio* 20 (Summer, 1993).

_____."Christological Aesthetics and *Evangelium Vitae*: Towards a definition of liberalism", *Communio* 22 (Summer, 1995).

_____.*Heart of the World, Center of the Church*, Grand Rapids MI: William B. Eerdmans, 1996.

_____."The historical-critical claims of modernity: on the need for metaphysics," *Communio* XXX (Spring 1979).

Schleiermacher, Friedrich, *The Christian Faith*, Edinburgh: T&T Clark, 1999.

Schillebeeckx, Edward, *Christ the Sacrament of the encounter with God*, New York: Sheed and Ward, 1963.

_____.*Ministry: Leadership in the Community of Jesus Christ*, trans., John Bowden, New York: Crossroad, 1981.

Schmitz, Kenneth L., *At the Center of the Human Drama: The Philosophical Anthropology of Karol Wojtyła/Pope John Paul II*. Washington D.C.: CUA Press, 1993.

Stein, Edith, *The Collected Works of Edith Stein VI: The Science of the Cross*, trans., Josephine Koeppel O.C.D., Washington D.C.: ICS Publications, 2002.

Taylor, Charles, *A Secular Age*, Cambridge Massachusetts: Belknap Press of Harvard University Press, 2007.

Torrell, O.P., Fr. Jean-Pierre, "Saint Thomas et l'histoire: État de la question et pistes de recherches," *Revue Thomiste*, 105 (2005).

Walker, Adrian, "Fundamentalism and the Catholicity of Truth," *Communio* 29 (2002).

Wilken, Robert Louis, "*In Dominico Eloquio*: Learning the Lord's Style of Language," *Communio* 24 (Winter 1997).

-oOo-

www.ingramcontent.com/pod-product-compliance
Lightning Source LLC
Chambersburg PA
CBHW060940230426
43665CB00015B/2005